CRIMINOLOGY

CRIMINOLOGY

RAM AHUJA

RAWAT PUBLICATIONS
Jaipur • New Delhi • Bangalore • Guwahati • Kolkata

ISBN 978-81-7033-609-9 (Hardcover)

Reprinted, 2024

Published by
Prem Rawat for **Rawat Publications**
Satyam Apts., Sector 3, Jawahar Nagar, Jaipur - 302 004 (India)
Phones: 0141 265 1748 / 265 7006
E-mail : info@rawatbooks.com
Website: rawatbooks.com

New Delhi Office
4858/24, Ansari Road, Daryaganj, New Delhi 110 002
Phone: 011-23263290

Also at *Bangalore, Guwahati* and *Kolkata*

Typeset by Rawat Computers, Jaipur
Printed at Nice Printing Press, New Delhi

Contents

Preface

In the last few decades, crime has become not only a subject of great interest for students of sociology and law but it has also become a topic of major public interest because of the rising rate of crime, the changing attitude of liberal judges to crime and criminals and entering of criminals into politics. The interest is shifting from causes of crime and theory-building to enacting of laws, interpretation of laws and the law enforcement agencies. Thus, not only sociologists and criminologists, but even police, judiciary and politicians have started thinking seriously about crime.

Sociology deals with social action and social behaviour; criminology deals with criminality; and sociological criminology deals with the behaviour of criminals and with sociology of crime, i.e., crime as behaviour emerging from social structures or as an outcome of social pressures. It talks of control over crime through social engineering and changing and improving social order, as well as protecting the interests of victims and criminals.

In western society, criminology changed over the decades from conservative to liberal, to radical thought. It is difficult to point out precisely when criminology began in India. The teaching of criminology as a subject was introduced in the late 1940s at Lucknow while at the postgraduate level, it was started in the early 1950s when it was taught in the departments of sociology, psychology, social work, or law in various universities. Earlier, the teaching of criminology depended mostly on literature from the United States. It was only after professors like J.J. Pannakal, Haikerwal, Sushil Chandra and M.J. Sethna published articles and books on criminology in the 1950s and the 1960s that real interest in Indian criminology developed.

In America, England and other countries, empirical and theoretical studies in criminology in the last 6-7 decades and in India in the last five decades were mostly undertaken by scholars who had academic training in sociology and social psychology. In the western countries, the early theorists of this science had background of medicine, law, psychiatry and biology. After criticising conservative criminologists, the liberal criminologists of the 1940s looked for etiology of law-breaking in institutions and social structures, human ecology (social and physical environment) and in the weakening/reducing of social controls, through the process of learning within criminogenic culture. Reacting to the question, why people exposed to "crime-producing" structures do not take to crime and why some of those not so exposed do commit crimes, some liberal criminologists tried to explain it with a "social process" perspective. The later new liberal criminologists talked of crime as "status" and of criminality as resulting from struggle to defend individual and group interests. The radical criminologists of the 1970s and the 1980s rejected not only the idea of origin of criminogenic forces in the basic institutions and structures of society but also the idea of liberal reformism. They explained crime as a result of the enacting of laws by the 'power elite' for protecting their vested interests and for keeping the people weak, docile and powerless. Crime came to be explained as a result of rational response to the legal structure and as a means of survival in a society. It was maintained that crime could be eliminated only by changing the political and economic structures of society, and by preventing the rulers from undermining the interests of the people through legal machinery. This position, however, is not accepted by many scholars today. They ask: how do we explain crime of the rich and the influential people? How can crime be explained only in terms of class biases of the state? How do we explain crime in non-capitalistic societies? In India also, we find that a good number of decisions of some High Courts and the Supreme Court in recent years indicate that law enforcement agencies are not exploiters but protectors of the people.

Emphasis from time to time on factors like social environment, learning, social interaction, socialisation and the exploitation of the weak indicates that crime can be more satisfactorily explained with a sociological perspective. Developing feelings, beliefs, values, attitudes, motivations, preferences or developing a sense of 'self' asserts relationship between personality, environment and behaviour. With growing sociological interest in crime, it will, therefore, be more appropriate to use the phrase "Sociology of Crime" in analysing crime and criminals in a society.

In India, criminology as a science has developed rather tardily. Only a few scholars have undertaken empirical studies on some selected issues. One has to depend more on the crime data made available by agencies like National Crime Research Bureau and National Institute of Social Defence. Collecting material from empirical and secondary sources is a painstaking task. Yet it was a necessary task to make Indian students of criminology and deviant behaviour aware of the reality of crime in our society. An endeavour has been made to provide a relatively complete, comprehensive and valid account and analysis of crime situation in modern India. An effort has also been made to analyse criminological issues related to political crime, crime against women, youth crime, police and judiciary, etc., which as yet are not prescribed as topics of study in Indian universities teaching criminology. It is hoped that these themes will be considered crucial by teachers of criminology.

I express my sincere thanks to all those persons who provided me valuable help in collecting the required material. I am grateful to my wife and my two sons who made it possible for me to devote so much time to writing work. I earnestly hope, the book will be of interest and use to all those who are keen to have an up-to-date volume on crime and criminals in India.

RAM AHUJA

Chapter 1

Crime, Criminal and Criminology

It looks as if crime has become a topic of recent public debate; in fact, it has always been a subject of keen interest. The present interest, however, unmistakably reflects growing public concern over the ever-rising rate of crime, increasing influence of criminals in society, criminalisation of politics, politicisation of police, and over what ought to be done about all these serious developments. The debate, *inter alia*, deals with variability of what is defined as crime. What is considered to be crime differs between and within societies over time. For example, the sale of alcohol was a legitimate activity in all states in India till the early fifties but it came to be described as an illegitimate activity in a couple of states with the introduction of prohibition policy, and has once again become a legitimate activity after the withdrawal of prohibition. Similarly, it has in the recent past, come to be debated whether we actually need so many laws. The Chairman of the Law Commission, in one state in northern India, some time back revealed that out of 211 laws prevalent in the state, only 73 were being actually used. Why not do away with the remaining laws? Again, do we need to re-examine the word 'criminal'? At least, many sociologists think so. While most criminologists receive their academic training today in the social sciences, usually in sociology, the pioneers in criminology, like Lombroso (physician), Garofalo (professor of Law), Ferri (lawyer) Healy (psychiatrist), Sutherland, etc., were trained in various other disciplines. We will, therefore, first try to understand what criminology is and then how traditional criminology differs from liberal and radical criminology.

WHAT IS CRIMINOLOGY

Criminology in a narrower sense is described as the "scientific study of crime as a social phenomenon", or "a science that deals with different aspects of behaviour that violates criminal law" (Bloch and Geiss, 1970: 79). In its broadest sense, it is referred to as the "entire body of knowledge regarding the causes and prevention of crime, punishment and correction of criminals, and operation of correctional institutions and agencies" (*see*, Gibbons, 1977: 3). It is also defined as a "discipline or a branch of knowledge which embraces etiology of criminal behaviour, societal responses to crime, control of crime, and the correction of criminals." Walter Reckless (1955: 11) has described criminology as a "science which studies violation of criminal codes or set of rules and regulations in society." On this basis, a criminologist is defined as "one whose professional training and occupational role are concerned toward a scientific approach, study, and analysis of the phenomena of crime and criminal behaviour (Wolfgang, 1963: 155-102). The branch of criminology dealing specifically with the punitive aspect is known as 'penology.' One thing on which all criminologists agree is that criminology today is vastly different from what it was twenty-five or fifty years back or when it originated about a hundred years ago.

GROWTH OF CRIMINOLOGY

The origin of the term 'criminology' can be traced back to the French anthropologist Topinard, whose major work appeared in 1879. In the eighteenth and early nineteenth centuries, however, the emphasis was on the reform of criminal law and not on the causes of crime. Scholars, including the Italian scholars Beccaria and Bentham, were more concerned with the humanitarian aspects in dealing with criminals and reforming severe criminal laws. Great progress in criminology was made after the first quarter of the twentieth century. The first American textbook on criminology was written in 1920 by sociologist Maurice Parmalee under the title *Criminology*. Programmes were developed for the specific purpose of training students to be criminologists, but the developments were rather slow.

In India, the teaching of criminology started in 1940 at the Jail Officers Training School at Lucknow. In 1949, a diploma course in criminology was started at the Lucknow University. In subsequent years criminology as a subject came to be taught in several universities. Four universities/institutions deemed to be universities soon introduced independent departments of criminology: Tata Institute of Social

Sciences, Bombay (1954); University of Saugar, Saugar (1959); University of Madras, Madras (1965) and University of Karnataka, Dharwad (1970). Diploma courses in criminology today are run by the Lucknow University, Lucknow and Rajasthan University, Jaipur. At the postgraduate level, criminology as a paper was started between 1950 and 1959 by the Sociology Departments of Lucknow University, Gorakhpur University and Institute of Social Sciences, Agra and by the Psychology Departments of Baroda University, Baroda and Utkal University, Bhubaneshwar. Between 1960 and 1969, criminology paper was started by the Sociology Departments of Marathwada University, Nagpur; Kashi Vidyapeeth, Varanasi; Kalyani University, Calcutta; Rajasthan University, Jaipur; Udaipur University, Udaipur and the Psychology Departments of Andhra University, Bhagalpur University, Madras University, Nagpur University and Ranchi University. Lastly, between 1970 and 1980, it was introduced by the Sociology Departments of Annamalai University, Hyderabad; Gujarat Vidyapeeth, Ahmedabad and by the Psychology Departments of Himachal Pradesh University, Shimla; Osmania University, Hyderabad and S.V. University, Tirupati. In Social Work Institutes, criminology is taught at Udaipur, Baroda, Madras, Indore, Dharwad, Delhi, Waltair, Bangalore and Mangalore. At the undergraduate level, criminology is taught either in Sociology or Psychology Department as a compulsory paper in sixteen universities and as an optional paper in eleven universities. Greater growth of criminology, thus took place between 1970 and 1980—in disciplines like sociology, psychology, social work and law—than between 1950 and 1970.

Gibbons and Garabedian (Cf. Charles Reasons, *The Criminologist: Crime and the Criminal*, 1974: 51-65) have recently identified three major perspectives in the growth of criminology: conservative, liberal, and radical (or critical). *Conservative criminology* incorporates the following ideas: (1) criminal law is given; (2) criminals are 'morally defective' people; (3) criminologists have to study how morally defective people are produced and how society can protect itself against criminals; (4) in dealing with the question of causation of crime, conservative criminologists advocate the 'multiple factor' approach, emphasising combinations of personality, biological, and environmental factors; and (5) conservative criminologists tend to have faith in efficient police and criminal justice machinery (*see*, Barlow, 1978: 26).

Liberal criminology emerged in the 1940s and in the early 1950s, while radical criminology emerged in the 1970s. Since liberal criminology has dominated the field over the past fifty years, it is also called mainstream criminology. Early liberal criminology retained the emphasis of conservative criminology on offenders and their behaviour but pushed the search for the cause of crime in institutions and structure of society. Three major views of liberal criminology are: (1) crime is the result of learning process occurring within a criminogenic culture; (2) criminality is the result of breakdown of personal and social controls; and (3) crime is a normal response to a situation of cultural discontinuity between ends and means (Gibbons and Garabedian, *op.cit.*: 53). These views affirm that criminals are not perceived as 'morally defective' persons but are seen as law-abiding people in society, who commit crimes to achieve culturally supported goals—wealth, prestige and power.

While early liberal criminology laid emphasis on crime as behaviour and on a criminal as a law-violator, liberal criminology of the 1960s and the 1970s laid stress on crime as status and on the process of making and enforcing criminal laws. According to the new liberal criminology, society is characterised by conflict and criminality is the product of power differentials and of struggle to defend individual interests. Criminals in society are those who are lacking in power and who are unsuccessful in the struggle to defend their interests. Police and courts are viewed as failures in living up to the ideals of justice.

Radical criminology rejects liberal reformism like probation, parole, juvenile court system, Borstal schools, and correctional reformatories because all these "strengthen the power of the state over the poor". The main thrust of radical criminology is: (1) a relatively small number of politicians, bureaucrats, and military men (what C. Wright Mills has called the 'power elite') comprise a close-knit power structure bent upon exploiting people; (2) laws have been created as devices for compelling the masses to remain docile; (3) the police are the mercenaries of oppression, serving the interests of the 'power elite'; (4) criminals are held captive as innocent victims of a corrupt, capitalistic and exploitative society; and (5) unless the present political-economic structure of (capitalistic) society is changed, criminality will remain and the legal machinery will continue to undermine the interests of people (Barlow, 1978: 28).

THE FIELD AND SCOPE OF CRIMINOLOGY

The interests of criminologists include the study of nature of crime and criminals, origins of criminal law, etiology of crime, social reactions to crime, and the functioning of law-enforcement agencies and penal institutions. It can be said that broadly criminology directs its enquiries along three lines: first, it investigates the nature of criminal law and its administration and conditions under which it develops; second, it analyses the causation of crime and the personality of criminals; and third, it studies the control of crime and the rehabilitation of offenders. Thus, criminology includes within its scope the activities of legislative bodies, law-enforcement agencies (police), judicial institutions (courts), correctional institutions (prisons and reformatories) and educational, private and public social agencies.

Walter Reckless (*The Crime Problem*, 1955: 6-7) has also talked of the territory or the contents that criminology should cover. He suggests the following boundaries to be covered by criminology: (1) It should study how crime is reported to official sources and acted upon officially. (2) It should study the development of and changes in criminal laws as they relate to social, economic, and political systems and to the social values in various societies. (3) It should study the characteristics of criminals, like sex, class, marital condition, occupation, employment, psychological characteristics, physique, pathological conditions of mind and body etc.; and compare these with those of non-criminals. The effort here is to discover what kinds of people do and do not get involved in crime. (4) It should study the area and regional variation in the amount of crime as well as variation in specific patterns of crime. (5) It should attempt to shed light on the causative factors of crime and should formulate causal theories. (6) It should study the special manifestations of crime that are quite different from ordinary crime, like organised crime, white-collar crime, etc. (7) It should study the relation of closely affiliated problems to crime, especially alcoholism, drug abuse, prostitution, gambling and vagrancy. In many societies, most or some of these problems may or may not be defined as crimes but these problems have a very close connection with crime. (8) It should study the effectiveness of law enforcement and of special laws in the control of crime. (9) It should study the effectiveness of the measures to treat offenders, like imprisonment, probation, parole, institutional treatment and aftercare. (10) It should study various efforts and experiments to prevent crime and delinquency.

In studying the field of criminology, it should, however, be remembered that this discipline is composed of knowledge drawn from such fields as sociology, law, medicine, public administration, social work, religion, and education. The interest of sociologists has primarily been in the science of criminal behaviour, while scholars of law are more concerned with criminal law. Attempts have been made recently by scholars interested in criminal behaviour and criminal law to conduct interdisciplinary research or integrate the findings of various disciplines on criminality.

RADICAL CRIMINOLOGY

The emergence of 'radical' approach to deviance can be traced through a gradual process of shift from the liberal pluralist positions which characterised 'mainstream' criminology in the 1940s and the 1950s. Early criminology—now popularly called conservative, traditional or orthodox criminology—concerned itself, up to late 1930s, with the pathological nature of the deviant act. In 1939, Sutherland (Cf. Sutherland and Cressay, *Principles of Criminology*, 1965: 74) offered a "social process" view of criminology. The "social structural" theories of Merton (1938) and Cloward and Ohlin (1960) drew attention to the functioning of social structures in the causation of crime. For locating the cause of crime, they advised criminologists to look for socially structured sources of 'strain' within society. The social structural and social process theories shared in common the view that crime is 'normal' rather than a pathological condition, and that a criminal is like any other person. The higher and lower rates of crimes in different societies were explained in terms of different social conditions and social experiences. Then developed a view in the 1960s which described crime as nothing more than a label attached to conduct and people, and what needed to be explained was variations in labelling behaviour (Becker, 1963). Crime came to be thought of as a status applied to behaviour, not as a particular kind of act. This was followed by the development of anew criminology or anew deviancy theory in the 1970s (Hunt, 1976) which focused on 'reaction' and 'social control' in giving rise to deviance. According to it, too much control is irrational and dysfunctional. The overreaction of those in power creates more deviance which further raises the level of coercive strategies necessary to maintain control. The key to controlling crime then lies not in structural change in society but in the control of reaction against deviance. The 1970s also saw the emergence of 'critical' perspective. Gouldner's (1970) questioning the validity of 'value neutrality' in social sciences, including sociology, sharply affected criminologists also, from which emerged a number of critical and radical strands. Conflict theory was revived and theorists such as Turk (1969), Chambliss (1969), and Quinney (1970) applied conflict theory directly to criminology. After the attack on 'value neutrality', many sociologists and criminologists took up a clear 'partisan' stance. One consequence of this was the growing 'politicisation of deviance'. There evolved a structural critique of dominant institutions, of big business, and of political rulers, who came to be regarded as 'true' criminals. This analysis of the political consequences of 'criminalisation' of deviance led to the growth of 'Union of Radical Criminologists' in the United States, School of Criminology at

Berkeley (USA), and National Deviancy Conference in Britain. These organisations provided framework for the convergence of critical theory with radical political ideology. They took up a 'politics of support' for prisoners, drug users, homosexuals, etc.

It was realised that a "new fully social theory of deviance" was required which could demonstrate theoretically the connections between law and the state, legal and political relations, the economic basis and functions of crime. On this terrain were forged the links between a 'radical politics' of deviance and a 'critical' version of Marxist and neo-Marxist theories (*see*, Fitzgerald, *et al.*, *Crime and Society*, 1981: 465). Taylor, Walton and Young published *The New Criminology* which laid emphasis on a "fully social theory of deviance" and talked of "abolition of inequalities in wealth and power". They argued that the study of crime was to be grounded in material conditions, the capitalist division of labour and the structural inequalities of wealth and power which the law helped to preserve. Thus, 'new criminology' attempted to forge a synthesis between neo-Meadean interactionist theories and a neo-Marxist political economy.

A social theory of criminality was at the heart of this critical enterprise. According to it, "criminality did not arise from biological inheritance or personality disorder or evil intent but is politically, economically, and socially induced." It (criminality) arose from 'material necessity' and 'material incentive'. A criminology not committed to 'the abolition of inequalities of wealth and power' was bound to be correctional. Its (new criminology's) objective was 'containing the consequences of crime'.

The 'new criminology' opposed traditional correctional criminology. Instead, it chose to consider issues like (Taylor, *et al.*, 1973: 270-76): (i) the wider origins of deviance in terms of cultural, structural and socio-psychological conflicts within wider society; (ii) the situated background specific deviant action; (iii) a grasp of the actual act in terms of wider origins; (iv) the immediate origins of social reaction; (v) wider contexts of social reaction; (vi) the effect of social reaction by and on the deviant and (vii) the subsequent persistence and change in action. The programme (of new criminology) not only proposed to retain the focus on the immediate interactions between the deviant and the agencies of control but also to locate them in a broader, historical and structural framework. This was a bold programme but it proved difficult to defend it.

This programme was developed further in a new book, *Critical*

Criminology in 1975 edited by Taylor, Walton and Young. In this book, the authors adopted a Marxist materialist analysis. 'Critical criminology', however, failed to answer many questions. In 1975. Hirst argued against developing a 'Marxist criminology'. It may, thus, be said that new critical and radical criminology was mainly concerned with the relationship between law, crime, and class, and the fact that crime is the product of class conditions.

Features of Radical Criminology

The major features of radical criminology are described as under:

1. Radical criminologists reject the individualistic approach to crime causation. They hold that not only the personality maladjustment theories (like biological, psychological) have to be rejected but even those sociological theories cannot be accepted which are dependent on notions of an individual's defects owing to inadequate socialisation or peer group pressures. The question is not of identifying those objectively-determined characteristics which distinguish criminal from non-criminal but of determining those social processes which stigmatise some individuals by labelling them as criminals but not others.

2. The radical criminologists question the rightfulness of law. They even describe that assumption as unrealistic according to which criminal law expresses a widely shared set of values. Richard Quinney maintains that we cannot accept Michael's and Adler's view that most of the people in any society would probably agree that most of the behaviour prescribed by the criminal laws is socially desirable. We cannot accept the view that all laws promulgated by a government, which is considered legitimate by almost all people, represent the collective moral judgements of society. The operation of legal agencies in fact is based on the self-conscious use of the law to maintain the status of those who hold power in society. Activities of legal agencies aim at self-interest and careerism. Criminal law and its enforcement are deliberately designed for the control of one social class by another.

3. The radical criminologists instead of explaining the fact of deviance with reference to the society within which it occurs, give importance to the social power.

4. The radical criminologists do not believe in the accuracy of government figures relating to crime because government officials either overstate or understate figures. Peten Manning has also said (Cf. Douglas, ed., *Crime and Justice in American Society*, 1971: 169) that the crime rate is simply a construction of police activity and the actual volume of crime is

unknown and probably unknowable. Richard Quinney (*The Problem of Crime*, 1970) submits that actual criminality is not the issue. The crucial question is: why societies and their agencies report, manufacture, or produce the volume of crime that they do. We must look for a systematic distortion that is part of the machinery for social control.

5. The radical criminologists hold that the law is used only against the poor, the illiterate, the powerless and the members of the minority groups. The ruling class uses legal apparatus mainly with three objectives: (a) to impose its morality and standard on the society; (b) to protect their persons and property from the depredations of the poor; and (c) to compose such definition of criminal behaviour which may enable them to maintain dominance over the poor and the middle classes.

Difference between Conservative and Radical Criminology

The following points of difference may be pointed out between conservative/traditional/orthodox criminology and radical criminology: (1) Conservative criminology remains concerned with the causation of crime and punishment and correction of criminals, but radical criminology focuses on the legislation enacted by the ruling class, or the materialist analysis of law. (2) The conservative criminologists explain deviance by reference to some social or personal pathology, but the radical criminologists argue that deviant action must always be examined in terms of political-economic structure of society, and in terms of the 'power elite' wanting to strengthen power of the state over the weak and the poor. (3) While functional paradigm is dominant in conservative criminology, conflict paradigm is dominant in radical criminology. (4) Conservative criminology attempts to correct and control the excesses of a punitive and repressive judicial system, but radical criminology does not take interest in the amelioration of environment or the building of a social work. (5) The conservative criminologist focuses his attention on the activities of the violator of law, the radical criminologist focuses on the activities of the powerful, most of which (activities) are either not defined as illegal or else are not apprehended in practice, like financial swindles, moral scandals, high-class prostitution, upper-class fraud, bribery, corruption, civil rights violations, government burglaries, and business malpractices. No wonder, the 'expose (new radical) criminology' is useful in demasking the crime-free facade of the ruling class, and in pointing to inequalities in apprehension, definition and punishment of the crimes of the powerful people, or the ruling groups. (6) The conservative criminologists characterise the social order as consensual, with a minority of deviants existing in society, the radical criminologists argue for the existence of a diversity of values and various subcultures or of cultural diversity within the society. (7) The conservative criminologists are more concerned with correctionalism or effective management and reform in the penal system, the radical criminologists reject liberal reformism and correctionalism. They criticise the role of the police, the prison administrators, the judges, and the social workers taking them to be agents of social control. They claim that probation, parole, juvenile court system, children homes, Borstal schools, observation homes, the indeterminate sentence system, etc. only "serve to strengthen the power of the state over the poor and the exploited". (8) The conservative criminologists explain the deviancy of a person in terms of forces beyond his control (i.e., determinism), the radical criminologists explain it in terms of 'free-will' of deviants.

Criticism of Radical Criminology

The question arises: are statements/arguments given by the radical criminologists valid? The answer is that the question of right or wrong arguments does not arise. Radical criminology is not a body of precise and systematic theoretical propositions. It is simply a perspective or an orientation. A theory explains relationship between variables which may be proved or disproved; but a perspective can only be considered logical or illogical. We can only point out some faults in the perspective of radical criminology. Some of these faults are: (1) The radical criminologists' belief that law is used only against the poor, the illiterate, the powerless, and the members of the minority groups is not based on any concrete evidence. (2) The belief that the intended and the recognised object of implementing law by the ruling elite is only to maintain its dominance is not correct. Even if some examples may be cited in support of this view, contrary examples can also be located in the society. A striking example is the recent decision of the Supreme Court of India against politicians illegally occupying government bungalows, after ceasing to hold political power. Equally noteworthy are the court's decisions/observations criticising the CBI for not taking interest in expediting the Hawala probe, instructing the government to save the Taj Mahal from polluting industries in the region, instructing the Delhi government to get the streets cleaned up, instructing the CBI to investigate the animal husbandry fodder scam in Bihar, and criticising highly placed government officials for not respecting the decisions of the courts (this includes the awarding of one month's imprisonment to an IAS officer in Karnataka). (3) The radical criminologists use model of social stratification which is ambiguous. Again, they only talk of the powerful and the powerless. They portray the middle class sometimes as the victim of the powerful class and sometimes as the co-opted agent of the elite class. The fact is that the reactions against the criminal law and its administration vary from class to class. On this basis, to hold the view that law is predominantly used by the powerful to impose their power on the powerless is not valid. (4) The radical criminologists' view that all of us commit acts in our lives for which we can be labelled as deviants may be correct but this does not mean that all of us are criminals. Isolating individuals who are considered a threat to society and social order by identifying them as criminals does not mean that they are being 'labelled'/condemned as criminals. It is totally illogical to aver that legal stigma of being a criminal is necessarily based on irrelevant factors, such as income, education, etc.

In spite of this criticism of radical criminology, it is possible to argue that there are merits in this perspective. These are: (1) It affects our outlook on legislation—its enactment and its administration. (2) It compels us to determine how the internalisation of legal norms varies in different segments in our society. (3) It prompts us to examine how the methods designed to control crime result in some unintended effects. (4) It lays stress on explaining the relationship between political order and deviant behaviour. In a way, this revitalises the profound sociological theme of relationship between individual and the state. (5) It points out the importance and the necessity of legal equality in a democratic society. If radical criminologists succeed in creating awareness about the desirability of having legal equality in society, they may do great service to society.

Radical criminologists have yet to demonstrate analytically that rule breaking is institutionalised, regular, and widespread amongst powerful men, be they ministers, bureaucrats, judges, policemen or businessmen. We do not wish merely to suggest that certain powerful individuals are engaged in deviance, or that corruption is on the increase. Were this the problem, the political answer would be, in the first instance, that the 'bad apples' should be rooted out and subjected to the force of law, and that secondly, a change of government or government policy should occur with a view to eradicating corruption, reducing crime, and re-establishing justice. The focus of the radical criminologists, however, is on fundamental and radical changes so that double-standard moralities and inequalities could be eliminated. Granting bail in a case to a big capitalist by a magistrate at his home at night in Delhi and denying bail to a petty offender only because he cannot provide a surety and thus forcing him to remain in judicial lock-up for months together are examples of double-standard moralities. The radical criminologists' interest is in eradicating such practices. On occasions, the operation of double standards immunises the powerful rule breaker from prosecution itself. A chief minister is only asked to resign when a corruption charge is proved against him, but, a lowly clerk is awarded two years' imprisonment for a similar charge. A senior central cabinet minister who did not pay income tax for eleven years was not indicted on the grounds that prosecution might undermine the confidence of the public in the government. The fact that the last four decades have seen an unprecedented number of such cases and revelations in India must be seen as significant in itself. It should prompt us to give due attention to the viewpoint of the radical criminologists that the authoritative dominance of the powerful and the ruling group can cause our society to collapse unless very significant transformation in the economic and institutional structure is brought about.

The researcher in radical criminology remains faithful to the researched population in the sense that he is expected to feed back his results not to the powerful but to those most immediately and directly affected by the inequalities he is researching. If the interest of conservative/traditional criminology in correctionalism is significant, so is the need for radical criminology which is normatively committed to the abolition of inequalities in wealth and power. If there is need for radical sociologists in India today who focus on "management of social change in a planned way", and use sociology for the uplift of the underprivileged and the weaker sections of people in our society, there is also need for radical criminologists who may take normative position on crime and criminals.

CRIMINOLOGY AS A SCIENCE

When it is said that criminology is the scientific study of crime and criminals, one or two questions crop up: Is criminology a science? What does the word 'science' mean? Science is an approach to the problems of human knowledge based on the attempt to develop general principles about phenomena, derived from empirical observations. The generalisations are so stated that they can be tested by any competent person (Theodorson, 1969: 368-69). Further, the generalisations of a science do not reflect individual experiences, but rather the consensus of the scientific community. Science is based on the assumption that the biases and values of the observer can be relatively controlled so that a reasonable degree of objectivity is possible.

Scientific observation has certain characteristics. The more important ones are (*see*, Horton and Hunt, *Sociology*, 1984: 4-6):

- *Scientific observation is based upon verifiable evidence*, i.e., factual observations which other observers can check for accuracy.
- *Scientific observation is accurate*, i.e., facts are exactly described as they are without any exaggeration or underestimation.
- *Scientific observation is precise*, i.e., the observer precisely refers to the measurement or the degree. For example, he states how many people exactly were interviewed (say 500 or 1,000 or 2,000) instead of saying that "a lot of people were interviewed"; or how many people were exactly in favour of a certain programme instead of saying that "most of the people" were in favour. A poet may say "every moment dies a man and every moment one is born" but a scientist will say that 45 persons are born in a minute in India or the population of the country increases by 1.7 crore every year.
- *Scientific observation is systematic*, i.e., observations are not casual but are collected in an organised and systematic way.
- *Scientific observation is recorded*: Human memory being notoriously fallible, unrecorded facts may be difficult to recall. Trustworthy statements are, therefore, made only on the basis of recorded data.
- *Scientific observation is objective*, i.e., observation is unaffected by the observer's own beliefs, values, attitudes, and feelings. In other words, objectivity means the ability to see and accept facts as they are, not as one might wish them to be.
- *Scientific observations are made under controlled conditions*, i.e., even though laboratories are not used where all variables may be totally controlled, yet it is possible to control quite a few variables even when studying human behaviour.
- *Scientific observations are made by trained observers*: Untrained observers do not know where to look for facts and how to collect them and analyse and interpret them. Their inaccurate observations, biases, and casual impressions may impinge upon their efforts, which may adversely affect the results or generalisations.

There are several steps in the scientific method of investigation. These are: (i) defining the problem; (ii) reviewing the literature; (iii) formulating the hypotheses or making tentative propositions to explain certain facts; (iv) planning the research design; (v) collecting the data and (vi) drawing conclusions or making generalisations regarding the uniformities and regularities found in the facts through an inductive method (i.e., proceeding from the particular to the general). These generalisations may or may not be in agreement with the working hypotheses and may even lead to their complete rejection. Conclusions are further drawn from the formulated generalisations by proceeding from the general to the particular, i.e., through the process of deduction. Thus, science moves from observation through induction and deduction to verification in a never-ending process. The findings of science that have been tested and appear to be correct are known as scientific truths, though these scientific truths are subject to continuous re-examination and modification in the light of new evidence. The findings of science are classified as hypotheses, theories, and laws. A scientific law is a universal and predictive statement of a relationship among facts that has been repeatedly corroborated by scientific investigation. It is universal in the sense that the stated relationship is held always to occur under the specified conditions. It is predictive in that if the specified conditions are found, the relationship may be predicted to follow. A scientific theory is a set of logically interrelated and empirically verifiable propositions, while hypotheses are the propositions which have not been well verified. The proportions in the theory are those which have already been subjected to empirical testing. Thus, according to Theodorson (1969: 437), a theory is a generalisation intermediate in degree of verification between a law and a hypothesis.

With these concepts of science and scientific method, criminology may be described as a science because it uses the method that is defined as science. However, if 'science' is referred to in terms of the 'content', i.e., "the body of scientific findings", then criminology is not a science.

CRIMINOLOGY: THEORY AND PRACTICE

Criminology may be described as including two separate but interdependent branches: one, which conducts scientific studies and the other, which uses theoretical principles in practice for preventing crime and treating criminals (Johnson, 1978: 53). This development of interdependence between theory and practice depends on the one hand on the willingness of the scientists to participate in applied research and on the other hand on the openness of the criminal justice agencies (police, prisons, courts, correctional institutions, probation department) to alternative interpretations of their purposes and work patterns. Criminologists with their professional training, occupational roles, and commitment to research remain concerned with scientific research in issues like nature of crime, causes of crime, types of persons who commit crimes, factors which encourage crime, institutions engaged in controlling criminal behaviour, societal reaction to crime, functioning of structures of law-enforcement agencies, and so on. They insist that criminology is a separate and an autonomous discipline of knowledge because "it accumulates its own set of organised data and theoretical conceptualisations that use the scientific method, approach to understanding and attitude in research." Though it is true that other disciplines make important contributions, yet refined analysis of crime and criminal behaviour demands "devoted and disciplined concern with the special subject". People in criminal justice administration are excluded because they are at most consumers of the products of criminological science. Criminology, as a theoretical discipline has to be a self-contained and independent discipline. It has to present a distinctive intellectual identity, a broad organisational base and an established flow of qualified persons (teachers, researchers) for continuity of a distinctive occupational community. Theoretical criminology has to develop as a collection of criminological sciences, rather than as a single autonomous science. In this, sociology of course has to be dominant and has to play a major role, though psychology, biology, psychiatry, physical anthropology, law, and medical science also have to make contributions in their own way. While it is not easy to say whether the development has to be based only on sociological approach or on multidisciplinary approach, one thing is quite clear: criminology has to develop as a special science. Does this mean that 'practitioners' have to be excluded from the ranks of criminologists? According to Johnson (*op. cit.*, 55), though some people might question it, yet the reality is that only theoreticians in criminology can take serious interest in research; practitioners still hesitate to use criminological principles. They have yet to realise that they will gain from the closest contact with the theoreticians in criminology. Of course, the theoreticians too have to realise that they too will be made more aware of the many problems, of which they would otherwise be unaware, if they maintained communication/contact with the courts, the police and the prison officials. Theory and practice in criminology have to be kept interlinked. A theoretician criminologist cannot be accused of abstract thinking and a practitioner cannot claim that only his thinking is concrete. The researcher derives his knowledge from empirical studies and from direct contact with criminals, prisoners, policemen, probation officers, judges, etc. The practitioner, when criticising the theoretician criminologist, by declaring that "he tells only what we already know" is erroneous. Both have to maintain a sustained interest in each other's work as well as in mutual partnership. The growth of criminology depends on the professional interests of both researchers and practitioners of criminological principles.

METHODS AND TECHNIQUES IN CRIMINOLOGY

What are the methods mostly used in data collection in criminology? While scientific methods are basically alike for all sciences, scientific techniques differ, for techniques are the particular ways in which scientific methods are applied to a particular problem. Each science, therefore, develops a series of techniques which fit the body of material studies. What are the techniques used in criminological research? The criminologists generally use survey method, case study method, and statistical method in studying criminal behaviour. Occasionally, experimental method is also used.

The *survey method* collects facts by putting questions to a large number of persons under scientific controls. The three tools often used in this technique are questionnaire, schedule and interview guide. A questionnaire is filled out by the informant personally, while a schedule is filled out by a trained investigator. Questions in both are pre-structured. An interview guide consists of only points on which questions are put to the informants; it does not have structured questions. These tools have their pitfalls. The informants may not understand a question; they may pick up an answer even though they may not have any firm opinion on the matter; they may give an 'acceptable' answer rather than the real one; or they may be swayed by the way the question is worded. Even though these tools may have a margin of error, yet they are very useful, for they are more reliable than guesswork. While non-participant observation may be used in criminology, the use of participant observation is almost impractical. The participant observer seeks insight by wishing to take part in whatever is being studied, and, this is not feasible in criminological studies.

The *case study* method is a method of studying social phenomena through an intensive and in-depth analysis of an individual case. The case may be a person (a juvenile delinquent), a group (youth criminals), an institution (Borstal School), an event (riot in prison), a situation (collective violence), an organisation (the police), or any other unit of social life. This method provides an opportunity for a thorough analysis of many specific details that are often overlooked in other methods.

The investigator delves into the social, medical, psychological and sometimes psychiatric and mental background of the individual.

Attention is given to attitudes and perceptions as well as to behaviour, following the theory of W.I. Thomas that "if individuals define situations as real, they are real in their consequences". Information is gathered from families, school records, neighbours, peers, work-groups, and other sources; numerous interviews with the individual are also made. This approach rests on the assumption that the case being studied is typical of cases of a certain type so that, through intensive analysis, generalisations may be made which will be applicable to other cases of the same type.

The greatest value of the case study is in the suggestion of hypotheses which can then be tested by other methods. Much of our reliable knowledge about juvenile delinquency, for instance, has developed through the testing of hypotheses which were suggested by early case studies of delinquents (Thomas, 1923; Shaw, 1931). Similarly, much of our present knowledge about female criminals in India stems from hypotheses suggested by Ram Ahuja (1969) and others. These hypotheses are often not tested by the case study method but by other methods.

The *statistical method* enables us to reduce a complex mass of data to simple units of measurement. For example, the researcher can calculate an average (a mean, a median, or a mode) and point out the central tendency of the whole group of items and can also give another figure (standard deviation) to measure the dispersion of items around the central tendency. For example, a criminologist can collect data pertaining to the period for which criminals remain under trial and are detained in prisons without any work, or the period for which petty offenders are imprisoned, pointing out the lack of utility of such imprisonment in the reformation of criminals. By means of statistical device, known as coefficient of correlation, a criminologist can also compare the figures of one group with those of other groups in order to reveal potential relationships.

In statistical technique, quite frequently the *correlation technique* is used in criminology. Investigators pick up a variable considered to be relevant to the study of crime or delinquency and measure the correlation between that variable and crime. The *correlation coefficient* measures the degree to which variables occur together. Perfect correlation is 1.00, and the direction may be positive or negative. For example, age and vision are usually negatively correlated, i.e., as age increases, vision decreases. In criminology, suppose in one study, we find a correlation coefficient of -0.51 between median years of education and juvenile delinquency, and a correlation coefficient of +0.70 between the rate of delinquency and the percentage of low-caste persons, it would mean that as the rate of delinquency increases, the median years of education decrease. But this relationship is not as strong as the relationship between class and delinquency. The strong correlation found by Kewalramani (*Child Abuse*, 1991) in his study of sexual abuse of children was negative to correlation of -0.56 between poverty and rate of sexual abuse. That is, as the percentage of children who lived in well-off homes increased, the rate of sexual abuse of children decreased.

The criticism against the statistical technique is that it can give us bases upon which to predict delinquency/crime but it tells us nothing about causation. For example, the correlation between the social contacts a prisoner is able to maintain and his adjustment in prison is high. We can predict that one will occur when the other occurs; but we would certainly not argue that maladjustment in prison is caused by lack of social contacts. More likely, in many cases of correlation, factors other than those correlated may be the 'cause'. Could we say that because more rapes occur in homes than in streets, sleeping in the streets is safer for women than sleeping at home? This type of correlationship will be ludicrous. Other factors have to be considered in the analysis of statistics. A correlation only directs inquiry; it does not show a causal relationship. A sociologist has wisely said: "Where there is causation, there is also correlation, but where there is correlation, there may be no corresponding causation." In short, statistical analyses are used by criminologists only to measure the frequency with which certain factors—such as age, income, education, intelligence, and others—occur with regard to delinquency and crime.

The *experimental method*, often used used by physical scientists, is not as adaptable to use in the social sciences because control is more difficult to achieve. The closest the criminologist has come to the use of this method is through controlled observations. We may take an example: Suppose we attempt to measure the differences between short-term and long-term methods of detention of male juvenile delinquents. Knowing the failure of traditional methods used in the reformation of juveniles in Children Homes, a new type of treatment facility is introduced in a selected Home that would treat boys for a short period, say, up to three months. The new programme could be a guided group interaction combined with work and recreation programmes, all aimed at changing the self concept of the juvenile. Its results then would be compared with those of the longer treatment period at the same Home where the sentences ran from twelve months to eighteen months. Thus, in an experimental method, ideally an experiment begins with two or more equivalent groups and an experimental variable is introduced only in the 'experimental group'. The 'control group' does not experience the experimental variable. The investigator measures the phenomenon under study before and after the introduction of the experimental variable, thus getting a measure of the change presumably caused by the variable.

In using the experimental method in criminology, the investigator encounters the problem of selecting equivalent groups which proves to be an insurmountable problem. Thus, the difficulty of equalising the experimental and control groups, the difficulty in getting sufficient data, the difficulty of isolating all variables that are not being tested are only some of the problems which make the use of the experimental design in delinquency and crime research doubtful.

All the above-mentioned methods have thus relative merits as well as limitations. As such, no one method can be described as superior to the other. Each is important for its own purpose. The merit of the survey method lies in the fact that it makes the study of criminal behaviour in its natural setting (family, prison, police station, court, correctional reformatory, etc.) eminently practicable; but the great weakness of this method is that the convicted and the incarcerated criminals often do not give accurate information. They only say what they think a researcher wants to hear, either because they just wish to get rid of the researcher, or because they think that the researcher might help them with the official agency. However, the greatest advantage of this method is that researchers get out of their armchairs and move into the field and study criminals in their own environment.

CONCEPT OF CRIME

Now, we take up the concept of crime. Since official statistics are based on the legal definition of crime, since the system of criminal justice is perceived from a legal approach, since all empirical studies on criminals focus on crime as defined by law, and since legal definition of crime is considered to be precise, unambiguous and capable of measurement, let us first examine the legal definition of crime.

Legal Definition of Crime

The legal definition of crime is that it is behaviour or an activity in violation of the legal code. Paul Tappan (1960: 10) has defined crime as "an intentional act or omission in violation of criminal law committed without defence or justification and sanctioned by the state for punishment as a felony or a misdemeanour". Six elements as under are important in this definition:

1. The act should be *actually* committed or it should be an omission of a legal duty (as different from moral duty), i.e., a person cannot be punished for his/ her thoughts. In some cases, however, even words may be considered as acts, as in treason or in aiding or abetting another person to commit a crime. In such cases, it is reasonably argued that some action has taken place. The omission of a *legal* duty is also a crime. Let us illustrate by taking a couple of examples. Suppose a person has a visitor and this visitor suddenly has a heart attack. As the host fails to call a doctor, his friend dies. In this situation, the host cannot be convicted for omission of a duty because he was not legally obliged to try to save his visitor's life. Moral duty will not suffice for prosecution. Now, suppose a person is running a creche. A child in the creche gets injured, but, the person fails to call a doctor and the child dies. The owner of the creche can be convicted for omission of his legal duty to save the child's life.
2. The act must be *voluntary* and committed when the actor has control over his actions. Suppose a person has a dog and he always keeps it chained. A neighbour's child approaches the dog, teases it and throws stones at it. The dog breaks the chain and bites the child. The dog-owner cannot be prosecuted. The case would be different, however, if the man does not chain his dog, knowing well that it is in the habit of biting people. A visitor, if is bitten by the dog, can file a case against him.
3. The act should be *intentional*, whether the intent be general or specific. A person may not have specific intent to shoot another person and kill him, but he is expected to know that his action might result in injury or death of others. Thus, if he shoots a person even when having no specific intent to kill him, he commits a crime because he knows well that his action might injure or cause the death of a person.
4. The act should be a *violation of a criminal law*, as distinct from a non-criminal law or civil and administrative law. This is necessary so that the state can take action against the accused. Non-criminal laws refer to laws which regulate the rights between individuals and organisations; for example, divorce laws, contract laws, laws regulating property rights, etc. We can differentiate between criminal wrongs and non-criminal or civil wrongs. In a criminal wrong, the state brings an action against the accused wrong-doer, while a non-criminal wrong is a wrong against a particular individual (and

not the state) and it is this individual (against whom the wrong is done) who has to take action against the wrong-doer. Some acts, however, may be both criminal and non-criminal and could invite action on the basis of both criminal and non-criminal laws. For example, a person who assaults another person can be prosecuted by the state as well as the assaulted person for damages.

5. The act should be committed *without defence or justification*. Thus, if the act is proved to be in self-defence or to have been committed in insanity, it will not be considered a crime even if it causes harm or injury to others. Ignorance of law is usually no defence.
6. The act should be sanctioned by the state as a felony or a misdemeanour. Persons can be punished only for those acts that may be considered to be *socially harmful* and for which society has provided punishment. A child of four who has killed his mother cannot be convicted for crime because the state has provided no penalty for a child of this age, even if the act is socially harmful.

Hall Jerome (*General Principles of Criminal Law*, 1947: 8-18) has defined crime as "legally forbidden and intentional action which has a harmful impact on social interests, which has a criminal intent, and which has legally-prescribed punishment for it." According to him, no action is to be viewed as crime unless it has following seven characteristics: (1) The behaviour must be harmful in terms of its impact on social interests. The mere intention of causing harm is not crime unless it is actually committed. (2) The harm which occurs must be legally forbidden. (3) The act which brings harmful consequences must be intentional. (4) The act, to affect the harm, must have deliberate motivation. An insane person causing harm does not commit a crime, for the necessary intention is not present. (5) There must be a fusion of criminal intent and conduct. A maid-servant who regularly enters a house to clean utensils, if commits a theft therein, cannot be prosecuted as a trespasser; she can only be convicted for committing a theft. (6) There must be a 'causal' relation between the legally-forbidden harm and the act/conduct. When a teacher slaps a child and his ear-nerve is accidentally ruptured, and he later dies, we are treading a slippery terrain. The relationship between conduct and harm (death) is not so clear in a situation of this kind. (7) There must be legally prescribed punishment for the harmful conduct.

It will be relevant here to discuss the viewpoints of three types of scholars---the classicists, the new deviancy theorists, and the Marxists---who consider the legal rather than the social definition of crime as paramount.

The *classicists* regard crime as behaviour which violates the social contract, which is detrimental not to the state but to the personal safety and property of those individuals in society whose decision to 'contact in' founded the authority of the state (*see*, Fitzgerald, *et al.*, *op. cit.*: 248-307). Thus, for social contract theorists, corruption—including tax-evasion—might be widespread and generally condoned as 'normal' but it would be necessary to legislate against it because it is anti-social and against social justice. They concentrate not on circumstances and influences but on the criminal act itself. If judged as illegal as the law defines it, the act should be punished proportionately—with unwavering certainty, severity and impartiality. Neither discretionary application of justice nor arbitrary exercise of terror are acceptable to them.

The *new deviancy theorists* (like Howard Becker), who believe in the notion of labelling, hold that crime is a behaviour which violates the interests of the powerful. An action, to be termed criminal or deviant, demands not one but two activities: an individual or a group must act in a particular fashion, and second, another individual or group with different values must label the initial activity as deviant. Human beings constantly generate their own systems of values. But within a pluralistic order of society, certain groups, having more power than others, variously termed as 'the elite', 'the powerful', 'the bureaucrats', 'the moral entrepreneur', impose their values upon the less powerful and label those who infringe their rules with stereotyped tags. Thus, a person who in fact is existentially free and evolves different values or experiments with various forms of behaviour, is labelled by the authorities, as, in essence, 'a homosexual', 'a thief', 'a psychopath', 'a drug addict', or 'an alcoholic'.

The *Marxists* accept the legal definition of crime. While the new deviancy theorists believe that crime is an action which is severely against the interests of the powerful, the Marxists have a different opinion. They maintain that law protects the interests of not only the ruling class but also of the working class in a society. According to them, every society is a class society, consisting of the ruling class and the working class. Legal institutions represent the interests of the ruling class but the state—being and remaining the state of the ruling class—nevertheless sustains universal law and thereby guarantees at least a modicum of equality and security for the whole society. Law not only legitimises ruling class domination but also protects working class interests. The Marxists, thus, define crime as violation of law enacted by the society.

Social Definition of Crime

Crime has also been defined in social or non-legal terms. The social definition of crime is that it is behaviour or an activity that offends the social code of a particular community. Mowrer (1959) has defined it as "an anti-social act". Caldwell (1956: 114) has explained it as "an act or a failure to act that is considered to be so detrimental to the well-being of a society, as judged by its prevailing standards, that action against it cannot be entrusted to private initiative or to haphazard methods but must be taken by an organised society in accordance with tested procedures."

Thorsten Sellin (1970: 6) has described crime as "violation of conduct norms of the normative groups". Marshall Clinard (1957: 22) has, however, maintained that all deviations from social norms are not crimes. He talks of three types of deviation: (i) tolerated deviation, (ii) deviation which is mildly disapproved, and (iii) deviation which is strongly disapproved. He perceives the third type of deviation as crime. Let us take an example. Gandhiji not only himself deviated from caste norms but also prompted others not to follow them. Yet, Gandhiji was not considered a deviant because his deviation was for the good of the society. The deviation that harms the society is strongly disapproved.

Positivists, conservatives, and those who explain crime in terms of 'strains' accept the social definition of crime (*see*, Jock Young, *Crime and Society*, 1981: 269). Positivists, like Ferri (1901), Eysenck (1969) and Miller (1958), believe that there is a consensus of values in society that can be scientifically ascertained. Against this it can be judged whether an act is deviant or not. Positivists prefer the word 'deviant' to 'criminal' as the latter merely refers to violation of legal codes which (a) may not reflect consensual values at all (e.g., tax evasion as normal behaviour); (b) do not encompass all acts of deviance (e.g., sexual promiscuity/homosexuality may be deviant but perfectly legal); or (c) are based on legal concepts which are unscientific.

According to conservatives like Nisbet (1970), crimes are the activities which threaten social order, offend morality, and endanger person or property. Attacks on tradition as well as on people's respect for authority are a considerable threat to an ordinary society. Pornographic books and sexy films undermine morals of people and are, therefore, as much a danger to society as enemy agents.

Strain theorists, like Clinard (1964), Merton (1964) and Matza (1969), consider crime as an action which is dysfunctional to society as well as an individual. Thus, they consider not only theft, robbery and homicide etc., as crimes but also truancy, drug addiction, vandalism, suicide, etc. as crimes. All these acts create circumstances in which a wide range of disorder occurs. As functionalists, they note that some crimes may be directly functional to the social order, being the result of 'normal' behaviour rather than strain, and should not be considered as major indications of disequilibrium. Strain theorists do not, therefore, limit themselves to using the official crime statistics, but, rather see them, along with other social indices, as useful and usable.

Criminologists with a sociological perspective have not claimed that there is no place for legal definition of crime in criminology. They have only drawn attention to situations in which people who engage in 'criminal' behaviour are either not caught or are acquitted by the courts because of inadequate evidence or legal loopholes or pressures. Taking a reconciliatory position between legal and social definitions of crime, Reid (1976: 5) has said that legal definition may be used for compiling statistics on crime and for assigning the label 'criminal', but, the studies undertaken for studying causation of crime should include such persons also in their sample of 'criminals' as admit their crime and were not convicted by the courts.

Thus, the legal and non-legal definitions of crime do not always coincide because the legal and the social codes of a society can often differ. For example, accepting a bribe (or corruption) is illegal, but, in reality it is a normal activity indulged in by a large number of people, including the rulers of a country (as happened in the Hawala case in India in which a large number of politicians, bureaucrats, and public servants (about 115) were alleged to have received millions of rupees----65 crore in all---between 1988 and 1991 from Jain brothers in the garb of donations for political parties). Similarly, accepting dowry may be seen as a crime by virtue of the Anti-Dowry Act, making it illegal, or, it may be seen as part and parcel of sanctioned social behaviour of people in the Indian society. Since the legal definition of crime is precise and unambiguous and since the system of our criminal justice is based on legal approach, it is this (legal) definition which is used for all operational purposes, in all official actions, in compiling statistics, and in empirical investigations.

TYPES OF CRIMES

Crimes have been classified on varied bases. Sutherland has given two types of crimes on the basis of their atrocity and seriousness---felony and misdemeanour. The distinction between the two is made in terms of the sentence that can be imposed. Felonies are the more serious crimes for which a person can be imprisoned for a long period of time or sentenced to death. Misdemeanours are the less serious offences for which either a short-term confinement in a jail may be provided or a fine may be imposed. This classification is not much useful because some misdemeanours can be more dangerous than some felonies. A person having committed a theft can be imprisoned for two to three years (if he is a recidivist) or for two to three months only (if he is a petty first-offender). Similarly, theft of ornaments and money from a house, where a girl is to be married, and where her parents have kept jewellery and cash worth thousands of rupees in an almirah, may be more serious than theft of one or two lakhs of rupees from the house of a multi-millionaire. Another objection to this classification is that it is used for classifying criminals as felons (more dangerous) and misdemeanants (less dangerous) who are more susceptible to reformation. But it is quite fallacious to judge danger to group/society or probability of correction and resocialisation on the basis of one act. Suppose an individual commits a theft (misdemeanour) and within a month thereafter, a murder. The two crimes do not represent changes in his character. Yet another argument against this classification is that what is considered a misdemeanour in one society may be considered felony in another society, or what is considered a misdemeanour in a society at one point of time may be considered a felony after a few years in the same society. On these grounds, there seems to be good reason to abandon this classification.

Bonger (*Criminality and Economic Conditions*, 1916: 36-37) has classified crimes into four groups on the basis of their motives: economic, sexual, political and miscellaneous (with vengeance as chief motive). But it cannot be maintained that all crimes are committed only with one motive. A politician who gets his politician father-in-law killed may have a political motive, vengeance motive, as well as an economic motive of getting his (father-in-law's) property through his wife who may be the only daughter of the politician killed. The classification is thus clearly inadequate.

Crimes are also classified for statistical purposes into four groups: against person (assault, murder), against property (theft, robbery), against public decency or morality (drunkenness, disorderly conduct) and against public justice (embezzlement, breach of trust). This classification may be useful from the legal point of view but not for theoretical analysis.

Lemert (*Social Problems*, 1958: 141-49) has classified crimes as situational and systematic. The former are those which are committed because of the pressure of situation while the latter are those which are committed in a planned and systematic way. This classification is important in the treatment of criminals.

Clinard and Quinney (*Criminal Behaviour Systems: A Typology*, 1967: 14-18) have given six types of crimes:

(i) *Violent personal crime*: This crime is based on the use of violence and is committed by a person who does not have earlier record of crime against him. Murder, rape, assault are some examples of this crime. The reaction of society against those who commit this crime is very harsh.

(ii) *Occasional property crime*: This crime is violation of individual property rules. Shoplifting is one example of this crime.

(iii) *Occupational crime*: This crime is committed, during the course of one's occupation, with an economic motive. The criminals who commit this crime accept the traditional norms of society except that of honesty. Embezzlement, blackmarketing, misleading advertisements are some examples of this crime.

(iv) *Political crime*: This is committed by an individual with vested political and economic interests. Treason, spying, passing secrets to enemy country are examples of this crime.

(v) *Public order crime*: This crime is one in which an individual violates the rules of conduct in society. Some examples of this crime are alcoholism, vandalism, prostitution, homosexuality and violation of traffic rules.

(vi) *Conventional crime*: This is a crime in which an individual violates the sacred norms of individual property. Theft, robbery, dacoity, kidnapping, and riot are some examples of this crime. Individuals commit these crimes on a part-time basis, and these crimes are not the main source of their income. However, these criminals are more committed to criminal subculture.

Besides the above kinds of classification, crimes are also classified as white-collar crime (committed by persons of high status with an economic motive), professional crime (committed as a profession and as the main source of livelihood because of which crime becomes a way of life which gives criminals a status in their criminal group), and organised crime (committed in a planned way by a group of criminals).

CONCEPT OF A CRIMINAL

Legally speaking, a criminal is one who is convicted by a court for violating the law of the land. A person who is arrested by the police but is let off by the court cannot be designated as a criminal, i.e., technically the term criminal cannot be applied to one who has not been convicted of a crime. However, the law has never specified whether the criminal status of a person ends after completing the term of imprisonment imposed upon him, i.e., when the status begins and when it ends. A serious problem thus occurs when society refuses to erase the label of criminal. In practice, a person who is once labelled a criminal is often not permitted to forget that status. Caldwell (*op. cit.*: 18) has stated that a question is often asked today: Is criminal a victim of adverse circumstances, unsavoury environment and changing social conditions and social values or is he, as Lombroso claimed, a moral degenerate? Is he a mental imbecile as claimed by psychiatrists? Is he a hardened desperate individual or a dangerous beast as penologists would have us believe? It is not easy to answer the question why he is a criminal. But one thing that is accepted mostly by all scholars today is that he is not a born criminal and efforts can and should be made to correct and resocialise him. Those who commit crime as a matter of choice or as a means of livelihood are few indeed. A large number of criminals are victims of situations or criminals by accident who entertain in the heart of their hearts the same ideals, the same hopes, and the same ambitions which ordinary people have.

CLASSIFICATION OF CRIMINALS

Criminals have been mainly classified as first offenders, casuals habituals, professionals and white-collars. However, different criminologists have classified criminals on the basis of different criteria. Garofalo (*Criminology*, 1914: 111-32) has classified them into four groups: murderers, violent criminals, criminals deficient in probity and lascivious (with feeling of lust) criminals. Ferri (*Criminal Sociology*, 1917: 138-39) has classified them as follows: the insane, the born, the habitual, the occasional, and the passionate. Alexander and Staub (*The Criminal, the Judge and the Public*, 1931: 145-52) have classified criminals as: the accidental and the chronic. The accidental criminal is one who commits a single crime or only a few crimes because of unusual circumstances, while the chronic criminal is one who commits crime repeatedly either because of his association with criminals (*normal* criminal) or because of his anxieties, guilt feelings and personality conflicts (*neurotic* criminal) or who engages in criminal behaviour because of an organic condition (*pathological* criminal). Thus, of the three subcategories of chronic criminals, the 'normal' criminal is a product of sociological factors, the 'neurotic' is a product of psychological factors, and the 'pathological' is a product of biological factors.

Lindesmith and Dunham ("Some Principles of Criminal Typology", *Social Forces*, March 1941: 307-14) have suggested two types of criminals: the social criminal and the individualised criminal. The *social* criminal is one whose criminal behaviour is supported and prescribed by his cultural milieu. In this milieu, crime is customary, and by committing it skillfully, he achieves status and recognition within a certain minority group. In this group, he learns to be a criminal because of his association with criminals. For committing crime, he uses means which are generally regarded as illegitimate. The best example of this type of criminal is the professional criminal. The *individualised* criminal is one who commits crime only for his personal ends. He may commit crime under the stress of economic needs or in a state of emotional disturbance, etc.

Ruth Cavan (*Criminology*, 1948: 30-3Z) has classified criminals in the following six categories: (1) Criminals who live in non-criminal world. These include: the *casual* (who violates minor laws, including local laws, for his convenience), the *occasional* (who occasionally commits crime of a minor nature), the *episodic* (who commits crime, usually a serious one, under some great emotional strain), and the *white-collar* (who commits crime, usually financial in nature, while engaged in some legitimate business). (2) *Professional*, who depends upon crime for his livelihood, moves in the world of criminals, and develops a philosophy in support of his activities. (3) *Organised* (racketeer), who systematises his criminal activities much as some business is organised, with specialised personnel and permanent gradations of leadership. (4) *Habitual*, who repeats his crime. (5) *Mentally abnormal*, whose crime satisfies his psychological need. (6) *Non-malicious*, who is law-abiding in terms of the norms of his own group and in general conforms to the laws of the larger society except in some few instances where his small group norms contradict these laws.

The categories, as given by Cavan, however, are not mutually exclusive. A professional criminal may also be engaged in organised crime and/or be a habitual criminal. Similarly, a criminal who lives in a non-criminal world may also be a habitual criminal and/or a non-malicious criminal, and so on in varying combinations of the categories. In fact, Cavan's classification is based on three criteria: the number of crimes committed, the kind of crime committed, and the kind of person committing the crime. These criteria are loosely fitted together in various combinations. Nevertheless, the classification of criminals into more homogeneous subgroups (as above) does provide deeper insight into criminal behaviour.

CRIME, CRIMINAL AND CRIMINOLOGY

Six questions are important in criminology today (Jock Young, *Crime and Society*, 1981: 249-52), These are: (1) How is an individual's criminal behaviour explained? At the point of committing crime, is the offender perceived as acting out of free will or is he seen AS compelled by some forces beyond his control? (2) How is the functioning of social order perceived? Is order in society understood as based on consent of the vast majority or is it largely based on coercion? (3) How is crime defined? Is crime seen as the violation of the legal code or as behaviour that offends the social code of a particular community? (4) How is extent and distribution of crime viewed? Is crime viewed as a limited phenomenon committed by a small number of people, or as an extensive phenomenon engaged in by a large proportion of the population? (5) How are the causes of crime explained? Are the causes of crime located primarily within the individual (i.e., his personality) or is crime seen as the product of the wider society within which the individual lives? (6) What is the policy regarding criminals? Is the policy of punishing the offender appropriate or is the policy of treatment of the criminal accepted?

Jock Young has framed the following six questions on the basis of dichotomies:

- Individual's behaviour : free will versus determinism
- Functioning of social order : consensus versus coercion
- Definition of crime : legal versus social
- Extent and distribution of crime : limited versus extensive
- Causes of crime : individual versus social
- Policy towards criminals : punishment versus treatment

Following Jock Young, the following chart (on p. 30) can be presented to point out the dichotomous reactions of seven different paradigms to these six questions.

STATISTICS ON CRIMES AND CRIMINALS

The use of statistics in all social sciences, including criminology, is looked at with suspicion for explaining a criminological phenomenon on the ground that the given statistics are either unreliable or inadequate. Howsoever true this allegation may be, statistics are important.

Reactions of Different Paradigms to Important Questions of Crime and Criminals

	Questions and Dichotomous Reactions	*Classicism*	*Positivism*	*Conservatism*	*Strain Theory*	*New Deviancy Theory*	*Liberalism/ Reformism*	*Marxism*
1.	How is individual behaviour determined? (Free will v/s determinism)	Free will	Determinism	Freewill	Determinism	Determinism	Determinism	Determinism
2.	How is functioning of social order perceived? (Consensus v/s coercion)	Consensus	Consensus	Coercion	Consensus	Coercion	Coercion	Coercion
3.	Definition of crime (Legal v/s social)	Legal	Social	Social	Social	Legal	Legal	Legal
4.	Extent of crime (Limited v/s extensive)	Limited	Limited	Extensive	Limited	Limited	Limited	Limited
5.	Causes of crime (Individual v/s social)	Individual	Social	Individual	Social	Social	Social	Social
6.	Policy towards criminal (Punishment v/s treatment)	Punishment	Treatment	Punishment	*	*	Treatment	*

* (They emphasise changing the functioning of social structures and social systems.)

According to Caldwell (1956: 1415), statistics in criminology furnish us with much valuable information. *First*, they tell us about the magnitude of crime, types of crimes, and the nature of criminals in a society. This information is very useful in corrective and preventive programmes. *Secondly*, statistics can inform us about the number of persons arrested for committing crimes, number of persons prosecuted, convicted, imprisoned, placed on probation, or acquitted, i.e., how the criminals have been handled. This can help in determining the efficiency of the law-enforcement agencies and the problems that confront them. *Thirdly*, they can explain the characteristics of criminals and delinquents and their backgrounds (sex, age, marital status, education, occupation, income, residence, etc.). This information enables us to compare criminals with non-criminals and thus gain some insight into the possible causes of crime and juvenile delinquency. Similarly, it indicates the kind of preventive and remedial measures that are needed to cope with these problems.

Caldwell has, however, maintained that the use of statistics in criminology involves certain difficulties. *First*, the laws keep on changing from time to time and place to place. Consequently, increases or decreases in the figures shown in reports may reflect the action of legislatures in the reduction of offences and not any changes in the habits or activities of people. For example, in India before the enactment of the Juvenile Justice Act,1986, children (both boys and girls) on attaining the age of 21 years were included in the statistics compiled on juvenile delinquents. But from 1988 onwards, boys below the age of 16 years and girls below 18 years of age were described as juvenile delinquents. The result was that crime cases attributed to juveniles got much reduced. While the percentage of juvenile crimes in the total crimes under the Indian Penal Code (IPC) was 3.7 in 1987, it got reduced to 1.7 in 1988. Similarly, the share of juvenile crimes in the total crimes under the local and special laws fell from 2.4 per cent to 0.7 per cent. This reduction was due to a change in the law and not any change in the attitudes of children. *Secondly*, all required statistics are not always available. Absence of complete record on crimes, therefore, provides us only a sample of actual criminality. The ratio between sample and totality may not always be the same, because of which the criminologist may fail to ascertain the actual size of the problem. Thorsten Sellin (*Law Quarterly Review*, October 1951: 496-98) has also said that all statistics on crime are in fact statistics of law enforcement agencies which may not necessarily reflect 'total' criminality in a given geographical area. Therefore, police statistics, court statistics or prison statistics cannot always be accepted as the index of actual criminality. *Thirdly*, the recorded criminality in order to be meaningful must be related to the population of the society. This is generally not done. The result is that what is interpreted as increase in criminality may actually reflect an increase in population. For example, the total crimes committed under the Indian Penal Code and the Local and Special Laws in 1971 were 38.6 lakh when the population of the country was 54.82 crore. This means that 0.7 per cent people were involved in crimes. On the other hand, the total number of crimes committed under the Indian Penal Code and the Local and Special Laws in 1998 was 61.8 lakh and the total number of persons arrested was 71.49 lakh when the population of the country was 97.09 crore. This means 0.13 per cent of people were involved in crimes (*Crime in India*, 1998: 263-65). Thus, if we take only the total number of crimes committed in 1998 as against those committed in 1951, crime shows an increase of 2.7 per cent, but, if it is seen in terms of increase in population in 47 years, crime shows a meagre increase from 179.9 per one lakh population in 1951 to 183.2 per one lakh in 1998 (*Crime in India*, 1998: 12). This clearly reveals the difficulty involved in compiling statistics. *Fourthly*, the number of persons arrested by itself does not give the correct picture of crime because other information is also needed if we are to have a clear picture of what is happening in our society. For example, the enacting of new laws or the repealing of old laws, the changing attitudes of citizens, and the efficiency of law enforcement agencies also affect the crime scenario in the society. A researcher in criminology has to give due weight to all these factors in analysing crime rather than merely depend on crime statistics compiled by the Ministry of Home Affairs or some other agency in the country.

SALIENT CHARACTERISTICS OF CRIME IN INDIA

In India, in an hour about 193.2 cognisable crimes under the Indian Penal Code and 464.9 crimes under the Local and Special Laws are committed (1991 to 1998 figures, *Crime in India*, 1998:42). Taking the average of 8 years from 1991 to 1998, in one day, the police grapples with 850 thefts, 264 riots, 397 robberies and burglaries, and 3,145 other criminal offences (*Crime in India*, 1998: 15-16). Between 1978 and 1988, crime registered a rise of 15-16 per cent (from 13.44 to 14.40 lakh) while between 1988 and 1998, crime increased only by 20.0 per cent (from 14.40 lakh to 17.79 lakh) (*ibid.*, 1998: 16). The rising graph of crime might cause alarm among the public but our police and our politicians remain unruffled about the deteriorating law and order situation. The non-ruling political parties are concerned with these figures only in one way—they use them to criticise the policies of the ruling party so that it could be defamed and removed from power, yielding place to a new governing elite.

Given the limitations of official criminal statistics, it is perhaps unwise to attempt to set forth vitally important facts about crime in the Indian society. It is conceivable that with adequate and valid methods, many of these 'facts' would change drastically. Nevertheless, there seems to be enough evidence to support at least the following brief description of crime in our country:

1. Taking the average of four years—from 1995 to 1998—of the total 62.20 lakh crimes committed in India every year, about 17.26 lakh are cognisable crimes under the Indian Penal Code (IPC) (including theft, burglary, robbery, dacoity, murder, riot, kidnapping, cheating, breach of trust...), and about 44.94 lakh are offences under the Special and Local Laws (SLL) (like Dowry Prohibition Act, Prohibition Act, Gambling Act, Excise Act, Arms Act, Immoral Traffic Prevention Act, Narcotic Drugs and Psy-Substances Act, Indian Railways Act, Explosive Substances Act, etc. (*Crime in India*, 1998:27). Thus, the crime rate is not very high in our country. Whereas crime rate per one lakh population in India is 636.6, in Canada it is 12,735, in Britain it is 8,576, in Germany it is 8,030, in Denmark, it is 10,021 and in New Zealand it is 13,087 (*Crime in India*, 1997: 24).
2. Of about 74 lakh cases of crimes investigated by the police every year, about 31 per cent are cases of cognisable crimes under the IPC and about 69 per cent are offences committed under the SLL (*ibid.*, 136-40).
3. The pattern of crime under the IPC indicates that of the total offences every year, 15 per cent are violent crimes (murder, rape, kidnapping, riots, etc.), 23 per cent are property crimes (theft, burglary), 3 per cent are white-collar crimes (cheating, breach of trust, counterfeiting) and 59 per cent are other (uncategorised) crimes (*ibid.*, 1998:30).
4. Of the total (cognisable) crimes under the IPC, about one-fourth (24.7%) are related to theft (16.2%), burglary (1.7%), robbery (1.3%) and dacoity (0.5%). Further, crime rate is almost same (26.4%) for offences against persons (murder, abduction, hurt, rape, kidnapping, cheating, cruelty, molestation, sexual harassment). The same is *not* true of the United States where about three-fourths (77%) crimes are property crimes (burglary, larceny, auto-theft, etc.) and only one-fourth (23%) are crimes against person (Backer, 1966: 211).
5. Of the total persons arrested for offences under the SLL, about

one-fifth (19.7%) are arrested under five Acts: Prohibition Act—12.3 per cent; Gambling Act—2.6 per cent; Excise Act—2.5 per cent; Indian Railways Act—0.9 per cent; and Arms Act—1.4 per cent. The remaining four-fourths (80.3%) are arrested under the Immoral Traffic Act, the Narcotic Drugs Act, the Explosives Act, the Dowry (Prohibition) Act, the Essential Commodities Act, TADA, and so on (*Crime in India*, 1998: 37-38).

6. Of the total IPC crimes, about half (54.8%) are committed in six states of Uttar Pradesh (10.4%), Maharashtra (10.1%), Madhya Pradesh (11.3%), Bihar (6.5%), and Rajasthan (9.4%) and Gujarat (7.1%). About one-fourth (26.9%) crimes are committed in four southern states of Tamil Nadu (8.4%), Karnataka (6.2%), Andhra Pradesh (6.9%) and Kerala (5.2%) (*ibid.*, 1998: 33).
7. For about 17.8 lakh IPC crimes committed every year, about 26.6 lakh persons are arrested, that is, on an average 15 persons are arrested for every 10 crimes. On the other hand, for every 10 offences committed under the SLL, 10.2 persons are arrested (*ibid*: 16, 263, 265).
8. More than four-fifths of the offenders (85%) commit crimes under the IPC for which they get less than six months imprisonment, that is, their crimes are misdemeanours.
9. Crime rate is much higher for males than females. Out of every 100 offenders, 95 are males and five are females (*ibid.*, 1998: 271).
10. The percentage of urban offenders is much lower as compared to rural offenders.
11. Crime rate is the highest among those in the destitute class (income up to Rs. 500 p.m.), the lower class (income between Rs. 501 and Rs. 1,000 p.m.) and in the lower-middle class (income between Rs. 1,001 and Rs. 2,000 p.m.).
12. Crime rate (IPC and SLL together) is the highest (51.3%) in the age group of 18-30 years. The percentage in other age groups is 0.2 in age group below 16 years, 1.2 in 16-18 years age group, 41.3 in 31-50 years age group and 6.0 in 51 plus age group (*ibid.*, 1998: 299-300).
13. A characteristic feature of the Indian criminal scene is an increase in organised crime—the emergence of large-scale organisations for criminal activities. What is being systematically organised is the control and distribution of illicit goods and services—drugs (narcotics), girls for prostitution (in India and in the Arabian countries), smuggling of gold, etc. In addition, there are the organised

efforts of the mafia groups to control various legitimate business activities, such as coal mines, unions in industries, and the like. Although the total number of major crimes charged to 'organised crime' is probably small, its cost and its pattern in cities provides a distinctive element.

In presenting these facts and features, the idea is to point out the weakening of motives for conformity to social norms and the disruption of social relationships and social bonds. The unrest is increasing almost in all sections of our society. There is unrest among youth, peasants, industrial workers, students, government employees, and the minorities. Social unrest increases frustrations and strains which lead to violation of legal and social norms. It is true to say that organisation and the functioning of the existing subsystems and structures in our society are largely responsible for the increase in crime. Various sets of ideas about crime causation have been developed by a number of scholars, stemming primarily from Durkheim, moving to scholars like Merton, Cohen, Miller, Cloward and Ohlin, and recently to Hermann Manheim, Radzinowicz, Jock Young, Ian Taylor and others. We shall attempt to analyse some of these viewpoints in the following chapter.

References

Barlow, Hugh D., *Introduction to Criminology*, Little, Brown and Co., Boston, 1978.

Block, Herbert A. and Geis Gilbert (2nd edn.), *Man, Crime and Society*, Random House, New York, 1970.

Caldwell, R.G., *Criminology*, Ronald Press Co., New York, 1956.

Fitzgerald, Mike, McLennan Gregor, Pawson Jennie, *Crime and Society*, Routledge and Kegan Paul, London, 1981.

Gibbons, Don C., *Society, Crime, and Criminal Careers* (3rd edn.), Prentice-Hall, Englewood Cliffs, New Jersey, 1977.

Johnson, Elmer H., *Crime, Correction and Society*, (4th edn.). The Dorsey Press, Illinois, 1978.

Reckless, Walter C., *The Crime Problem* (2nd edn.), Appleton-Century-Crofts, Inc., New York, 1955.

Reid, Sue Titus, *Crime and Criminology*, The Dryden Press, Illinois, 1976.

Taylor, Ian, Walton Paul, Young Jock, *Critical Criminology*, Routledge and Kegan Paul, London, 1975.

Chapter 2

Theories of Criminal Behaviour

What is it that causes crime? Various scholars have attempted to build different theories to explain crime systematically. Some have even tried to modify the existing theories so that different parts of a theory fit coherently, ironing out inconsistencies and contradictions of position. It is not even uncommon to adopt different explanations for different types of crime and different categories of offenders. Thus, white-collar (or occupational) crime is theorised differently from a common thief's petty property crime. Female crime is explained differently from male crime. Crimes by juvenile delinquents and also youths (between 16 and 24 years of age) are explained differently from adult crimes. In fact, variability in crime has led some criminologists to question the search for a single all-embracing theory which will explain all types of crimes. It may well be that we may not require a single theory, no matter how systematic it may be, to account for all types of crime.

Criminological theories indeed differ in their explanation of crime. Reid (1976: 103-251) has classified theoretical explanations as follows: (1) classical and positive theories, (2) physiological, psychiatric and psychological theories, and (3) sociological theories. He has further subclassified the sociological theories in two groups: (i) social structural theories (including Merton's, Cohen's, Cloward and Ohlin's, Matza's, Miller's and Quinney's theories), and (ii) social process theories (including Sutherland's and Howard Becker's theories.

We shall consider in this chapter seven major theoretical explanations of criminal behaviour: (i) classical and neo-classical theories, (ii) biological and constitutional theories, (iii) psychological, psychiatric

Theoretical Explanations of Causes of Crime

No.	*Theoretical explanation*	*Propounder*	*Year*	*Main thesis that crime is result of*
1.	Classicist	Beccaria	1764	(i) Man's rational motivation (ii) Hedonism or pain/pleasure principle
2.	Biogenic	....	....	Inherited traits
	(i) Evolutionary Atavism Theory	Lombroso	1876	Physical stigmate or defective organisms
	(ii) Goring's Theory	Charles, Goring	1919	Defective anatomical factors
	(iii) Hooton's Theory	Hooton	1939	Biological inferiority
	(iv) Physiological Make-up Theory	Sheldon	1940	Mesomorphic physique
3.	Psychogenic....	....	....	Defective personally
	(i) Psychological Theory	Goddard	1919	Inherited feeble-mindedness
	(ii) Psychiatric Theory	William, Healy	1919	Mental disorders or emotional disturbances
	(iii) Psychoanalytical Theory	Adler, Abrahamsen, etc.	1930 1952	Instincts, or undeveloped ego, or guilt feelings, or inferiority complex
4.	Economic (Theory)	Fornasari and Bonger, etc.	1894 and 1916	Economic conditions or poverty and riches
5.	Geographical (Theory)	Dexter, Quetlet, etc.	1904	Geographical factors like climate, temperature, humidity, etc.
6.	Sociogenic	....	....	Conditioned by social environment
	(A) Ecological or Delinquency Area Theory	Clifford Shaw	1929	Disorganised neighbourhood or pathological living conditions
	(B) Structural Theories....	....	....	Social structures create crime
	(a) Differential Association Theory	Sutherland	1939	Associations with and social influences of criminalistic norms
	(b) Anomie Theory	Merton	1938	Strains caused by disjunction between goals and means

Contd...

Contd...

	(C) Subcultural Theories			
	(a) Differential Opportunity Theory	Cloward & Ohlin	1960	Differentials in legitimate and illegitimate means to achieve success-goals
	(b) Delinquent Subculture Theory	Cohen	1955	Rejection of dominant values and development of delinquent values
	(c) Theory of Techniques of Neutralization	Matza & Sykes	1970	Delinquent denies responsibility, injury and victim and thus reduces the forces of social control
	(D) Social Process Theories	....	....	Process of a person becoming a criminal
	(a) Labelling Theory	Howard Becker	1963	Consequence of application by others of rules and sanctions to an offender
	(b) Containment Theory	Walter Reckless	1967	Unfavourable self-concept and lack of strong inner and reinforcing outer control
	(c) New Deviancy Theory	Richard Quinney	1972	Exploitation of the powerless by the powerful. It focuses on 'Reaction'.
	(E) Conflict Theories:			Conflict among conduct norms
	(a) Culture Conflict Theory	Thorsten Sellin	1938	Crime caused by combination of biological, psychological, economic and social factors.
7.	Multiple-Factor Theory	Cyril Burt	1915	

and psychoanalytical theories, or mental subnormality, mental illness and psychopathological explanations, (iv) economic theory, (v) geographical or topographical theory, (vi) sociological theories, or ecological, structural, subcultural and social process theories, and (vii) multiple-factor theory.

CLASSICAL AND NEO-CLASSICAL THEORIES

Classicist explanations of crime and punishment were developed in the second half of the eighteenth century. In fact, these theoretical explanations developed as a reaction of enlightened thinkers and political reformers to arbitrary systems of justice and barbarous codes of punishment which prevailed up to the end of the eighteenth century. They demanded a legal system that would defend the interests of criminals and protect their rights and liberties. They believed in the 'contract theory' of the origin of state (propounded by Rousseau), that is, regulating the conduct of free individuals who were bound to one another within the society by a fee and 'legal' contract between free and equal individuals. (According to Rousseau's doctrine of social contract, men were absolutely free and independent in a state of nature but surrendered a small part of their freedom through a social contract in order to secure the benefits of union. The doctrine of social contract has no foundation in history, and Rousseau himself probably knew that it was a fiction, but it gave him a basis upon which to plead the cause of liberty and to protest against tyranny.) Thus, individuals were conceived as free, rational and sovereign individuals, capable of defining their self-interests and rationally thinking of the consequences of their actions. They, therefore, thought of state/society not as something sovereign but as something which individuals had contracted to establish for their individual and mutual benefits. In this way, they sought to limit the power of the state to the defence of rights and liberties, as well as safety and security of the individual.

The classicists define crime as behaviour which violates the social contract, which is detrimental not to the state as such, but to the personal safety and property of those individuals in society whose decision to 'contract in' founded the authority of the state. Thus, for classicists, an act like tax-evasion might be widespread and generally condoned as 'normal' but it would be necessary to legislate against it because it is anti-social and against social justice. For them 'legal' rather than 'natural' definitions are paramount in the definition of crime, i.e., crime according to them is infringement of legal code, not of a social norm. It is only by "due process of law" that it can be ascertained whether a particular act is a crime or not.

Classicists concentrate not on circumstances and influences but on the criminal act itself. If illegal, judged as the law defines it in the light of the social contract, then the act should be punished proportionately, with unwavering certainty, severity, and impartiality. Classicists thus accept neither the arbitrary exercise of terror not the discretionary application of justice. They also maintain that the law should not be involved in the control of any activities which do not harm others or do not threaten the social contract. Individuals should be free to do anything they like, provided what they do is not proscribed by law. Law and morality should be regarded as separate spheres: the one regulating the public concerns; the other, the individual judgement and private reasoning.

The cause of crime in the classicist paradigm relates to the question of rational calculation where the 'benefit' is greater than the 'cost'. For this reason, punishment must be made so strict that an individual would be deterred from committing crime again.

The propounder of the classicist explanation was an Italian thinker, Beccaria who was influenced by the writings of scholars like John Howard. Beccaria (*Essays on Crime and Punishment*, 1764) maintained that: (a) human nature is rational, free and governed by self-interest, (b) social order is based on consensus and social contract, (c) crime is infringement of the legal code and not of social norm, (d) distribution of crime is limited and is to be ascertained through a 'due process', (e) crime is caused by an individual's rational motivation, (f) crimes should be judged by a jury of one's peers, i.e., by other rational and equal individuals. The judges should be guided by a clear and systematic legal code, and (g) in punishing the offender, the principle of 'restraint' should be observed, i.e., sentencing should be limited to applying a prior, agreed and fixed set of penalties.

The classical school of criminology had four important principles. *First*, the rights and liberties of an individual must be protected. *Second*, all persons who commit the same crime should be punished alike. *Third*, crime is a judicial abstraction and therefore a definite penalty should be attached to each crime and invariably inflicted. *Fourth*, punishment should be limited by the social need. Its social utility consists in its deterrent influence and as much of it should be inflicted as is necessary to prevent others from committing the same crime.

The main postulates of Beccaria's classical explanation (Cf. Schafer Stephen, 1969: 106) are:

1. Man's behaviour is purposive and rational and is based on hedonism or pleasure-pain principle, that is, he consciously chooses pleasure and avoids pain.
2. Punishment should be assigned to each crime and the measure of punishment should be the injury done to the public welfare by a crime. Pain should outweigh any pleasure derived from the commission of crime.
3. Punishment should not be very severe and deterrent and it should also be proportioned to crime, pre-determined, prompt and public. Torture should be abolished, more use should be made of imprisonment instead of corporal punishment, and a fair trial should be insured.
4. Law must apply equally to all citizens.
5. Legislatures should clearly enact the law and prescribe specific punishment for its violation. Judges should not interpret the laws according to their own ideas of justice but should only decide whether or not a person had committed a crime (violated the law). In other words, courts should only determine innocence or guilt and thereafter prescribe the set punishment.

The major arguments against the classical explanation are: (1) Classicists assume that all men are free, rational and equal. None has priority of rank or status, and no prior handicaps or advantages. But the real world does not in any way resemble this ideal model. Even classicists accept the competitive model of man, where seeking advantage (acquiring property, accumulating wealth) is precisely the most rational of motivations. These generate, as the necessary consequence of a competitive system, massively unequal distribution of advantages and disadvantages. There is, thus, contradiction in classicism. Jock Young (Cf. Fitzgerald, *et al.*, *Crime and Society*, 1981: 264) has also said that all problems in classicism flow from this central contradiction. (2) If men are equally rational, as claimed by classicists, why do they violate the law at all? Should not reason regularly prevail? Further, if all individuals are equally endowed with reason, why do the poor regularly commit so much more crime than the rich? Young also asks a question: if classicists are right in their view (that all individuals are equal and rational) why do statistics on crime in the United States (and for that matter in any other country) take the shape of a pyramid (as shown below) in which a labourer is found fourteen times more likely to go to prison than a professional? (3) All criminals are to be treated alike without differentiating them on the basis of age, sex or intelligence. (4) No importance is given to the nature of crime (that is, whether the crime is a felony or misdemeanour) or the type of the criminal (that is, whether he is a first offender, a casual offender, a habitual offender, or a professional offender). (5) Explaining an individual's behaviour merely on the basis of doctrine of 'free will' and suggesting punishment on the principle of 'utilitarianism' is only an armchair philosophy which considers crime in the abstract and lacks scientific approach in objective and empirical measurement. (6) There is no provision for *justifiable* criminal acts. (7) Beccaria and Bentham were more concerned with reform in the criminal law (like mitigation of severity of punishment, removal of defects in the jury system, abolition of transportation and capital punishment, and in the adoption of a prison philosophy) and regulating morality, than in controlling crime or in the development of criminological theories.

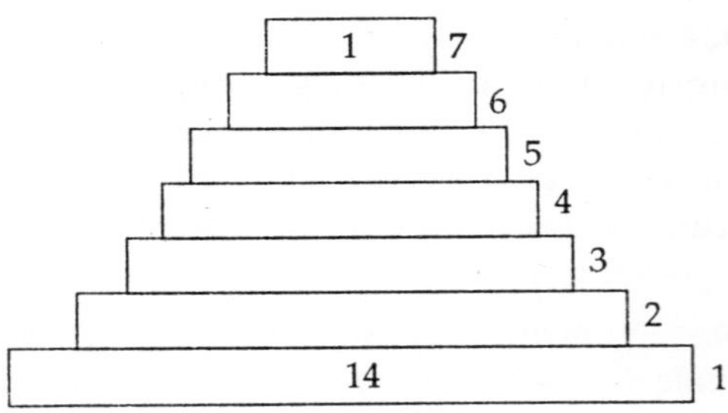

[1. Labourers; 2. Service workers; 3. Operatives; 4. Craftsmen; 5. Clerks; 6. Managers; 7. Professionals]

The British neo-classicist criminologists revised the classical theory in 1810 and 1819 and (a) provided for judicial discretion under objective circumstances, (b) introduced the idea of minimum and maximum sentences, (c) recognised the principle of extenuating circumstances, and (d) described the concept of equal justice as unreal, suggested giving importance to age, mental condition and situations in fixing punishment to criminals. Children under seven years of age and mentally diseased persons were to be exempted from the law (Vold, 1958: 25-26; Reid, 1976: 113-14). In spite of these changes, the neo-classicists continued to accept the principles of free will of man and hedonism. Besides, unlike the classical school, this school did begin to deal with the problem of causation. By making exceptions to the law, varied causation was implied. However, this school also has not been considered a scientific school of criminology.

BIOLOGICAL THEORIES

The positivists (who used experimental or inductive method in making generalisations) rejected the concept of 'free will' advocated by the classicists and the neo-classicists and laid emphasis on the doctrine of 'determinism'. They paved the way for a philosophy of individualised scientific treatment of criminals, based upon the findings of the physical and social sciences. Lombroso, Ferri and Garofalo were three major positivists who laid stress on the physiological incapacity of an individual or the biogenic or hereditary aspects of criminal behaviour. (Heredity is the parental contribution made through 46 chromosomes. Of these, two determine sex of the infant and 44 affect other qualities of the body. Combinations and permutations among genes determine an infant's particular genotype, that is, genetic contribution of an organism).

Lombroso, an Italian physician and professor of clinical psychiatry and criminal anthropology, and described as the "father of criminology", propounded the theory of evolutionary atavism (also called theory of physical criminal type, or theory of born criminals) in 1876. He claimed that: (1) Criminals constitute a distinct 'born' type. (2) This type of criminal can be identified by certain physical abnormalities or stigmata or anomalies such as asymmetrical face, large ears, excessively long arms, flattened nose, retreating forehead, tufted and crispy hair, insensibility to pain, eye defects, and other physical peculiarities. (3) The stigmata are not the causes of crime but rather the symptoms of atavism (reversion to a more primitive type) or degeneracy. Thus, according to Lombroso, atavism and degeneracy are the basic causes of crime. (4) A person who is the criminal type cannot refrain from committing crime unless he lives under exceptionally favourite circumstances. (5) Not only criminals differ from non-criminals in physical characteristics but they (criminals) can also be distinguished according to the type of crime they commit.

Initially, Lombroso came out with only one type of criminals—the born criminals (a term which, in fact, was introduced by Ferri)—but later on he identified two other types of criminals too: *criminaloid* or *occasional* criminals (who differed from born criminals only in degree, and who indulged in crime owing to precipitating factors in environment, i.e., when they got an opportunity to commit crime), and *criminals by passion* (who were in complete contrast with the born criminals in terms of nervous and emotional sensitiveness, and in motives of crimes such as love or politics). Although Lombroso obviously emphasised the biological causes of crime, he did not entirely neglect, as erroneously claimed by many critics, the sociological causes. While going through his later works, one reaches this obvious conclusion.

Lombroso's research had serious methodological problems. Of these, Reid (*op. cit.*: 117) has pointed out four: *One*, he depended on collection of facts which were limited to organic factors. Although, he realised the importance of psychic factors, yet he found them hard to measure. *Two*, his method was mainly descriptive and not experimental. *Three*, his generalisations about atavism and degeneracy left a large gap between theory and fact. *Four*, his method was largely one of analogy and anecdote, from which he drew his conclusions. Such a method is unscientific for drawing generalisations.

As for the policy towards criminals, Lombroso was of the opinion that if the criminal was not responsible for his or her actions, it made no sense to punish him/her. Instead, we must replace punishment by treatment. A panel of experts should diagnose the condition of the individual and prescribe appropriate treatment. He thus holds that punitive response, as advocated by classicist theorists, is applicable.

Charles Goring, an English psychiatrist and philosopher, criticised Lombroso's theory on the basis of his own study in which he measured the characteristics of 3,000 English convicts and a large number of non-criminals in 1913. He maintained that there was no such thing as a 'physical criminal type'. However, he himself explained crime on the basis of hereditary factors (1919: 11), using statistical treatment of facts, or what is called statistico-mathematical method. Goring's work was also criticised because (Reid, 1976: 120-21): (1) he committed the same errors in statistical analysis for which he had criticised Lombroso. He measured intelligence not by the available Simon-Binet tests but by his own impression of the mental ability of criminals; (2) he completely ignored the impact of environment on crime; (3) the sample of non-criminals which included undergraduate university students, inmates of a hospital, mental patients and soldiers was defective; and (4) he was violently prejudiced against Lombroso.

Garofalo and Ferri had supported Lombroso in his biological school. Garofalo in his book *Criminology*, published in 1885 (its English translation appeared in 1914), talked of physical differences between criminals and non-criminals, but he differed from Lombroso in the emphasis he (Lombroso) placed on the physical abnormality of the criminal. Garofalo was not sure whether or not physical abnormality of the criminal was caused by physiological factors. Rejecting Lombroso's 'physical anomaly', he focused on 'psychic anomaly' of the criminal and referred to 'moral degeneracy'. He admitted that environmental factors might play a role in individual's criminality but there was one element (organic deficiency) in the criminal which was inherited or somehow acquired early in infancy. He did not believe in the 'casual' offender and disagreed with Lombroso (as well as Ferri) in the classification of offenders. He himself (*Criminology*, 1914) classified them as typical criminals (murderers), violent criminals, criminals deficient in probity and lascivious criminals. Garofalo believed that since crime was basically the result of an inherited organic deficiency, the criminal could not be reformed. He also criticised the reform plans as suggested by Ferri.

Ferri was another Italian scholar who supported Lombroso's biological school. He not only coined the term 'born criminal' for Lombroso's 'atavistic criminal' but he also talked of three other types: the 'insane' (who suffers from some clinical form of mental alienation), the 'habitual' (who has acquired the habit of crime), the 'occasional' (who commits insignificant criminal acts), and the 'passionate'. His classification, thus, closely parallels that of Lombroso.

Referring to causes of crime, Ferri (*Criminal Sociology*, 1917: 54) rejected the classicists' doctrine of free will and talked of criminal behaviour as the result of interaction between the personality and the environment of a man. In order to be a criminal, it is necessary that the individual should face such personal, physical, and moral conditions and social environment which draw him towards crime. Ferri believed that crime was primarily caused by society. It can be corrected by making economic, social and political changes in society, like freedom of emigration, changes in tax structure (lower tax on necessities and higher tax on luxuries), providing employment opportunities, cheap houses, electoral reforms, changes in marriage and divorce laws, and so forth. Ferri was also in favour of penal reforms.

Taking Lombroso's, Garofalo's, and Ferri's views together, we may analyse contribution of the positive school of criminology. *First*, it placed emphasis on empirical research and use of scientific approach to the study of criminal behaviour and on reform of the criminal law. *Two*, it drew attention to the principle of determinism in criminality. *Three*, it introduced the concept of environment in the study of crime. *Four*, it advocated substituting the indeterminate sentence for the definite sentence.

However, Lombroso's theory in particular and positivist school in general have been criticised. The main criticisms against Lombroso's and positivists' theoretical explanation are: (1) Lombroso's collection of facts was confined to organic factors and he neglected psychic and social factors. Garofalo and Ferri, however, did place emphasis on these factors. Hans Eysenck (1977: 77-79) has said: "Criminality is a social concept, not a biological one. The very notion of crime would be meaningless without a context of learning or social experience and of human interaction. What the studies on heredity have demonstrated is that it is a very strong predisposing factor as far as committing crimes is concerned. But whether the crime is actually committed by an individual or not and the way in which he carries it out is subject to the changing vicissitudes of his everyday life." (2) Positivists' method was mainly descriptive. (3) Their research samples were often too small and not representative, being taken only from prison populations. (4) They made no use of control groups or follow-up studies. (5) Operational definitions of their terms were not always clear and concise. (6) They did not use sophisticated statistical analysis. (7) There were logic-of-science errors in their research as they assumed that institutionalised populations represented criminals. (8) Their approach has no predictive value because many who have the characteristics they attribute to criminals do not become criminals and many who do not have these characteristics do become criminals.

PHYSIOLOGICAL THEORIES

Interest in biogenic variables got revived when emphasis on physiological characteristics came to be placed. The science of endocrinology (glands) devoted itself to the study of the glands of internal secretion. Schlapp and Smith (*The New Criminology*, 1928) explained crime as the product of endocrine deficiencies, excesses and disturbances. Barnes and Shalloo (*Contemporary Social Theory*, 1940: 688-89) are of the opinion that though this theory contributes something or a good deal to our understanding of crime, yet it does not completely explain it. Glands do affect personality but personality is something more than glands. Crime cannot thus be related to the functioning of glands alone.

Hooton, a Harvard physical anthropologist, was another scholar who tried to determine whether there was any relation between anti-social conduct and physiological characteristics. On the basis of his 12-year study of 13,873 male prisoners compared to a small number of 3,203 male non-criminals, he concluded (*Crime and the Man*, 1939) that the primary cause of crime is 'biological inferiority'. He did not claim that inferiority directly causes crime but he asserted that crime was the result of biological and social forces because of which mentally and physically inferior individuals were selected for criminality. The four conclusions he drew from his study were: (1) Criminal behaviour is the direct result of inherited biological inferiority as shown by characteristics like sloping forehead, thin lips, straight (and not curved) hair, body hair, small ears, long thin neck and sloping shoulders. (2) Particular types of crime are caused by particular types of biological inferiority. Tall and thin men tend to be murderers and robbers, tall and heavy men tend to be cheats, short-statured and thin men tend to be thieves and burglars, and short heavy men are prone to commit sexual crimes. (3) Criminals are organically inferior. (4) Increase in criminality can be checked only by the sterilisation of the physically and mentally defective persons. Hooton further held that in every society, there were a few genuises, hordes of mediocres, masses of morons, and regiments of criminals. He named three types of biologically inferior people: organically unadaptable, mentally stunted, and sociologically warped.

His theory was, however, criticised by Albert Cohen, Alfred Lindersmith, Karl Schuessler, and others (*see*, Sutherland,1955: 118-19; Vold, 1958: 59-64; Gibbons, 1977: 139-40) on the following counts: (1) his studies were based on biased samples. The non-criminals represented types that could be expected to be superior intellectually (university students) and physically stronger (firemen), military men, members of a bathing house, and outpatients of a hospital. The sample of criminals was unrepresentative as criminals were drawn only from an imprisoned population; (2) his research methodology was defective; (3) he had no explicit criteria of 'biological inferiority' as he did not operationally define it; and (5) he offered no evidence that physical inferiority is hereditary.

Sheldon related crime to physiological make-up or body constitution in 1940. He classified individuals on the basis of their physique (or body types) into three groups: endomorphic, ectomorphic, and mesomorphic. Individuals with the first type of physique (with small bones, short limbs, and soft, smooth and velvety skin) love comforts and luxury and are essentially extroverts; those with the second type of physique (with lean, fragile, delicate body, small delicate bones) are introverts, full of functional complaints, sensitive to noise, complain of chronic fatigue, and shrink from crowds and individuals; and those with the third type of physique (with strong muscles and bones, heavy chest and large wrists and hands) are active, dynamic, assertive and aggressive. Sheldon developed scales for measuring the body-type dimensions in which individuals were scored on each component between 1 and 7 scores However, Sheldon's hypothesis that there is a relationship between delinquent behaviour and body-types and that delinquents are somewhat more mesomorphic in body structure than are the non-delinquents has not been convincingly proved. Crime is a social process and not a biologically determined pattern of behaviour.

Besides the above theories, some studies on identical twins have also laid emphasis on heredity as an important factor in crime. For example, the German psychiatrist Johannes Lange (*Crime as Destiny*, 1931) compared the behaviour of male twins in several prisons with those of non-institutionalised twins. He found that in the case of identical twins (bom of a single fertilised ovum), 10 of the 15 pairs were 'concordant' (both members of a twin pair having the same characteristics) while in the case of fraternal twins (born of separate ova),15 of the 17 pairs were 'discordant' (both twin members having different characteristics).

Kranz (Cf. Rosenthal, *Genetic Theory and Abnormal Behaviour*, 1970), in his study of twins and criminality in 1936, found 66 per cent twins concordant among identical twins and 54 per cent among fraternal twins. Christiansen (Cf. Reuck and Porter, *The Mentally Abnormal*, 1968) in his study of 6,000 pairs of twins bom between 1880 and 1890 in Denmark found that with respect to criminal behaviour, male identical twins were concordant in 35.8 per cent cases as compared to 21.3 per cent in the case of male fratemal twins.

The criticism against explaining criminal behaviour in terms of inherited factors is that similarities in the behaviour of identical twins could be the result of living in the same environment and be totally unrelated to heredity. Secondly, if heredity is the cause of crime, there should be no cases of identical twins where one is a criminal and the other is not. On similar lines, the studies of family lines (Jukes by Dugdale in 1877; Kallikaks by Goddard in 1911, etc.) as evidence of inherited criminality have also been rejected.

PSYCHOGENIC THEORIES

The psychogenic theories trace crime to some defect in the personality of the offender or "in the inside of the person". The psychological theory emphasises "feeble-mindedness" (low Intelligence Quotient or IQ), the psychiatric theory "mental disorders", and the psycho-analytical theory "undeveloped ego, or drives and instincts, or guilt-feelings or inferiority complex."

Psychological Explanation

The psychological approach to the problem of crime causation has been concerned largely with an exploration of the relationship between mental deficiency and crime. Charles Goring (*The English Convict*, 1919: 269) on the basis of his study of English convicts claimed that there was more 'weak-mindedness' in the prison population than in the general population. This led many to assume that mental deficiency was an important cause of crime.

Henry Goddard (*Human Efficiency and Levels of Intelligence*, 1920: 73) reported results on intelligence tests conducted in 1919 and maintained that the greatest single cause of delinquency and crime was low-grade mentality or feeble-mindedness (or very low IQ). He said that feeble-mindedness was inherited and was very little affected by life events. He emphasised the point that a criminal was not born but made. But Goddard did not believe that every feeble-minded person was a criminal. He might be a potential criminal but whether he became one would be determined by two factors: his temperament and his environment. Thus, though feeble-mindedness may be hereditary, criminality is not hereditary. "It is hereditary feeble-mindedness and not hereditary criminality that accounts for the conditions" (Goddard, *Feeble-mindedness: Its Causes and Consequences*, 1914: 8-9).

The validity of the intelligence test by Goddard has been questioned. Does the test really measure intelligence, or do the cultural factors blur that possibility? Further, the test did not seem very objective when it is considered that the more skilled the person giving the test, the greater the number of feeble-minded persons (Fink, *Causes of Crimes*, 1939: 238-39). The results of the test were used to define feeble-mindedness only in terms of the physiological setting, ignoring the sociological one. The relationship between feeble-mindedness and crime was seriously questioned when intelligence tests were used on army recruits during World War I by L.D. Zeleny ("Feeble-mindedness and Criminal Conduct", *American Journal of Sociology*, January 1933: 569). As many as 47.3 per cent soldiers were found to be below the mental age of 13 and 30.3 per cent below the mental age of 12. These results led even Goddard to conclude that it was absurd to think that one-third of the army recruits were feeble-minded.

In 1928-29, Sutherland (Cf. Kimball Young, *Social Attitudes*, 1931 357-75) reviewed 350 research reports on intelligence tests, covering little less than two lakh criminals and delinquents, to examine the relationship between crime and mental deficiencies. He discovered that: (1) Fifty per cent criminals were diagnosed as feeble-minded in the studies conducted between 1910 and 1914 but only about 20 per cent criminals were found feeble-minded in studies in the period between 1925 and 1928. The drop in the percentage of feeblemindedness was not caused by a change in the phenomenon but rather by changes in methods of testing and in interpreting intelligence tests. (2) There was a negligible difference in the mental age of criminals and non-criminals. (3) The discipline among low intelligence prisoners was the same as among high-intelligence prisoners, and (4) Conformity to parole conditions of the feeble-minded and the ordinary parolees was almost equal. He, thus, concluded that low intelligence of the feeble-minded was not a significant cause of criminality. These findings, thus, led to the abandonment of the theory of feeble-mindedness as a cause of crime.

Psychiatric Explanation

Psychiatry is such a field of medicine which specialises in the understanding, diagnosis, treatment and prevention of mental problems. It postulates that each person is a unique personality and it can be understood by means of a thorough or diagnostic case study. The study includes family environment, relationships in the family, neighbourhood, school history, childhood diseases, work experiences, conduct on the job, and so on.

William Healy (*The Individual Delinquent*, 1915), a psychiatrist in Chicago, disagreeing with his physician colleagues that juvenile delinquency is caused by defective organism or anatomical factors emphasised personality defects and disorders, or 'psychogenic traits' as the cause of crime. In broader terms, psychogenic traits cause those ways of behaviour which are established in the infant or the young child through emotional interaction within the family. These traits refer to extroversion or introversion, dominance or submission, optimism or pessimism, emotional independence or dependence, self-confidence or its absence, egocentrism or sociocentrism, and so on (Johnson, 1978: 155). In narrower terms, however, the term 'psychogenic' is referred to as the 'mental factor or disorders' or 'emotional disturbances'. Analysing psychological factors, Healy found a greater frequency of personality disorders among delinquents than among non-delinquents.

In 1935, Healy and Bronner enunciated their theory, based on case studies of 1,953 delinquents in three cities, that delinquency was purposive behaviour that resulted when children met frustration in their attempts to fulfil some of their basic drives, such as, the need for secure social relations both inside and outside the family for recognition, for freedom and so forth. They found in their study that delinquents had a higher frequency of personality defect and disorder, like illness, neurosis, food idiosyncrasies, dislike of school, too much liking for movies and so forth. Healy's explanation runs like this: Frustration of the individual causes emotional discomfort, personality equilibrium demands removal of such pain; the pain is eliminated by substitute behaviour, i.e., delinquency. In order to treat the individual, we must subject him to a thorough examination, utilising physical, mental, sociological, and psychiatric analysis for this purpose. This constitutes "case study of the individual in its most highly developed form".

Psychiatrists have given three types of mental disorders or psychoses (that is, individuals manifesting severe decompression, distortion of reality and loss of contact with reality): (i) schizophrenia (exhibiting tendency to retreat from reality through delusions and hallucinations), (ii) manic-depressive disorder (exhibiting fluctuations in mood), and (iii) paranoia. Evaluating mental disorders in delinquency, it was estimated that only 1.5 per cent to 2.0 per cent criminals are psychotic, of which the schizophrenic is the most common among such offenders. This indicates methodological errors in Healy's research; hence its inadequacy.

A study of 10,000 felons in New York between 1932 and 1935 also pointed out that only 1.5 per cent were psychotic, 6.9 per cent were psycho-neurotic, 6.9 per cent were psychopathic and 2.4 per cent were feeble-minded. Thus, 82.3 per cent of offenders were diagnosed as 'normal'. Another study of Paul Schilder (*Journal of Criminal Psychopathology*, October, 1940: 152) in 1937 in New York pointed out that 83.8 per cent offenders were 'normal'. Dunham's (1939: 352-61) study of 500 males in Illinois hospital showed that schizophrenia is a negligible factor in the causation of crime. Thus, all these investigations show that the psychiatric theory has proved untenable (Bromberg and Thompson, 1939: 70-89).

Other deficiencies, different from the serious methodological errors, have also been pointed out in Healy's researches: (1) His samples were small and unrepresentative. (2) His terms were either not defined or vaguely defined; for example, 'normal emotional control', 'good living conditions', 'stable home', etc. How are these factors to be measured? (3) Research failed to explain why some children who had the traits believed to be characteristic of delinquents did not become delinquents and why some children who did not have those traits became delinquents. (4) They do not explain why one sibling becomes a delinquent and the other does not. We, therefore, conclude that psychiatric theory stands rejected.

Psychoanalytical Explanation

Psychoanalysis is a special branch of psychiatry, employing a particular personality theory and a particular method of psycho-therapy. The approach utilises the method of individual case study. Sigmund Freud, who developed the psychoanalytical theory at the end of the nineteenth and the beginning of the twentieth century, did not advance a theory of criminality. But his approach and the three elements of id, ego, and super-ego have been used by others like Alfred Adler, David Abrahamsen, August Aichorn, Friedlander, etc. to explain criminal behaviour. Id is an individual's raw instincts or desires or derives or urges; ego is the reality; and super-ego is an individual's conscience or more pressure. Super-ego constantly tries to suppress id while ego is the acceptable balance between id and super-ego. Id and super-ego are basically *unconscious* while ego is the *conscious* part of personality.

The three propositions of psychoanalytic thought are: (1) behaviour is largely the product of unconscious psychological-biological forces (drives or instincts); (2) criminality arises out of conflicts related to these basic drives; and (3) to modify undesirable (criminal) behaviour, the person must be guided towards insight into the unconscious roots of his responses so that he can develop control over such impulses. In a well-balanced personality, id, ego and super-ego work in relative harmony. But in abnormal cases (neurotic individuals), imbalance and disharmony occur. When super-ego is not sufficiently developed, the released repressed instincts may lead to anti-social behaviour. Conflict in the unconscious mind gives rise to feelings of guilt with consequent desire for punishment to remove the guilt feelings and restore a balance of good against evil. The individual then commits the criminal act, leaves clues for apprehension in order to be caught and punished (George Vold, 1968: 93).

August Aichorn (1955: 30) was the first scholar to use Freud's psychoanalytical approach for studying delinquents. According to him, 'dissocial' behaviour results from the inner play of psychic forces. He found several kinds of delinquents: some neurotic, some aggressive and lacking in super-ego development, some with little capacity for repressing their instinctual drives, and some having distorted cravings for affection. Psychoanalysis enables a therapist to discover the unconscious motives behind the 'dissocial' behaviour and guide the patient towards social conformity. Alfred Adler explained crime in the first quarter of the twentieth century in terms of 'Inferiority complex'. An individual commits crime to 'get attention' which helps him to compensate for his sense of inferiority. But Adler's theory has been criticised by Mannheim (*Comparative Criminology*, 1917: 331) for placing greater emphasis on the 'rational' side of an individual's behaviour and for oversimplification.

David Abrahamsen (1952) explained crime in terms of an individual's resistance to tendencies and situations. He developed a formula: $C = \dfrac{T+S}{R}$, where 'C' stands for crime, 'T' for tendencies, 'S' for the situation, and 'R' for resistance to impulses. Criminal behaviour will result if the individual has strong criminalistic tendencies and low resistance. Abrahamsen held that "in general, the causes of child's delinquent behaviour may be traced to his parents' emotional attitude toward his early instinctual manifestations and also by the way his ego and super-ego develop." In simple terms, all past experiences are important in individual's further behaviour, particularly delinquent behaviour.

Sociologists have not reacted very favourably either to Abrahamsen's explanation or to psychoanalytic explanation that causes of crime are unconscious. They say that early emotional conflicts and traumas might have influence on personality development and delinquent behaviour, but it is an oversimplification to reduce causative factors to three factors in mathematical terms. Likewise, the explanation that the criminal commits crime because he subconsciously desires to be punished as a result of some of his guilt feelings cannot be accepted for all crimes because in some cases, the individual commits crime, feels guilty, and is then punished which enables him to atone for his action.

Thus, arguments against the psychogenic theories (i.e., psychological, psychiatric and psychoanalytical theories) are: (1) There are methodological and logic-of-science errors in the theories. They all commit dualistic fallacy, assuming that there are two distinct groups of people—criminals and non-criminals—and that these exclusive groups commit behaviour that can be distinguished. One commits criminal acts and the other commits non-criminal acts. In fact, criminal behaviour is just like any other behaviour. (2) The terms are vague as no operational definitions (say of id, ego, super-ego, or unconscious) are given. (3) Projective techniques are open to subjective interpretation of the analysts. (4) The researches are based on small samples and inadequate control groups. (5) So long as an individual is the focus of the approach, generalisations cannot be made regarding patterns of behaviour. Individualistic approach cannot be used for making generalisations for larger populations.

ECONOMIC THEORY

Some scholars using social-structural approach have explained crime in terms of the economic structure of society. They focus on the impact of economic conditions on criminal behaviour. This explanation holds that a criminal is a product of the economic environment which provides him his ideals and his goals. It was the Italian scholar Fornasari who talked of the relationship between crime and poverty in 1894. He maintained that 60 per cent of the population of Italy was poor, and of the total crimes in Italy, 85 per cent to 90 per cent criminals belong to this section of the poor. Economic system thus provides 'climate of motivation' for criminal behaviour. In 1916, a Dutch scholar Bonger also emphasised relationship between crime and the capitalistic economic structure. In a capitalistic system man concentrates only on himself and this leads to selfishness. Man is interested only in producing for himself, especially in producing a surplus which he can exchange for profit. He is not interested in the needs of others. Capitalism, thus, breeds social irresponsibility and leads to crime.

A British criminologist Cyril Burt (*The Young Delinquent*, 1925), analysing juvenile delinquency, found that 19 per cent juvenile delinquents belonged to extremely poor families and 37 per cent to poor families. He concluded that though poverty was an important factor in crime, yet it was not the only factor. In 1915, William Healy and Augusta Bronner (*Delinquents and Criminals: Their Making and Unmaking*, 1926) studied 675 juvenile delinquents and found that 5 per cent belonged to the destitute class, 22 per cent to the poor class, 35 per cent to the normal class, 34 per cent to the comfort class, and 4 per cent to the luxury class. Thus, since 73 per cent delinquents belonged to classes which were economically normal or well-off, poverty cannot be considered to be a very important factor in delinquency.

While Bonger used *facilitating* approach, Karl Marx used *deterministic* approach. Marx's view of economic determinism affirms that private ownership of property results in poverty which distinguishes those who own the means of production from those whom they exploit for economic benefit. The latter turn to crime as a result of this poverty. Thus, though Marx did not specifically develop a theory of criminal causation but he believed that the economic system was the sole determinant of crime.

According to Marxian approach, crime is caused by a criminogenic milieu which is created by the ever-present disparity between effort and reward, emphasis on equal opportunities yet the unequal reality of a class society, and stress on individual competition yet the handicapped nature of the race. Such contradictions are hard on the marginalised groups who are denied full access to consumer society. Thus, the very process which binds the worker to his bench turns the mind of the unemployed to crime. The unequal distribution of property and power in capitalism will always result in the privileged reproducing inequalities of opportunity areas. Thus, according to Marxists, the solution to the problem of containing crime lies in creating a world where formal and substantive inequalities disappear.

In India, two studies may be referred to in this context. Ruttonshaw (1947: 49) studied 225 juvenile delinquents in Poona and found (when the value of a rupee was one rupee in comparison to seven paise in 1999) that 20 per cent belonged to families whose income was less than Rs.150 per month (i.e., lower class), 58 per cent belonged to families with an income of Rs. 150-500 per month (i.e., middle class), 12.2 per cent belonged to families with an income of Rs.500-1,000 per month (i.e., middle-middle class),4.8 per cent belonged to families with an income of Rs.1,000-2,000 per month (i.e., upper-middle class), and 2.7 per cent belonged to families whose income was more than Rs. 2,000 per month (i.e., upper class). This study shows that poverty may not be given undue or excessive importance in crime.

Similarly, Sutherland (1965) has said that: (1) we find more criminals in poor families because it is easy to locate them; (2) criminals belonging to upper classes use their influence and pressures in escaping arrests and convictions; and (3) reactions of administrators are more biased towards the upper class people. No wonder, most behavioural scientists today reject the theory of economic determinism in criminal behaviour. Reid (*op. cit.*: 174-75) has also said that the problem of defining poverty, the impossibility of isolating other variables so that poverty can be seen as the cause of criminal behaviour, and the future crime to decrease when attempts are made to reduce or eradicate poverty, all these create problems in relating poverty to crime.

GEOGRAPHICAL THEORY

This explanation evaluates crime on the basis of geographical factors like climate, temperature, humidity, etc. It is supported by scholars like Montesquieu, Quetelet, Dexter, Kropotokin, Champneuf, and many others. Montesquieu (*Spirit of Laws*, 1748) laid down the law that criminality increases in proportion as one approaches the equator, and drunkenness increases in proportion as one approaches the poles. About a century later, Quetlet formulated his famous 'thermic law' of delinquency in which he claimed that crimes against person predominated in the south and increased in summers, while crimes against property predominated in the north and increased during the winter time. Champneuf supported this hypothesis of the relationship between the nature of crime and the climate on the basis of his study conducted in France between 1825 and 1830. He found 181.5 property crimes against every 100 crimes against persons in north France, and 98.8 property crimes against every 100 crimes against persons in south France. On the basis of his study of property crimes conducted between 1825 and 1880, the French scholar Laccasagne also found the highest number of property crimes in December, followed by January, November and February. In a study on the effect of climate on an individual's behaviour made in 1904, the American scholar Dexter found that crime and geographical conditions like barometric pressure, heat, humidity, etc., were highly related with one another. He found that crimes of violence were most numerous during the warm months of the year, during periods of low barometric pressure, and during periods of low humidity. (Cf. Joseph Cohen, *The Geography of Crime*, September 1941) In 1911, a Russian scholar Kropotkin established that the rate of murder in any month/year can be predicted by calculating the average temperature and humidity of the preceding month/year. For this, he gave a mathematical formula $2(7x+y)$, where x is temperature and y is humidity. Multiplying the average temperature x of the last month with 7 and adding the average humidity of the last month y to it, and then multiplying the total figure with 2, we will get the number of murders to be committed in a given month.

The geographical explanation has been criticised on the ground that geographical factors may affect individual behaviour but the direct relationship between crime and geographical factors cannot be accepted as claimed by these scholars. The geographical theories over-simplify the problem of crime and exaggerate the geographical factors. Had such relationship really existed, the number and nature of crime in a given geographical environment would have been the same at all times, which is not so. Hence, the invalidity of this theory.

SOCIOLOGICAL THEORIES

While the biological, physiological, psychiatric and psychological theoretical explanations emphasise the point that crime is either inherited and results from a physical or a mental factor, or is the consequence of suppressed childhood experiences, sociologists argue that criminal behaviour is learnt and is conditioned by social environment. Sociologists have used different approaches in studying the causation of crime: one approach explains crime in terms of pathological living conditions and breakdown of harmonious relations (social disorganisation approach), another approach studies the relationship between crime and the social structure of society (structural approach), the third approach studies the process by which an individual becomes a criminal (processual approach) and the fourth approach relates crime to cultural conflict (subcultural approach). We will briefly discuss all these theories by classifying them in four groups: (i) social disorganisation or Ecological theory which includes Clifford Shaw's theory, (ii) structural or affinity or adaptational theories which include Sutherland's and Merton's theories, (iii) subculture or affiliation theories which include Cloward and Ohlin's, Cohen's, and Matza's theories, (iv) social process theories which include Howard Becker's, Walter Reckless' and new deviancy theories, and (v) conflict theories which include Thorsten Sellin's culture conflict and Richard Quinney's modern conflict theories.

Social Disorganisation or Ecological Theory

Social disorganisation theorists were not primarily concerned with the study of crime itself but with the sociological problems of urban living. Criminals and deviants were seen by these theorists as a small minority occupying the margins of society principally because of their 'defective' socialisation, and were depicted as existing in a state of social disorganisation within these marginal areas or culture transmission.

Clifford Shaw's and Henry McKay's ecological theory was developed in the 1920s with the emergence of Chicago-based 'ecological' approach to crime. According to this approach, crime rates vary from area to area, neighbourhood to neighbourbood. In their book *Juvenile Delinquency and Urban Areas* (1942), Shaw and McKay demonstrated that the zone of 'delinquency area' which contains the highest rate of delinquency is characterised by physical deterioration, congested population, economic insecurity, poor housing with cheap rents, low standards of living, family disintegration, cultural heterogeneity, and absence of social controls. Thus, it is an area of social disorganisation and as such tends to produce disorganised personalities and delinquent careers. Shaw's and McKay's major conclusions may be summarised as follows: (Cf. Caldwell, *Criminology*, *op. cit.*: 221-22): (1) The rates of delinquency vary widely from one neighbourhood to another. (2) The highest rates tend to be near the central business areas and large industrial areas and decrease from the centre of the city outward. (3) The areas of high rates have had high rates for a long time. (4) The nationality composition of the population in areas of high rates changed almost completely over a period of several decades, while the relative rate of delinquents in these areas remained virtually unchanged. (5) Like the delinquency rate for the entire population, those of the various nationality groups tend to decrease from the centre of the city outward.

In Shaw's opinion, the environmental rather than the personal factors predominate in the causation of crime and delinquency in the 'delinquency area'. The population in the area changes but the high rates persist because they are primarily and functionally related to the environment in which people live. In the absence of social solidarity, crime and delinquency gain a foothold and persist over a period of years.

The ecological approach is, however, inadequate because it does not show how the causal factors operate in an individual to produce these problems. It has been pointed out that crime and certain other conditions, such as poverty, may coexist without being causally related. In fact, many persons living in the transitional zone remain law-abiding citizens throughout their lives.

The main criticisms against the ecological theory (or 'delinquency area' theory) are: (1) The 'delinquency area' concept does not give adequate recognition to the selective migration. Low rents, social obscurity and reduced social controls attract the poor, the unsuccessful, the inefficient, the handicapped, and the defective. These are the people who have already developed delinquent tendencies elsewhere. (2) It is based on unreliable statistical comparison. (3) In some cities, especially the smaller ones, the 'delinquency area' is in an isolated part of the town or on the outskirts. (4) The delinquency area concept does not satisfactorily explain the presence of negative cases, i.e., those people who are not delinquents or criminals, a fact which should have a sobering effect upon extreme environments. (5) It neglects the psychological and biological factors in criminality.

Structural Theories

Differential Association Theory

Sutherland proposed 'differential association' theory in 1939 and elaborated it in 1947. Initially, he applied his theory only to 'systematic criminal behaviour', but, later on, extending his theory, he applied it to all criminal behaviour. Sutherland forwarded mainly two explanations for criminal behaviour: situational and genetic or historical. The former explains crime on the basis of situation that exists at the time of crime, and the latter explains crime on the basis of a criminal's life experiences. He himself used the second approach in developing his theory of criminal behaviour. Let us take an example. If a hungry boy comes across a 'dhaba' (restaurant) and finds the owner absent, he steals a 'roti' (loaf of bread). In this case, the boy steals not because the restaurant owner was absent and he himself was hungry but because he had learnt earlier that one could satisfy one's hunger by stealing things. Thus, it is not the situation which motivates a person to commit a theft; it is his learnt attitudes and beliefs.

Sutherland's main thesis (*Principles of Criminology*, Philadelphia, 1947) is that individuals encounter many inharmonious and inconsistent social influences in their lifetime and many individuals become involved in contacts with carriers of criminalistic norms and as a consequence become criminals. He called this process 'differential association'.

The theory of differential association presented nine propositions: (1) Criminal behaviour is learnt. (2) It is learnt in interaction with other persons in a process of communication. (3) The principal part of the learning process (of criminal behaviour) occurs within intimate, small, personal groups. (4) The learning includes techniques of committing crime, and specific direction of motives, drives, rationalisations, and attitudes. (5) The specific direction (of motives and drives) is learnt from definitions of legal codes as favourable or unfavourable. (6) A person becomes a criminal or a delinquent because of an excess of definitions favourable to violation of law over definitions unfavourable to violation of law, i.e., criminal behaviour is determined in a process of association with those who commit crime. This is the principle of differential association. Differential association is possible because society is composed of various groups with varied cultures. Thus, cultural conflict is the underlying cause of differential association. The origin and persistence of culture conflicts are due to social disorganisation. (7) Differential associations may vary in frequency, duration, priority and intensity, i.e., the chance that a person will participate in criminal behaviour is determined roughly by the frequency and consistency of his contacts with patterns of criminal behaviour. (8) The processes of learning criminal behaviour by association with criminal and non-criminal patterns are fundamentally the same in form as the processes which result in lawful behaviour. Individual differences among people in respect of personal characteristics or social situations cause crime only as they affect differential association or frequency and consistency of contacts with criminal patterns. (9) While criminal behaviour is an expression of general needs and values, it is not explained by these general needs and values since non-criminal behaviour is an expression of the same needs and values.

Sutherland's theory was supported by James Short Jr. on the basis of his study of 176 school children (126 boys and 50 girls) in 1955 (*see*, Rose Giallombardo, 1960: 85-91). Short measured degree of presumed exposure to crime and delinquency in the community, frequency, duration, priority and intensity of interaction with delinquent peers, and knowledge of and association with adult criminals.

Sutherland's theory, however, has been attacked by many scholars like Sheldon Glueck, Mabel Elliott, Robert Caldwell, Donald Cressey, Paul Tappan, George Vold, Herbert Bloch, Jeffery Clarence, Daniel Glaser, and others. The major criticism is that it is difficult to empirically test principles, and measure 'associations', priority, intensity, duration and frequency of relationships. According to Paul Tappan (1947: 96-102), Sutherland has ignored the role of personality or the role of biological and psychological factors in crime. Sutherland has relegated these factors to an entirely subordinate position. He has said that "individual differences cause crime only as they affect differential association"; but the individual, as a unique combination of heredity and environment, has a reality apart from the group. Therefore, in opposition to Sutherland's contention, one may argue that differential association causes crime only as it gives expression to individual differences. George Vold (1958: 194) has maintained that Sutherland has ignored the role of secondary contact and formal groups in criminality. Clarence Ray Jeffery (Cf. Johnson, 1978: 158) holds that Sutherland's theory fails to explain the origin of criminality since criminality has to exist before it can be learnt from someone else. Mabel Elliot (1952: 402) says Sutherland's theory explains only 'systematic criminal behaviour' by which Sutherland apparently means criminal behaviour that has become a way of life for an individual and is supported by a philosophy in terms of which it is justified. According to Donald Cressey (*Journal of Criminal Law and Criminology*, May-June 1952: 51-52), Sutherland does not fully explore the implications of the learning process itself as it affects different individuals. He (Cressey) has further said: "It is doubtful that it can be shown empirically that the differential association theory applies or does not apply to crimes of financial trust violation or even to other kinds of criminal behaviour." Herbert Bloch (1962: 158) is of the opinion that it is virtually impossible to measure associations in comparative quantitative terms. Glueck (1951:

309) maintains that an individual does not learn every kind of behaviour from others; many acts are learnt naturally. Caldwell (1956: 183) says that individuals become what they are largely because of the contacts they have but both constitutional or inborn hereditary structure and intensity of environmental stimuli must be appraised evenly. He has further said: "If the claim is made that this theory explains all criminal behaviour, then it is doubtful whether the theory can be proved. But if the theory merely means that many persons learn to be criminals through association with others who do not have proper respect for the law, then it has been reduced to an elaboration of the obvious—a fate that has befallen many other oversimplifications of human behaviour."

Daniel Glaser (*American Journal of Sociology*, March 1956: 433-44) modified Sutherland's theory a little to explain from whom an individual learns crime. He called this new theory as 'differential identification theory' and said that a person pursues criminal behaviour to the extent that "he *identifies* himself with real or imaginary persons from whose perspective his criminal behaviour seems acceptable". He further said that one of the persistent problems in the theory of differential association was the obvious fact that not everyone in contact with criminality adopts or follows the criminal pattern. What, therefore, is the difference in the nature or quality of the association that in one case it leads an individual to accept the attitudes and behaviour of a group, but, in another case, it only leads to an individual's acquaintance with but not the acceptance of the behaviour characteristic of the group. The answer lies in the choice of persons with whom an individual identifies himself, and who serve as models for his behaviour.

It may be concluded that although Sutherland's theory has some serious weaknesses, it does have some merit too. It calls attention to: (a) the importance of social factors, (b) the similarity between the process of learning criminal behaviour and that of learning lawful behaviour, and (c) the fact that criminality cannot be explained entirely in terms of personality maladjustments.

Anomie Theory

In 1893, Durkheim proposed that deviant behaviour was a normal adaptation to living within a society, which was structured by a high division of labour and was based on values of competitive individualism. He said that a society without deviance was impossible because it was inconceivable that no person would deviate from the norm or ideal. Moreover, deviance was not only inevitable but also necessary for the progress of any society. The deviant behaviour became a new approach to problem and without the introduction of new approaches to problem solving, society would remain static. The causes of individual deviation were thus related to the degree of integration and cohesiveness by which society was governed at a particular time. But Durkheim focused only on one type of deviant behaviour, viz., suicide.

In 1938, Merton used the concept of anomie beyond suicide to all forms of deviance. While Durkheim believed that aspirations were limitless, Merton argued that they were socially produced and thus regulated to some extent, but they could exceed what was obtainable through available opportunities. While Durkheim claimed that anomie resulted from a social failure to control and regulate individual behaviour, Merton proposed that anomie resulted from 'strains' in the social structure that pressurised individuals and encouraged the development of unrealistic aspirations. Anomie was thus dependent on the interaction between cultural goals----aims that define success and status in society----and institutionalised means----acceptable methods of achieving such goals.

Merton, reacting against the biological and psychiatric theories (that crime is the result of inherited traits), first attempted to explain deviant behaviour in 1938 in a paper published in the *American Sociological Review*. He further elaborated his thesis in 1949 and 1957 and distinguished between social and cultural structures (*see*, Merton Robert, *Social Theory and Social Structure*, enl. edn., 1968). Cultural structure, according to him, refers to goals and interests men pursue, while social structure refers to means or approved methods which regulate and control the pursuit of goals and interests. The cultural system of society enjoins upon all men to strive for goals by means of normatively regulated or approved forms of behaviour. However, opportunities to reach these goals through socially approved means are unequally distributed. Deviant behaviour ensues when social structure restricts or completely closes a person's access to the approved modes of reaching these goals. In other words, the disjunction between goals and means causes strains which in turn leads to a weakening of men's commitment to the culturally prescribed goals or institutionalised means, that is, to a state of anomie. Thus, Merton's thesis is that certain social structures exert pressure on some persons to engage in non-conformist rather than conformist conduct.

The focus in Merton's theory is not at all on the individual (criminal) or the act (of crime), but on the 'tensions' which lie not within the individual but between culture and structure. These tensions are experienced not so much by isolated individuals as by whole groups of individuals in certain structural positions. It is here that strain theory introduces the concept of subculture. Subcultural responses are jointly elaborated solutions to collectively experienced problems. Groups of people have both collective goals and legitimate means fixed for them by the determining agency of society. In their positions as housewives or teenagers or executives of clerks or employees or workers, they evolve subcultures—specialised parts of the general culture suitable for their needs. Often these are non-deviant, but where there are significant discrepancies between aspiration and opportunity, deviant subcultures occur. Deviant behaviour is then viewed as being a meaningful attempt at solving the problems faced by groups of individuals, in particular structural positions.

Merton (*Social Theory and Social Structure*, 1968) has identified five modes of adaptation available to those who react to the goals and means of society: conformity, innovation, ritualism, retreatism and rebellion. *Conformity* describes acceptance of the prevailing state of affairs, i.e., accepting both goals and means of society. *Innovation* represents acceptance of the goals but rejection of the means for obtaining these goals and substituting alternatives in their place. For example, a student accepts the goal of passing an examination and obtaining a degree but uses unfair means to pass. Merton says that the social class structure which imposes goals also prevents some people from attaining them by the socially approved means. Low status and low income of lower class people and the basic occupational opportunities open to them do not permit them to achieve high status in terms of power and income; they, therefore, often turn to deviant behaviour. The social structural pressure to attain goals, along with social structural limitations of legitimate means, produces pressure toward deviant behaviour. The cause of widespread deviant behaviour is that social structure proclaims that all should achieve these goals but blocks legitimate efforts of large numbers of persons to do so. This situation helps to explain high rates of crime in poverty areas. Merton further points out that poverty does not cause crime, but, when poverty is linked to cultural emphasis on monetary success as a dominant goal, and, a poor individual cannot compete because of his poverty for the culture values, criminal behaviour is the normal outcome.

Ritualism, according to Merton, is rejection of the goals but acceptance of the means. For example, a student goes to college but doesn't attend classes and spends time in college canteen. Merton says that while innovation as a mode of adaptation is more characteristic of the lower class, ritualism is more characteristic of the lower-middle class. The middle class places greater emphasis on the socially approved means of obtaining goals. Is this form of adaptation really deviant behaviour? Merton thinks so because "it clearly represents a departure from the cultural mode in which men are obliged to strive actively to move onward and upward in the social hierarchy."

Retreatism involves rejection of both culturally supported goals and institutionalised means. Merton suggests that this occurs after a person has accepted both goals and means of society but has repeatedly failed to achieve goals by legitimate means. At the same time, because of prior socialisation and internalised values, individual is not able to adopt illegitimate means. Thus, he is cut off from both legitimate and illegitimate methods of obtaining goals. He, therefore, rejects both goals and means and takes to drinking or becomes a drug-addict or a vagabond. *Rebellion* is characterised by rejection of goals and means and substitution of new goals and means, i.e., establishing a new social order or changing the social structure. The individual not only himself adopts new goals and means but also attempts to *institutionalise* these new. goals and means for the rest of society.

While Merton considers the last four modes of adaptation as deviance, he offers his category of 'innovation' in support of the link between anomie and crime. The innovator, in rejecting institutionalised means and substituting alternatives, is likely to find that the 'new' means are illegal ones and his actions crimes. Merton thus uses 'innovation' to explain the high crime rates among the lower-class or the poor segments of population. Their disadvantaged status, coupled with high cultural priority given to pecuniary success as a dominant goal for all, make high rates of crime a 'normal outcome' for those (poor) segments of population.

Merton's theory has been criticised by Albert Cohen, Marshall Clinard, Lemert, and a few others. Their main arguments are: (1) Merton's theory is incomplete because he has not explained who will reject the goals and who will reject the means; (2) only structure has been given importance; an individual's personality has been ignored; (3) strains do not necessarily lead to deviant behaviour; (4) the theory neglects the important role of social control; (5) Merton's assumption that deviant behaviour is disproportionately more common in lower classes is not correct; (6) anomie may be the cause rather than the effect of circumscribed life chances; (7) Merton has not explained what the determinants which determine the mode of adaptation of an individual are; (8) Merton has failed to account for 'non-utilitarian' crime and juvenile delinquency in which people engage only for fun and not to meet specific goals of society; for example, vandalism, car-theft for joy-ride, etc.; (9) the theory does not take into account social-psychological variables or social structural elements which might explain adoption of one adaptation over the other by individuals; and finally, (10) the theory has not been empirically tested.

Subcultural Theories

Herman Mannheim (*Comparative Criminology*, 1965: 499) has said that there are often conflicts among different classes because of their characteristic features. There also exist conflicts among the subcultures created by them. Some theories have, therefore, concentrated on the 'subculture' of social class. The subculture theories were preceded by Thrasher's study who saw the emergence and development of gangs as a result of social disorganisation in a zone of transition. But Thrasher did not specifically talk about subcultures. Subculture theorists have attempted to understand delinquent behaviour as sanctioned by status requirements of a gang or subculture. We will discuss here a few of these theories of subculture.

Differential Opportunity Theory

Cloward and Ohlin integrated Sutherland's and Merton's theories and developed a new theory of criminal behaviour in 1960. Whereas Sutherland talks of illegitimate means and Merton talks of differentials in legitimate means, Cloward and Ohlin (*Delinquency and Opportunity*, 1960) talk of differentials in both legitimate and illegitimate means to success-goals. The important elements of this theory are: (1) an individual occupies position in both legitimate and illegitimate opportunity structures; (2) relative availability of illegitimate opportunities affects the resolution of an individual's adjustment problems; and (3) faced with limitations on legitimate avenues of access to goals and unable to revise his aspirations downward, he experiences intense frustrations, resulting in the exploration of non-conformist alternatives. Solving adjustment problems thus depends upon relative access to these systems. If in a given social structure, a person has little or no access to illegal or criminal means, he would not be expected to adopt criminal means to solve his problems.

Clarence Schrag (1972: 167) systematically organised Cloward and Ohlin's theory and gave its four postulates: (1) middle-class goals, specially economic goals, are widespread, (2) every organised community provides legitimate opportunities for attaining these goals, (3) access to legitimate means varies from class to class, and (4) within a given community, illegitimate opportunities may or may not be available. But Schrag himself has criticised the theory of Cloward and Ohlin based on the above postulates on two counts: (1) the theory fails to explain why a young person who belongs to the lower class does not become involved in the activities of delinquent gangs, and (2) who will use illegitimate means to achieve goals? Schrag has answered the second question himself. He says that three types of persons are susceptible to indulging in deviant behaviour or joining delinquent gangs: (1) those who blame the system for their failures and/or adjustment problems, (2) those who think they possess the official criteria but not the pragmatic criteria, and (3) those who are alienated from conventional norms or a legitimate system.

Cloward and Ohlin (*ibid.*, 1960: 50-52) have identified three major types of delinquent subcultures: the criminal, the conflict, and the retreatist. A particular one that emerges in any given socio-cultural setting will be a function of the availability of illegitimate opportunities. The first is characterised by illegal money-making activities, the second emphasises acts of violence and gun-fighting, and the third emphasises drug use and other 'kicks'.

Criminal subculture tends to arise in lower-class neighbourhood where successful and big-time criminals reside and are also willing to associate with them (juveniles). Juveniles in this social class do not have conventional role models of successful people who have achieved their success through legitimate channels; but they do have access to criminal success models. The child has an opportunity to actually perform illegitimate roles because such activity finds support in his immediate neighbourhood milieu. The rewards—monetary and other—of successful learning and performance are immediate and gratifying. Further, in this subculture, integration of conventional and criminal values also exists. Since the youth 'fix' politicians, police officials and law enforcement officials and seek their support, they maintain necessary relationships with these people. As a consequence of the integrative relationships, a new opportunity structure emerges, one which permits and facilitates illegitimate instead of legitimate activities.

Conflict subculture is found in areas where there is no alliance between the criminal and the conventional elements. This subculture features violence and/or threat of violence as method of getting status. In such neighbourhoods, young people tend to organise themselves in a community of gangs contending with one another for 'rap' through a show of violence and toughness. These areas are populated by failures from conventional society as well as failures from the criminal world. Social controls are also weak in these areas. With no organised way to solve their frustrations, the youth in these areas "seize upon the manipulation of violence as a route to status." In the world of violence, all that is needed is guts and the ability to endure pain.

Retreatist subculture is manifested through or in the use of drugs. It is found in areas where either repressive police measures make street-fighting quite dangerous or where moral and other inhibitions against the use of violence exist. Individuals denied access to 'criminal' and 'conflict' opportunities tend to withdraw into a world of narcotic drugs. Referring to the availability of illegal or criminal means, Cloward and Ohlin have said if there is little or no access to drugs, it is not likely that the retreatist subculture would develop. Similarly, where the means of violence are not available to juveniles, a violence-oriented subculture would most probably not develop.

Short, Tennyson and Rivers have supported Cloward and Ohlin's theory on the basis of their study on the perception of legitimate and illegitimate opportunities pertaining to education and occupation among 500 Negro and white lower-class gang boys and middle-class non-gang boys from the same neighbourhood. Walter Reckless also undertook a project to examine Cloward's theory. Some of the questions pertaining to the perception of opportunities were: (1) I probably won't be able to do the kind of work that I want to do because I don't have enough education; (2) if a kid like me works hard, he can get a lead; (3) my family can't give me the opportunity that most kids have; (4) most people are better off than I am; (5) I am as well-to-do as most people are; (6) a guy like me has a pretty chance of going to a college. On the basis of the responses received, Reckless found that Cloward's theory is partly correct, that is, it explains some crimes but not all crimes.

The important criticisms against Cloward and Ohlin's theory are: (1) The main contention of the theory that there are two kinds of opportunities---legitimate and illegitimate---is not so simple as it seems. The distinction, although real, is 'analytical' rather than 'concrete', that is, there are not *some* things that are legitimate opportunities and *other* things that are illegitimate opportunities, but the *same* things are always both; for example, notes prepared by students on small pieces of paper when used in examinations become unfair means, but, when used a day or two before examinations for remembering important points, these very notes are nothing but legitimate simple means. Similarly, a gun can be used for killing as well as defending oneself. (2) Cloward and Ohlin maintain that the lower-class youths have two orientations: orientation towards membership in middle-class, called 'lifestyle' orientation, and orientation towards economic improvement, called 'economic' orientation. Cloward and Ohlin's thesis is that candidates for delinquent subculture are those who wish to retain lower-class membership but aspire to improve their economic status (Cf. Johnson, 1978: 179). Gordon, however, says that these two orientations do not exist separately. (3) Cloward and Ohlin have not specified the initial conditions for the emergence of various types of subculture. (4) There is class-bias in this theory. (5) Clarence Schrag has said that the concepts used in the theory cannot be operationalised; for example, 'opportunity structure', 'perception of opportunity', 'denial of legitimacy', 'double failure', etc. (6) Personality factor has been completely ignored.

Value Orientation or Middle Class Measuring Rod or Delinquent Subculture Theory

Albert Cohen's value orientation theory mainly deals with the problems of status adjustment of working-class boys. Cohen holds (*The Delinquent Boys: The Culture of the Gang*, 1955) that the young children's feeling of themselves depends largely upon how they are judged by others. The situations in which they are judged, most notably the school situation, are largely dominated by middle-class values and standards, which in fact is the dominant value system. These standards include such criteria as neatness, polished manners, academic intelligence, verbal fluency, high levels of aspiration, drives for achievement, etc. Young people of different origins and backgrounds tend to be judged by the same standards in society, so that young people of lower classes find themselves competing for status and approval under the same set of rules. However, they are not equally well-equipped for success in this status game. For this and other reasons, lower-class children are more likely to experience failure and humiliation. One way they can deal with this problem is to repudiate and withdraw from the game and refuse to recognise the rules as having any application to them. But, it is not quite that simple because the dominant value system is also, to a degree, their value system. They have three alternatives before them (*ibid.*, 1955: 75): (i) to adopt the 'college-boy response' of upward mobility (thrifty, hard work, cuts himself from activities of peers), (ii) to adopt 'stable corner-boy response' (does not surrender the upward mobility ideas but is neither thrifty nor cuts himself from peers nor incurs hostility of either middle-class persons or delinquent boys), and (iii) to adopt 'delinquent response' (completely repudiates middle-class standards). Of these alternatives, most of the children adopt the third response. They resort to reaction formation. They reject the dominant value system and develop a subculture within which their values and activities are *non-utilitarian* (because they do not benefit economically), *malicious* (because they enjoy themselves at others' cost and suffering), and *negativistic* (because they are opposed to the accepted values of the larger society).

The delinquent subculture is also characterised by *short-run hedonism*. The boys are interested in momentary pleasures, giving no thought to planning activities or budgeting time and money for the future. Finally, the gang is characterised by *group autonomy*, i.e., the gang is intolerant of restraint except informal pressures from within the group itself. The gang members tend to have intensely solidaristic relations among themselves, while their relations with other groups are indifferent, hostile, or rebellious. The members of the delinquent subculture gang tend to resist efforts of social institutions to regulate their lives. Cohen is not trying to explain how individual boys become delinquents. Rather, he is attempting to explain the development of the delinquent subculture.

The propositions in Albert Cohen's theory may be stated briefly as follows (Kitsuse and Dietrick, 1966: 20): The working-class boy faces a characteristic problem of adjustment which is qualitatively different from that of the middle-class boy. His problem is one of 'status-frustration'; His socialisation hinders him from registering achievement in the middle-class status system. Nevertheless, he is thrust into this competitive system where achievement is judged by middle-class standards of behaviour and performance. Ill-prepared and poorly motivated, he is frustrated in his status aspirations by the agents of middle-class society. The delinquent subculture represents a 'solution' to the working-class boy's problem, for it enables him to 'break clean' with the middle-class morality and legitimise hostility and aggression without moral inhibitions. Thus, the delinquent subculture is characterised by *non-utilitarian* (delinquents steal, for example, "for the hell of it"), *malicious* (they derive "enjoyment in the discomfort of others"), and *negativistic* (they take pride in doing things precisely because they are wrong by middle-class standards) values since it is an attack on the middle-class culture where their egos are most vulnerable. It expresses contempt for a particular way of life by making its opposite a criterion of status. Thus, even when Cohen assumes that the subculture affects the young boy, he does not overlook the possibility that the family structure may also be instrumental or a factor. He thus does not minimise the role of family; rather he magnifies it. He only emphasises the ways in which the consequences of family life/environment depend upon the social world outside the family. Cohen's theory primarily attempts to explain why the young lower-class boy develops a subculture (i.e., new values). He is denied access to status within society, so he must find status within the subculture.

Albert Cohen's theory has been critically examined both as a theory of the delinquent subculture and as a theory of delinquency. Sykes and Matza, Merton, Reiss and Rhodes, Kobrin and Finestone, Kitsuse and Dietrick, Wilensky and Lebeaux, etc., have questioned various propositions and implications of his thesis. The main criticisms are: (1) A gang member does not reject middle-class values and standards but adopts techniques of neutralisation to rationalise his delinquent behaviour (Sykes and Matza, 1957). (2) If Cohen's theory is accepted, the delinquency rate of lower-class boys should be higher in areas where they are in direct competition with middle-class boys and their rate should be the lowest in areas where lower-class is universal. But Reiss and Rhodes (1951) found that the more the lower-class boy was in minority in school and in his residential area, the less likely was he to become a delinquent. (3) Kitsuse and Dietrick ("Delinquent Boys: A Critique" in Harwin Voss (ed.), *Society, Delinquency and Delinquent Behaviour*, 1970: 238-45) have challenged Cohen's statement that the working-class boy measures himself by middle-class norms. In fact, he does not care what the middle-class people think of him. (4) His description of delinquent subculture as non-utilitarian, malicious and negativistic is inaccurate. In fact, most of the activities of the lower-class gangs are much more serious than Cohen indicates. The facts thus do not support Cohen's theory. (5) Cohen's description of the working-class boys ambivalence towards the middle-class system does not warrant the use of the psychological concept of 'reaction formation' to describe the culture of the delinquent gang. Cohen's development of this concept is based on the assumption that the lower-class boy has developed a desire to improve himself in terms of middle-class status. Interestingly, Cohen also suggests that the lower-class boy is constantly confronted by middle-class standards, by the people who are in charge of various agencies within his community. In order to win favour of these people, he must change his habits, values, ambitions, speech, and associates. Having failed in that, he turns to the street where he finds human relations more satisfying. According to Kitsuse and

Dietrick, this does not support the theory of 'reaction formation', as believed by Cohen, but, on the contrary, it suggests that the lower-class boy does not want to strive for middle class standards and resents the intrusion into his community of those who hold such values and try to impose these on him. (6) The theory is ambiguous concerning the relation between the emergence of the subculture and its maintenance. (7) Finally, Kitsuse and Dietrick (*ibid.*: 245) question Cohen's theory from methodological point of view. First, the theory is dependent upon a historical method of research, i.e., it attempts to explain why the subculture developed. Kitsuse suggests that it may be reasonable to approach the theory from a functional point of view, attempting to ascertain what function is performed by the delinquent subculture, or what consequences of participation in the delinquent subculture for the participants are.

Sykes and Matza ("Techniques of Neutralisation" in Wolfgang's, *Sociology of Crime and Delinquency*, 1970: 292-99) in developing their theory attacked Cohen's theory in its assumption that delinquents respond to values that differ from those of the adult society. They argue that: (i) if delinquents had established a subculture with different norms and had accepted those norms in place of the norms of society, they would not exhibit shame and guilt when violating the norms of society; (ii) the juvenile delinquent often admires the person who is a law-abiding citizen. He also resents the attribution of criminal or immoral behaviour to those who are important to him, say, his mother. He, therefore, appears to be recognising the moral validity of the dominant normative system in many instances; (iii) juvenile delinquents distinguish appropriate victims and consider other persons or groups to be inappropriate targets for their activities; and (iv) the delinquent has probably internalised some of the norms of society. He is not totally immune to the demands for conformity made by the dominant social order. For these reasons, they argue, the delinquent is at least partially committed to the dominant social order.

Delinquency Drift and Techniques of Neutralisation Theory

David Matza's and Syke's approach (1964) marked a mid-position between classicists' free will and positivists' determinism (i.e., crime is the result of forces beyond the control of the perpetrator). Matza's approach of 'soft determinism' or 'drift' (*see*, *Delinquency and Drift*, 1964) suggests that the delinquent 'drifts' between conventional and criminal behaviour and also into delinquency. He is neither compelled nor is committed to deeds nor freely chooses them; rather he responds to the demands of each (i.e., conventional and criminal behaviour), flirting now with one, now with the other, but postponing commitment and evading decision.

Later on, Matza along with Sykes, developed the theory of "techniques of neutralisation" in 1970. In fact, their theory was an attack on Cohen's theory. Their theory (*see*, *Techniques of Neutralisation*, 1970) was that the delinquent justifies or rationalises his deviant actions. These justifications maybe valid for the delinquents but not for the legal system or society at large. Sykes and Matza, therefore, call them "techniques of neutralisation" and point out their five (neutralisations) major types: denial of responsibility, denial of injury, denial of the victim, condemnation of the condemners, and appeal to higher loyalties. These techniques of neutralisation reduce the impact of forces of social control on delinquents even if they do not shield them. Albert Cohen later on agreed with Sykes and Matza and described his 'reaction formation' as really a "technique of neutralisation and that the subculture itself is a neutralising factor".

Labelling Theory

Howard Becker propounded his Labelling theory in 1963. Before him, Frank Tennenbaum (1938), Edwin Lemert (1915), John Kitsuse (1962) and K. Erikson (1962) had also used an approach called the 'social reaction approach' or the 'social interaction approach' as different from the 'structural approach' used by Merton or the 'cultural approach' used by Cohen, and Cloward and Ohlin. Becker's theory (*see*, *Outsiders: Studies in the Sociology of Deviance*, 1963) does not deal with the question why a person becomes a criminal but tells why society labels some people as criminals or deviants. Some men who drink heavily are called alcoholics while others are not; some men who behave oddly are committed to hospitals while others are not. Thus, according to this theory, what is important in the study of deviance is the *social audience*, not the individual *person*. What is important in crime is not the act of the individual but the reaction of the society in terms of rules and sanctions. Kai Erikson has also said that what distinguishes a delinquent from a non-delinquent is not the characteristic *found* in him but the characteristic *assigned* to him by others. According to Becker (1963: 9), deviance is not a quality of the act a person commits but rather a consequence of the application by others of rules and sanctions to an 'offender'. The deviant is one to whom that label has successfully been applied; deviant behaviour is behaviour that people so label. An experiment was performed in the United States of America (Reid, 1976: 232) in which eight sane persons of varied backgrounds got themselves admitted for feigned mental illness to psychiatric wards of different hospitals in various parts of the country. All gave the same account of their life situations. All but one were labelled schizophrenic. Once labelled insane, they were presumed insane by the staff who interacted with them daily. This shows that it is the reaction of others which labels an individual in a specific way. In the case of criminals also, it is the society which brands some people but not others as criminals. If a lower-class boy steals a car, he is branded a 'thief', but if an upper-class boy does so, he is described as a 'mischievous pleasure-seeker'.

In another experiment conducted by Richard Schwartz and Jerome Skolnick in 1962 in the USA, one person with a criminal record was introduced to 100 potential employers with four different versions—he was found a criminal and convicted; he was not found a criminal and acquitted; he was found a criminal but acquitted; he was not found a criminal but was convicted. It was found that employers would not offer a job to a person with a criminal record. Thus, the labelling theory shifted the focus to those who label, that is, to persons responsible for the process of rule-making and rule enforcement.

According to Becker, whether or not labelling occurs depends upon: (1) the time when the act is committed, (2) who commits the act and who the victim is, and (3) the consequences of the act. Thus, whether a given act is deviant or not depends in part on the nature of the act and in part on what other people do about it. Becker suggests that a distinction be made between *rule-breaking behaviour* and *deviance*. Deviance is not a quality that lies in the behaviour itself, but in the interaction between the person who commits an act and those who *respond to it*. Becker has also suggested that certain types of groups are more likely to be labelled deviant than others; for example, groups that do not have political power and, therefore, cannot put pressure on officials for not enforcing the law, groups which are seen to threaten persons in power, and groups which have low social status.

What are the effects on the individual who is labelled. The official response to the behaviour in question may initiate processes that push the 'delinquent' individuals towards further delinquent conduct, and at least, make it more difficult for them to re-enter the conventional world. If on the other hand, the individual does not receive official response to his delinquent acts, he may continue committing them while receiving no help in changing his behaviour (Wheeler and Cottrell, 1966: 22-27).

Criticism against the labelling theory is that it employs good logic but does not explain the cause of crime. It entirely avoids the question of causation. Jack Gibbs (1982: 219) has posed four questions. What elements in the scheme are intended to be definitions rather than substantive theory? Is the ultimate goal to explain deviant behaviour or to explain reactions to deviation? Is deviant behaviour to be identified exclusively in terms of the reaction to it? Exactly what kind of reaction identifies behaviour as deviant?

Self-Concept and Containment Theory

Walter Reckless, the propounder of this theory (1967: 522), has said that the important question that must be answered in explaining criminal behaviour is why, given the alternatives of law-abiding and law-violating behaviour, do some people turn to one or the other behaviour. He suggests that self-concept is the key factor in explaining the choice among alternatives of behaviour. A favourable self-concept directs an individual towards law-abiding behaviour, and an unfavourable self-concept directs him towards delinquent behaviour. Reckless has further said that there are two important aspects of control: inner control and outer control, and that depending upon the balance of these control systems, the individual can take either a deviant or a conformist route. His assumption is that strong inner and reinforcing outer containment constitutes an isolation against normative deviancy, that is, violation of the socio-legal conduct norms.

In 1955, Reckless and Dinitz studied white 'good' boys (who, their teachers thought, would not get into trouble with the law) of sixth grade of about 12 years age, selected from high delinquency areas. The schedule, administered in the boys' homes, contained 50 items designed to measure self-concept. Likewise, in 1956, they interviewed 101 'bad' boys (who, their teachers thought, would become delinquents) and studied their self-concept. They concluded, on the basis of this study, that a good self-concept is evidence of favourable socialisation and the development of a 'strong inner self' (self-control, well-developed super-ego, high frustration tolerance, resistance to diversions, ability to find substitute satisfactions, tension-reducing rationalisations, etc.) which directs a person towards middle-class values. Poor self-concept is indicative of unfavourable socialisation and 'weak inner direction', which in turn does not deflect the boy from bad companions and street corner society, does not enable him to embrace middle-class values, and gives him an awareness of being cut off from upward movement in the legitimate opportunity system.

The evaluation of this theory has pointed out that though this is the only research by sociologists in the area of delinquency which handles variables of personality and self, nevertheless the measure of self-concept has been questioned and the lack of control groups has been noted. The samples have also been questioned. Was the selection of 'good' boys related to their performance in schools? What about boys with 'bad' self-concepts who might not be delinquents?

Culture Conflict Theories

Thorsten Sellin's Theory

Thorsten Sellin in his article "Culture Conflict and Crime" (1938) presented an analysis of the role of culture conflict in crime causation. Sellin says that crime is caused by conflicts among norms. He suggests that criminologists should study crime not as 'violation of law' but as 'violation of conduct norms', which are the rules that prohibit persons from acting in a certain specified way in certain circumstances. Such norms are not necessarily embedded in the criminal law, and if they are not, their violation should not be termed crime. Sellin says: "This extension of the meaning of the term is not desirable. It is wiser to retain the term 'crime' for the offence made punishable by the criminal law and to use the term 'abnormal conduct' for the violation of norms whether legal or not" (*ibid.*: 30-32).

Sellin has further said that in the study of conduct, it is necessary to think of culture conflict as a conflict of conduct norms. Such conflict may arise as a result of a process of differentiation within a cultural system or area or as a result of contact between norms drawn from different cultural systems or areas. We may study these conflicts either by an investigation of the person in whom the conflict is assumed to be internalised or by a study of violations in groups or areas within which the conflicts are assumed to occur.

Sellin distinguished between 'primary conflict' and 'secondary conflict'. The former is the conflict of culture norms when two different cultures clash, while the latter occurs within the evolution of a single culture. The first is illustrated by a man from Italy who, while living in America killed the man who seduced his adolescent daughter. The father was surprised to be arrested because in his country, such an act by a father was the expected behaviour for the purpose of defending the honour of the family. But in the United States, it was a crime. This is a case of conflict between the norms of two different cultures. The second type of conflict occurs during the normal growth of cultures from homogeneous to heterogeneous.

The criticism against this approach is that identification and measurement of such conduct norms is very difficult.

Richard Quinney's Modern Conflict Theory

Most criminological theories are based on the assumption that societies have a general consensus concerning goals, values and norms that should regulate behaviour, and that this is reflected in *law*. Thus, the assumption is one of *consensus*. On the other hand, conflict theory views law as a consequence of interests rather than (merely as) an instrument that functions outside of interests to resolve conflicts between interests. Law is a tool of the ruling class. Criminal law is a device used by the ruling class to preserve the existing order. Thus, the modern conflict theorists question the legal order or talk of sociology of law.

Richard Quinney's conflict theory is significant in this context. He has categorised traditional criminological approaches as under: (i) the post positivistic, (ii) the social constructionist, and (iii) the phenomenological. The first approach attempts to study crime empirically and objectively. The second approach looks into the subjective meaning of social reality to the actors involved and questions whether objective reality can exist apart from the social meaning attached by the actors to that reality. The third approach analyses the process by which an individual understands the world (against the first two approaches which are concerned with explaining social life). Phenomenologists look for reality in consciousness. Besides these approaches, Quinney himself has suggested one more approach—that of 'critical philosophy'. It questions the present order and radically talks of developing a new form of life—an active life in which we transcend the established existence. For bringing about this change, we do not think negatively; we only try to bring something to replace what we reject. Quinney proposes a socialist society in which the goal is a world that is free from oppressions produced by capitalism. In the capitalist society, crime is the result of exploitation of the powerless by the powerful. In a socialist society, all will be equal and all will share equally in the material benefits of society. A new human nature will arise and there will be no crime.

How do the conflict theorists explain the cause of crime? Chambliss says that "criminal acts occur as a consequence of social relations which stem from a society's mode of production."

This new conflict theory is criticised on the ground that it does not offer evidence for their new viewpoint (that crime is caused by mode of production). Secondly, what is the evidence that in socialist societies there is no crime? How truthful is the argument that criminal laws are passed to maintain the economic interests of the ruling class?

New Deviancy Theory

New deviancy theory emerged in the 1960s and early 1970s. It was primarily a radical response to positivist domination of criminology (that crime is the result of individual, physical, and social conditions). The new deviancy theorists believed in free will and creativity. According to this theory, crime is that behaviour which violates the interests of the powerful. The definition of crime or deviance depends upon two activities: one, an act of an individual or a group, and second, another individual or group with different values must label the initial activity as deviant. Human beings constantly generate their own system of values. Within a pluralistic society, certain groups—termed as "the powerful", "the bureaucracy", "the moral entrepreneurs"—with more power than others impose their values upon the less powerful, labelling those who infringe their rules with tags of 'deviants' or 'criminals'.

Thus, people who evolve different values or experiment with various forms of behaviour are labelled by the authorities as 'an alcoholic', 'a homosexual', 'a drug addict', 'a thief', 'a psychopath' and so on.

For example, a college girl who may be good at studies and is likely to get a position in the university examination, but, because she conceives without being married, would be labelled an 'unwed-mother' or 'a deviant girl'. An officer who may be very efficient, hard-working and competent but if he takes alcohol everyday, would be labelled an alcoholic.

In explaining the causes of crime, people usually talk about motivation, i.e., why a person indulges in a deviant act. They hold that the basic difference between one who deviates and one who conforms lies in the character of their motivations. Thus, psychological theories find the cause of deviant motivations or acts in the individual's early experiences. Sociological theories look for socially structured sources of 'strain' in society, or social positions which have conflicting demands placed upon them so that these position-holders seek an illegitimate way of solving the problems their position produces. In this way, some theories focus on individual characteristics (positivism), some on structural antecedents of the criminal act (sociological), and some on the act itself (classicism), but the new deviancy theory focuses on 'reaction'. It holds that administration of crime and not its origin is the key to understanding criminal phenomenon (Duster, 1970: 10).

EVALUATION OF SOCIAL, STRUCTURAL AND SUBCULTURAL THEORIES

Social structural and subcultural theories of criminal behaviour (by scholars like Clifford Shaw, Thorsten Sellin, Bonger, Quetlet, Sutherland, Merton, Cloward and Ohlin, Cohen, etc.) have been in existence for more than fifty years. These criticised the physiological, biological, and psychological theories of crime etiology and focused our attention on environment—economic, geographical and social. Thus, the emphasis shifted from the personality of the deviant to the social milieu of the criminal. However, these theories have not been free of methodological errors (as discussed in earlier pages) because of the serious problem in defining terms, specially the development of operational definitions; for example, Bonger's 'climate of motivation' or 'egotistic tendency' or 'poverty' or Clifford Shaw's 'disorganised neighbourhood' or Sutherland's 'differential associations' or Cloward and Ohlin's 'differential opportunity', etc. Secondly, the empirical base of these theories is questionable. Sampling problems exist in most of researches. Further, some of the theorists did not conduct any empirical research. The assumptions of some of the theories have also been questioned by later empirical research. Some scholars focused their researches on lower-class populations. Control groups and follow-up studies were usually not a part of the research design. Finally, in many of the theories, unwarranted assumptions and generalisations have been made, e.g., poverty as the cause of crime or broken homes as the cause of juvenile delinquency, or learning crime from criminals in intimate groups, etc. Thus, though these theories have taken the focus off the individual criminal—who earlier was presumed to be 'defective' in some way, yet these (structural theories) have failed to explain why those persons who are exposed to the type of the structure being associated with crime do not become criminals, or, how so many persons, who are not exposed to those social structures, do become criminals. It, therefore, becomes necessary to look beyond the social structure as well as the culture and seek an explanation of the process by which people become criminals. Perhaps, emphasis on holistic approach, including the role of various type of environment and personality characteristics. could help in understanding law-violating citizens.

MULTIPLE-FACTOR APPROACH

Early theories of criminal behaviour have been criticised because they emphasised a single factor as the cause of crime. Factors like inherited physical traits, biological inferiority, feeble-mindedness, emotional disturbances, or poverty were described as the single cause of crime. The multiple-factor approach in criminology grew out of discrepancies in single-factor approach. Its adherents argued that crime should be understood in terms of varied contributions made by a variety of factors. The assumption was that crime is the product of many factors---biological, psychological, economic and social---and that different crimes will be the result of different combinations of factors. Hence, 'proper' approach in criminology is an eclectic one emphasising identification and analysis of multiple factors. Scholars who believe in this approach are William Healy, Cyril Burt, and Sheldon and Glueck. On the basis of his study of 1,000 juvenile delinquents, William Healy (*The Individual Delinquent*, 1915) identified 138 factors and classified them as psychological, biological and social-environmental factors in the causation of delinquency. Influenced by Healy's work in the United States, Cyril Burt (*The Young Delinquent*, 4th edn.1914) pursued a similar investigation in England in 1925. He found no less than 170 factors which he classified into nine major categories. Sheldon Glueck ("Theory and Fact in Criminology", *British Journal of Delinquency*, October 1956) in his study of 500 delinquents and 500 non-delinquents in 1950 extensively analysed social background, home-life, physical characteristics, intellectual ability, psychiatric states, emotion and temperament of the respondents and identified socio-cultural, biological, and psychological factors in delinquency. He concluded that while a host of different factors show associations with delinquency, the major causes of delinquency are "problems in the home" (parental separation, parental drunkenness, physical or mental ailments, poor home management, lack of child supervision, little show of affection), and so forth.

The multiple-factor approach has been criticised by scholars like Albert Cohen and many others. While recognising that the multiple-factor approach made a useful contribution to criminology through the compilation of factors associated with delinquency, Cohen (1955: 5-13) mainly gave three arguments against it: (1) the advocates of multiple-factor approach have confused a single theory with single-factor explanations. A single theory does not necessarily explain crime in terms of a single factor. Theories are concerned with 'variables' and 'factors' and a single theory usually incorporates a number of different variables. To explain crime, we need theories which consist of logically related propositions asserting particular relationships among a number of variables. (2) Cohen objected to a major assumption of the multi-factor approach, namely, that factors have intrinsic crime-producing qualities. Factors found statistically associated with crime are often asserted to cause crime, or to be one cause among others. Each factor is presumed to carry a fixed amount of criminogenic power. But Cohen argues that not only the factors have no intrinsic crime-producing qualities but also they should not be confused with causes. Causal power cannot be assumed on the basis of a discovery that a certain factor, or combination of factors, shows a statistical association with crime. (3) Many, if not most, multi-factor studies talk of 'evil causes'. The fallacious notion is that evil consequences (crime) must have evil precedents (biological pathologies, low IQ, pathological mental states, poor living conditions). Sutherland (1965: 61) has also referred to this argument against explaining crime or any other social problem. He says: "When we explain crime, we tend merely to catalog a series of ugly circumstances which any 'decent citizen' would deplore, and attribute causal power to those circumstances. In criminology, this fallacious procedure might stem from a desire to eradicate crime without changing other existing conditions which we cherish and esteem; that is, criminologists tend to identify with the existing social order and seek 'causes' of crime in 'factors' which might be eliminated without changing social conditions which they hold dear, or which may be safely deplored without hurting anyone's feelings."

References

Ahuja, Ram, *Apradhshastra*, Rawat Publications, Jaipur, 1999.

Barlow, Hugh D., *Introduction to Criminology*, Little, Brown and Co., Boston, 1978.

Becker, Howard (ed.), *Social Problems: A Modern Approach*, John Wiley and Sons, New York, 1966.

Bloch, Herbert A. and Geis, Gilbert, *Man, Crime and Society*, Random House, New York, 1962.

Burt, Cyril, *Young Delinquent*, University of London Press, London, 1944.

Caldwell, Robert G., *Criminology*, University of Pennsylvania Press Philadelphia, 1956.

Clinard, Marshall, B., *Sociology of Deviant Behaviour*, Holt, Rinehart and Winston, Inc., New York, 1957.

Cloward, Richard and Ohlin Lloyd, *Delinquency and Opportunity: A Theory of Delinquent Gangs*, The Free Press, Glencoe, Illinois, 1960.

Cohen, Albert K., *Delinquent Boys: The Culture of the Gang*, The Free Press, New York, 1955.

—, *Deviance and Control*, Prentice-Hall Inc., Englewood Cliffs, New Jersey, 1966.

Elliot, Mabel, *Crime in Modern Society*, Harper and Bros., New York, 1952.

Fitzgerald, Mike, *et al.*, *Crime and Society*, Routledge and Kegan Paul London, 1981.

Gibbons, Don, *Society, Crime and Criminal Careers*, (3rd edn.), Prentice-Hall, New Jersey, 1977.

Johnson, Elmer H., *Crime, Correction and Society*, (4th edn.), The Dorsay Press, Homewood, Illionis, 1978.

Merton, R.K., *Social Theory and Social Structure*, The Free Press, New York, 1968.

Reckless, Walter, *The Crime Problem* (2nd edn.), Appleton Century Crofts, Inc., New York, 1955.

Reid, Sue Titus, *Crime and Criminology*, The Drydon Press, Hinsdale, Illinois, 1976.

Schafer, Stephen, *Theories in Criminology*, Random House, New York, 1969.

Taylor, I., Walton P., Young J. (ed.), *Critical Criminology*, Routledge and Kegan Paul, London, 1975.

Sutherland, E.H. and Cressay D.R., *Principles of Criminology*, (6th edn.), The Times of India Press, Bombay, 1955.

Vold, George, *Theoretical Criminology*, Oxford University Press, New York, 1948.

Chapter 3

Factors in Crime

In spite of the fact that so many empirical studies have been conducted in the last several decades with refined techniques and new insights, it is difficult to say that we have fully acquired the knowledge regarding causes of crime. While we no longer accept the unscientific and ludicrous views like one that crime is caused by the possession of evil spirits, we refuse to accept explanations holding a single factor—like poverty, defective family, strain, value conflict, etc.—as the cause of crime. In fact, the cause of crime varies from case to case, individual to individual and situation to situation. Today, it is generally held that crime is caused by a combination of personal and environmental factors. The more important personal factors have been identified as physiological handicaps, personality conflicts, fear, and mental abnormalities and diseases, while major environmental factors have been pointed out as defective family, disorganised neighbourhood, peer group associations, and movies and obscene literature. We will analyse each of these factors separately.

PERSONAL FACTORS

It is said that a person inherits many traits from his parents through heredity and some of these traits become the cause of his criminal activity. However, it is also said that the raw material carried by the germ plasm is moulded by social environment and greatly modified by social experiences. Thus, it is established that heredity endows man with potentialities and imposes limits upon his development as well as behaviour. Human personality emerges out of the interaction of heredity with many factors in man's life—both personal and environmental. Personality, which ultimately determines human behaviour, is composed of sentiments, ideas, attitudes, beliefs, values, skills, styles, intelligence, will-power, habits, and so forth.

The inherited characteristics may depend on germ plasm but the acquired traits are not inherited. And the development of personality depends upon both the inherited and the acquired traits. The cultural traits based on the discoveries of science and the achievements of the arts are transmitted to persons through the process of education and learning. A man has the capacity to benefit by these processes. It is difficult to say how much a human being is the product of heredity and how much of the environment. Many of the hereditary qualities remain latent and there is no method to identify them. A normal person carries both latent as well as manifest traits. Certain characteristics in one individual may be found inherited but environmental in another. The situation is further complicated by the fact that some inherited characteristics appear only gradually through the process of maturation. In view of these facts, we may hold that personal factors in a human being have in them a bit of both heredity and environment, and both are present in an individual in indeterminable proportions.

Physical Handicaps

The old contentions of some scholars that physical degenerative stigmata (Lombroso) or body-build (Sheldon and Kretschmer) or endocrine glands (Schlapp) etc. cause crime have not been substantiated. However, physical defects and handicaps like crippleness, dwarfism, ugliness, lameness, baldness, lack of bodily symmetry, blindness, deafness involve self-concept of inferiority and the resultant behaviour of protest. Persons with these defects are shunned and avoided by normal people which creates emotional disturbances and inferiority complex. Being handicapped in social relationships, a person faces personality problems and a feeling of guilt. These feelings sometimes lead to aggressive behaviour. However, this behaviour does not always lead to crime because sometimes the desire for security and recognition may lead a person to devote more time to his hobbies and interests which may make him a good artist, a famous musician, a renowned painter, etc. Thus, persons with physical defects and handicaps are found both as law-abiding citizens as well as law-violating citizens.

Frustrations, Wish Blockages and Personality Conflicts

Every person feels frustrated in many situations in his/her life. Similarly, every person is not able to fulfil all his wishes in life due to various types of blockages faced. But ordinarily, the frustrated persons suppress, sublimate, find substitute satisfaction, resign themselves to fate and come through wish blockage with a moderate amount of restlessness and discontent. However, some people become emotionally disturbed or supercharged in the process and come to indulge in deviant activities.

As a person grows in age, he develops new needs and dependence on more and more persons for the gratification of these needs. Failure to maintain and continue social relationships for satisfying these needs makes a person frustrated and disorganised and causes personality conflicts. The failure to develop social relationships may be caused either by environmental obstacles like poverty, caste restrictions, lack of education, etc. or personal obstacles like physical deficiencies, feeble-mindedness, etc. Personality conflicts are also the result of conflict between two wishes, say, whether to side with mother or with wife. Supporting one may displease other who may become more nagging. To escape such behaviour, a person may assault the nagging individual. The assault here is deviant behaviour which is caused by personality conflict. Similarly, the conflict may be caused owing to two opposite wishes of getting money and passing out the country's military secrets to the enemy, or of giving bribe and getting a job of a subinspector in police. Some people manage to face such conflicts realistically by seeking others' help or through one's own resources but in a few cases the conflicts persist and the individual struggles with them through mechanisms like sublimation, repression, regression, rationalisation, day-dreaming, compensation and projection. Sometimes, a person solves this conflict by blaming others or his luck or by belittling himself. However, some individuals fail in these efforts and commit crimes due to personality conflicts. If an individual does not adopt such behaviour, the conflict may dominate his personality and may push him to mental imbalance. For example, day-dreaming may take a person away from the realities of life and he may develop hallucinations and become a psychotic case. Likewise, persistent repression may make him a neurotic person. This shows that adopting mechanisms to deal with personality conflicts may express itself in law-abiding behaviour or it may lead an individual to conflict with the law. In one case, the tendency to blame others for one's failure may cause a person to commit the murder of the person whom he considers responsible for his behaviour; in the other case, the failure to gratify the need through normal social relationships may force him to become a thief; while in third case, rationalisation may provide an opportunity to a woman to become a prostitute or commit a sex offence. The fact that personality conflicts may lead a person into crime or juvenile delinquency does not necessarily mean that he has become mentally ill. It may also be pointed out that even when personality conflicts may develop aggressiveness, shyness, disagreeableness, conscientiousness or even rebellious behaviour, all these do not necessarily express themselves through criminal behaviour. It is possible that sometimes criminal behaviour may also lead to personality conflicts. It may thus be said that personality traits alone are not the cause of crime, but that in the analysis of causation, they must be seen in their functional relationship with many other factors.

Mental Abnormalities

Mental abnormalities include: (a) mental deficiency, and (b) mental disease.

Mental Deficiency

Mental deficiency or retardation implies subnormal intelligence, i.e., lack of mental development or low intelligence level (i.e., IQ of less than 75). A person with an IQ of more than 75 is considered a mentally normal person while a person with an IQ of 50 to 70 is called a moron, with 20 to 50 is called an imbecile and with less than 20 is called an idiot. A person with a low IQ is said to be a *mentally deficient person*, i.e., a person with incomplete development of intelligence. The development of normal social relationships and performing one's roles depends upon a person's ability to adopt himself to his environment and to maintain existence independently of external support. This, in turn, depends upon one's IQ Idiots (with a mental age of a child under three years) and imbeciles (with a mental age of a child of 3-7 years) are incapable of managing themselves or their affairs but they are physically strong enough to be dangerous when provoked or frustrated. Morons (with a mental age of a child of 7-12 years) often have a normal appearance, yet they require care and supervision. In the absence of proper care and control, the morons come to be involved in such crimes as theft, vagrancy, drunkenness, sexual offences and so forth. Their indulgence in these anti-social behaviour patterns is due to the fact that they are confused, emotionally unstable or easily exploited by others. But it cannot be said that all mentally deficient persons indulge in crimes. Manual Shulman's (*Journal of Criminal Law and Criminology*, March-April 1951: 763-81) evidence indicates that only a small proportion of mentally deficient persons are delinquent or criminal, and that the offenders and the general population have about the same distribution of intelligence levels. Thus, like physical defects and personality conflicts, low intelligence is also described as a factor in criminal behaviour. However, it may be a major factor in one particular case but it is never the only factor in crime.

Mental Disease

Mental disease or mental disorder is defined as "a state of mental imbalance or derangement which prevents a person from assuming responsibility for his own support or causes him to be a positive menace to the safety of the community." Mental disease refers to a mind that has developed normally, almost always to maturity, but has become disordered or deranged. Mental disease is distinguished from insanity which is a legal term. An insane person is considered to be incapable of having any criminal intent. The mental disease may either be of *psychosis* type or *neurosis* type.

Psychosis

The symptoms of psychosis and neurosis differ from each other not qualitatively but quantitatively. A psychotic person loses contact with the world of reality completely or partially owing to mental breakdown. He requires medical and special institutional care, but he may not manifest his abnormality continuously. At times, he may act quite rationally.

Neurosis

Neurosis is a mental disease which makes a person socially and personally less efficient but does not incapacitate him to the point that he may be institutionalised. Most neurotic persons behave in a socially normal manner but their 'compulsions' may find expression in crime and delinquency, like compulsive stealing, fire setting or exhibition of self. The disorderly conduct of young person may be a compensation for his feeling of inferiority or timidity which may embarrass him. It is also possible that his crime may be the result of a desire for punishment.

Psychopathic Personality

Some mentally diseased persons are not classified as psychotics or neurotics but are described as having a psychopathic personality. Persons with this type of personality are believed to possess some abnormal or psychopathic trends like being ruthless, indisciplined, defiant, vindictive, unstable, etc. It is because of these characteristics that they are found lacking in conscience and empathy. Dealing with a person of psychopathic trends is almost like dealing with a child who never became cooperative, reciprocal, socialised or with someone who developed such an outer shell of defence as to insulate himself against society.

It is difficult to say how many mentally diseased persons (i.e., psychotics, neurotics and psychopaths), commit crimes, as it is difficult to accept that all mentally diseased persons indulge in criminal activities. Bromberg and Thompson (1937: 70) have said: "We have some evidence derived from the studies of prisoners which indicates that only a very small percentage of prisoners (about 20%) are clearly psychotic and that even the percentages of neurotic and psychopathic prisoners are not very large." Schilder (1940) also found that of the convicted felons examined in one study, hardly 13 per cent were found psychotic, neurotic, psychopathic or feeble-minded. It may thus be concluded that though mental disease may be a factor in crime yet it does not inevitably cause crime or delinquency.

Personality Traits

Aggressiveness, assertiveness etc. are character traits which affect social contacts as well as an individual's behaviour. They are an approach to life situations, the way an individual handles life. Sometimes, these traits become the cause of failures and limitations of individuals involving inability to cope with problems. A person accumulates problems which he seems unable to solve or manage. For example, a young girl develops the habit of taking loans knowing that she would not be able to repay, sales her wristwatch, steals her friend's money, develops illicit relations, becomes pregnant, goes for illegal abortion, fails in examination, tries to find a job but fails to get it, gradually loses love and affection of her parents and siblings, runs away with a boy who promises to marry her, is cheated by him, and ultimately takes to a life of a call-girl.

ENVIRONMENTAL FACTORS

The analysis of individual case histories of delinquents and criminals provides an insight in the causative environmental factors. But the causative factors are more readily discernible in the case of juvenile delinquents than in the case of adult offenders. Adults so face complicated situations, sequences and experiences that they obstruct a clear view of causation. Nevertheless, the pattern of life and activity set by milieu determines individual's role in society. When an individual fails to fit himself in this role, he develops a life organisation of his own in a milieu that gives him scope and opportunity for a criminal career. It is, therefore, more realistic to look for behaviour patterning processes in the search for the causative factors in crime.

Most studies have shown that crime is caused because of social and economic environment. We will discuss here the role of a few selected social factors in criminality, namely, family, neighbourhood, peer group, and movies.

Family

All sociologists are of the opinion that family exerts a deep influence in the life of an individual. It not only gratifies an individual's essential and nonessential needs but it also transmits cultural values which socialise an individual and train him in survival patterns. However, family situations vary from individual to individual. All individuals may not be able to live in 'normal' families and experience socialising interpersonal relationships. Lowell Carr (*Delinquency Control* 1950: 166-68) has given six characteristics of a 'normal' family: (i) *structural completeness*, i.e., presence of both natural parents in the home; (ii) *economic security*, i.e., reasonable stability of income necessary to maintain health, working efficiency and morale; (iii) *cultural conformity*, i.e., parents speaking same language, eating same food, following same customs and holding substantially the same attitudes; (iv) *moral conformity*, i.e., conformity to the mores of the community; (v) *physical and psychological normality*, i.e., no member is mentally deficient or deranged or chronically invalid; and (vi) *functional adequacy*, i.e., members have harmonious relations with one another and there is a minimum of friction and emotional frustration. Further, children are not rejected by parents, there is a minimum of sibling rivalry, and there is no effort to escape from reality.

However, it is impossible to find a home with all these characteristics, which does not mean that there are no 'normal' homes at all in our society. What is important is the level or degree of the presence of these characteristics.

Retrospectively speaking, a large number of experimental studies were carried out in the 1930s, the 1940s, the 1950s, the 1960s, and the 1970s on the families of juvenile delinquents and criminals. The object was to ascertain factors in a criminal's family life or the so-called 'under-the-roof culture' responsible for his delinquent or later criminal activities. Identifying factors such as lack of control, too strict or too lenient discipline, parental neglect or rejection, physical abuse, and broken homes appeared to corroborate much of the popular but wise notion that family influence in general and parents' erratic disciplining of children in particular had an influence on subsequent criminality. Later on, however, it was found that these studies had serious methodological and conceptual deficiencies which limited their validity. In spite of this criticism, it is worthwhile to go through these retrospective studies on the role of broken homes, insecure homes, immoral homes, etc. in delinquencies.

Broken Home

The broken home is one in which one parent is absent due to death, divorce, desertion, separation or imprisonment. The absence of a parent may result in lack of affection, lack of control and supervision, development of bad habits like smoking, drinking, gambling, etc. falling into bad company, and so forth. A number of studies have been conducted on the role of broken homes in juvenile delinquency. The broad conclusion of these studies conducted between 1939 and 1950 is that 30 to 60 per cent delinquents come from broken homes (Sutherland, 1965: 176). Healy and Bronner's study of 4,000 juvenile delinquents in two cities in the United States showed that about 50 per cent had a background of broken homes. Glueck's study (1950) of 500 delinquent boys from two correctional institutions and 500 non-delinquent boys showed that the parents of the delinquent boys employed rather unsuitable methods of disciplining their children: lax, over-strict, or erratic. They were also either indifferent or hostile or used physical punishment against their children. In their later study (1962), they also found that the hostility became reciprocal and children also developed indifference and hostility towards their parents.

In India, Ruttonshaw's study in Poona, a study conducted in Ahmedabad, and a study conducted in Varanasi (by Manju Kewalramani in 1982) also noted the significant role of broken homes in juvenile delinquency. The value of such studies depends upon the comparison of experiment groups with control groups, i.e., in determining how many non-delinquents belong to broken homes is compared to delinquents.

Such studies were conducted by Shildeler and Merrill who found that about twice as many delinquents as non-delinquents came from broken homes. Shaw and McKay found that 42.5 per cent delinquents and 36.1 per cent non-delinquents were from broken homes showing that broken home is not an important factor in delinquency. Studies by Silverman, Hirsch and Campbell also pointed out that broken home itself is a relatively unimportant factor in the causation of delinquency. However, Harny Shulman (1949) is of the opinion that the majority of research studies have shown that the incidence of broken homes is higher for delinquents than non-delinquents, which suggests that some relation does exist between delinquency and broken homes. Sutherland (1965), however, believes that evidence in general indicates that broken home is less important than it was formerly believed to be. My own contention is that causation must be seen as a functional relationship in which many factors interact in a changing situation, and broken home is just one factor in it. But the term 'broken home' is too broad. The role of the father of a child may be taken over by his brother, mother etc. in his absence and if the father happens to be unemployed or a drunkard, his absence would not affect the upbringing of the child. Similarly, before divorce, the relations between the husband and the wife might have already been shattered and, therefore, separation of parents might be more functional than dysfunctional for the child.

Poor Home

A poor home is not able to provide economic security to its members. It not only fails to satisfy the basic needs of members but it also fails to provide security against various exigencies of life, like accident, illness, unemployment etc. Sometimes, poverty operates directly to produce criminal activities. A poor person who is not able to provide dowry for his daughter's marriage may indulge in embezzlement, accepting bribes or committing fraud, etc. A child who fails to get pocket money may steal from his father's purse. A father may steal to supply his children food, clothing, and other necessities of life. Often, poverty operates indirectly too. A child from a poor family may run away from his home to escape worry, irritability, desperation and discord of parents and may come to associate with delinquent gangs. Scholars like Stephan Hurwitz (1952: 319-24) maintain that the great majority of criminals and delinquents come from poor economic conditions, and the incidence of poverty in the homes of offenders far exceeds that of the general population.

Functionally Inadequate Home

This home is one in which tensions and discords are common in interpersonal relations amongst family members over question of status, role dominance, values, attitudes, rights, and acceptance. But the person who is the subject in any case-history of delinquency or criminality must be at the apex or one pole of the conflict. He must be a part of the conflict. In some cases, however, a child may not be directly in conflict with his parents but his two parents may have conflicts with each other, and the child may like to escape from such home environment, fall into bad company and become a delinquent.

Defective Discipline

Defective discipline in family may be found in various forms, like lax supervision, immoral home, etc. Lax family supervision means lack of parental guidance and direction which may be caused by varied reasons, like ill health, large family, mother being busy with her job outside the home, and so on. Homelessness in adults means not having parents and siblings, living away from home in a rented house or in a hostel/lodge, etc. Homelessness leads to considerable mobility which becomes the cause of detachment from family controls. Andry's study in 1971 suggests that the fathers of delinquent children are particularly significant in that they show less affection and have less contact with children than the fathers of 'normal' (non-delinquent) children.

Sears made a study in 1957 to find out whether criminal activity was a result of the acquisition of a faulty morality or of conscience. This was in fact the study of the effects of child-rearing practices in delinquent and non-delinquent families. The study indicated 'latent' pre-disposition to crime as well as actual 'performance'. Children treated in certain ways in non-delinquent families do become equally (latently) 'immoral' but various other factors suppress their performance of delinquent/criminal acts. The general finding was that *psychological* techniques of discipline (like praise, withdrawal of love, and isolation, i.e., sending a child to his room) were positively associated with moral development, while *physical* techniques (such as withdrawal of rewards, deprivation of privileges and physical punishment) were negatively associated with it.

This study and several such other studies on family have a methodological drawback. They 'pre-label' a family as delinquent-prone and then analyse child-rearing practices. The right way is to undertake studies which take not a pre-labelled group as the starting point but normal population of children who are then followed through their development in order to see which ones become 'delinquent' and which do not. Another criticism of these studies is that they fail in accounting for 'within-family' differences, i.e., why one child rather than another becomes delinquent. Do factors like school, friends, social opportunities for need gratification, etc. mitigate the family influence?

In sum, it may be said that all these studies provide considerable data, albeit some of dubious validity, of the 'family life' of delinquent children. It is apparent that these studies employed certain moralistic ideologies which essentially served to 'blame' parents for the treatment of their children and their subsequent criminal activity. However, this begs the question of where the causal chain starts. That is to say, why are the parents behaving in such a way? Were they (parents) maltreated by their parents?

The studies, however, presented three views on the role of family in crime: (i) psychoanalytic explanation, (ii) behaviourist explanation, and (iii) cognitive explanation. The *psychoanalytic* explanation focused on difficulties in children's early development leading to their 'sickness' causing them to commit crimes like thefts, arson, sexual attacks, etc. Since crime was caused by 'sickness', children were not considered totally responsible for them. This view had its impact on the punishment and the treatment policies, leading to the rise of psychiatric treatment for offenders. The *behaviourist* explanation given in the 1950s and the 1960s rejected psychoanalytic explanation owing to its lack of rigorous testability. Instead, it proposed that people's actions are controlled by a system of rewards and punishments and crime is caused by 'inappropriate learning experiences' or 'social mis-learning'. Criminals were thus seen not as 'sick' persons but those who suffered from 'mis-learning'. In the 1960s and the 1970s, there was a shift away from behaviourist explanation towards *cognitive* developmental explanation. According to it, a person's predisposition to commit crime is 'cognitive' rather than 'emotional', that is, a person's actions are regarded as guided by his moral development or awareness which reflects his ability to distinguish between 'right' and 'wrong' or 'good' and 'bad'.

In all these explanations, family has been chosen as the focus of causal agency. This stops short of a question: what is the wider influence of society? There is no doubt that family is an influential institution. It needs to be borne in mind that some of the problems which appear to be generated by the family are a function of its basic nature as a structure for living in society. If family determines action, it also constrains and constructs individual's actions. This influence of family on the members is complex and cannot adequately be explained in simple causal terms.

PEER GROUP

Many children as well as adults pick up criminal habits from their friends. In many cases, individuals get support of their peers in committing crimes. Drug trafficking, picking someone's pocket, stealing, eve-teasing etc. are crimes which are learnt as well as committed more in association with peers. These associations affect attitudes, morals as well as ideals. In fact, peer group may even surpass the family as an educational agency. The delinquent gang, which emerges from peer relations, has a somewhat permanent membership and definite organisation. It provides an outlet to children for indulging in suppressed activities which are always anti-social activities. These criminal peer groups supply adventure and excitement to their members and give them recognition for their skills, and protection against their cruel parents and teachers, and security from the police. Healy, Shaw, Gluecks, Cyril Burt and many others have shown that a good number of delinquents and criminals usually act in association with their peer delinquents. Walter Gluecks in his tabulation of 107 factors in delinquency gave first rank to 'delinquent companions' and seventh to 'gang companions' (Reckless, 1955: 74).

NEIGHBOURHOOD

In rural areas, neighbourhood continues to be a primary group while in urban areas, it is emerging as a secondary group. Neighbourhood is an important agency of social control and contributes much to the development of the child. The child plays with his neighbours and gets the required recreation. But the neighbourhood also contributes to crime and delinquency by blocking basic personality needs, fostering anti-social values and creating subcultural conflicts. When a family migrates from one neighbourhood to another, in the new neighbourhood the children of the migrated family may find the prevalent values shocking and may ultimately come into conflict with the enforcement of law. This is so because the new neighbourhood may affect their attitudes and may handicap them in their social adjustment. Influences in a neighbourhood can destroy the moral precepts of home, and the informal education provided by groups in the neighbourhood can easily nullify the effects of the teaching of family and school. Video parlours, cheap hotels and picture houses etc. in neighbourhood can also focalise the anti-social forces and create criminal attitudes in children.

Such places often become the centres of meeting-places of local 'goondas' (anti-social elements) and 'hang-outs' for members of the organised criminal gangs and petty politicians who indulge more in criminal activities than social activities. In the causation of delinquency and crime, neighbourhood plays an important role in "delinquency area". Lawlessness in these areas is transmitted through groups operating in the neighbourhood.

MOVIES

Movies exert colossal but harmful influence on the young minds. Today's movies are so full of sex and violence that the youth easily pick up new values, attitudes and personality traits. On the one hand, movies create social awareness against evil customs, arouse public opinion against undesirable social conditions, and stimulate public demand for civic, social and political reforms, and on the other hand, movies provide vicarious experience to the young people, draining off their tensions and converting their anti-social tendencies into imaginary adventures.

A number of cases are reported in the newspapers where young persons have used the same techniques of committing crimes as were shown in the movies they had watched. The most recent example is the case of a boy in Calcutta reported in January 1996 who, along with two of his accomplices, murdered his parents by using the same methods they had seen in an English movie a few days earlier. Such cases are often reported from cities like Mumbai, Delhi, etc. However, children and young persons from the lower and middle classes are more likely to be driven towards crime by watching movies rather than those from the upper classes. Further, already acquired delinquent or criminal tendencies through intimate association with peers are likely to get more aggravated by watching motion pictures which may not result in the acquiring of totally new conduct norms. It may also be added that children are more susceptible to the influence of movies than adults.

The television now faces almost the same charges that were once hurled at the movies. The English movies, particularly those shown on the cable TV, glamourise life, stimulate desire for a life of luxury and arouse sexual passion. Both English and Hindi movies as well as serials on the TV provide new philosophies of life, new ideas of rights and privileges, and fashions in dress and behaviour. They also teach the adolescents and the youths modern techniques of love-making and some deviant techniques of achieving things and earning money. The youths impersonate actors and imitate them in their conduct. Herbert Blumer and Philip Hauser (Cf. Sutherland, 1965: 216) have also said: "The motion pictures were found a factor of importance in the delinquent or criminal careers of about 10 per cent of the male and 25 per cent of the female offenders studied. Movies display criminal patterns of behaviour, arouse desires for easy money and luxury, suggest questionable methods for their achievement, induce a spirit of bravado, toughness and adventurousness, arouse intense sexual desires and invoke day-dreaming of criminal roles."

INTERACTION BETWEEN PERSONAL AND ENVIRONMENTAL FACTORS: A CONJUNCTIVE APPROACH

The above analysis of personal and environmental factors has clearly indicated that in both individual and situation lies the riddle of crime and delinquency causation. Walter Reckless's formula (1955: 79-80) on causation of crime is simple.

$$c = \frac{S}{I} \text{ or } \frac{\text{Situation}}{\text{Individual}}$$

In this formula, '*S*' stands for pressure of the situation and weaknesses in the social order. The former (situational pressures) refers to adverse impact and the latter (weaknesses) refers to an inability to guide, direct, control or contain the individual. The *I* (individual) can be equated in terms of inherited or acquired strength to withstand pressure or to control self without a strong supporting social order. Or, the "*I*" can be equated in terms of inherited or acquired weaknesses in the individual: anxiety, low frustration toleration, weak ego (conscience) structure, restlessness, suggestibility, uncontrollable temper, immaturity, instability, poor attitudes, absence of goals and ideals, and so forth. According to Reckless, actually the "*I*" represents the precedence of strengths over weaknesses in certain predicaments or the procedure of weaknesses over strengths in some other situations. The "*I*" is, therefore, the differential response that the individual makes, according to his weakness or strength components.

A situation may play on the weakness components and be too overpowering for the strengths of an individual. At the same time, there may be no backlog of support from family, friends, neighbourhood and group affiliations to help bolster up the individual or rescue him from his plight. The pressures of a situation become greater in their impact when social order fails to provide support. Tension, disruption, lack of direction, weak social controls, absence of structured roles and statuses are all weakness ingredients of the social order that make it impossible for the social order to cushion the pressures on individuals. Consequently, the pressures are thrown against the individual's strengths and weaknesses.

If the impact of the situation is too great for the available strengths of the individual, or if it plays directly on weaknesses, the individual breaks through the lines of control: succumbs to pressures, runs away, aggrandises himself, steals, assaults, and so forth. The less the impact of "*S*", the less the weaknesses of the individual come into play, and the more the strengths can hold the line. A person with unusual character strengths can steer his course without deflection even in the face of terrific external pressure. On the other hand, if "*T*" is charged with weaknesses and emotional disturbances, it takes very little in "*S*" to drive him off course.

David Abrahamsen (1946: 7), as already stated, has presented a formula in this connection:

$$C = \frac{T+S}{R}$$

in which *C* is crime, *T* is tendencies, *S* is situation, and *R* is resistance. According to him, crime depends upon the abilities of an individual to resist his tendencies and situational pressures.

Sheldon and Glueck (1950: 281-82) have pointed out five factors (individual and environmental) in the causation of crime: (1) *physical* (mesomorphic in constitution), (2) *temperamental* (restless, impulsive energetic, aggressive, extrovert, destructive), (3) *attitudes* (being hostile, defiant, resentful, suspicious, stubborn, assertive, adventurous, unconventional, non-submissive to authority), (4) *psychological* (being less methodical, in approach to problems), and (5) *sociological* (defective family rearing, parents immorality). Of these five factors, one is situational and four are individual ingredients.

Lowell Carr (1950: 160-61) has given a different formula (on the role of individual and situation in crime) in terms of deviation and conformity pressures. The formula is as follows:

$$\begin{array}{rcl} CF\ (I \times E) - DF\,(I \times E) = & CD \rightarrow & CB \\ & \text{or} & \text{or} \\ & DD \rightarrow & DB \end{array}$$

The conformity factors (*CF*), both internal (*I*), and external (*E*), minus the deviation factors (*DF*), both internal and external, equal a conformity differential (*CD*, if greater) or a deviation differential (*DD*, if greater), which leads to conforming behaviour (*CB*) or deviant behaviour (*DB*). If deviation factors exceed a certain number, delinquency is the end-result. According to Carr, the environmental aspects of deviation pressures or factors include: (a) anything that frustrates or blocks the satisfaction of a normal need, and (b) any external stimulus towards a departure from the cultural norm of behaviour necessary for the satisfaction of such a need (*ibid*: 165). The internal deviation factors consist of inadequacies, maladjustments, instabilities, aggressiveness, hostilities, and so on. Conformity factors, both internal and external, would represent the absence of pressures or drives for deviation.

Albert Cohen (*Deviance and Control*, 1966: 41-44) has also referred to the role of personality structure and situation in deviant behaviour. In personality structure, he includes individual's perspectives, values, goals, interests, temperament, needs, and drives. Any act we can think of could have turned out differently if some other person had stood in the actor's shoes, or if the situation had been in some respect different. The processes through which the variables interact and which determine the outcome, whether these processes are located within the actor or in the conjunction of actor and situation, are called 'motivational mechanisms' by Cohen.

Let us try to understand his explanation of motivational mechanisms (*see*, Albert Cohen, 1966). Let us assume that two persons have two different personality structures—P_1 and P_2— each having a propensity to certain kinds of behaviour. These two types may be conceived of in terms of biological characteristics (hereditary or acquired) or in terms of purely psychological characteristics (such as temperament or dominant underlying needs). The person with P_1 personality will conform to social norms and his behaviour will be law-abiding while person with P_2 personality will deviate from social norms and his behaviour will be law-violating. Similarly, suppose these two persons function in two different situations—S_1 and S_2. The person with P_1 personality functioning in situation S_1 will be law-abiding while the person with personality P_2 functioning in situation S_2 will be a law-violator. This means that personality (P_2) and situation (S_2) together cause crime. In other words P_1 functioning in S_2 or P_2 functioning in S_1 will not commit crimes. This is diagrammatically shown in Diagram 1.

Diagram 1

Personality Variations and Behaviour

Kinds of Personality	*Behaviour*	
	Law-abiding	*Law-violation*
P_1	√,	
P_2		√

Situational variations and behaviour

Kinds of Situation	*Behaviour*	
	Law-abiding	*Law-violation*
S_1	√,	
S_2		√

Personality and situational variations and behaviour

Kinds of personality	*Kinds of situation*	*Behaviour*	
		Law-abiding	*Law-violation*
P_1	S_1	√,	
P_2	S_2		√

Further, 'situation' (S) means "varied situations taken together" ($S_1 + S_2 + S_3$) in which the person acts. It is the presence of all situations ($S_1 + S_2 + S_3$) that will cause 'crime'. Let us understand it in detail. In situation S_1, the act of the person P is a, while in situation 'Not S_1', it is 'b'. Following situation S_1, in situation S_2, the act of P will be *aa* while in situation 'not S_2', his act will be *ab*. Following both situations S_1 and S_2, in situation S_3, the act of P will be *aaa*, i.e., 'crime', while in situation 'not S_3', his act will be *aab*. This means that three situations together (or $S_1 + S_2 + S_3$) will create crime. If either S_1 or S_2 or S_3 is absent, there will be no crime.

We may take an example to understand this theoretical approach. A woman with a certain personality structure P fails to get her husband's love and affection (let us call it situation S_1). Her in-laws also hate her (situation S_2). She then develops illicit relations with somebody (situation S_1). Being instigated by her paramour, she murders her husband. Thus, murder (crime) is caused only when three situations ($S_1 + S_2 + S_3$) combine. Had she got her husband's attention (not S_1) or had she been supported by her in-laws (not S_2), she might not have developed illicit relations (not S_3) and thus she might not have committed crime (husband's murder). This is what is called 'multiplicity of situations' leading to crime. This is shown in Figure 2.

Figure 2

Multiplicity of Situations

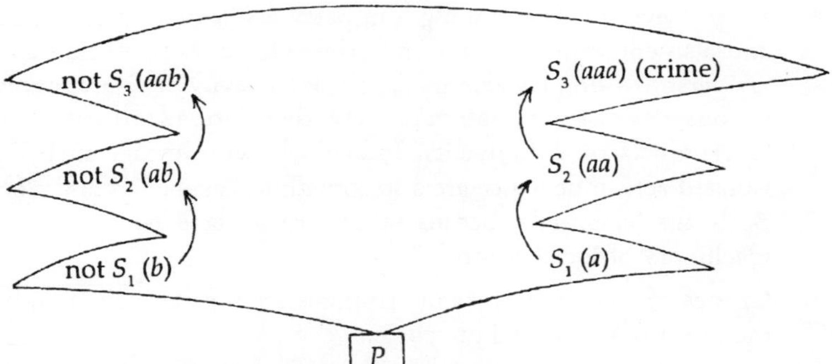

S_1+S_2+S_3 → lead to act '*aaa*' i.e., crime

It may be concluded that the varying combinations of these factors differ greatly from one case to another. The personal factors contribute to crime and delinquency by decreasing the adjustment potentialities of the individual, and the environmental factors by blocking the satisfaction of the personality needs of the individual and/or by instilling values that bring him in conflict with the values of the organised society. In short, crime is the outcome of interaction between actor and situation.

SOCIOLOGICAL CONTENTIONS ABOUT THE CAUSES OF CRIME

A sociologist has his own perception of looking at human behaviour. He does not ignore personality traits but lays stress on learning and acquired aspects of behaviour. Crime is also one aspect of individual behaviour. The analysis of criminal behaviour should therefore focus on the following facts (Gibbons, 1977: 244-46):

1. Learning of values, attitudes, and behaviour patterns depends upon the process of socialisation and interpersonal associations. It is therefore meaningful to approach individual's crime by paying attention to his collection of social roles picked up from the

structure of society.

2. The etiological process that leads to criminalistic role behaviour involves a number of causal variables, i.e., criminal behaviour is the product of multiple causation.
3. Situations which block the achievement of goals contribute much to crime and delinquency.
4. Almost every person indulges in petty law violation in his lifetime and also entertains deviant and criminalistic motives; but criminals are persons who play criminalistic roles 'heavily', i.e., are involved in serious acts of law-violation and are, therefore, identified by society as criminals or delinquents. Individuals who engage in petty and isolated acts of deviance are also sometimes labelled as law-violation. Both are 'criminals' because they are so labelled by the official machinery of social control.
5. Crimes of a large number of criminals are not premeditated but are the result of situational pressures.
6. Male and female criminals and juvenile and adult offenders require different approaches in their motivational mechanisms for committing crimes.
7. There are character variations among criminals. The variations are both in their social characteristics as well as in deviant behaviour. Also, there are some persons who consider themselves as criminals but there are many who have no self-image as a criminal.
8. Criminals play not only anti-social role but also many social roles as husband, father, employee, and so on.
9. Variations in societal reactions to criminality of different kinds as well as punitive handling determine continuation in criminality.
10. More the laws in society, more the police becomes ineffective. Thus, excessiveness of laws and ineffectiveness of police increase criminality.

References

Carr, Lowell, *Delinquency Control* (rev. edn.), Harper and Brothers, New York, 1950.

Cohen, Albert K., *Deviance and Control*, Prentice Hall Inc., New Jersey, 1966.

Journal of Criminal Law and Criminology, March-April, 1951.

Reckless, Walter, *The Crime Problem* (2nd edn.), Appleton-Century Crofts, New York, 1955.

Sheldon and Glueck, *Unravelling Juvenile Delinquency*, The Commonwealth Fund, New York, 1950.

Sutherland E.H., and Cressay, D.R., *The Principles of Criminology* (6th edn.), The Times of India Press, Bombay, 1965.

Chapter 4

Juvenile Delinquency

Different approaches have been used to define and explain the term 'juvenile delinquency', like the legal approach, the social work approach, the psychological approach, and the sociological approach. The *legal approach*, which is based on normative formalism, tends to explain delinquency in *specific* terms in order to protect the public from dangerous conduct and to protect the delinquent from unjust acts by the police and the courts. The *social work approach* is informal and therapeutic. The *psychological approach* is analytical. These two approaches (i.e., social work and psychological) are primarily concerned with the welfare of the individual delinquent and attribute only secondary importance to the security of the social group in which he committed his delinquency. The *sociological approach* views the delinquent as a member of his social group, and the delinquency as a deviation from group norms and as a disruptive force in the smooth functioning of organised social life (*see*, Knudten and Schafer, *Juvenile Delinquency*, 1970: 29).

In the legal approach to misconduct of a juvenile, the stress is on the following requirements: (1) that a specific charge be levelled against the defendant, (2) that it be defined in definite terms by law, (3) that the offence be proved rather conclusively, (4) that protection be given to the accused during trial against conviction by false, misleading, irrelevant or immaterial evidence.

In the sociological approach, the focus is on two aspects: *age* and *conduct* or *status*. Age is important from the point of view of maturity—chronological, mental and social. A child below a certain age is considered to be irresponsible by reason of immaturity. The 'conduct' concept of delinquency has evolved from an appreciation of the danger that the young offender may easily become an adult criminal if no deterrent or rehabilitative influences play upon him. Hence, the effort to curb anti-social traits in their incipience.

In terms of age, a juvenile delinquent is considered an underaged criminal, i.e., one who is between the age of 7 and 16 or 18 years, as prescribed by the law of the land. The maximum age today for juvenile delinquents according to the Juvenile Justice Act of 1986 is 16 years for boys and 18 years for girls, but earlier, according to the Children Acts, it was different in different states. In states like Uttar Pradesh, Gujarat, Kerala, Maharashtra, Punjab, and Madhya Pradesh, it was 16 years but in states like Bengal and Bihar, it was 18 years. In states like Rajasthan, Assam, and Karnataka, it was 16 years for boys and 18 years for girls. Apart from age, the nature of offence is vitally important.

Children who are involved in 'status offences' such as truancy, vagrancy, immorality, and ungovernability also fall within the definition of juvenile delinquents. Neumayer, Ivan Nye and James Short Jr, Richard Jenkins, and Walter Reckless have also emphasised 'type of behaviour' in the concept of juvenile delinquency. According to Walter Reckless (1956), the term 'juvenile delinquency' applies to the "violation of criminal code and/or pursuit of certain patterns of behaviour disapproved of for children and young adolescents". Thus, *age* and *behavioural infractions* prohibited in the statutes are important in the concept of juvenile delinquency.

The 'behaviour content' in juvenile delinquency is important in the sense that there is a difference in the approach/attitude of judiciary and that of administrators. The judicial approach requires the proof of fairly definite offences. The administrative view, to the contrary, is that since delinquents are not criminal in character, and the courts are designed to aid children who are unadjusted, the courts should not seek to define and segregate delinquency but to discover and treat the maladjustments of children who appear before them. This raises the central issue of who should be brought before the court and who should the court adjudicate as delinquent? Is the child who has run away from home once or several times, a delinquent? Is the child who reacts rebelliously to the hostility of his step-mother at his home, a delinquent? Is the boy who stays out with his friends till late hours in the evening and causes much anxiety to his family, a delinquent? Is the boy who wants more freedom and behaves in a very independent fashion, a delinquent? How then, may one distinguish the problem child, the adventurous child, and the delinquent? To solve this problem, five categories of deviation have been set up to consider the level at which the court may take control (*see*, Knudten and Schafter, *op. cit.*, 43):

1. *Deviant situational factors*, where the child is exposed to deleterious home and community influences, e.g., broken home, economic insecurity, vice in the home, unhealthy recreation, slum neighbourhood, places of moral risk like cheap hotels, etc.
2. *Behavioural problems of personal unadjustment* to the environment; e.g., temper tantrums, nail-biting, etc.
3. *Antisocial attitudes* wherein the child reveals reactions antagonistic to authority but without serious overt aggressiveness; e.g., hostility, guilt-feelings, isolation, anxieties.
4. "*Waywardness*" or "*Incorrigibility*" or the violation of relatively non-serious community conduct standards; e.g., truancy, running away from home, disobedience, fighting, etc.
5. *Serious illegalities* or the violation of criminal conduct norms; e.g., theft, burglary, rape, assault, robbery, homicide.

Some scholars are of the opinion that certain types of attitudes and deviant conduct, as in the above-mentioned categories 1, 2, and 3, may better be dealt with by non-judicial social agencies—public or private—and by non-court personnel. This, however, raises an important question. If there are no appropriate agencies in the society, such as case-work organisations, psychiatric resources, etc., should the court then take over the cases of maladjustment of juveniles? In a society like India, this is indeed a crucial problem. What is needed is differentiating between 'slight' deviation and 'extreme' deviation to work out a systematic philosophy and programme for treatment.

The difference between a delinquent child and an adult criminal is important from the case-work approach. The difference between the two is made in the conduct involved, in the methods employed by the court, in the philosophy and methods applied in treatment, and in the individual's status, reputation and civil rights in the community after adjudication.

NATURE AND INCIDENCE

Of the total delinquencies committed by the juveniles, hardly 2 per cent come to the notice of the police and the courts. The statistics compiled by the National Crime Records Bureau give some indication of the incidence of juvenile delinquency in India. Up to 1987, every year about 50 thousand delinquencies were committed under the Indian Penal Code and about 85 thousand under the local and special laws. But the new definition of a juvenile, after the enforcement of the Juvenile Justice Act in October, 1987 (passed in 1986) excludes males in the age group of 16 to 21 years and females in the age group of 18 to 21 years. Crime cases attributed to juveniles naturally have been reduced now. This is why juvenile delinquency in and after 1988, compared to 1987 and earlier years has decreased both under the IPC and the Local and Special Laws. In 1988, about 25 thousand (to be exact 24,827) delinquencies under the IPC and about 25 thousand (to be exact 25,468) delinquencies under the Local and Special Laws were committed. In 1998, about 15.3 thousand juveniles were apprehended (9,339 or 61% under IPC and 6,005 or 39% under the Local and Special Laws) for different crimes (*Crime in India*, 1998: 238-241). The percentage of juvenile crime to total cognisable crime in India in 1998 was about 0.5 per cent (in 1988, it was 1.7%). Before 1988, this percentage (of juvenile delinquency to total cognisable crime in India) was about 4 per cent.

The highest number of delinquencies committed by juveniles under the IPC are money motivated, that is, theft, burglary, robbery and dacoity. In 1998 (*ibid.*: 240) these four crimes accounted for 40 per cent of the total cognisable (under IPC) crimes committed by juveniles (theft---25.5%, burglary—13.3%, robbery—0.8%, and dacoity—0.4%). This is about 10 per cent more as compared to the percentage of the same crime committed by adult criminals. After economic crimes, 8.5 per cent juveniles were apprehended for riots, 3.1 per cent for murder, 1.8 per cent for rape, and 1.4 per cent for kidnapping and abduction.

The largest contribution, under the SLL (Special and Local Laws), was from offences under the Prohibition Act (27.9%), the Gambling Act (4.6%) and Immoral Traffic Prevention Act (3.8%) (up to 1987, it was 27%, 21%, and 9% respectively) (*ibid.*, 241). The incidence of juvenile delinquency varies widely in different states. Four states—Maharashtra (24.1%), Madhya Pradesh (25.2%), Rajasthan (7.3%), and Gujarat (11.1%) ---account for about 68 per cent of the total juvenile delinquencies in the country under IPC. For crimes under the Local and Special Laws, two states---Maharashtra (18.4%) and Tamil Nadu (56.6%)---account for about 75 per cent of the total offences (*ibid.*, 1998: 233-34).

Out of 18,964 juveniles apprehended and sent to courts in 1998 for delinquencies under the IPC and SLL, 13.8 per cent were sent to their homes after advice/admonition, 24.9 per cent were released on probation,

9.2 per cent were sent to special homes, 4.8 per cent were fined, and 11.1 per cent were acquitted. About 36.2 per cent cases remained pending (1998: 255).

CHARACTERISTICS

A number of studies have been conducted on juvenile delinquency between 1947 and 1999, quite a few among them being for Ph.D. degrees. Of the published works, eight studies by Ruthonsha (1947), R.K. Singh (1948), Hansa Sheth (1960), B.K. Bhattacharya (1962), A.D. Attar (1964), Sushil Chandra (1967), S.C. Verma (1969), and Harjeet S. Sandhu (1977) and three studies by the Government of India (1952, 1954 and 1970) are considered to be more significant. On the basis of these studies and on the basis of data compiled by National Crime Records Bureau, 1998, following characteristics of juvenile delinquency in India may be given:

1. The delinquency rates are many times higher for boys than girls, that is, girls commit fewer delinquencies than boys. The percentage involvement of girls in juvenile delinquency up to 1987 was about 6-7 per cent. This suddenly increased to 13.4 per cent in 1988 due to a change in the definition of juveniles, by which girls in the age group of 7-18 years only were considered as juveniles. If we take the figures pertaining to the earlier years and work out the percentage of girls within the newly defined range of age, it comes to 13.1 per cent which compares well with 13.4 per cent in 1988. Thus, the present figures (in 1998) suggest an overall arrest ratio of 2.8 boys for each girl. Of the 18,964 juveniles apprehended under the IPC and the SLL crimes in 1998, 26.1 per cent were girls (*ibid.*, 1998: 246).
2. The delinquency rates tend to be highest during early adolescence (12-16 years age group). After the new definition of the age of juvenile delinquency in 1988, if we calculate the average of ten years from 1988 to 1998, about three-fifth delinquents (61.0%) fall in this age group of 12-16 years. Earlier (between 1978 and 1987), it was observed that a large number of delinquents (71%) belonged to 18-21 years (late adolescence) age group, 15 per cent belonged to 16-18 years age group, 9 per cent to 12-16 years age group, and 5 per cent to 7-12 years age group. Now, the percentage share of two age groups has changed. About 17.5 per cent belong to 7-12 years age group and 21.4 per cent to 16-18 years age group (1998: 247). The share of 12-16 years age group has increased from 10 per cent in 1978-87 to 61 per cent in 1998 because from 1988, 18-21 years age group has entirely gone out of the ambit of juvenile consideration.

3. Juvenile delinquency is more an urban than a rural phenomenon. The metropolitan cities like Delhi, Mumbai, Chennai, Calcutta, Ahmedabad, Hyderabad and Bangalore produce more juvenile delinquents than small cities and towns. If we take 23 metropolitan cities in India, of the 1,981 delinquents apprehended under the IPC in 1998 in these 23 cities, about three-fifths (62.3%) committed crimes in six cities (Bombay: 9.1%, Delhi: 17.5%, Indore: 8.8%, Jaipur: 13.7%, Nagpur: 5.9%, and Pune: 7.3%) (*Crime in India*, 1998: 253).
4. Children living with parents and guardians are found to be more involved in the juvenile crimes. At the time of arrest, about three-fourths (73%) of the delinquents were found living with their parents, about one-fourth (22%) with their guardians, and about one-twentieth (5%) were homeless (1998: 256). This shows the role of family environment in juvenile delinquency.
5. Low education background is the prime attribute of delinquency. About two-fifths (38.1%) of the juveniles are illiterate, two-fifths (39.3%) are primary passed, one-fifth (18.5%) are middle and secondary passed, and a very small number (4.1%) is educated up to the high school level and above (1998: 256). Thus, most delinquents come from illiterate and less educated families.
6. Poor economic background is another important characteristic of juvenile delinquency in India. About half (52%) of the delinquents come from homes with an income of less than Rs. 500 per month (i.e., destitute and very poor classes), about one-fourth (27%) from homes with income between Rs. 501 and Rs. 1,000 per month (i.e., poor classes), about one-tenth (14%) from homes with income between Rs. 1,001 and Rs. 2,000 per month (i.e., lower-middle class), and a very small number (5%) from homes with income between Rs. 2,001 and Rs. 3,000 per month (i.e., lower-middle class) or with income above Rs. 3,000 per month (2%) (i.e., middle-middle class) (1998:257). This shows that juvenile delinquency is more a lower-class phenomenon. Almost all studies conducted in our country on juvenile delinquency and its relation to the socioeconomic order show that those belonging to the bottom strata have been found to have the highest rates. The extent to which this is true varies under different conditions; but one general point that has been made in almost all studies (Ruttonsha, Hansa Seth, Sushil Chandra, Verma, etc.) is that the impact of socio-economic status is revealed most strongly the deeper one goes into the delinquency adjudication process.
7. Nine out of 10 juvenile delinquents are first-offenders and only one-tenth are recidivists or past-offenders. The 1998 figures show that

89 per cent were new offenders (*ibid.*: 257). The number of total juveniles apprehended between 1988 and 1998 has gradually declined every year. From about 38,000 (IPC+SLL) in 1988, the number declined to about 30,000 (29,591) in 1991 and about 19,000 (18,964) in 1998 (*ibid.*: 246).

8. Not many delinquencies are committed in groups. In the United States, Shaw and McKay in their study found that 90 per cent children had companions in their delinquencies. In India, it appears, a large number of delinquencies are committed all alone.
9. Though some delinquencies are committed in groups yet the number of juvenile gangs having support of organised adult criminals is not large in our country.

TYPES OF JUVENILE DELINQUENCY

Delinquency exhibits a variety of styles of conduct or forms of behaviour. Each of the patterns has its own social context, the causes that are alleged to bring it about, and the forms of prevention or treatment most often suggested as appropriate for the pattern in question. Howard Becker (1966: 226-38) has referred to four types of delinquencies: (a) individual delinquency, (b) group-supported delinquency, (c) organised delinquency, and (d) situational delinquency.

(a) *Individual delinquency*: This refers to delinquency in which only one individual is involved in committing a delinquent act and its cause is located within the individual delinquent. Most of the explanations of this delinquent behaviour come from psychiatrists. Their argument is that delinquency is caused by psychological problems stemming primarily from defective/faulty/pathological family interaction patterns. Researches of Healy and Bronner, Albert Bandura and Richard Walters, Edwin Powers and Helen Witmer, and Henry Meyer and Edgar Borgatta are based on this approach. Healy and Bronner (1936) compared delinquent youths with their non-delinquent siblings and analysed the difference between them. Their most important finding was that over 90 per cent of the delinquents compared to 13 per cent of their non-delinquent siblings had unhappy home lives and felt discontented with their life circumstances. The nature of unhappiness differed: some felt rejected by parents and others felt either inferior or jealous of siblings or suffered from mental conflict. They indulged in delinquency as a solution to these problems, as it (delinquency) either brought attention from parents or provided support from peers or reduced their guilt feelings. Later studies also identified important aspects of family relations leading to delinquencies. Bandura and Walters compared the aggressive actions of white delinquents with those of non-delinquent boys with no clear sign of economic hardship. They found that delinquents differed from non-delinquents a little in their relationship with their mothers but more in their relationship with their fathers. Thus, father-son rather than mother-son relations seemed more crucial in delinquency, as delinquent boys could not internalise moral values because of the absence of good role models in their fathers. In addition, their discipline was also more harsh and stern.

(b) *Group-supported delinquency*: In this type, delinquencies are committed in companionship with others and the cause is located not in the personality of the individual or in the delinquent's family but in the culture of the individual's home and neighbourhood. The studies of Thrasher and Shaw and McKay talk of this type of delinquency. The main finding in understanding why the young became delinquent was their association and companionship with others already delinquent. This was later put very clearly by Sutherland, who developed the theory of differential association. Unlike the psychogenic explanations, this set of ideas focuses on what is learnt and who it is learnt from rather than on the problems that might produce motivation to commit delinquencies.

(c) *Organised delinquency*: This type refers to delinquencies that are committed by formally organised groups. These delinquencies were analysed in the United States in the 1950s and the concept of 'delinquent subculture' was developed. This concept refers to the set of values and norms that guide the behaviour of group members, encourage the commission of delinquencies, award status on the basis of such acts and specify typical relationships to persons who fall outside the groupings governed by group norms. Cohen was the first person to refer to this type of delinquency. He was followed by Cloward and Ohlin and a few others.

(d) *Situational delinquency*: The above-mentioned three types of delinquencies have one thing in common. In all of them, delinquency is viewed as having deep roots. In individual delinquency (according to the psychogenic explanation), the roots of delinquency lie primarily within the individual; in group-supported and organised delinquencies (the sociogenic explanation), the roots (of delinquency) lie in the structure of the society with emphasis either on the ecological areas where delinquency prevails or on the systematic way in which social structure places some individuals in a poor position to compete for success. Situational delinquency provides a different perspective. Here the assumption is that delinquency is not deeply rooted, and motives for delinquency and means for controlling it are often relatively simple. A young man indulges in a delinquent act without having a deep commitment to delinquency because of less developed impulse-control and/or because of weaker reinforcement of family restraints, and because he has relatively little to lose even if caught. David Matza is one scholar who refers to this type of delinquency. However, the concept of situational delinquency is undeveloped and is not given much relevance in the problem of delinquency causation. It is a supplement to rather than a replacement of other types.

CLASSIFICATION OF JUVENILE DELINQUENTS

Juvenile delinquents have been classified by different scholars on different bases. For example, Hirsh (1937) has classified them in six groups on the basis of the kinds of offences committed: (1) *incorrigibility* (for example, keeping late hours, disobedience, etc.), (2) *truancy* (staying away from school), (3) *larceny* (ranging from petty theft to armed robbery), (4) *destruction of property* (including both public and private property), (5) *violence* (against community by using weapons), and (6) *sex offences* (ranging from homosexuality to rape).

Eaton and Polk (1969) have also classified delinquents into five groups according to the type of offence. The offences are: (1) minor violations (including disorderly conduct and minor traffic violations), (2) major violations (including automobile thefts), (3) property violations, (4) addiction (including alcoholism and drug addiction), and (5) bodily harm (including homicide).

Robert Trojanowicz (1973: 59) has classified delinquents as accidental, unsocialised, aggressive, occasional, professional and gang-organised.

Psychologists have classified juvenile delinquents on the basis of their individual traits or the psychological dynamics of their personality into four groups: mentally defective, psychotic, neurotic and situational.

FACTORS IN JUVENILE DELINQUENCY

Researchers generally agree that a number of factors play an important part in a youngster's delinquencies. We may divide these factors into two groups: individual factors and situational factors. The former include personality traits like submissiveness, defiance, hostility, impulsiveness, feeling of insecurity, fear, lack of self-control, emotional conflict, etc., while the latter may be subdivided into five groups: family, companions, school environment, movies, and work environment. We will mainly discuss here the family's contribution to delinquency.

Family

Many theorists consider family as the most significant factor in the development of juvenile delinquency. Class status, peer group relations, class mobility, etc., are also directly or indirectly related to the family environment. Psychological theorists like Irving Kaufman (1959: 15), Sidney Burman (1964: 142), August Aichhorn (1969: 16), etc., relate the causation of delinquency to early childhood experiences, emotional deprivations, child-rearing processes, etc., which influence the formation of the personality and the development of attitudes, values, and life-style. The abnormal expression of behaviour expressed in an anti-social form, is the result of these factors according to psychologists. Whereas the psychologist is concerned with the identification of individual variables, such as motivation, drives, values, and needs, the sociologist is concerned more with the social environment, the factors in the social system, and the functioning of the institutions that affect delinquency. Thus, the psychologists focus on internal control and the sociologists focus on external control.

Family environment producing delinquent behaviour may be analysed with reference to a broken home, family tension, parental rejection, parental control, and family economics. A *normal* family, according to Carr, is described as one which is structurally complete (with both parents alive), functionally adequate (each member performing his expected role which reduces conflicts), economically secure (gratifying important needs of the members) and morally strong (each member conforming to the moral values of the family/social culture). The family is *abnormal* if it lacks any of these characteristics.

The *broken family* (where one parent is absent because of parental separation, divorce or death) fails to provide affection and control to the children. Sheldon and Glueck (1968: 12) found in their study of delinquents and non-delinquents that more than half of the delinquents studied were reared by one parent, whereas only 10 per cent of the non-delinquents were reared by one parent. Monahan (1957: 250-58), Browning (1960: 37-44), Gold Martin, Slocum and Stone (1965), and Peterson and Becker (1965) also found that a significantly greater number of delinquents than non-delinquents were from broken homes.

Factors in Juvenile Delinquency

- **Individual factors**
  - Submissiveness
  - Defiance
  - Hostility
  - Impulsiveness
  - Feeling of insecurity
  - Fear
  - Emotional conflicts
  - Lack of self-control
- **Situational factors**
  - Family
    - Parents' discipline
    - Parents' affection
    - Cohesiveness of family
    - Conduct standards of home
    - Substitute parents
    - Father's work habits
    - Economic condition of family interest
    - Conjugal relations of parents
    - Broken homes
    - Affection of siblings
    - Household duties
    - Cultural refinement of home
  - Peer group relations
  - School environment
    - Adjustment to school mates
    - Attitudes towards school
    - Failure in classes or lack of academic interest
  - Movies
  - Work environment

Family tension is also a major contributing factor to delinquent behaviour. Abrahamsen (1960: 43) found that family tension results from hostility, hatred, etc. The youngster does not feel secure and content in the tension-filled family environment. Long-term tension reduces family cohesiveness and affects the parents' ability to provide a conducive atmosphere to satisfactory childrearing and family problem-solving. McCords and Zola (1959) also found that cohesive homes produce fewer delinquents whereas homes where tension and hostility exist are good breeding grounds for future delinquents. Gluecks (1968: 8) found that one in three delinquent families, as compared with one in seven non-delinquent families, was disrupted when one of the parents left the family because of a tension-filled and quarrelsome relationship.

Parental rejection or emotional deprivation has much to do with juvenile delinquency. If a rejected or neglected child does not find love and affection as well as support and supervision at home, he will often join groups of a deviant nature outside the family. Studies have found that mutual rejection of parent and child markedly affects positive relationship and can ultimately result in delinquent behaviour. Jenkins (1957: 528-37) found that parental rejection had a direct effect on the child's development and growth of conscience. He averred that lack of adequate conscience, combined with feelings of hostility for being rejected, led to aggression. Andry (1960: 64) also has maintained that delinquents were recipients of less parental love both in quantity and in quality than were non-delinquents.

Just as a broken home, family tension, and parental rejection can affect the capability of the family structure, methods of *parental control* or forms of discipline also can play a part in the development of delinquent behaviour. The type of discipline enforced by parents in rearing children varies from situation to situation and from child to child. An authoritarian approach to discipline affects the child in his peer group relationships as the child will not be able to interact freely with his peers. Conversely, rather lenient discipline will not provide the child with the necessary controls to guide his behaviour. Unfair or partial discipline fails to form an adequate conscience in the child, prevents the adults from serving as a model to be imitated by the child, and reduces the adolescent's wish to avoid hurting parents and delinquent behaviour. Gluecks (1968: 15-16) found that parents of delinquents used physical punishment more than verbal discussion. Both parents were less consistent in their disciplinary measures than were the parents of non-delinquents. If the methods of disciplining are classified as love-oriented discipline, punitive discipline, lax discipline, and erratic discipline (punitive and lax), the last three types can be related to delinquency.

Emotional instability and behavioural disturbances in one or both of parents also lead to a child's delinquent behaviour. A child of the parents who are constantly in conflict often exploits the situation and gets away with a great deal of misbehaviour.

Lastly, *family economics* is also an important contributing variable in delinquency. A family's inability to provide for the material needs of the child can create insecurity and affect the amount of control that the family exerts over the child, because he often seeks material support and security outside the home. Peterson and Becker (1965) have pointed out that the homes of delinquents are often physically deteriorated which can affect a delinquent's perception of himself and can act as a repellent, driving him away from the home. It should, however, be pointed out that economic status and material possessions do not explain middle and upper class delinquency. The economic condition of the family can be one of many contributing factors in a multi-problem family.

Neighbourhood

The impact of neighbourhood on the child is greater in urban areas than in rural areas. After the family, the child spends a good part of the day in the company of children in his neighbourhood. The neighbourhood can contribute to delinquency by blocking basic personality needs, engendering culture conflicts, and fostering anti-social values. On the other hand, it can supplement the influence of the home in the maintenance of social values. Congested neighbourhoods with inadequate recreation facilities deny the natural play impulses of children and encourage the formation of delinquent gangs. Picture houses, cheap hotels, video-halls, etc. in neighbourhood become breeding places of vice and delinquency.

Cinema and Pornographic Literature

Movies and story books featuring immorality, smoking, drinking and brutality leave a strong impression on the young minds of children and adolescents. Many a time, they teach techniques of crime and delinquency. Several children are arrested in different parts of our country for using cinema techniques to commit thefts, burglaries and kidnapping, etc. They claimed to have seen such procedures in the movies. These movies also develop attitudes conducive to delinquent behaviour by arousing desires for easy money, suggesting questionable methods for their achievement, inducing a spirit of toughness and adventurousness, arousing sexual desires, and by invoking day-dreaming.

SOCIOLOGY OF JUVENILE DELINQUENCY

The major sociological theorists who have contributed to the criminological knowledge of delinquency are Merton, Frederick Thrasher, Clifford Shaw and Henry McKay, George Herbert Mead, Albert Cohen, Cloward and Ohlin, Walter Miller, and David Matza. Since we have described their theories in detail in the preceding chapter, we may only briefly summarise them here for ready reference.

Merton's Anomie Theory (1938: 672-82) is that when there is a discrepancy between the institutionalised means that are available within the environment and the goals that individuals have learnt to aspire for in their environment, strain or frustration is produced and norms break down and deviant behaviour may result. Merton, thus, does not discuss individual motivational factors in deviance, (that is, in selecting one of the five alternative modes of behaviour suggested by him) or he fails to explain why all persons in similar situations do not choose deviance.

Frederick Thrasher's Gang Theory (1936: 381) concentrates on group delinquency and explains positive peer influence as Cohen's, Cloward's, and Miller's theories did later on. Thrasher does not say that the gang is a cause of delinquency but he says that gang facilitates delinquency. Explaining the process whereby a group takes on certain behavioural characteristics and then transmits them to its members, he says that a gang originates during the adolescent years from spontaneous play groups and conflict with other groups, transforms it into a gang for protecting its members' rights and satisfying the needs which their environment and their family could not provide. Gradually, the gang develops distinct characteristics such as a mode of operation, and disseminates criminal techniques, excites mutual interests and attitudes and provides protection to its members. Thrasher emphasised the point that not all gang activities were necessarily devious and that much of the gang members' time was spent in normal athletic activities as well as in other teenage endeavours. His thesis, thus, mainly describes how environmental pressure is conducive to delinquent behaviour.

Shaw and McKay's Cultural Transmission Theory (1931: 386) holds that delinquency is transmitted through personal and group contacts and that lack of effective social control agencies contributes to the high incidence of delinquency in some parts of the large cities. The 'delinquency areas' are the low income and physically deteriorated areas whose members suffer from economic deprivations. Furthermore, the boys in these areas are not necessarily disorganised, maladjusted or anti-social. It is the exposure to delinquency traditions present in these areas which makes them delinquents. But for this exposure, they would have found their satisfaction in activities other than delinquency. Shaw and McKay acknowledge that other factors may cause certain youngsters to become involved in delinquent activities, but they feel that these factors are secondary to the economic and social factors that exist in the community. It is this learnt phenomenon of delinquency which is developed in Sutherland's theory also.

George Herbert Mead's Role Theory and Theory of the Self (1918: 577-602) explains why only a limited number of persons assume criminal identities while majority of the people remain law-abiding. He says, becoming a delinquent and assuming a criminal identity involves more than merely associating with law violators. Such association has to be meaningful to the individual and supportive of the role and self-concept that he wants to be committed to.

Albert Cohen's Working-Class Boy and Middle-Class Measuring Rod Theory (1955: 119) maintains that delinquency is mainly a working-class phenomenon. He states that the working-class boy finds himself at the bottom of status hierarchy whenever he moves into the middle-class world. To the degree to which he values middle-class status either because he values the good opinion of middle-class persons or because he has, to some degree, internalised middle-class standards himself, he faces the problem of adjustment. A delinquent subculture deals with the problems of adjustment (that is, of status problems) by providing a criteria of status which these children can meet. Not having learnt the behaviour that will equip them to deal with competitive struggle for their success, the working class boys feel frustrated, react against middle-class values and standards, and adopt their very antithesis, that is, non-utilitarian, malicious, and negativistic values. Group or gang delinquent activity legitimises and supports aggression against middle-class institutions.

Cloward and Ohlin's Success Goals and Opportunity Structures Theory (1960: 86) copes with the discrepancies of Sutherland's, Merton's and Mead's theories and explains the types of alternatives available as a result of strain and lack of legitimate alternatives to satisfy needs. Faced with limitations or legitimate avenues of access to their goals and unable to revise their aspirations downward, the lower-class youths experience intense frustrations which fact results in their exploring non-conformist, and illegitimate alternatives. Cloward and Ohlin's theory is difficult to test and evaluate empirically.

Walter Miller's Lower-Class Boy and Lower-Class Structure Theory (1958: 6) rejects 'delinquent subculture' and talks of 'lower-class culture' itself which comes about as a result of the processes of immigration, migration and mobility. Those persons who are left behind as a result of these processes comprise the lower-class. They develop a distinct pattern of behaviour (which is not necessarily reactive against any other class) based on distinctive (lower-class) traits like toughness, smartness, excitement, fate, autonomy. The street group provides the lower-class adolescent boy an opportunity to act tough and become involved in masculine activities. Many of his activities, thus, revolve round his desire to become a 'real man'. The major criticism of Miller's theory is that today with mass communication, it is difficult to believe that the distinct lower-class culture, which Miller describes, can exist in such a pure form. Lower-class is bound to be influenced by the other classes.

David Matza's Delinquency and Drift Theory (1964: 11) rejects the deterministic orientation of the positive school that delinquent behaviour is caused almost entirely by emotional and environmental factors. Matza feels that man is neither totally free (as the classical school assumes) nor is he totally constrained (as the positive school assumes), but he is somewhere between being controlled and being free. Drift stands midway between freedom and control. A youngster, therefore, drifts between criminal and conventional action. Even though most of a youngster's activities are law-abiding, he can periodically drift into delinquency because the normal conventional controls that usually inhibit delinquent behaviour become neutralised as a result of the drifting process. Once he indulges in delinquency, he drifts back to conventionality. Matza, thus, emphasises the 'will to crime'. It is this 'will' which explains why some youngsters choose delinquent behaviour while most of their peers within the same environment choose socially acceptable modes of adaptation. He also explains why delinquency is not an 'either-or' proposition. Most youngsters exist somewhere along the continuum between convention and crime. Total commitment to delinquency is uncommon.

If we now take all the sociological theories of juvenile delinquency together, it may be said that all sociologists have placed emphasis on environment, social structures, and on the learning process unlike the psychologists who consider the individual and his motivational patterns important in delinquency.

METHODS OF TREATING DELINQUENTS

Many approaches and methods can be used in treating a delinquent. Some important methods are: (1) psychotherapy, (2) reality therapy, (3) behaviour therapy, (4) activity therapy, and (5) milieu therapy. Punishment is not discussed as a treatment method because it is no longer viewed as a viable technique of treatment, though some do feel that pain serves as a deterrent to further criminal action. Restrictions and reprimands can be effective supplements to the major treatment approach utilised but punishment cannot become an end in itself.

The two basic approaches in dealing with youngsters are the *individual* and the *group* methods of treatment. Of these, it is generally the individual method which is used by psychologists, psychiatrists, sociologists and social workers, though psychologists sometimes do use group method as well. Sociologists usually take a 'social engineering' approach to delinquency, that is, they deal with the conditions of the social structure that breed delinquency, while psychologists treat the individual and emphasise his interpersonal dynamics. Sociology is regarded as a theoretical discipline researching the causes and effects of crime and delinquency. The profession of social work is the 'practical arm' of the sociologists (Trojanowicz, 1973: 229). As such, the above-mentioned five therapeutic methods are generally utilised by psychologists, psychiatrists and social workers. We will briefly discuss each method separately.

Psychotherapy treats emotional and personality problems by psychological means, that is, by changing the attitudes and feelings about significant persons (say, parents, etc.) in the client's (delinquent's) past. When the early relationship of a youngster with his parents was not satisfactory, his emotional development was often retarded, with the result that he was often impulsive in his attempt to satisfy his infantile urges, not satisfied with the normal manner within his family. Satisfying these urges and impulses can take the form of anti-social behaviour. Through psychotherapy, the delinquent is allowed by the therapist to operate in an atmosphere of love and acceptance where the person does not have to fear severe rejection or physical punishment. This is due to the transference established in which the client and the therapist feel comfortable in exchanging communication. Thus, this therapy involves facilitating the solving of conflicts and providing positive alternatives to behaviour adaptation by the client.

Reality therapy is based on the view that people, unable to fulfil their basic needs, act in an irresponsible manner. The object of the reality therapy is to help the delinquent person act in a responsible manner, that is, refrain from antisocial activity. For example, if a boy does not attend school classes owing to the harshness of the teacher, he is made to understand that the teacher is not harsh but is interested in helping him shape his career. Here, the present is delinked with the past as the past cannot be changed. This therapy can be given by any one (police officer, counsellor, teacher, social worker, family member, or a friend), because it does not emphasise nebulous psychiatric terms, extensive testing, or time-consuming case conferences. This method differs from the psychotherapeutic method in the sense that the latter is concerned with the past behaviour, while this is concerned with the present behaviour. Whereas the basis of psychotherapy is that a person cannot change his present behaviour unless he clearly ties it to the events in the past, the basis of the Reality Therapy is that the past is insignificant. In this therapy, since a child is treated as a responsible person and not as an unfortunate youngster, the treatment transmits strength to the youngster. The child is expected to obey rules but he is not rejected when he breaks one.

Behaviour therapy modifies the learned behaviour of the delinquent through the development of new learning processes. Behaviour can be changed through positive or negative reinforcements, that is, rewards or punishments. Negative or unpleasant reinforcements (like restrictions) will reduce/eliminate negative behaviour (that is, delinquent activity), while positive or pleasant reinforcements (like rewards), will maintain/increase positive behaviour (like success on the job and in school). This requires determining each individual's 'reinforcers', that is, those aspects which the individual (delinquent) will strive to achieve to gain personal satisfaction. Money, praise, attention, food, privileges, admission in school, freedom to play with children, good clothes, etc. can be considered as positive reinforcers, while threats, confinements, ridicule, physical punishment, depriving of money, etc., are negative reinforcers. For modifying behaviour, both the reinforcers can be employed.

Activity therapy: Many children do not have the verbal ability to communicate effectively in a conventional individual or group situation. In activity therapy method, a group of six to eight children are gathered/invited to meet at a specific time/place to engage in play or some artistic endeavour. The atmosphere is permissive and the youngsters can use their time as they wish. Thus, a moderately neurotic child finds great release in a permissive environment where he can express his hostility and aggression in creative work, play, or mischief. Because his behaviour does not call for retaliation, punishment or disapproval, pent-up emotions find appropriate discharge.

Milieu or environment therapy attempts to produce an environment that will facilitate meaningful change and satisfactory adjustment. This is used for persons whose deviant behaviour is a reaction to unfavourable life conditions.

Besides using the above methods, three more methods are also used in the treatment of juvenile delinquents. These are: (1) *Social case-work*, that is, assisting the maladjusted youngster in coping with his problems. Although similar to psychotherapy in many respects, technically social case-work is different from psychotherapy. Whereas a social case-worker, could be a probation officer, prison counsellor, mental health worker, or hospital social worker, a psychotherapist is essentially a doctor by profession. The caseworker prepares the case history of the client to explore his background, environment and relationships with his family, friends, school-fellows, etc. and evaluates his personal strengths and weaknesses so that a treatment plan can be devised and carried out. This method, however, is often not successful with delinquents because on the one hand, it is difficult to obtain the delinquent's cooperation as he has no trust in the case-worker and on the other hand, the delinquent's family also resists and feels threatened by the case-worker's 'probing'. (2) *Individual counselling*, that is, re-educating a delinquent to enable him to understand his immediate situation and solve his problem. In this method, no attempt is made to effect a fundamental change in the client's personality. (3) *Vocational counselling*, that is, increasing the delinquent's knowledge of his career choices, job specifications and qualifications and training needed for successful employment. The positive attitudes, skills and habits that the youngster develops and refines in the work situation can be carried over to the community and can positively affect his relationships with others.

CUSTODY IN JUVENILE INSTITUTIONS

Remand Homes (now renamed Observation Homes), Certified Schools, Reformatory Schools, Borstal Schools and Probation Hostels are some of the important institutions used for custody and correction of juvenile delinquents in India.

Children Acts were enacted back in different states for the treatment and protection of young offenders, and for custody, trial and punishment of juvenile delinquents. Madras (present Tamil Nadu) enacted such an act in 1920, Bengal in 1922, and Bombay (Maharashtra) in 1924. After that, all states passed these acts. Besides juvenile delinquents, these acts also dealt with the neglected, destitute and socially handicapped children, victimised children, and uncontrollable children. But these acts have now-been replaced by the Juvenile Justice Act, 1986. A review of the situation shows that besides the Children Act 1960, passed by the union and state legislatures, all the states except Nagaland and Jammu and Kashmir had already enacted their laws. Around 55 districts of the country, however, were not covered by any of the Children Acts. With the new 1986 Act, which supersedes different Children's Acts in different states and union territories, the whole country has now been brought under it.

The Children Acts suffered from many deficiencies in the absence of a uniform law for the country as a whole. Some of these deficiencies were: (1) the upper age limit in defining a 'child' varied from state to state; (2) all states had not provided for juvenile courts; (3) the institutional facilities were devoid of any well-defined criteria and norms to regulate capacity, staff, programmes, etc.; (4) no minimum standards for basic needs, living conditions, or therapeutic services existed; and (5) in most of the states, neglected children were huddled together with juvenile delinquents.

An important feature of the 1986 Act is that it provides a differential approach in dealing with the 'neglected juvenile' as opposed to the 'delinquent juvenile'. The former category includes juveniles who are likely to be abused, exploited and inducted into criminogenic life and are in need of legal support to be weaned away from such situations. The juvenile delinquents under no circumstances are to be lodged in jails with other prisoners. The neglected children will have to be kept in Children's or Observation Homes. Under the Act, boys up to 16 years of age and girls up to 18 years will be dealt with under the juvenile law in case of commission of crimes. While neglected juveniles are to be produced before the Juvenile Welfare Board, delinquents are to be dealt with by the juvenile courts. The neglected juvenile is to be sent to a juvenile home only if his care with a parent, guardian, or a fit person or an institution is not found feasible. For juvenile delinquents, special homes are required to be set up with facilities for accommodation, education, vocational training, and character building. The Act requires the state governments to create a fund and to exclusively utilise it for the welfare and rehabilitation of juveniles dealt with under the Act and also to constitute Advisory Boards to advise the authorities concerned on matters relating to establishment and maintenance of homes, mobilisation of resources, and so forth.

Juvenile Courts

Juvenile courts have been established in some states to try and convict specifically juvenile delinquents. The first juvenile court was established in Calcutta in 1922, followed by Bombay in 1927 and by Madras in 1930. Since then, some more states have also created such courts. The methods used by the juvenile courts are quite different from those used by the adult criminal courts. Generally, the presiding magistrates of these courts are female magistrates. Police officers in official uniform are not permitted in these courts. In trial also, complete secrecy is maintained. Members of the public are not permitted to be present at the sittings of the juvenile courts, except by special permission. Lawyers are not entitled to appear in any case before the juvenile courts. However, if a juvenile court is of the opinion that in the public interest, the appearance of a legal practitioner is necessary, he is authorised to appear in ordinary dress in particular cases. The conviction by this court does not affect the trial for another crime in some other court. The main features of he juvenile courts are: informality of procedure, de-emphasis on deterrent or retributive justice, protection and rehabilitation of juveniles, and use of socialised treatment measures. Structurally, the juvenile courts are an integral part of the judicial hierarchy, as all appeals from juvenile courts are forwarded to higher adult courts. The methods used for the disposal of cases by the juvenile courts generally are: restoring delinquents to guardians, release after admonition, imposition of fine, release on probation, commitment to reformatories, schools and borstals, and imprisonment.

Remand Homes or Observation Homes

These homes are meant for children during the pendancy of trial in the courts, but they are also used for keeping the homeless, destitute and neglected children. The stay here is used for evaluating their personality traits and behaviour. As such, these Homes are viewed more as observation homes than as places of detention.

The more important characteristics of a good Remand (Observation) Home are supposed to be: segregation, education, training, recreation facilities, health care, controlled discipline and effective supervision. Since a child in an Observation Home comes into contact with the law for the first time, if the environment is not cordial/sympathetic, the child might become suspicious and defiant towards the court.

In India, Remand/Observation Homes do not exist in all states.

According to 1998 figures, Remand/Observation Homes are found only in 14 out of the 25 states and in one union territory. The highest number of Observation Homes are found in Maharashtra, followed by Gujarat, Karnataka, Tamil Nadu, Kerala, Uttar Pradesh, Bihar, Andhra Pradesh and West Bengal. Of about 154 Remand/Observation Homes, a little more than a half are run by various governments and little less than a half are voluntary. There are separate homes for boys and girls. Of the total inmates in Observation Homes, 15 to 20 per cent are juvenile delinquents and the rest are homeless, destitutes, neglected children and so forth. Of the total inmates, two-thirds belong to 714 years age group while the remaining one-third are either below seven years or between 14 and 18 years.

About 50 per cent inmates are kept here for less than six weeks, 35 per cent between six weeks and six months and 15 per cent for more than six months. Doctors are appointed for health care on both full-time and part-time basis. While the average expenditure per inmate per month in a Remand Home in 1973 was about Rs. 60, in 1998 it was believed to be Rs. 400.

Certified or Reformatory Schools

Juveniles given detention order by the court are kept in Reformatory Schools for a minimum period of three years and a maximum period of seven years. Inmates of about 18 years age are transferred to Borstal Schools. These schools, meant only for boys, remain under the supervision of prison department. Each school having a capacity of 80 to 100 inmates is divided into four to five dormitories and each dormitory has four to five cells. Each school has superintendent, a deputy superintendent, a deputy jailor, an assistant jailor, a doctor, three to four instructors, two to three teachers, and some wardens. Training is given in tailoring, toy-making, manufacturing leather goods, and agriculture. Each training programme is of two years. The inmate gets raw materials from the school and the things manufactured by him are sold in the market and the profit deposited to his account. After the deposits have reached a certain amount, the inmate has to produce things only for state use. The inmate even gets basic education up to the fifth standard and he has to appear in the examinations conducted by Inspector of Schools at the end of the year. If an inmate wants to study beyond the fifth standard, he is admitted to an outside school. Since no work is forced upon the inmates here, they live like family members. However, no follow-up records are maintained by the schools after the release of the inmates. Besides, the training programmes are too old and traditional.

Borstal Schools

Provision was made in the 1920s for the segregation of adolescent offenders from adults so that correction services, free from authoritarian atmosphere, be made possible for the young offenders. Borstal schools were thus established for youthful offenders in the age-group of 16-21 years. Up to 1998, there were Borstal schools in only nine states in the country: Tamil Nadu (1926), Andhra Pradesh (1926), Bihar (1926), Punjab (1926), Madhya Pradesh (1928), Maharashtra (1929), Uttar Pradesh (1938), Kerala and Karnataka (1943), (*Social Defence*, 1998). The capacity of each school varies from 100 to 350 inmates. Though these schools function under the general supervision of the Inspector General of Prisons, but each school has its own Visiting Committee consisting of a session judge, a district magistrate, a district level school officer, and four non-government members. No inmate is kept here for less than two years or more than five years. Thus, only those delinquents are sent to these schools who are awarded more than three years' term. Each school is divided into houses and each house has a house-master. Each house is further divided into groups and each group has a monitor. These monitors are selected from among the inmates. There is a grading system too in these schools: ordinary, star and special-star grades. Those inmates who violate norms are demoted to penal grade, but generally, they are promoted from the lower to the higher grade. No inmate is eligible to be released from school unless he has reached the special-star grade. On being admitted to school, he is first observed for three months and given some ordinary work like gardening, etc. On being placed in the ordinary grade, he is assigned some training programme, depending on his education and potentialities. Each promotion entails more freedom and more privileges. The total number of inmates in the nine Borstal schools in the country was estimated to be 1,400 in 1998 (*Social Defence*, 1998), of which 35 per cent belonged to 16-18 years age group, 60 per cent to 18-21 years age group and 5 per cent to either 15-16 years or 21-22 years age group. The inmates of last category are admitted as special cases. The expenses per inmate, per month are estimated at present (1998) to be about Rs. 800. This is about double the expenses in the Children's Home. The daily routine includes two hours' basic education and five to six hours' vocational training. Every inmate gets 15 days' leave in one year to visit his home. Normally, the inmate remains in continuous contact with his family members through correspondence and their visits. Some schools have created a panchayat system too and have thus associated the inmates with the management of the schools. In many cases, inmates are released from the schools before the expiry of the term. For example, out of 1,200 inmates who left the various borstal schools in 1997 in the country, 50 per cent were released after the expiry of the term, 10 per cent on bail, 10 per cent on 'licence', 5 per cent on appeal, 8 per cent on some other basis, and 2 per cent escaped. Around 15 per cent were transferred to some other institutions. Before release from a borstal school, the Discharged Prisoners Aid Society is informed so that it can chalk out after-care programme for the released inmate.

Probation Hostels/Homes

These institutions, established under the Probation of Offenders Act, are meant for providing residential care and treatment to offenders released on probation with the supervision of the probation officer. The inmates are given complete freedom for going to the market and also for taking up jobs of their choice.

Evaluation of Homes

An evaluation of all types of juvenile institutions shows that lifestyle in these institutions is not at all satisfactory and inmates enjoy little freedom. The institutions are mostly over-crowded, management is centralised, training programmes are very traditional, individualised attention is not paid, life is by and large dull, their budgets are rather low, and the number (of institutions) is very inadequate. On study made long ago (1968) to evaluate juvenile correctional institutions was by the Indian Council of Social Welfare under the directorship of S.D. Gokhale. In this study (1969: 83-89), 229 inmates released during the period of five years were interviewed. It was found that: (1) training given in the institutions does not help the inmates in getting jobs; (2) institutions do not provide facilities for formal school/college education; (3) counselling and case-work facilities are inadequate; (4) individual attention is not paid to inmates; and (5) institutions have limited budgets which prevents them from adequate planning.

Two recent studies of Observation Homes---one conducted in early 1995 by a non-governmental organisation (NGO) called BOSCO in Bangalore and another conducted in November 1995 in three cities—Mumbai, Delhi, and Ujjain—by a popular weekly magazine (*Sunday*) reveal horrible conditions in the Observation Homes. Escapes from these homes have been a regular feature now for many years. Six escapes hit the headlines in the last five years (1991-96). The most recent one was the escape of 22 inmates from Observation Home, Delhi (November 1995). The second was the escape of 29 inmates from the Juvenile Home, Ujjain (Madhya Pradesh) in June 1995, two months after it was opened. One teenager even attempted suicide. There were reports of torture and a confirmed case of sexual exploitation. The third incident was reported in February 1994 in Delhi in which 14 boys escaped by cutting through a false ceiling and crawling out through a ventilator. The fourth case was reported from Patna (Bihar) in August 1993 in which 35 youngsters, aged 7-20 years, were so unhappy with the inhuman behaviour of the staff that they assaulted the guards before escaping. The Umerkhadi Remand Home, Mumbai reported the escape of 49 inmates in July 1992. Of these, 24 were rearrested. Lastly, ten juvenile delinquents escaped from the Shilyayan Centre, Behrampur, West Bengal in December 1991 because of the inhuman conditions at the home. Children are found in the homes even after the stipulated period of three to six months is over. In Bangalore it was shocking to discover a boy who had been in the home for six years while one boy had landed in it for the eleventh time (*Sunday*, 26 November-2 December 1995: 87).

An inmate of one home of Mumbai about five years ago (November 1995) revealed in his interview that "the younger boys in the homes virtually live under the dictatorship of the senior boys. They make them wash their utensils and clothes and even snatch their share of food. The warden and the security staff never bother to intervene. On the contrary, the complainants are beaten up by the authorities. Sexual abuse of younger children is common in the homes and authorities turn a blind eye to it. Beatings are a regular affair". An inmate of a home in Surat pointed out: "if an inmate did not want to be beaten, he had to be friendly with the master". The life of juveniles who languish in the homes means an endless series of days spent trying to save themselves from being bullied and tortured by older boys and sadistic officials. Since there is no way they can retaliate, in most cases they have to submit, unconditionally, to the whims and fancies of their tormentors.

Additional Sessions Judge (ASJ), Delhi visited one of the three Observation Homes for juvenile delinquents in January 1995 in North Delhi run by the Delhi Administration. She was so shocked by visible flouting of the rules that as a member of the Delhi Legal Aid and Advice Board, she moved the High Court seeking directions to the Delhi Administration authorities to implement the Juvenile Justice Act in the Observation Homes. Young boys were herded in the home like cattle.

When the juvenile justice rules stipulate minimum space of forty square feet for each inmate, the ASJ found that 92 young inmates were packed in two small rooms, each inmate having hardly space of 4.5 square feet. No special classes were being held as stipulated by law. In the name of recreational facilities, only one small TV set was kept in the room. The inmates were being given tailoring instructions two hours everyday. There was no systematic attempt at reformation. The welfare staff and teachers too were in short supply. Instead of three welfare officers, a teacher and a psychologist, there was only one welfare officer in the home. While it is mandatory on the part of the administration to provide free education to juvenile undertrials, the authorities were callously ignoring even this obligation. Medical facilities were also absent. The rules require medical examination of inmates in two to three days of their admission. This rule was being followed more in breach than in observance. Resident doctors, even where appointed were hardly present in the home when required. The security was also very lax. No wonder, 72 out of 105 inmates escaped from this home in November 1995 after tying up the two caretakers. The caretakers were found to be in the habit of becoming friendly with the young offenders permitting them to hide liquor bottles and organise drinking sessions quite frequently. The idea is not to turn Observation Homes into jails but reformation is surely needed if homes like this are to be properly used in handling juveniles under trial (*The Hindustan Times*, December 1995).

Official response to such charges is dismissive. Staff members generally aver that "after all, these kids belong to the streets and it takes time to mend their ways. The allegations of maltreatment and sexual abuse of juveniles in these homes are unfounded. The media blow up only the stray negative cases." However, it is a fact that exposure of conditions in these homes in the press forces the authorities to do some self-examining. The Umerkhadi Remand Home in Mumbai is one such example. After the escape of inmates from this home was reported in July 1992—because of the intolerable conditions created by an apathetic staff—the home has been trying to bring about improvement in its functioning. Even if conditions really improve in these Observation Homes, the best place for a child's rehabilitation is the home and not an institution. An institution has to be the last resort for juvenile delinquents. The sooner a child is restored from the home to his parents, the better for the child, the parents as well as the state because the institution can never offer real affection to children who are usually at an age when they need it the most. Care and counselling can never be expected from untrained and callous staff in the homes. The traumatic experiences of the children remanded to these homes only turns them into bigger criminals. The society needs to be sensitised to their plight.

A study of 27 institutions for socially handicapped children in Rajasthan (including Juvenile Reformatory, Observation Homes, Probation Home, Children Home, etc.) conducted by M.S. Bedi about fifteen years ago also pointed out that: (1) institutional facilities are underutilised and occupancy rate of institutes is much below their capacity; (2) the quality and the content of vocational training is poor. It does not equip the inmate to rehabilitate himself economically after being discharged from the institute; (3) space and physical amenities for inmates fall short of the minimum standards laid down by the Central Social Welfare Board; (4) protection services during institutionalisation (against tough and aggressive inmates, homosexual assaults, snatching of eatables and other things by fellow inmates) and after discharge (against old accomplices, police harassment, immoral traffickers, etc.) are not provided; and (5) facilities to inmates for communicating with family members, kin and friends are inadequate. Even if it is assumed that some changes have been introduced in these Homes in the last few years, it can be safely said that there is great need of restructuring these Homes.

PREVENTIVE PROGRAMMES

Juvenile delinquency being mainly an urban phenomenon, both private and public agencies have to be involved in delinquency prevention, keeping in mind the complexities of the urban society

The three approaches to delinquency prevention are: (1) organising activities that contribute to healthy personality development and adjustment of children, (2) controlling environment of children contributing to delinquency, and (3) organising specific preventive services for children. The *first* approach links delinquency prevention to (i) general improvements in the institutional structure of the society, for example, family, neighbourhood, school, etc., (ii) helping the poverty-stricken families in getting cheap rations and clothes, etc. from the licensed shops, (iii) providing job opportunities to children in institutions where they are not exploited, (iv) establishing schools, (v) improving job conditions, (vi) providing recreational facilities in neighbourhoods, (vii) improving marital relations through family counselling services and family social work, and (viii) imparting moral and social education in schools. Preventive activities of the *second* type also include community organisation, welfare efforts and child-care agencies, etc. Preventive activities also include probation and parole services, Certified and Borstal Schools, Children Homes, Probation Hostels and so forth.

The preventive programmes have been classified as (Trojanowicz, 1937: 188) (1) pure prevention or primary prevention, which attempts to inhibit delinquency before it takes place, and (2) rehabilitative prevention or secondary prevention, which deals with youngsters who have been adjudicated delinquents by the courts.

Peter Lejins (1967: 3) has classified the prevention programmes as: (1) punitive prevention, (2) corrective prevention, and (3) mechanical prevention. The first is the threat of punishment based on the idea that punishment will forestall criminal acts; and second refers to an attempt to eliminate potential causes before the criminal behaviour actually takes place; and the third emphasises placing obstacles (like increased security measures or increased police protection) in the way of the potential criminal so that he will find it difficult to commit an offence.

The agencies concerned with the prevention of delinquency between the 1950s and the 1999s in India are voluntary children's organisations administering child welfare and schools, social welfare departments, rescue homes, orphanages, psychiatric centres, and so on. The efforts of voluntary organisations are less coordinated, while those of government departments are more planned and systematically organised.

An overview of the functioning of the government institutions (Children Homes, Certified Schools, etc.) for 'rehabilitative prevention' has been given in the earlier pages. We may briefly discuss here the 'pure prevention programmes'. The most important areas where the government needs to take up some measures like providing educational, recreational, and vocational training facilities for preventing delinquencies are the slum areas in cities. A big chunk of population lives in slums in urban areas. If theories propounded by Thrasher, Shaw and McKay, Cohen, and Cloward and Ohlin, etc., regarding the learning of delinquencies from environment and lack of neighbourhood cohesiveness have some justification, it is necessary that the government take up some measures for the welfare of children in these areas and for their better integration into community life.

Family is another institution which needs greater attention. The role of functionally inadequate families, structurally incomplete or broken families, poor families, immoral families and indisciplined families in juvenile delinquency has already been elaborated. Unless these disorganised families are reorganised, unless environment or milieu therapy is provided, frustrated and emotionally disturbed children cannot be prevented from developing a relationship with delinquents.

Police running recreation units for children is a new concept. Juvenile units in the police department in cities like Mumbai and Delhi have undertaken these tasks. The police-school liaison programme on similar lines will go a long way in removing hostility and mutual suspicion between the police and youngsters, with the police helping teachers in handling problem youth, and by improving the police image in general.

Initiating community programmes for educating youngsters regarding the detrimental effects of using drugs and becoming involved in devious social behaviour is yet another measure in the prevention of juvenile delinquency. Drug abuse in recent years has increased among school children and slum-dwellers. Providing counselling services to these children experimenting with drugs will be an effective means of combating illicit drug use in particular and juvenile delinquency in general.

Programmes for run-away children also need attention. Homes for these children, to give them a chance to reflect on their own situations, with the assistance and guidance of staff members, need to be established in big cities and towns. These homes can help in promoting positive communication between run-away children and their parents and guardians and resolving serious problems.

It may be concluded that the development of a sound public policy regarding all aspects of delinquency prevention and control needs both planning and evaluation by rigorous research methods. This requires coordination between government agencies (like social welfare department), educational institutions, police, judiciary, social workers, and voluntary organisations.

References

Becker, Howard S., *Social Problems: A Modern Approach*, John Wiley and Sons, Inc., New York, 1966.

Berman, Sidney, "Anti-social Character Disorder", in Ruth S. Cavan, *Readings in Juvenile Delinquency*, J.B. Lippincott and Co., Philadelphia, 1964.

Cohen, Albert, *Delinquent Boys: The Culture of the Gang*, The Free Press, Glencoe, Illinois, 1955.

Giallombardo, Rose, *Juvenile Delinquency*, John Wiley and Sons, Inc., New York, 1966. Gibbons, Done C., *Deviant Behaviour*, (2nd edn.), Prentice-Hall, Inc., Englewood Cliffs, N.J., 1976.

Glueck and Sheldon, *Delinquents and Non-delinquents in Perspective*, Harvard Univ. Press, Cambridge, 1986.

Gokhale, S.D., *Impact of Institutions on Juvenile Delinquents*, United Asia Publications Ltd., Bombay, 1969.

Knadten, Richard D. and Schapter, Stephen, *Juvenile Delinquency: A Reader*, Random House, New York, 1970.

Legins, Peter, "The Field of Prevention", in *Delinquency Prevention: Theory and Practice* ed. William Amos and Charles Wellfond, 1967.

Martin, Gold, "Status Forces in Delinquent Boys", in Rodman and Grams, *Juvenile Delinquency and the Family*, New York, 1976.

Miller, Walter, "Lower Class Culture as a Generating Milieu of Gang Delinquency" *Journal of Social Issues*, No. 3, 1958.

Monahan, Thomas P., "Family Status and the Delinquent Child", in *Social Forces*, 1957.

Neumayer, *Juvenile Delinquency*, New York, 1977.

Reckless, Walter G., *Handbook of Practical Suggestions for the Treatment of Adult and Juvenile Offenders*, Government of India, 1956.

Shaw, Clifford and McKay Henry, *Juvenile Delinquency and Urban Areas*, Univ. of Chicago Press, Chicago, 1942.

Slocum and Stone, "Family Interaction and Delinquency", in Herbert C Quay, *Juvenile Delinquency*, Van Nostrand Co., Princeton, 1965.

Tappan, Paul W., *Crime, Justice and Correction*, McGraw-Hill, New York, 1960.

Trojanowicz, Robert C., *Juvenile Delinquency: Concepts and Control*, Prentice Hall Inc., Englewood Cliffs, N.J., 1973.

Venugopal, Rao, *Juvenile Delinquency: Role of the Police*, working paper in a seminar organised by CBI, Ministry of Home Affairs, Delhi, Nov 25-27, 1965.

Chapter 5

Female Crime

It was believed till a few decades ago that crime is predominantly a male phenomenon and the world of crime is only a man's world. The subject of female criminality was totally neglected. No attention was paid to research on women's crime which resulted in paucity of theoretical material on crime amongst women. In India, it was after this author undertook research in 1967-68 and published a book in 1969 (*Female Offenders in India*) presenting a new theoretical paradigm on the causation of female crime that gradually newer studies came to be undertaken in this field.

My study conducted in Rajasthan, Madhya Pradesh and Punjab not only analysed the nature and magnitude of crime among women but also explored the causes of crime and developed Social Bond Theory to explain the etiology of female criminality. The issue of adjustment in prisons was also examined to point out the need for change in punitive philosophy. My hypothesis of "family maladjustment" or "role conflict in family" was supported by some other studies that followed in the 1970s, the 1980s, and the 1990s by R.K. Sharma, Rani Bilmoria, Mishra and Gautam, Eswar Shariff and Sekar, Śanyal and Agrawal, and Neera Kuckreja Sohony. R.K. Sharma (*Women Offenders of Uttar Pradesh*, 1963) studied female offenders in Uttar Pradesh and highlighted social and psychological factors in female crime. In 1985, she also worked on murders committed by women. Rani Bilmoria (1980) studied 120 female convicts in Andhra Pradesh. By explaining crime in terms of unhealthy marital and family relations, she supported this author's theory of family maladjustment as the main cause of female crime. Eswar Shariff and Sekar (1982) studied female inmates of Remand Home in Bangalore and pointed out defective family environment (pathological family patterns), faulty discipline by parents, broken homes, parental rejection, etc. as causes of deviant behaviour. Mishra and Gautam (*Female Criminality: Causes and Consequences*, 1982) too in their study have pointed out that female criminality is largely due to broken homes and crisis of changing social values. Sanyal and Agarwal (1982) studied a sample of 69 female convicts and found that about 75 per cent criminals had a feeling of insecurity and 80 per cent had a feeling of low self-esteem. Neera K. Sohony (*A Socio-demographic Study of Women Prisoners*, 1986) studied prisoners in Pune and found some of the hypotheses of this author on female crime developed in 1969 as true and valid. B.R. Sharma (*Crime and Women*, IIPA, New Delhi, 1993) studied 36 female offenders in Tihar Jail, Delhi and Borstal Jail, Hissar (Haryana) in 1991-92. Of these, 39 per cent were below 25 years of age, 39 per cent belonged to the age group 26-43 years,16 per cent belonged to the age group 44-53 years, and 6 per cent were of 53 and more years. Further, 78 per cent were illiterate, 78 per cent were married, 56 per cent were from the rural areas, and 83 per cent had monthly income of less than Rs.2,000. In terms of nature of crime, 73 per cent females were convicted for very serious crimes like murder (59%) and bride burning (14%), 11 per cent for serious crimes like drug trafficking (5%), dacoity (3%) and abatement to suicide (3%), and 10 per cent for mild and petty offences like immoral trafficking (8%), theft (5%) and vagrancy (3%). However, Sharma's study was more psychological than sociological. He mainly administered RorSchach's test in studying female criminals, while he collected information on socio-demographic background and social factors in crime through an interview-schedule.

A few studies conducted on female criminality in the United States deserve mention here. Mabel Elliott, a female criminologist presented two chapters on female criminality in her book *Crime in Modern Society* published in 1952. The first of the two chapters presented a review of theories on female crime, including sex role formulation to account for low rates of crime among women. She also discussed a number of socio-demographic characteristics of women offenders in the US. The second chapter contained some case studies of prostitutes, women gangsters and other types of female offenders. Otto Pollak (*The Criminality of Women*, 1950) has said that though the crime rate among women equals to that among men yet it has a 'masked character'. On the one hand, all female crimes are not reported to police and on the other hand, the police and the courts are very sympathetic towards them due to their paternalistic and protective attitudes. The policemen do not like to arrest them and prosecutors and judges do not like to convict them. No wonder, crime rate is inadequately reflected in statistics. The unreporting and underreporting of female crime is also due to the fact that the social roles of women are excellent covers and homes serve as a smoke screen for hiding crime. Studies on female crime made by Parker (1965), Franklin (1967), Edith de Rham (1969), and Sparrow (1970) while supporting Pollak's proposition of hidden crimes through case studies throw little light on causes of female criminality.

Rita Simon analysed various dimensions of female criminality like extent and types of crimes committed and their treatment by court and prison officials in her book *Women and Crime* in 1975. She, however, did not study the issue of etiology of female crime. According to her, increase in female crime is due to expanding occupational opportunities for women.

Carol Smart has criticised all above studies in her study of prostitution and rape in 1976 and pointed out the need for developing a new theory. However, she herself did not attempt to propound any new proposition. Laura Crites (*Female Offenders*, 1976) studied women criminals but she made no important contribution in any respect except pointing out that women criminals are neglected and are given discriminatory treatment in prisons. Balman, Berger and Schmidt's article on "Women, Crime and Deviance" (in *Crime and Deviance in America*, 1980) used a Marxist perspective and submitted that women commit crime as a result of their socialisation under capitalist structures.

NATURE OF FEMALE CRIME IN INDIA

Statistically speaking, crime amongst females is not a significant problem in India. Of the total crimes committed in our country in 1998, about 5.4 per cent are committed by females (*Crime in India*, 1998: 271). While between 1971 and 1980, the quinquennial average of female crime was 29,300 (Surat Mishra and Arora, 1982), between 1981 and 1990, it was 64,680. In 1998, of 26.57 lakh persons arrested for crimes under the Indian Penal Code in the country, 1.43 lakh (or 5.4%) were females (*ibid.*: 271). It is true that there has been increase in female criminality from 1971 onwards. From 1.7 per cent in 1971, female crimes under the IPC increased to 1.9 per cent in 1978, 3.1 per cent in 1990, 3.5 per cent in 1992, and 5.4 per cent in 1998; but this increase is not so high when compared to the increase in male criminality. While incidence of crime under the

IPC among males increased by 9.44 per cent during the period from 1953 to 1963, by 63.49 per cent during 1963 to 1973, by 25.2 per cent during 1973 to 1983, by 20.7 per cent during 1983 to 1993, and by 9.2 per cent during the period from 1993 to 1998, the IPC crime among females increased by 48.5 per cent from 1983 to 1993 and by 50.4 per cent from 1993 to 1998 (*ibid.*, 16; 1993: 153). Thus, statistically, female criminality is not yet a serious social problem for our society.

There are more female crimes in America, England, France, Canada, Japan, Thailand, etc. in comparison to India. For example, against nine female crimes per one lakh of population in India, there are 1,154 crimes in America, 561 in West Germany, 316 in Thailand, 138 in France, and 133 in Japan. [The general crime rate (i.e., males and females together) per one lakh of population in 1998 in different countries was: India: 636, Canada: 8,452, England: 10,403, America: 5,897, Japan: 1,459, France: 6,095, Germany: 7,868 and Austria: 5,940 (*Crime in India*, 1998: 23)]. Sociologically, however, female crime in India may be considered a crucial problem because of its impact on the upbringing of children, and the overall fabric of society.

The difference in the rate of male and female crime is basically the result of the difference in their respective roles. The basic role of wage-earning by men is performed outside the home for which they have to compete with others. In the process of competition, sometimes when they are not able to achieve their goal through legitimate means, they use illegitimate means. On the other hand, the basic role of a householder is performed by women within the four walls of home for which they have not to compete with anybody and are not forced to use anti-social means for achieving their goal. Moreover, compared to men, women are more god-fearing, moral and tolerant. They are also subject to greater social restrictions. Further, some crimes require masculine skills and techniques or active independence on the part of the offender and the use or threat of violence (e.g., auto-thefts, chain-snatching, etc.). Women's participation in such crimes is very low. Lastly, the police and the courts take a more sympathetic attitude towards female offenders. In short, the important factors of difference in rate of male and female crime may be described as: (i) differential sex role expectations, (ii) sex differences in socialisation patterns and application of social control, (iii) differential opportunities to engage in crime, (iv) differential access to criminal subcultures and careers, and (v) sex differences built into crime categories (*see*, Dale Hoffman Bustamente, "The Nature of Female Criminality", in *Issues in Criminology*, Fall 1973: 117-36).

CHARACTERISTICS OF FEMALE CRIMINALS

Who are the women who commit crimes? Their social and economic background will be discussed here in terms of five variables: marital status, age, income, education, and residence. These variables then may be used for developing a hypothesis pertaining to the causation of female criminality. The background shall be analysed on two bases: (a) on the basis of all India official crime statistics, and (b) on the basis of my own empirical study of 325 female offenders conducted in the three states of Rajasthan, Punjab and Madhya Pradesh between 1967 and 1977. The difference between these two bases is that whereas all-India official statistics include all types of female offenders in the country, my study was solely focused on a certain type of offenders, namely, those who got more than six months' imprisonment for their crime. I shall analyse the five variables in their socio-cultural background separately.

Marital Status

The all-India figures reveal that about 73 per cent of the female offenders in India are married, 15 per cent unmarried and 12 per cent widows. On the other hand, my study (of 325 offenders in three states) showed that 76 per cent offenders were married, 17 per cent were widows, 4 per cent were unmarried and 3 per cent were deserted women. Since nine out of 10 women committing crimes were either married or had lived for some time in the family of procreation after marriage, it may be legitimately inferred that marital life in particular and family life in general in a female criminal's career deserved special attention while analysing causes of female criminality.

Age

In terms of age, according to all India figures, taking the female offenders convicted for crimes under the IPC and under the Local and Special Laws together (1998), it may be said that 1.5 per cent offenders are below 18 years of age, a little less than half (46.5%) belong to 18-30 years age group, a little more than two-fifths (43.7%) belong to 30-50 years age group, and a little less than one-tenth (8.3%) are more than 50 years age (*Crime in India*, 1998: 299-300). Table 5.1 shows the age groups of female offenders in 1998.

My study showed that (out of 325 offenders) 5.7 per cent female offenders were very young (below 16 years of age), 52.8 per cent were young (16-30 years of age), 35.8 per cent were middle-aged (30-50 years of

Table 5.1

Age Groups of Female Offenders in 1998

Age group	Crimes under the IPC		Crimes under SLL		Total	
	No.	%	No.	%	No.	%
Below 16	773	0.6	119	0.1	892	0.3
16-18	2,360	1.7	1,707	0.9	4,067	1.2
18-30	67,167	46.7	86,586	46.2	1,53,753	46.4
30-50	60,129	41.8	84,392	45.1	1,44,521	43.7
50+	13,251	9.2	14,515	7.7	27,766	8.4
Total	1,43,680	100.0	1,87,319	100.0	3,30,999	100.0

Source: *Crime in India*, 1998: 299-300.

age), and 5.7 per cent were old (above 50 years of age). The mean age at the commitment of crime was 28.7 years and median was 26.1 years. Against this, the mean age at the beginning of the marital life of these offenders was 17.4 years. This is the age at which a girl is neither chronologically nor mentally mature and is biologically and socially incapable of understanding and performing the marital and other roles in the family. This clearly shows that since a large number of female offenders are young at the time of committing crimes, the interpersonal relations in the family after marriage create adjustment problems for women and sometimes force them to indulge in deviant behaviour.

Income

As regards the economic background of the female offenders, the all India figures have not compiled this variable. My study, however, pointed out that 85.7 per cent offenders belonged to the families, the monthly income of which was less than Rs. 300 (in late 1960s, and early 1970s), 10.3 per cent belonged to the families, the income of which was between Rs.300 and Rs.500 per month, and 4 per cent belonged to the families, the income of which was more than Rs.500 per month. Assuming that the value of a rupee between 1967 and 1977 has come down to eight paise in 1998, it could be said that 86 per cent female offenders today belong to families with an income of Rs. 2,000 per month, 10 per cent to families with an income of Rs.2,000 to Rs.4,000 per month (both classes described together as destitute class) and 4 per cent to families with an income above Rs.4,000 per month (extremely poor class). Even though economic condition does not necessarily indicate the role of poverty in female crime, yet it is significant in the sense that low income is an important contributory factor to family tensions, and a combination of unsatisfactory social relationships and poverty is conducive to criminal behaviour.

Education

The same thing is true of the educational background of female offenders. The all India figures show that 12 per cent female criminals in the country are literate. My study indicated that 79 per cent female criminals were illiterate, 11 per cent could read and write though they had no formal education, and 10 per cent had some school education. These figures point to the fact that like poverty, lack of education may also create the problem of family adjustment, forcing a few women to take to deviant behaviour.

Residence

Lastly, an analysis of the residential background of the female offenders showed that 23.5 per cent offenders belonged to the urban areas and 76.5 per cent to the rural areas. It should not, however, be inferred from this that female crime is basically a rural phenomenon, or that the rural areas produce more female criminals than the urban areas. Of the total population of the three states studied by us, 18.1 per cent was urban and 81.9 per cent was rural in 1971. It may, therefore, be concluded that women's crime is greater in the urban areas than in the rural areas. Furthermore, if female criminality is to be seen in terms of family maladjustment (as hypothesised by us), environment in urban family has to be analysed quite differently from the environment in rural family.

The analysis of these five variables helps us in hypothesising the role of family maladjustment, caused by early marriage, poverty, and illiteracy, in women's crime.

NATURE OF CRIME

What are the crimes mostly committed by women in our society? About 48 per cent of the crimes committed by females involved victims (VIC) and 52 per cent are without victims. Of the total convicted female offenders in India under the Indian Penal Code in 1998 (1,43,680), 16.1 per cent were convicted for riots, 3.8 per cent for murder/attempt to murder, 3.1 per cent for thefts, 1.1 per cent for kidnapping and abduction, 18.8 per cent for hurt, 15.3 per cent for cruelty, 3 per cent for

Table 5.2

Crimes under the IPC by Males and Females Committed in 1998

Offence	*Females*		*Males*	
	Number	*Percentage*	*Number*	*Percentage*
Theft	4,405	3.0	1,62,723	6.5
Murder, its attempt and homicide	5,537	3.8	1,48,987	5.9
Burglary	1,022	0.7	71,353	2.8
Riots	23,076	16.0	4,15,894	16.5
Cheating	1,185	0.7	31,213	1.2
Breach of trust	426	0.3	14,693	0.6
Kidnapping and abduction	1,522	1.0	28,998	1.2
Dacoity	200	0.1	25,021	1.0
Robbery	155	0.1	31,638	1.3
Rape	335	0.2	19,143	0.8
Hurt	26,970	18.7	4,17,311	16.6
Dowry deaths	4,322	3.0	13,561	0.5
Others	75,525	52.4	11,33,664	45.0
Total	1,43,680	100.0	25,14,199	100.0

Source: Crime in India, 1998: 271.

Table 5.3

Crimes under the Special and Local (SLL) Laws by Males and Females in 1998

Local and Special Laws	*Females*		*Males*	
	Number	*Percentage*	*Number*	*Percentage*
Prohibition Act	1,22,334	65.3	4,10,969	9.6
Immoral Traffic Act	11,617	6.2	1,262	0.02
Excise Act	5,917	3.2	1,13,320	2.6
Dowry Prohibition Act	1,902	1.0	6,980	0.2
Gambling Act	344	0.2	2,49,573	5.8
Narcotic Drugs Act	895	0.5	20,491	0.5
Explosives Act	10	0.00	5,727	0.1
Arms Act	122	0.06	66,746	1.6
Indian Railways Act	976	0.5	41,162	1.0
SC/ST Atrocities Act	860	0.5	24,268	0.5
Others	1,87,319	22.6	33,63,814	78.1
Total	3,32,296	100.0	43,04,312	100.0

Source: Crime in India, 1993: 176.

dowry death, 0.7 per cent for burglary, 0.8 per cent for cheating, 0.3 per cent for breach of trust, 0.2 per cent for rape, 0.2 per cent for dacoity, 0.1 per cent for robbery, and 36.5 per cent for other offences (1998: 271) Of those 1.87 lakh female offenders who were convicted under the Local and Special Laws, 65.3 per cent were convicted under the Prohibition Act, 6.2 per cent under Immoral Traffic Act, 3.8 per cent under the Excise Act, 1.0 per cent under the Dowry Prohibition Act, 0.5 per cent under the Narcotic Drugs Act, 0.2 per cent under Gambling Act, 0.5 per cent under the Railways Act, and 22.5 per cent under other Acts (1998: 286).

My study of 325 female offenders, however, presented a different picture. It showed that 63 per cent offenders were convicted for murder, 14 per cent for theft, 5 per cent for excise offences, 4 per cent for kidnapping, 4 per cent for vagrancy, 3 per cent for causing hurt, 2 per cent for immorality, one per cent for attempt to commit suicide, and 4 per cent for other offences.

When we compare the nature of female crime in India with that of female crime in the United States and Australia, we find some significant differences. While women's crime constituted only about 2 per cent of the total crime in our country in 1980 and 4 per cent in 1993, in the United States it constituted 16 per cent and in Australia 7.6 per cent in 1980. Thefts in the U.S. constituted 30.7 per cent and in Australia 15.6 per cent of the total female crimes in 1980 against 20 per cent in India; cheating constituted 32.6 per cent in the US, 0.1 per cent in Australia and 0.7 per cent in India, and murder constituted 14.6 per cent in the US, 4.1 per cent in Australia and 3.2 per cent in India (*see*, Mukherjee and Scutt, 1981: 81). These figures not only provide a tool of comparison of volume of participation in crime by women in India and in the two Western countries but also help in a meaningful assessment of the character of female criminals in our society.

The pattern of crime shows that women are moving out of traditional crimes like sex offences and shoplifting to thefts, burglary and crimes of violence like murder, abduction, etc. But there is no indication that their participation in these offences has increased much more markedly than has men's in recent years. This is evident from Tables 5.2 and 5.3. We therefore do not agree with the viewpoint of scholars like Freda Adler (*Sisters in Crime*, 1975: 59) that the breakdown of sexual inequality lies behind the involvement of women in various forms of crime. Nor can we agree with Rita James Simon (*Women and Crime*, 1975) that as labour-force participation increases, opportunities to engage in criminality should expand for women. I have a different opinion on the causation of women's criminality which is discussed below.

CAUSES OF CRIME

Darie Klein (*The Etiology of Female Crime: A Review of the Literature*, 1973) offered a summary of much of the literature on causes of female crime discussed by Lombroso, W.I. Thomas, Kingsley Davis, and Otto Pollak. According to Klein, the shared assumptions running through the works of all these persons include the proposition that female crime is the result of *physiological or psychological characteristics of individuals*, with little or no recognition being given to the importance of social-structural factors. These physiological or psychological traits of women offenders were usually viewed as pathological distortions or departures from the normal, inherent nature of women. As per this view, these females were seen as disposed towards characteristics such as aggressiveness which is a violation of their true nature. Individual counselling was therefore suggested for crime control, through which errant women could be drawn back into 'proper' feminine behaviour.

Freud (Cf. Simon, *Women and Crime*, 1975: 2-9) offered a physiological explanation of female criminality holding that normal women accept and internalise societal definitions of femininity but women criminals suffer from 'masculinity complex'. Thus, normal women exhibit 'normal' feminine traits but criminal women exhibit perversion of or rebellion against the biologically natural female role. Critics have described these arguments as defective because they contain erroneous assumptions about biological characteristics of women.

W.I. Thomas (*The Unadjusted Girl*, 1923) described female deviancy as departure from conduct that is biologically and psychologically 'normal' for women. Kingsley Davis ("Sociology of Prostitution", in *American Sociological Review*, October 1937) presented a functionalist interpretation of prostitution, arguing that it arises in circumstances where demands for sexual novelty cannot be supplied within the framework of marriage and/or where some males are cut off from access to sexual partners because they are unmarried or are at a sexually competitive disadvantage. Commercial prostitution arises as a blackmarket in sex. The problem with this theory is that it supports the thesis that the only proper role for women is that of a child-bearer and housewife.

Pollak (*The Criminality of Women*, 1950) asserts that women crimes are characterised by deceit and double standards. Just as physical weakness forces a woman to resort to deception, the use of physical charm enables her to attract the victim. Poisoning a child or an adult at home, sexual crimes, shoplifting and other thefts, abortions, etc. are easily hidden by them. Greater freedom has allowed them to enter new positions and new roles, thereby giving them more opportunities for participation in crime. Maintaining double standards by women also helps create female crime because it leads to frustrations and envy on their part. It pushes them to false accusation against men (charges of rape, for example). However, Pollak's propositions are not based on any evidence. In fact, some statements made by him are described as ridiculous and biased. Pollak has paid more attention to petty crimes committed by them and ignored their serious crimes like murder, robbery, etc.

Freda Adler (*op. cit.*, 1975) studied prostitution, drug addiction, and juvenile delinquency among females. She has attributed these crimes to the liberation movement of women and women's assertiveness. She contends that educated girls and women are more willing than ever to challenge traditional restrictions and social roles. The easing of restraints on women is further likely to increase female crime.

Empirical studies conducted on female crime in India have by and large supported this author's etiological explanation. B.R. Sharma (1963) concluded in his study that strained interpersonal relations with husband and other family members, husband's extra-family relations, deprivation and denial of basic needs of life (like affection, security, etc.) were the main causes of frustrations and ultimate crimes. Rani Bilmoria (1980) and Sohoni Neera Kuckreja (1986) also supported this author's theory of family maladjustment as cause of female crime. Let me, therefore, analyse my study on female crime and discuss the hypothesis regarding the role of "family maladjustment" or "role conflict in family" in female criminality. We will first examine the crime of murder.

Who are the victims of murder? My study revealed that in 77 per cent cases, the victim was the member of the offender's family, in 5 per cent cases, he/she had kinship relationship with the criminal, in 9 per cent cases, he/she was her neighbour, in 8 per cent, he/she was the member of her village community, and in less than 1 per cent cases, he/she was a complete stranger. This shows that in 99 per cent cases, the female offender had primary relationship with the victim. Of the 77 per cent cases in which the victim was a member of the respondent's family, in 92.2 per cent cases, he (the victim) was a member of respondent's family of procreation and only in 7.S per cent cases, was he a member of the family of orientation. This supports my earlier proposition that *family life after marriage* plays a very crucial role in women's criminality.

Of the 92.2 per cent cases in which the victim was a member of the female criminal's family of procreation, in 57.9 per cent cases, the victim was ego's husband, in 18.9 per cent cases, ego's own child, in 4.2 per cent cases, ego's secondary kin (SoWi, SoSo) and in 19 per cent cases, ego's husband's primary or secondary kin. This fact of the victim being usually a kin or a close associate of the offender in crimes of murder was also discovered by Bullock (1955: 572) in his study of urban homicides in Texas, by Svalastoga (1956: 40) in his study of 172 Danish cases, and by Sutherland (1950: 548) in his study of 324 murders by females. Wolfgang (1958: 212), however, had found such relationship only in 23.13 per cent cases in his study of 588 homicides in Philadelphia.

In the cases where the victim was the respondent's own child, the murder was committed either because the child was illegitimate and the woman was afraid of social ostracism, or in a moment of extreme anger because of an altercation with the husband. Thus, in about four-fifths cases, husband-wife relationship proved quite an important factor in the causation of murder. In 45.5 per cent cases, the cause was illicit relations of the offender with some man; in 10.9 per cent cases, it was illicit relations of the victim with some woman; and in 27.3 per cent cases, it was conflict with husband and/or ill-treatment by husband. This proves the validity of our hypothesis of family maladjustment as the main cause of female criminality.

Not only in murders but also in other crimes, family was found to be an important factor in criminality. For example, in excise offences, when husband was arrested for illicit distillation, his wife too was arrested for helping the husband in illegal activities. In these cases, the wife merely helped her husband in his economic pursuits because of her *dharma* (religious duty) and not because of any desire to violate the social or legal norms. Similarly, in one case of theft (in which 4 men and 3 women of a Gujar family were arrested, convicted and given one year's imprisonment), the male members of one Gujar family stole the cows and buffaloes of other Gujar family with which they had a family feud. While returning from the village with the animals, they were arrested by the police. Since women accompanied men, they too were arrested and penalised. This case also shows that women were labelled 'criminals' not because they had 'criminalistic tendencies' but because their family male members were so labelled. My contention is that most of the thefts committed by women are not the result of psychological or social aberrations but are due to family and economic compulsions. Women convicted for minor thefts are mainly housewives who usually lack money to be able to buy things which were later stolen. Many a time, they steal to 'stretch their budgets'. The lower-class social status of women convicted for thievery is a further proof of our hypothesis.

In crimes of above types, women arrested play secondary/supportive roles. Their involvement in the offence is closely tied to woman's role as a wife. They seem to commit crimes in roles auxiliary to men, in keeping with their sex roles. They are, therefore, not to be treated as sole perpetrators of these crimes. Our hypothesis regarding the role of family in female criminality is thus fully justified.

Simon (1975) and Adler (1977) have explained the recent increase in the incidence of female crime in terms of the breakdown of prevailing patterns of 'sexual inequality'. According to Simon, increased labour-force participation of women and other developments in the direction of sexual equality have expanded the crime opportunities and pressures towards law-breaking among women. According to Adler, a growing trend towards female assertiveness, manifested in the contemporary women's movement in the United States as well as in other ways, has led to consequences in the area of criminality.

These explanations do not explain crime situation in India in spite of the fact that in our country too there is a Women's Liberation Movement. But this movement is confined to the urban areas whereas a large number of female criminals in our society come from the rural areas where women never talk of equal rights with men and there is no breakdown of sexual inequality. We, therefore, cannot hold the view that in India as labour-force participation increases, opportunities to engage in criminality would expand for women as well.

Could we examine 'adult female crime' in terms of factors offered for explaining 'delinquency in young or adolescent girls'? Some of the factors suggested are: family tensions or 'under-the-roof culture' (Gibbons, 1976: 169), self-concept deficiencies and perceptions of lack of opportunity (Datesman *et al.*, 1975: 107), excessive weight or other physical problems (Cowie *et al.*, 1982). My contention is that it is not the physical and psychological factors which account for female crime but it is the non-harmony and instability in family relationships or disintegration of family life which mainly explain crime among women.

Theories About Female Criminality

Let us now move from 'causes' to 'theoretical explanations'. Various theories about crime have been propounded from time to time but only a few among them have dealt with female criminality. We will first review the old theories about female crime like those of Lombroso, Freud, Kingsley Davis, and Otto Pollak before examining the recent ones.

Lombroso (1903) maintained that his researches produced fewer indications of physical stigmata or biological anomalies among women, supporting his belief that women are organically conservative. This conservating tendency of women accounts not only for the lesser involvement of women in criminality but also for the cause of crime (atavistic features) among females.

Freud's (*see*, Klein Dorie, 1973) physiological explanation holds that law breaking by females represents a perversion of or rebellion against the biologically natural female role, or is evidence of 'masculinity complex'. He maintained that all females experience some degree of jealousy of males but 'normal' women manage to accept and internalise societal definitions of femininity, centred about a single-minded interest in motherhood.

Kingsley Davis (1937) presented a functionalist interpretation of one specific type of crime by women, namely, prostitution. He argued that commercial prostitution arises as a blackmarket in sex. It arises in circumstances where demands for sexual novelty cannot be supplied within the framework of marriage and/or where some males are cut off from access to sex partners because they are unmarried, ugly or deformed.

Otto Pollak (1950) claimed that women engage in hidden crimes like abortions, murder by poisoning, offences against children, etc. because of their greater skill at deceit and cunning behaviour acquired through sexual socialisation. Besides the surreptitious and cunning nature of women acquired through differential socialisation process, Pollak also suggested that biological factors including lesser physical strength, as well as psychological concomitants of menstruation, pregnancy, etc. enter into the etiology of female crime.

The shared proposition of all these four scholars is that female crime is the result of physiological or psychological characteristics of individuals. They have not given any importance to socio-cultural factors but have viewed the biological characteristics as pathological distortions or departures from the normal inherent nature of women. Obviously, the assumptions in all these explanations about biological and psychological traits of 'normal' and criminal women are questionable. Rita James Simon (1975) has also contented that all the above explanations are incorrect because they contain erroneous presuppositions about 'normal' traits of women.

After the analysis of the viewpoints of the scholars of the past few decades, let us now examine some recent theoretical contributions. A few criminologists have used Role Theory to explain women's crimes. While advocating this theory, it is pointed out by scholars like Frances Heidensohn (1968: 170), Marie Andree Bertrand (1969: 74), etc. that owing to close supervision and social restrictions on women, socialisation, development of consciousness, and self-perception vary considerably between boys and girls. Girls are usually trained to be passive, domesticated and non-violent and are not allowed to learn how to fight or use weapons. Contrary to this, boys are aggressive, ambitious and outward-going. Girls thus shrink from violence and do not possess the necessary technical ability or strength to engage in crimes of violence, armed robberies, gang fights, etc. At worst, they engage in petty or domestic offences. Talcott Parsons (1949) also held that the low incidence of female crime was due to the ready availability of a female adult (since mother normally stayed at home) upon which the female child modelled her behaviour. The male child, however, in the absence of the role model (since father normally remained away from home for obvious reasons) and as a protest against the femininity of the mother, engaged in delinquent behaviour. Grosser (*see*, Mukherjee and Scutt, 1981: 72) maintained that it was the inability of females to express themselves through their criminality that accounted for the high disparity in the sex ratio in crime statistics. Cohen (1955) contended that the subculture of delinquency which presented a solution to the status problems of adolescents was uniquely male in character. Females were unable to 'prove' themselves by acts such as theft or vandalism as they represented the very antithesis of their sex role expectations. Smart (1976: 71) and Scutt (1976: 28) attempted in 1976 to update the role theory by incorporating within the role of school, peer group and occupational group, besides family, as socialising agents. But both of them had strong reservations about the value of role theory as an explanation for female criminality.

My argument against the role theory is that it does not explain the *cause* of committing of crime by females; it only explains the differential rates of male and female criminality. The role theorists highlight the way in which opportunity structures predispose males rather than females to crime. I, however, hold that woman's criminality can be theorised in terms of "contradictory or ill-defined roles in the family". *Role collision* (in which husband and wife, or daughter-in-law and parents-in-law, etc., have roles which are in conflict in some respect), *role incompatibility* (in which the woman plays roles which have contradictory expectations) and *role confusion* (in which there is lack of agreement among family members about expectations of a given role)—all these create a situation for a woman which compels her to indulge in deviant acts.

NEW THEORETICAL PERSPECTIVE

After analysing the important outlines of prevailing sociological explanations of trend towards sexual equality, patterns of differential sexual socialisation, and separation of adult social roles characteristic of males and females regarding the causation of female crime, let us now present a new sociological approach towards understanding the etiology of female crime. In fact, it is the failure of theorists to explain the cause of female criminality that prompts me to present this new perspective.

The first question is: is it possible to develop one broad theory which may explain all types of crimes committed by females, or has attention to be directed at specific patterns of law-breaking among women, say, amateur thieves, rioters, cheats, murderers, kidnappers, vagrants, excise offenders, etc.? My contention is that the analysis of crime among males may be focused on particular forms but female crimes *en masse* can be viewed in terms of one broad theoretical context. I believe that though female crime results from linking together of various influences yet we can identify the most important etiological influence. This causal factor is *family maladjustment*. Stated another way, in my perspective I am primarily concerned with the pattern of family relationships. Through analysing the structural problems of family organisation and through studying the types of functional problems in women's families of procreation, crimes committed by women are examined in terms of *maladjustment in interpersonal relationship within the family*. This 'family-centred explanation' or more broadly the 'pressure of primary relations perspective' can be explained through a diagram.

The above diagram shows that factors endogenous or exogenous to family create provocation, temptation, strains, and stresses in a woman's life. These provocations or stresses produce a desire or a need to deviate from social and/or legal norms. The personality structure or the socio-psychological characteristics like temperament, attitudes, frustrations, deprivations or dominant underlying needs prevent some

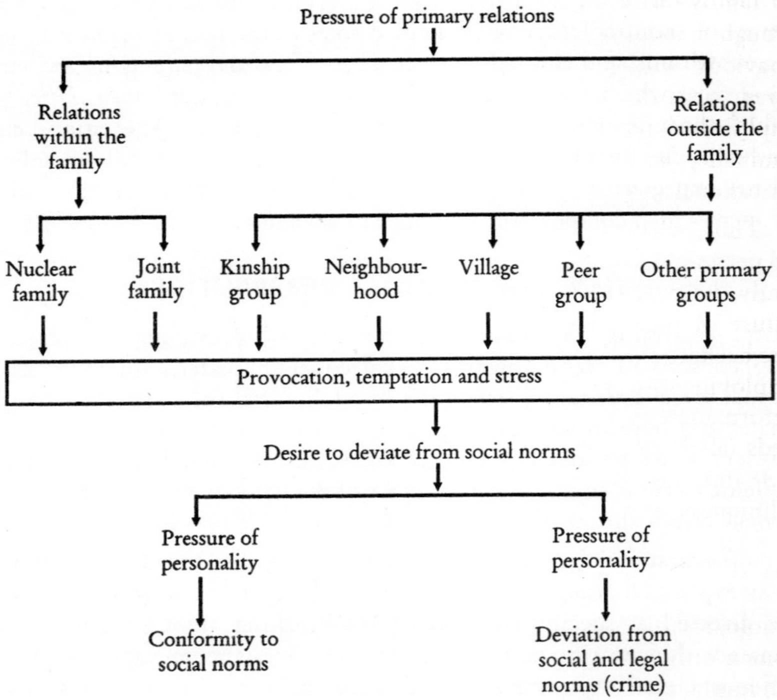

women from this deviation but fail to do so in other cases. Thus, both personality system and pressures of environment in which woman functions contribute to woman's criminality.

This theoretical model focuses on 'strength of character', 'role conflict' (role collision, role incompatibility, role confusion), 'opportunity', and 'totality of situation' in family. Totality of situation includes varied situations in family taken together. Suppose a woman fails to get her husband's love and affection (situation S_1), and in-law's care and support (situation S_2), and has illicit relations with a person (situation S_3), it will be the totality of the three situations together ($S_1 + S_2 + S_3$) that will lead her to criminality (say, husband's murder). Further, her personality characteristics (say, either personality P_1, or personality P_2) will determine whether she will really commit murder (one type of behaviour) or suicide (other type of behaviour) or elope (third type of behaviour) or continue to live in the family (fourth type of behaviour).

Thus, woman's 'crime' (husband's murder) will be the outcome of interaction between her personality system and 'totality' of situations in her family. It (crime) will develop in (interaction) process over time through a series of stages. In this process (spread over time), 'criminal behaviour' will emerge not because of the *past* alone but because of the *current* situation and triggering or precipitating circumstances too. In simplified form, our *conjunctive* theoretical model in women's criminality accounts for differences in women's families and other institutional structures as well as in their personalities.

Thus, what needs to be analysed in the diagnosis of environmental and personality factors in female crime is: (i) family composition (type of family, its size, economic background, etc.), (ii) interactional situation (nature of relations with husband, in-laws, children and parents), (iii) class-background (lower, middle and upper class status), (iv) role career (employment, domestic roles, etc.), (v) attitudes (towards religion, role performance, etc.), perceptions (or rights and duties, values and norms), needs (affection, control, support, etc.) and values (honesty, morality, etc.) and (vi) offence behaviour (nature of crime, crime skills and techniques employed, help received from others, and so forth).

CORRECTIONAL PROCESSES

Sociological inattention to female offenders has extended to dealing with women only through the law-enforcement and correctional machinery. The implicit assumption is that female criminality is relatively low, and female criminals are 'properly' handled by the criminal justice system. My contention, however, is that female criminals get unequal and discriminatory treatment within the correctional apparatus, if not within the justice apparatus, in our society. Though the courts do not discriminate against female offenders by imposing a sexual (double) standard upon them but in jails, we see sexual discrimination operating against female inmates at a variety of points.

The programmes and facilities in the correctional institutions for female offenders do not vary widely from one state to another. Most of the Female Reformatories are in poor condition as compared to institutions for male offenders. The social experiences ecountered by women inmates are decidedly negative ones, with the rules of conduct being more restrictive in women's prisons than in men's prisons. Treatment programmes for female prisoners are either non-existent or markedly inadequate. Female prisoners are often excluded from training programmes and parole facilities. The training programmes (mainly cleaning foodgrains, cutting vegetables, cooking and sewing) for female inmates are basically designed to prepare women to reenter the community as nineteenth-century domestics. No effort is made to introduce programmes that would adequately equip the women to deal with the variety of social adjustment problems they are likely to encounter in modern society (*see*, Ahuja Ram, *The Prison System*, 1981; and "Inmates' Adjustment to Prison Subculture", *Indian Journal of Social Work*, Bombay, 1983).

Two methods in the main are being used at present in punishing and correcting the female offenders: imprisonment and release on probation. Between the two, the former is used about 20 times more than the latter. Of the female offenders who are eligible to be released on probation, hardly 5 to 7 per cent are given the benefit of these services in India. Is imprisonment a correct method to deal with the female offenders? After all, what are the objectives of imprisonment? The main objectives suggested are: social isolation, repentance, punishment, deterrence, and reformation. Do criminal women need to be isolated from the society? Are they really a threat to social solidarity and social organisation? Do they repent of their wrong deeds only after being sent to prison? Do they really require punishment for correction? Will imprisonment deter potential offenders from indulging in similar offences? Do prisons function as correctional institutions? Do female prisoners get the right type of treatment and work in prisons? My contention is that since 'family maladjustment' or 'role conflict in family' or 'pressure of primary relations' is the main cause of crime in a large number of female criminalities, all female offenders do not need or deserve to be imprisoned. Unless monopolistic organisation of prisons is changed, unless frustrations and stresses and strains to which inmates are subjected by the authorities are contained, unless better work-milieu in jail administration is provided, unless prison officials are weaned away from excessive individualism so that they can adapt themselves to the new values of case-work, imprisonment cannot be a right method to deal with the female offenders.

The imprisonment of a woman is also dysfunctional to her family in the sense that the family has to face a crisis of what Hill calls 'dismemberment' and 'demoralisation'. The former refers to the crisis of absence of a member due to imprisonment and the latter refers to social disgrace and social stigma of the family due to its member's criminality. Both make a woman's husband and her children suffer emotional and social deprivations.

Furthermore, many women are forced to bring their young children to prisons. These children are so ill-treated and neglected that they suffer from serious problems. The age at which children ought to be educated and socialised is spent by such unfortunate children in jail without any opportunity to learn values and norms of society. Since a majority of female offenders get only a short-term imprisonment (about 85%) and since imprisonment stigmatises persons instead of reforming them, these women surely can be given the benefit of probation system.

This is not to suggest that imprisonment should be totally abolished for female criminals. My contention is that women offenders have to be classified in different categories and only *some* categories of offenders need be imprisoned. I categorise women criminals into five groups, namely, *frustrated*, *emotional*, *revengeful*, *accidental* and *misled* criminals, and believe that only the 'revengeful' and the 'misled' offenders deserve imprisonment. Of the 325 criminals in my study, 20.4 per cent belonged to the first type, 28.6 per cent to the second type, 13.2 per cent to the third type, 27.5 per cent to the fourth type, and 10.3 per cent to the fifth type (Ahuja, Ram, "Female Murderers in India", *Indian Journal of Social Work*, October 1970). On this basis, it may be maintained that only about one-fourth of the total female offenders in our society need to be imprisoned.

Besides finding suitable alternatives to imprisonment to deal with the large number of 'simple' female offenders, some reforms are needed in prisons also to make their functioning more effective. Generally speaking, women inmates get discriminatory treatment in prisons. When males are assigned productive work, women are given unproductive assignments. Males get special opportunities for earning remission which are mostly denied to women. Facilities of education and earning wages given to men in certain prisons are not provided to women in any prison. Thus, the greatest need today is of modernising work assignments for female offenders, giving them more facilities to earn extra remission, introducing wage system, providing facilities for education and passing primary examinations, giving training in crafts which will enable them to become self-reliant, and introducing leave and furlough systems. All these measures and extensive use of the parole system will help humanise female life in prisons.

A few other suggestions may also be made for dealing with women accused of crime and women in custody:

- After arrest, as far as possible, females accused of offences may be handled by women police.
- Free legal aid may be provided to female prisoners wherever necessary. In this connection, it may be suggested that: (a) a list of all

under-trial female prisoners be sent to the Legal Aid Committee of the district in which the jail is situated; (b) facilities should be provided to the lawyers nominated by the concerned District Legal Aid Committee to visit jail and interview the clients who have expressed their desire to have their assistance; (c) notices should be prominently displayed in jails regarding the proposed visits of lawyers of Legal Aid Committees.

- The courts could be more liberal in releasing women offenders on probation instead of awarding imprisonment of less than six months.
- New training programmes should be designed for female prisoners which may prove functional to their rehabilitation.
- Education should be made compulsory for illiterate women prisoners imprisoned for more than one year.
- A guarded parole release every six months for at least a week to long-term offenders will be a great help in their social rehabilitation.

The Government of India appointed a National Expert Committee on Women Prisoners in May 1986: (i) to review conditions governing the treatment of women offenders in penal and correctional institutions and in police lock-ups; (ii) to examine the efficacy of institutional services for the reformation and rehabilitation of women offenders; and (iii) to suggest measures for ensuring effective handling of women offenders at various stages of the criminal justice process. The Committee, appointed under the chairmanship of Justice Krishna Iyer, submitted its report in 1987. The important recommendations pertained to work, wages, training, education, social contacts, parole release, and care of children. Some of the recommendations were as follows (*Report of National Expert Committee on Women Prisoners*, 1989: 90-92):

- The treatment of female prisoners should emphasise not their exclusion from the community but their continuing part in it. Community agencies should, therefore, be enlisted wherever possible to assist the staff of the institution in the task of social rehabilitation of the prisoners.
- Every institution (prison) should have social workers charged with the duty of maintaining and improving all desirable relations of prisoner with her family and valuable social agencies.
- Treatment should be individualised and for this purpose a flexible system of classifying prisoners in groups should be adopted.
- Treatment should be such as will encourage prisoners' self-respect and develop sense of responsibility.

- Prisons should use all the remedial, educational and moral forces of assistance which may enable the female offenders to lead a law-abiding and self-supporting life.
- It is not necessary to provide the same degree of security for every group of prisoners. It is desirable to provide varying degrees of security according to the needs of different groups.
- The medical services of the institution should seek to detect and treat any physical or mental illnesses or defects which may hamper the prisoner's rehabilitation.
- Before the completion of sentence, it is desirable that the necessary steps be taken to ensure prisoners' gradual return to life in society. This may include release on trial under some kind of supervision which must not be entrusted to the police.
- Efficient after-care programme may be provided by the government and/or private agencies which may be directed towards the lessening of prejudice against the prisoner.

Very often women criminals are themselves responsible for becoming victims of crime or deviant or aberrant behaviour. Let us take the example of a woman who is criminally assaulted by her brother-in-law, frequently beaten by her husband, denied the legitimate share in her husband's/father's land and property by her kin, or forced by circumstances to help her husband in illegal economic pursuits. What happens when such a woman endeavours to free herself from the stultifying life her family imposes upon her? More often than not, the freedom and the redressal are sought, may be unintentionally, through behaviour which ultimately is labelled as 'crime'. Thus, since a large number of crimes committed by women are due to their adjustment problems of interpersonal relations in family and are not due to their criminal tendencies or disorganised personalities, there is a great need for a flexible sentencing policy for female criminals. Since almost all female offenders (about 99%) are first offenders, and since criminal behaviour is not a significant part of their life organisations, their imprisonment and banishment from society fail to bring about the required change in attitudes and values inimical towards society. The sentence has to be adjusted to the character and the treatment needs of the offenders and should take into account the causal factors in their crimes. The present system of police investigation and punishment needs to be replaced by a system based on *social investigation* and consideration of personality make-up and the circumstances in which the crime was committed. Sentences wholly unrelated to the feelings, attitudes and values of the offenders, and the compelling situations and circumstances in which these develop, are less likely to succeed in their retributive, deterrent or reformative aims.

References

Adler, Freda, M., *Sisters in Crime*, McGraw-Hill Book Co., New York, 1975.

Ahuja, Ram, *Female Offenders in India*, Meenakshi Prakashan, Meerut, 1969.

— "Female Murderers in India", *Indian Journal of Social Work*, Bombay, October 1970.

— "Inmates' Adjustment to Prison Subculture: A New Model and a New Perspective", *Indian Journal of Social Work*, Bombay, October 1983.

Bhanot, M.L. and Misra Surat, "Criminality Amongst Women", *Bureau of Police Research and Development*, New Delhi 1979.

Bilmoria, Rani, "Homicides by Females", *Indian Journal of Criminology*, Vol. 3, January 1983.

Cohen, A.K. *Delinquent Boys*, The Free Press, Glencoe, Illinois, 1955.

Devasia, L. and Devasia, V.V., *Female Criminals and Female Victims*, Dattsons Publishers, Nagpur, 1989.

Gibbons, Don C., *Society, Crime and Criminal Careers*, Prentice Hall, New Jersey, 1977.

Kingsley, Davis, "The Sociology of Prostitution", *American Sociological Review*, October 1937.

Klein, Dorie, "The Etiology of Female Crime", *Issues in Criminology*, Fall 1973.

Lombroso, Cesare, *The Female Offender*, Appleton, New York, 1903.

Misra and Gautam, "Female Criminality, Causes and Consequences", *Readings in Criminology*, Souvenir Volume, Calcutta 1982.

Mukherjee, S.K. and Scutt Jocelynne, A., *Women and Crime*, George Allen and Unwin Ltd., Sydney 1981.

Pollak, Otto, *The Criminality of Women*, University of Pennsylvania, Philadelphia, 1950.

Report of National Expert Committee on Women Prisoners, Vol. I. and II, Government of India, Department of Women and Child Development, New Delhi, 1990.

Scutt, Jocelynne A., "Role Conditioning Theory: An Explanation for Disparity in Male and Female Criminality", *The Australian and New Zealand Journal of Criminality*, Vol. 9, No. 1, March 1976.

Sharma, B.R., "Crime and Women: A Psycho-Diagnostic Study of Female Criminality", *Indian Institute of Public Administration*, New Delhi, 1990.

Simon, Rita James, *Women and Crime*, Lexington Mass, D.C. Heath and Co., 1975.

Smart, Carol, *Women, Crime and Criminology: A Feminist Critique*, Routledge and Kegan Paul, London, 1976.

Sohan, Neera Kuckreja, "A Socio-Demographic Study of Women Prisoners" (unpublished Ph. D. thesis), Poona University, 1986.

Chapter 6

Organised Crime

Organised crime is crime based on a cooperative effort like an organised business. Lindesmith ("Organised Crime", *The Annals of the American Academy of Political and Social Science*, September 1941: 19) has defined it as "crime that involves the cooperation of several persons or groups for its successful execution". According to Gordon Hawkins (Cf. Radzinowicz, *et al.*, *Crime and Justice*, Vol. I, 1971: 374), organised crime involves: (a) association of a small group of criminals for the execution of a certain type of crime, (b) chalking out plans by which detection may be avoided, (c) development of a fund of money for organising criminal activities and providing protection to members, and (d) maintaining political connections by means of which immunity may be secured in case of detection. Thorsten Sellin (1963: 12-19) has described organised crime as "an enterprise organised for the purpose of making economic gain through illegal activities". Pick-pocketing, robbery, burglary, smuggling, drug trafficking, prostitution, gambling are some of the crimes which involve association of a few criminals working as a team. The motive for committing these crimes is profit. Numerically, organised crime does not involve a large proportion of criminals, but, for society it is considered to be a serious problem.

CHARACTERISTICS

Organised crime has following important characteristics (Cf. Caldwell, 1956: 73-74):

1. *Team work*: It involves association of a group of criminals which is relatively permanent and may even last decades.
2. *Hierarchical structure*: It has a structure with grades of authority from the lowest to the highest, involving a system of specifically defined relationships with mutual obligations and privileges.
3. *Planning*: It involves advance arrangements for successfully committing crimes, minimising risks and insuring safety and protection.
4. *Centralised authority*: It functions on the basis of centralised control and authority which is vested either in the hands of one individual or a few members.
5. *Reserved fund*: It maintains a reserve fund from profits which serves as capital for criminal enterprises, seeking help of the police, lawyers and even politicians, and for providing security to the arrested members and their families.
6. *Specialisation*: Some groups specialise in just one crime while some others may be simultaneously engaged in multiple crimes. Those groups which are engaged in multiple crimes are more powerful and influential.
7. *Division of labour*: Organised crime involves delegation of duties and responsibilities and specialisation of functions.
8. *Violence*: It depends upon use of force and violence to commit crimes and to maintain internal discipline and restrain external competition.
9. *Monopoly*: It has expansive and monopolistic tendencies. Initially, organised criminal gangs operate in a limited area, and are engaged in a limited type of crime with a limited number of persons, but, gradually they expand into a wider range of activities extended over large geographical areas, involving a large number of carefully selected criminals. In whatever area they operate, they secure monopoly in their criminal enterprises. They do not hesitate to use violence or threats of violence to eliminate competition.
10. *Protective measures*: It arranges permanent protection against interference from law-enforcement authorities and other agencies of government. The protective measures include contacts with policemen, lawyers, doctors, politicians, judges, and influential persons in society. Giving money in cash or in gifts, providing help in elections, threatening their competitors, and arranging their (influential persons') foreign trips are some of the methods used by these gangs to secure protection and avoid arrest and conviction.

11. *Conduct norms*: It frames rules of conduct, policies of administration, and methods of operation for members and for the operation of crime. This helps in maintaining discipline, efficiency, loyalty, obedience, and mutual confidence. Penalties are imposed for violating rules.

ORGANISED STRUCTURE

Clinard and Quinney (*Criminal Behaviour Systems: A Typology*, 1967: 383) have stated that organised crime has a hierarchical structure of positions. Burgess (Cf. Clinard, *Sociology of Deviant Behaviour*, 1963: 273-84) has compared this hierarchical structure with a feudal system. At the top of the pyramid arc 'Lords'—powerful leaders who take important decisions and run the organisation. These leaders maintain a master-serf relationship with other persons in the feudal structure. A middle echelon of gangsters—'henchmen and lieutenants'—carry out commands of the leaders. At the bottom of the structure are 'runners', who are persons marginally associated with organised crime. These are criminals who work as prostitutes, carry narcotics or other illegal goods, pick pockets, supply alcohol, and directly deal with the public.

Hierarchical Structure

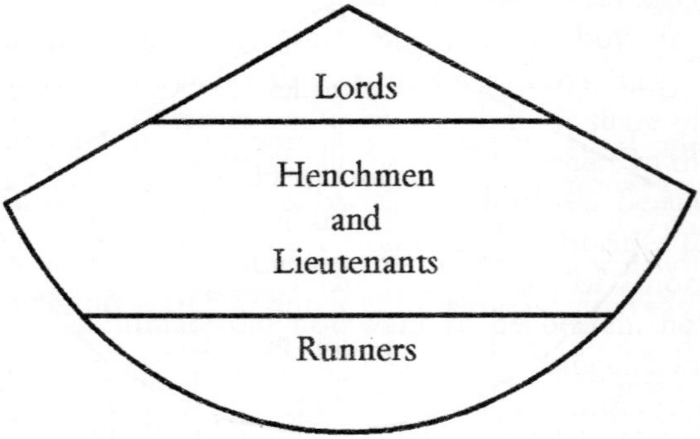

The hierarchical structure is held together by personal loyalties, a code of conduct, a chain of command, and antagonistic attitude towards conventional society. The hierarchical structure affects career of the criminals, especially those lower in the hierarchy. They have a long record of crimes against them and never think of ending their criminal careers. These bottom gangsters are either on the payroll of the organisation or get a cut of the profits. The gangsters at the middle level are sometimes pulled up from the lower levels and sometimes directly recruited from large cities, having criminal record of armed robberies and murders, and having a perception of themselves as 'tough' guys. Some 'lieutenants' sometimes become leaders at the top.

Leaders in the organised crime live segmented lives, retiring to the seclusion of respectability. Their commitment, nevertheless, remains with the world of crime, where, in detachment from the values of the larger society, they receive their prestige, power and a lifestyle of luxury.

Organised crime may thus provide a person with an opportunity for a lifetime career in crime. Walter Reckless (1955: 203) is of the opinion that selection of a career in organised crime is apparently dependent upon the existing social conditions of the area in which a person lives. However, little is known of the specific mobility of a criminal from one position to another, once he is a part of the hierarchy of organised crime. The career histories of organised criminals are not usually available because of the immunity of these persons from detection and imprisonment.

TYPES OF ORGANISED CRIME

Organised crime has three major types: gang criminality, racketeering, and syndicated crime. The first has simple characteristics while the last one has a fully developed form because of which it is considered to be most dangerous to society.

Gang Criminality

This type of criminality includes kidnapping, extortion, robbery, vehicle theft, etc. on a large scale. Gangs are composed of tough and hardened criminals who do not hesitate to kill, assault, or use violence. They are equipped with modern pistols, bullet-proof vests, cars, etc. The gang criminals are efficient, disciplined but dangerous. Barnes and Teeters (1951: 36) have said: "they live violently and expect violence." Their activities are spread over a large geographical area, moving from place to place but reuniting at prearranged hideouts. They are registered as hardened and habitual criminals in police records.

These criminals are recruited from among ex-convicts, escaped murderers, professional gangsters, and high-powered robbers. The Tyagi gang in Delhi, the Radha Yadav gang in Champaran district in Bihar, the Arun Gandhi gang in Bombay, the Vikram Singh gang in Uttar Pradesh, and the Shrikant gang in Bihar are some of the notorious gangs operating in different parts of our country, and, are engaged in robberies, kidnapping small children and wealthy individuals for obtaining ransoms, murder, extortion, and smuggling. There exist inter-rivalries among most of these gangs. Some of the gangs are also affiliated to the syndicates, operating on a very large scale.

Some gangs organise activities and furnish brains to individuals and groups engaged in anti-social activities, taking a cut of the loot or a fixed amount of money for the help rendered. The gangs float a score of satellites including restaurants, gambling dens, underworld messengers, women and children, and hangers-on. In December 1995, a boy was arrested at Marwar railway station in Rajasthan travelling by train and carrying Rs. 45,000 in cash in his especially stitched vest-pockets. He revealed working for a gang. From time to time, these gangs are hunted down by the police and destroyed, though most often the gangs operate with the active co-operation of the police. Occasionally, the law enforcement officers arrest some members and even kill some others, claiming the liquidation of an underworld empire.

Racketeering

This is an activity of an organised criminal gang engaged in extortion of money from both legitimate and illegitimate business through intimidation of force. It also involves dishonest way of getting money by deceiving or cheating people, selling worthless goods and articles, adulterated commodities, spurious drugs and so forth. The racketeers, unlike organised criminal gangs do not take away all the profits but allow the owners of the illegitimate business to continue their operations like prostitution, gambling, liquor trafficking, drug peddling, etc., but give them (racketeers) regular fixed money. Sometimes, businessmen engaged in fierce competition in legitimate business, employers and labour unions involved in conflicts, landlords unable to get their houses/shops vacated from tenants, and politicians trying to eliminate their rivals hire the services of gangsters and seek their 'help' by paying them their 'fees'. In some cases, these racketeers refuse to leave and continue to extort 'fees' from their former 'employers'. A favourite approach of these racketeers is to approach a businessman, suggesting that he needed protection and that it could be furnished at a stipulated monthly fee. The businessman, even if he does not need protection, is forced to accept racketeers' 'suggestion'. Once he starts paying the 'fee', he continues to pay till the racketeer functions. The racketeers thus do nothing but live on the blood and labour of others, collecting tribute by intimidation, force and terrorism. Assault and destruction of property often accompany the organisation of the racket.

Racketeering has found a fertile field in 'protecting' restaurant owners and big shop owners from possible harm. By means of intimidation, racketeers are able to extort large sums of money from the proprietors. Failure on their part to subscribe to the protection plan results in the destruction of furniture, in the forcible taking away of goods and commodities, in the creation of nuisance by constantly sitting in restaurants/shops, or in personal violence. Such demonstration of force by the 'protectors' usually convinces proprietors and other businessmen that protection is worth the money demanded for it.

According to Caldwell (*op. cit.*, 78), the racketeering gang is divided in two groups—the 'brains' and the 'muscles'. The former do the thinking, issue orders, solicit new business and arrange for protection. The latter do the beating, destroying, plundering and even killing, i.e., all what is called the 'rough stuff'. Fitzgerald (1951: 163-64) has stated that sometimes the 'brains' also do the jobs of the 'muscles' to maintain their leadership, enforce their authority, demonstrate proper techniques, to preserve their reputation.

Syndicate Crime

This is furnishing illegal goods and services by an organised criminal gang, often called 'mafia'. The illegal goods could be drugs, liquor, etc. while the illegal services could be call-girls, gambling and so forth. The syndicates create their own 'business' procedures, usually operating from established headquarters. They avoid using violence which differentiates them from organised criminal gangs, who frequently use violence or threat of violence. Society knows the members of these syndicates as respectable citizens living in posh residential areas, freely associating with high-status persons and engaged in lawful earning pursuits. The syndicates generally operate in big metropolitan areas which happen to be big centres of communication, transportation and distribution of goods.

The leaders of big crime syndicates periodically gather at fixed places to discuss problems of mutual interest and concern. While the scope and effect of the criminal operations of syndicates vary from one area to another, the wealthiest and most influential groups operate in Mumbai, Delhi, Chennai and Calcutta and the capital cities of some states like Patna, Lucknow, Ahmedabad, Hyderabad, etc. Each syndicate has a boss and an underboss. The underboss collects information and relays messages to the boss and passes instructions down to underlings. In some cases, there is no underboss but the boss has an advisor or a counsellor. Below the level of the underboss are criminals who act as 'intermediaries' between the upper and the lower level personnel. Some of these intermediaries act as chiefs of operating units. The lowest level members are ordinary criminals who report to the 'intermediaries'. Outside the structure of the syndicate are a large number of employees and agents who do most of the actual work in various criminal enterprises.

RULES OF CONDUCT

There is no evidence that various criminal organisations follow one particular code of behaviour. Cressey (*The Annals*, November, 1967: 163) has observed that no hard data is at all available on 'the law' of criminal organisations. Even if some groups have a code of conduct, it is unwritten. Yet, on the basis of information collected from different criminal organisations, Cressey has suggested that the members of the organised gangs, rackets and syndicates generally work on the basis of the following directives (*ibid.*: 175-78; *also see*, Barlow, Hugh D., *Introduction to Criminology*, Little Brown and Co., Boston, 1978: 274):

- Be loyal to the members of the organisation to maintain unity in the gang.
- Do not interfere with each other's interests.
- Do not be an informer.
- Be rational and work as a team-member.
- Do the assigned work quietly, safely and in a profitable manner.
- Keep your eyes and ears open and your mouth shut.
- Be a man of honour, and respect womanhood, and your elders.
- Don't engage in battles if you can't win.

Cressey points out that the conduct code of organised criminals is similar to the codes adopted by prisoners, professional thieves and other groups whose activities and conditions of existence bring them into confrontation with official authority and generate the need for 'private' government as a means of controlling the conduct of the members. Other authors have also made similar observations. Salerno and Tompkins (1969: 105; *also see*, Barlow, *op. cit.*, 74) have presented a more detailed code as the 'law' governing what they call the 'crime confederation'. Among the unwritten rules and directives are: maintain secrecy; put the organisation before individual, consider other members' families sacred, reveal nothing to your wife, do not strike another member, and do not disobey orders. While these two authors collected information from organised crime informants and police intelligence, Ianni (*Family Business*, 1973: 150-55) got information through participant observation of several groups and watching members' behaviour. After observing, he sought regularities that had enough frequency to suggest that the behaviour resulted from the pressures of shared social system rather than from idiosyncratic ideas and bahaviour. The three basic rules of bahaviour he found were: primary loyalty to the organisation rather than to individuals; doing nothing which brings disgrace on the organisation; and not reporting or discussing organisation's matters outside the group. Some other codes which he found stressed were: don't tell the police; don't cheat your partner in the network, don't be a coward; and try to "fit in" your attitudes and actions with the group.

The code adopted by any one criminal organisation reflects far more than the mere fact that it is a secret association engaged in regular criminal activities. The factors which are likely to influence the conduct rules, which are adopted and preserved are: how and why the participants came together in the first place (bonding relationships or linkages), how long the organisation has been operating, how small or big is the organisation, the cultural heritage of its major participants, and the nature and range of its activities.

SURVIVAL MECHANISMS OR PERMANENT IMMUNITY

What is it that makes organised crime persist and survive? Five factors appear to be important in this context: structural organisation and role performance, public tolerance, code of conduct, nature of criminal law, and immunity measures. Structural organisation and maintenance of secrecy by indulging in pseuclo-legitimate activities and code of conduct have already been analysed in the preceding pages. Here we will focus on permanent immunity and public tolerance.

The survival of the organised crime depends upon 'the fix'. To put the 'fix in' and maintain important connections with those in government and law, organised crime groups typically have one or more members assigned to corrupt officials to maintain good relations with them. These members may be called 'corrupters'. The corrupter may be found anywhere in the organisational hierarchy. His job is to bribe, buy, intimidate, negotiate and persuade policemen, public officials, politicians, judges, businessmen and anyone else who might help the organised crime group members to maintain immunity from arrest, prosecution and punishment. Cressey (*op. cit.*, 248) has called this (political) objective the 'nullification of government'. According to him, this is sought at two levels: (a) At the lower level are the agencies for law enforcement and the administration of justice, i.e., a policeman, a prosecutor, a magistrate, or a licence administrator. By giving bribes to these people, 'corrupter' in the organised gang/racket/syndicate 'nullifies' the law-enforcement process. (b) At the upper level are legislative agencies—central and state legislatures as well as municipal corporations. When a gang-boss supports a candidate for political office, he does so in an attempt to deprive honest citizens of their democratic voice, thus 'nullifying' the democratic process. As such, nullifying law-enforcement officers and legislators is 'nullification of government', which acts as an important survival mechanism in organised crime.

It could be said that permanent immunity is achieved by organised crime groups in several ways:

1. The leaders of organised crime are not usually arrested and prosecuted because they stay behind the scenes of operation.
2. Persons lower in the hierarchy, if arrested, are likely to be released by action taken by their superiors. Such release and avoidance of prosecution are assured through what is popularly known as the 'fix'. Persons (like policemen, judges, politicians, doctors, businessmen) not directly involved in criminal activity contribute, for various reasons, to the protection of organised criminals.
3. Protection is secured by gaining political power through contributions to political parties and political organisations, particularly for contesting elections, and 'purchasing' the support of members of the opposition parties. Many elected politicians thus owe their election to organised criminals.
4. Regular 'pay-offs' to law-enforcement officials also provide protection.
5. A certain amount of immunity results from public toleration of organised crime, since it provides the public with illicit and desired services, such as alcohol, narcotics, call-girls, etc.
6. Immunity is also provided by the functioning of law itself. Sometimes there are such loopholes in the laws that lawyers manage to save their clients (criminals) from legal action. Lack of effective legislation and weak law enforcement are a reflection of official toleration of organised crime.
7. Organised crime is able to evade law through infiltration in

legitimate business. Sometimes organised crime and legitimate business may even mutually assist each other. George Vold (1958: 237) has commented that the interdependence of the underworld of crime and the underworld of business assures the maintenance of both systems.

SOCIETAL REACTION

Society supports or tolerates many types of organised crime indirectly, if not directly. It has been persuasively argued that organised crime is the result of the particular structure of our society. Donald Taft (1964) has said that the motives for organised crime are largely the same as those valued so highly in the free enterprise system. Organised crime, like legitimate business, attempts to achieve maximum returns with a minimum of expenditure through efficient organisation and skilled staff. The difference is that legitimate business operates within the law and organised crime operates outside the law. Lindesmith has forcefully pointed out that factors like indifference to public affairs, general disregard for law, profit-motivated economics, and questionable political practices produce a fertile place for organised crime. People in society also tolerate this crime because it gratifies many of their needs. The claim of the people and the law-enforcement officials that they try to prohibit illegal practices is nothing but hypocrisy and self-deception. Robert Woetzel (1963: 8) has described the co-existence of law and lawlessness as follows: "The vast majority of people today would like to have their proverbial cake and eat it too, by theoretically affirming values which they hold dear and at the same time reserving for themselves a certain leeway in realising wishes which may not always correspond to these values. As a result, law and a high degree of lawlessness exist side by side, and moralists and gangsters complement each other. It is this situation as well as the toleration of illegal services which act as a serious handicap in the control and prevention of organised crime. The public demands action sporadically as intermittent, sensational disclosures (like sugar scandal, fodder scandal) reveal corruption caused by organised crime. Without sustained public pressure, law enforcement officers and politicians have little incentive to address themselves to combating organised crime. So long political corruption exists in the country (which in India has now assumed scandalous proportions), a drive against organised crime will have no meaning. The vicious circle perpetuates itself. Corrupt politicians will not act unless the public so demands; the public will not insist for action till it gets the required services provided by organised crime; and the police will not take prevention seriously till it gets its due share."

ORGANIZED CRIME IN INDIA

After independence, organised crime in India expanded into a wider range of activities and extended over larger geographical areas. The single event which brought about the greatest change in organised crime was the idea of prohibition, forbidding by law the sale and distribution of alcoholic beverages. Organised crime was able to provide illegal liquor demanded by a large number of people. So many groups/gangs came to be engaged in manufacturing illicit liquor that they started fighting with one another. Inter-rivalries amongst them led to widespread use of violence. Quite a few of these gangs, the strongest, finally dominated the scene. In the 1970s, many of these gangs extended their activity to drug trafficking. Political wranglings for separate states created a large demand for arms and weapons. Some gangs/syndicates started supplying illicit arms to insurgents, terrorists, naxalites and agitators. Some gangs further extended their activities to supplying girls to rich people in Islamic countries. Thus, the organised groups because of the large sums of money they had amassed and the elaborate organisation they possessed, not only widely expanded their illegal activities but also started acting as kings of the underworld.

The modern era of organised crime is represented by the crime syndicate. Organised crime has been expanded to the point where policemen, political leaders, law officers, etc. have also come to be associated with the gangs and syndicates. Many gang leaders contested elections to assemblies, parliament, municipal corporations, and gram panchayats, thereby securing political status which enables them to widen their social contacts, and use the influence of powerful people for escaping arrest after committing crimes. These gangs and syndicates today not only enjoy large financial gains but also enjoy immunity from interference and possess monopolistic control in large geographical areas.

Major Criminal Enterprises

Five major enterprises providing illicit profits in India are: Numbers betting (i.e., *matka*), drug trafficking, estate racketeering, automobile thefts, and supplying illicit weapons to terrorists and insurgents. On a lower level, the two main criminal enterprises are: kidnapping for extortion and supplying girls for prostitution.

Number Betting

Some people believe that illegal gambling in general and *matka* business (numbers racket) in particular are on the decline following the spread of state lotteries, but *matka* activities, as easy sources of money-making, continue to exist in a large number of cities. Numbers betting is predominantly a feature of urban poor life. One estimate is that more than one-fourth of daily wage earners and low-salary class workers (like rikshaw-pullers, sweepers, kerosene-oil sellers, auto-rikshaw drivers, masons, labourers engaged in construction work, and domestic servants) spend an average of twenty rupees a week on numbers. Numbers betting is simple in concept and easy to do. The gambler simply picks any one or two digit number and bets that this number will correspond to the winning number, selected in accordance with some predetermined procedure. The pay-off exceeds between five and twenty times the amount invested. Earlier, this betting business was done by individuals but now organisations have taken over this business because an organisation can manage money and muscle to keep off the cops and politicians from breaking up the game and shaking down the players and operators. Secondly, only a big organisation can pay up when the bank gets hit very hard. The organisation of this business is simple. The 'bets' are picked up by 'agents' in shops, office-buildings, factories, or simply on the street-corner. The 'agents' pass the money and betting slips on to local 'collectors' in charge of their neighbourhood. The 'collectors' pass the money to the 'controller' (boss) or 'owner'. At pay-off time, the money simply follows the reverse route. The agents and collectors get a commission on the money that is collected. Several states have banned *matka* business but it still operates on a large scale.

Drug Trafficking

This involves carrying drugs from one country to another country or from one city to another city, and their distribution to addicts. The need for organisation, contacts, and large sums of money puts the business outside the reach of most individuals and small criminal groups. There are millions of persons addicted to drugs including heroin, opium, cocaine, etc. These addicts get their supplies from 'pimps' who get them from organised groups engaged in this crime. It is a known fact that police knows the gangs engaged in these activities but because they are 'fixed up', nobody gets arrested. Not everyone who uses drugs becomes an addict, but for those who do, the addiction often leads to a life of violence and crime. Tragically, many of these casualties are teenagers and young persons.

Estate Racketeering

Some gangs are engaged in getting houses and shops vacated from tenants after 'charging' huge amounts of money from the house owners. These gangs have the support of the police who get a share of the 'earned' money.

Automobile Thefts

A good number of organised crime efforts are directed today at the kind of thievery that promises high returns while avoiding high risks, i.e., thefts of cars, motor-cycles, and scooters. Houses in big cities these days lack parking facilities which compel people living in them to keep their vehicles outside their houses. The 'experts' in stealing cars and two-wheelers have developed such skills of unlocking these vehicles that they can easily drive away these vehicles. Efficient organisation is required for changing paint colour, parts and number plates and for selling the stolen vehicles in different cities. This requires money, muscle power and contacts. This would explain the involvement of big crime organisations in this activity.

Supply of Illegal Weapons

States in the North-East, Kashmir, Punjab, Bihar, Bengal, and Tamil Nadu are some of the areas where insurgents, terrorists, naxalites, and agitators are engaged in fighting the police and the military and threatening the masses for achieving their political goals. They get the required weapons from organised criminal groups who get them from neighbouring countries at cheap rates. The arrest of six crew members of an aircraft owned by a London-based company run by a New Zealander, who dropped a large cache of sophisticated weapons in Puralia district of West Bengal on December 17, 1995 is a recent example of organised gangs engaged in systematic gun-running operations. Amongst the main accused Indians, one was from Bihar holding an Indian passport while the other held a Singaporean passport.

Taking all these crimes together, it may be pointed out that the conditions that support these organised crimes include: politics emerging as a source of personal profit, earning money by easy means, vast unemployment which frustrates the youth, corruption in getting jobs, changing cultural values stressing individualism, an entrenched philosophy of acquiring more and more material goods for leading a luxurious life, and a tolerance of the 'fix'.

Apart from their patently illegal enterprises, organised crime groups have infiltrated the world of legitimate business. While any complete list of different businesses in which organised crime groups are involved would be near impossible to compile, some pseudo-legitimate business enterprises could be identified. These are: restaurants and hotels, banking, real estate, construction, garment manufacture, stocks and bonds, automobile sales, and running liquor shops. Involvement of organised crime groups in legitimate business has been prompted by the following considerations: getting a cover for illegal activities, escaping from law-enforcement agencies, getting a respectable position in society, maintaining contacts with influential people, and finding an additional source of income. For example, owning a transport firm provides a means of transporting stolen property, running alcohol shops acts as a cover for bootlegging, and so forth.

Several gangs are engaged in organised crime in Mumbai. Of these, four are major gangs headed by Dawood Ibrahim, Chhota Rajan, Arun Gawli and Amar Naik. All other smaller gangs owe allegiance to one or the other of these four gangs. These gangs are mainly engaged in drug peddling, kidnapping and extortion rackets, real estate rackets, gold smuggling, contract murders, and running Hawala. Gang rivalries and feuds are now common in Bombay. The murder of the Managing Director of East West Airlines in Bombay in November 1995 was a brutal manifestation of gang feuds. Chhota Rajan was at one time described as the right-hand man of Dawood Ibrahim but now there is an ongoing feud between the two. After Dawood fled Bombay in 1985 and after his alleged role in bomb blasts in Bombay in March 1993, Chhota Rajan emerged as the new don of Bombay city's underworld. The rivalry between the two came into open when Chhota Rajan felt that Dawood was murdering his men to clip his wings (*Sunday*, December 1995). Dawood is now said to be operating from Dubai and Karachi through various underworld factions led by Chhota Shakeel, Abu Salem and Sharad Shetty. They get assistance from the Amar Naik gang. Chhota Rajan is operating from Kuala Lumpur (Malaysia). Arun Gawli (who at present is behind bars) is an arch-rival of Dawood. Though the activities of Bombay's underworld have been somewhat subdued since March 1993, the inter-gang fights continue. Dawood, at one time, was considered to be the king of Bombay's underworld. He had expanded the area of his operations to touch every aspect of the city's life—politics, film industry, construction, hotels, Hawala, horse-racing, etc. All these dons have the right political connections and the right men on the street operating for them. Their aides and supporters contest elections in assemblies and parliament. They also have many political functionaries on their pay-roll. They have thus the power of the gun, money, and musclemen to control the underworld. They have gained respectability to such an extent that it is almost a matter of privilege for any socialite to be seen at their get-togethers.

Over the last six years or so (i.e., between 1993 and 1999), organised crime in Mumbai's underworld has undergone a significant change in several ways. Most gangs, which survived for almost three decades on smuggling and extortion, have now got involved in real estate rackets. And thus has begun the builder-gangster nexus. Gangsters of the underworld get slums cleared and help builders in getting possession of the disputed properties. It is estimated that one don (Bhai Thakur, who earlier operated under Dawood but has now cut off all connections with him and surrendered to the police in early 1995) made over Rs. 2,000 crore by dealing in property. Gawli, Amar Naik, and Chhota Rajan also are engaged in estate rackets running into crores. In fact, to a large extent, these gangsters today depend heavily on real estate for their growth and indeed survival. Further, after the communal riots in 1993, the underworld gangsters are now organised on communal lines.

Organised crime will continue to persist till law-makers enact laws rendering illegal any activities, products and services demanded by significant numbers of the population. Organised crime makes bulk of its profits through supplying illegal commodities and services. The public helps organised crime survive by demanding illegal products and services. Change in public behaviour, attitudes, and perceptions is not easy to achieve. The public officials to whom we look for protection and guidance themselves present a warped picture. Politicians perhaps believe that too much effort spent exposing organised crime could be damaging to their future prospects. Given these numerous social, cultural, political, legal, and economic conditions, organised crime is there to stay, at least in the foreseeable future.

References

Bloch, Herbert and Geis, Gilbert, *Man, Crime and Society*, Random House, New York, 1962.

Clinard, M.B. and Quinney, R., *Criminal Behaviour Systems: A Typology*, Holt, Rinehart and Winston, New York, 1967.

Clinard, Marshall, *Sociology of Deviant Behaviour*, Holt, Rinehart and Winston Inc., New York, 1957.

Johnson, Elmer, *Crime, Correction and Society*, The Dorsey Press, Illinois, 1978.

Reckless, Walter, *The Crime Problem*, (2nd edn.). Appleton Century Crofts Inc., New York, 1955.

Radzinowicz, Leon and Wolfgang, M.E., *The Criminal in Society*, (Vol. I), Basic Book Inc. Publishers, New York, 1971.

Chapter 7

Occupational (White-Collar) Crime

Sutherland was the first criminologist who drew attention in 1939 to the nature and effects of white-collar or occupational crime in society. Occupational crime refers to "those illegal activities that occur in connection with a person's job or work". The conventional term 'white-collar crime' is narrower. It makes reference to the socio-economic status but not to the occupational status of the offender. According to Sutherland's original definition, white-collar crime is "a violation of the criminal law by a person of the upper socio-economic class in the course of his occupational activities." Sutherland added that "the upper socio-economic class is defined not only by its wealth but also by its respectability and prestige in the society" (Sutherland, *American Sociological Review*, Feb. 1940: 1-12; *also see*, *White-Collar Crime*, 1949).

Marshall Clinard (*The Black Market*, Rinehart & Co., New York, 1952: 127) has defined white-collar crime as "a violation of the law committed primarily by groups such as businessmen, professional men, and politicians in connection with their occupations". Frank Hartung (*American Journal of Sociology*, July 1950: 25-34) defines white-collar crime as "a violation of law regarding business which is committed for a firm by a firm or its agents in the conduct of its business".

Some people in their enthusiasm to widen the scope of white-collar crime have included those acts also in it which are immoral and unethical but not law-violations; for example, activities of a doctor who issues false certificates, performs illegal abortions, makes fraudulent reports, gives false testimony in accident cases and splits fees, or suggests all such pathological tests in a clinic of his choice which are not at all necessary for diagnosing the cause of the disease; or a lawyer who arranges the acquittal of his client through his contacts with the police without sending the case to the courts; or a politician who takes Rs. 5,000 to Rs. 10,000 for arranging transfer or a licence for a person. All these acts cannot be included in the definition of white-collar crime because they do not 'violate any law'. Morality and ethics are not the same as the law, and an immoral or unethical person is not necessarily a criminal. Anti-social acts or violation of conduct norms may be studied by criminologists but they cannot be defined as 'legal crimes'. It might be pointed out that Sutherland has labelled two types of persons as white-collar criminals who: (i) have been convicted by the courts, and (ii) who might have been convicted but through pressure or influence were able to avoid conviction, or for various reasons were taken before a commission or a board but not to a court. The focus is only on 'crime' as a legal term.

White-collar crime includes misrepresentation in advertising, violation of labour laws, violation of copyright and patent laws, and financial manipulations. However, all crimes committed by high-status people are not white-collar crimes. Only that crime which is specifically 'job-oriented', i.e., which occurs during the course of a person's job, is white-collar crime. A rich businessman who criminally assaults his lady secretary commits a crime but not an occupational crime to be termed as 'white-collar crime'. Sutherland's emphasis on 'high social status' of the offender results in the exclusion of a host of other occupation-related crimes that are similar to white-collar crimes but are committed by the lower-class people. For example, illegalities such as adulteration of milk by a milkman for public consumption, making unnecessary 'repairs' to radio and television sets, taking out few kilos of gas from the gas cylinder by the workman and so on are all occupational crimes (if law exists and prohibits them) but not white-collar crimes. Hence, the word that is preferred today for crime that is motivated by a person's legitimate occupation and context is 'occupational crime' and not 'white-collar crime'.

ELEMENTS OF OCCUPATIONAL CRIME

Several elements can be discerned in occupational crime. The more important ones are:

1. It involves violation of legal codes.
2. It takes place directly or indirectly in connection with a legitimate occupation.

3. It aims at gaining money.
4. The crime is not against a specific individual or a firm but is against society at large. There is therefore no specific victim who would complain.
5. Earlier only 'a person of high status' committing this crime was considered a (white-collar) criminal but now 'a person of any class violating law (different from one who commits an immoral or unethical act) in the course of occupational activity' is described as an occupational offender.
6. The organisation engaged in occupational (or white-collar) crime generally selects that crime which involves high stakes but carries the most negligible danger of detection and identification. Further, it is crime against which the victims are least likely to fight.
7. The offender (of this offence) does not regard himself as a criminal but considers himself as a respectable citizen. At the most, he regards himself 'a lawbreaker whose act has no victim'.
8. The organisation engaged in illegal occupational activity adopts a policy of 'fixing' cases. It is not only the law-enforcement officers who are 'fixed up' but the 'services' of politicians, bureaucrats and influential people are also used for 'protection'.
9. The effect of this crime is much more serious for society than an ordinary crime.

TYPES OF OCCUPATIONAL CRIMES

Herbert Edelhertz (1970: 73-75) has suggested the following four types of occupational crimes on the basis of motivation of the perpetrators:

1. Crimes committed by persons on an individual basis, e.g., income-tax evasion, bankruptcy frauds, credit purchases or taking loans with no intention to pay, and insurance fraud.
2. Crimes committed in the course of occupations by those operating in business, government, or other establishments, in violation of their duty of loyalty to the employer or client; e.g., bribery, kickbacks, embezzlement, and pilfering.
3. Crimes incidental to and in furtherance of business operations but not central to business purposes; e.g., food and drug violations, misrepresentation in advertising, and prescription fraud.
4. Crime as a business or as the central activity of a business; e.g., medical fraud schemes, lottery fraud schemes, mutual fund fraud

schemes, land and real estate frauds, charity and religious frauds and music pirating.

Block and Geis (*Man, Crime and Society*, 1970: 307) have classified occupational offenders into five groups on the basis of the nature of victim involved: (i) persons acting as individuals against other individuals (e.g., fraudulent lawyers, doctors), (ii) those committing crimes against business concerns that employ them (embezzlers), (iii) those in policy-making positions who commit crimes for their organisations (anti-trust violators), (iv) agents of an organisation who victimise the general public (advertising fraud), and (v) merchants victimising their customers (short-weighing). This method (of classifying occupational offenders on the basis of the nature of the victim involved) is simple. The victim could be employer, employee, public concern, government organisation, and so forth.

Some occupational crimes require less sophisticated complex technologies or social arrangements than others. "Commercial fraud" is one type of occupational crime which is found to be widespread in our country. It requires either a simple system of economic exchange like the manipulation of weights and measures or a simple division of labour. No wonder, consumer forums are becoming popular everywhere seeking justice from traders, shop-keepers, businessmen, and even government organisations like telephone departments (charging huge bills for phones which remain out of order for a long period), state electricity boards, water-works departments and so on. The consumer forums impose penalties and assess victim compensations.

Hugh Barlow (*op. cit.*: 227-30) has classified occupational crimes in six categories on the basis of special interests: embezzlement, financial fraud, adulteration, employee pilferage, consumer fraud, and shady land business. We will analyse each of them separately.

Embezzlement

This is a criminal activity which involves the conversion, to his own use, of funds or property by a servant, an employee, an agent, or any person who is entrusted all these (i.e., funds and property) by other person, say, master, employer, etc. Donald Cressay (1953: 19) has defined embezzlement as "the criminal violation of financial trust". This definition is, however, narrower. The broader definition considers those people as embezzlers who keep for themselves the goods that are in their legal possession by virtue of their roles as bailees for their employers/masters/other people. This crime (embezzlement) also includes selling/giving things in one's possession to some other person and pocketing the money received. With the expansion of commerce, trade, banking and business pursuits, the financial interests of the business community and employers necessitated additional protection under the criminal law because of which the existing laws were modified and their scope extended.

It is said that embezzlement by employees exceeds robberies. It has also been found that embezzlers generally belong to the middle income groups and rarely have a criminal record prior to their embezzling activities. They rarely think of themselves as criminals. One study revealed that the typical male embezzler is 35-45 years of age, married, and has one or two children. The main cause of his embezzlement is that either he has a daughter to marry, or construct a house of his own, or send his son for higher education, or has gambling habit. The number of female embezzlers is very small.

Financial Fraud

This is inducing someone to part with money or valuables through the use of deceit, lies, or misrepresentation. In simple words, this is also called cheating. Earlier, civil remedy was made available for 'trickery' but with the expansion of business and the growing complexities in commercial and industrial transactions, the business community asked for more legal protection and enactment of stringent laws for the offenders of this crime.

Adulteration or Violation of Laws Pertaining to Health and Safety

The production, distribution and sale of food and drug products are regulated by a variety of laws aimed at the protection of public health and safety. Adulteration of food products and sale of spurious drugs have gained prominence in the last five to six decades in all societies. Consumers' awareness of the threats posed to their health is enhanced partly through the changing experience of buying itself and partly through articles in newspapers, magazines and research findings in which dangers are spelt out in lurid and frightening details. The increasing alliance of quacks, vested interests of owners of industries supplying cosmetics, food products and pharmaceutical products, and corrupt doctors and crooks have all created dangerous situation for the people. But, as already stated, there exist many loopholes for avoiding the spirit of the law. The concerned law enforcement officials have failed to provide measures for safe and effective health devices. There are many food products which are not only adulterated since they contain toxic chemicals but are also prepared under insanitary conditions, mixed with unwholesome raw material—even manure—and often sold in deceptive and fraudulent manner. Lately, some state governments, having realised the inadequacy of legal controls and their ineffective enforcement have begun taking measures to control this occupational crime.

Employee Pilferage

This occupational crime is steadily increasing in our country in all government offices. It is virtually impossible to assess with accuracy losses caused by employee pilferage but estimates usually place them in millions of rupees annually. It is also said that employee theft is far more prevalent than shoplifting. The pilferage has now extended even to shop employees, university/college employees, warehouses, companies, etc. In non-retail business, the loss due to pilferage by employees is even harder to estimate because the companies find it difficult to keep track of all the property and valuables. It would be wrong to assume that employee pilferage is an exclusive activity of the lower-level employees. In one study in the United States by Norman Jaspen in 1964, it was estimated that 60 per cent of the pilferage is by employees at the executive or supervisory levels. Gerald Robin (*Journal of Research: Crime and Juvenile Delinquency*, 1969: 26-27) also noted that when executives are found stealing from the company, their thefts averaged larger amounts than those of the lower-level employees. Barlow (*op. cit.*, 1978: 233-34) has referred to four kinds of employee pilferage: (a) casual thievery, systematic thievery and repetitive thievery, (b) thievery by lone individuals and thievery by groups of employees working together, (c) thievery that victimises the company and thievery that victimises clients or other employees, and (d) theft of cash, tools, merchandise, parts, finished products, and materials.

Consumer Fraud

Consumers become victims of fraud in different ways. Three important ways are sales, advertising, and repairs. Sales fraud refers to selling products of low quality by describing them as products of high quality; refusing to change the defective product or repair it during the guarantee period; fraud concerning the effectiveness of a product; and fraud of concealing information regarding the product which may prove to be harmful. Many things which only a few decades ago were considered 'luxuries' are considered 'necessities' today—cooking gas, refrigerators, two-wheeler vehicles, pressure-cookers, germ-killing medicines, and so forth—largely because the companies selling them have convinced us that it is so. When things are considered necessities, people want to purchase them. Manufacturers and sellers use fraudulent ploys to attract people to purchase them, making false claims regarding the effectiveness of the product and assuring repair services, etc. But soon the people realise that they have been cheated by purchasing these products. Sales boys and sales girls misrepresenting the quality of products gain entry in consumers' homes and sell their products at concessional rates. But soon the fraud is discovered and cases of cheating are reported in newspapers.

Misrepresentation in advertising means that what the prospective buyers are told about the product is false, deceptive or misleading. For example, advertising that a particular scooter gives 60 kilometres a litre of petrol when actually it gives only 35-40 kilometres is advertising fraud. Advertising that a particular cream removes face pimples in seven days when it does not remove pimples at all or sometimes may even cause skin irritation and other troublesome reactions is advertising fraud. Similar misrepresentation may be found in the advertisements of cement, cooking 'masalas', medicines, cosmetics, etc. Millions and millions of rupees are spent annually on advertising products on television, radio, newspapers and magazines. This is an enormous investment in the art of persuasion. If the advertisement is only to promote the sale of the product by making people aware of it, spending money on it may be described as rational and logical, but companies try to make considerable profit by concealing harmful information about the product or exaggerating its efficacy. This dishonesty, misrepresentation, deception, and falsehood in sales promotion is a fraud on consumers.

Similar frauds may also be found when it comes to measuring and weighing things. A grocer may give short measure when he weighs out ten kilograms of sugar for a customer, who may be a loser by half a kilogram. Likewise, instead of giving five metres of cloth as demanded, the cloth-merchant may give only four and a half metres and charge for five metres. He too is guilty of giving short measure and customer is once again a loser. The actual content of a package or container may be less than what is printed on it.

The victim of fraud can be anyone but the most common victims are consumers—persons who buy goods and services from people in the business of selling. This is also called 'consumer fraud'. This reaches all the way from one-man small business to the manufacturers of consumer goods, large companies, retail business organisations, etc. With modern packaging practices, a shopper in a grocery shop rarely thinks of checking the weight or the quality of the packed commodity. If the consumer wants to inspect the packet he is forced in different ways to pay for the 'inspection'. While it is true that we have so many laws against consumer fraud, their implementation unfortunately has been rather slow to gain a real momentum largely because their implementation is not in the interest of businessmen, industrialists, bankers, advertisers and financiers, all of whom have considerable support of the powers that be.

Shady Land Business

Land, it is said, is perhaps the best investment. People of all classes—lower, middle and upper—wish to own a house. But many a time people find that far from making a good investment, they have inadvertently invested money in a plot of land which is already owned by someone else, or in a house which is a disputed property. Some people claim to have formed housing societies, and then start selling plots. Long after money was paid for a plot, it is found that the plot was a part of unauthorised land and there were little chances of it being approved and developed. As a result, the worth of the land is found to be far less than the paid price, and/or the purpose for which it was bought cannot be realised without extraordinary expense and inconvenience. In metro cities like Bombay, Delhi, Calcutta, and Madras or even big cities like Bangalore, Jaipur, Ahmedabad, Lucknow, Bhopal, etc. people pay huge amounts of money for flats under construction and later find that the construction company was bogus and the whole construction scheme was a shady one. Thus, a large number of fraud cases have been increasingly reported in the land development and investment business in recent years. For the poor and the middle-class victims, it often means loss of life savings or a future of substantial indebtedness; for the rich it means a bad investment. The picture that emerges from the press reports and some police investigations suggests that land fraud may well be tied to organised crime. The initial purchase of large land, advertising, and promotion campaigns, the construction of a few flats, sales programme and installment facilities, maintaining offices and staff, and arranging credit give an appearance of respectability to the 'fraud'. For the investor who thinks himself knowledgeable and cautious, the sales people have ready answers for critical questions and can show financial statements, printed brochures, company investment portfolios, and other 'official' documents to establish their legitimacy and the sound financial status of the operation. The investors discover rather late that they have thrown their money down the drain. The promoters take advantage of numerous loopholes in the legislation and the major responsibility for seeing that things are in order rests with the buyer himself.

SELF-CONCEPT OR CRIMINAL CAREER OF THE OCCUPATIONAL OFFENDER

The occupational offender does not conceive himself as a criminal, but perceives himself as a respectable citizen. His attitude is similar to that of an offender who is convicted for drunken driving, etc. The general public also is not able to condemn his activities openly as he remains engaged in a legitimate occupation. Many writers therefore do not regard occupational offenders as real criminals. Cressey (*Other People's Money*, The Free Press, New York,1953) in his study of 133 occupational offenders (imprisoned for violations of trust) found three elements common in all offenders: a financial problem, rationalisations about the violations, and knowledge of how to violate trust law. The violators were able to justify their criminal behaviour as non-criminal behaviour which allowed them to adjust themselves in business, home and society. They describe their behaviour as 'permissible' or 'irresponsible' or 'due to unusual circumstances' or 'to pay to higher ups' for which they were not to be labelled as criminals.

According to Clinard and Quinney (*op. cit.*: 33) the life organisation of the occupational offender is not built around a criminal role. By and large, he plays the role of a respected citizen. The reputations of occupational offenders have been observed in several studies. Clinard (1952: 295) noted in his study that less than one violator in ten was reported to have had a criminal record. In the studies of Hartung (1949) and Quinney (1962), it was found that the overwhelming majority of the offenders resided in the most desirable areas of the city. The Hawala scandal in India in 1995 pointed out that all persons involved were ministers, politicians, bureaucrats, and highly placed public servants.

OCCUPATIONAL (OR WHITE-COLLAR) CRIME IN INDIA

In India, occupational crime is found not only (a) of the type that Sutherland has called white-collar crime (i.e., embezzlement, fraud adulteration and employee pilfering, etc.) committed by respectable and *high-status* people, or (b) of the type that Barlow has called 'occupation-related crime' committed by the *lower-class* people, but also (c) of "personal non-business type illegal acts" committed by the *middle-class* people. The last category (i.e., '*c*' category) of illegal acts aims at concealment of income, avoiding payment of taxes, and obtaining personal advantages like false sales-tax or income-tax returns, showing lesser value of immovable properties to reduce the incidence of stamp duty, concealing capital gains tax, wealth and municipal tax, showing lesser rental income to evade income-tax, and concealing assets in insolvency proceedings, and so on. Including all the illegal acts of '*a*', '*b*', and '*c*' types in occupational crimes would mean modifying and expanding Sutherland's definition of 'white-collar crime' as well as Barlow's definition of 'occupational crime'. The above-mentioned '*c*' type crimes are 'non-business' and 'non-occupational' crimes but undoubtedly they are economic crimes. As such, we must consider not only crimes of 'respectable persons' in society related to their jobs or business (as stated by Sutherland) or crimes of "lower-class persons associated with their occupations (as stated by Barlow) but also crimes of middle-class persons" which, though not directly associated with their 'occupations', are yet full of adverse economic consequences to society. This points out the need for finding a new comprehensive term which encompasses all three types of illegal activities mentioned above, i.e., (a) illegal activities of the upper, middle and the lower classes, (b) illegal activities related to business and occupation, and (c) illegal activities not directly related to occupation yet full of economic consequences for society. In other words, we have to locate a term which may clearly define in our society "an illegal act achieving an illegal objective of gaining money for personal advantage committed by a person of any occupational status by non-violent means". Tentatively, we may call it 'occupational-economic crime'.

Some important occupational-economic crimes found in India in recent years are: Hawala transactions, tax and duty evasion, adulteration of food and drugs, banking and insurance frauds, foreign exchange violations, import/export violations, violation of industrial regulations, hoarding and blackmarketing, and chit-fund frauds.

Some of the *modus operandi* in occupational-economic offences are: evasion of excise duty and income-tax, obtaining loans from banks on the basis of false/inflated security, illegal sale of import licences, manipulation of accounts and showing reduced profits for the company, and showing false purchase of raw material.

What occupational (or white-collar) crimes or frauds do businessmen commit? Here are a few examples.

A manager of a soap factory sends a consignment which is to reach its destination in two days. The factory sends a fax that it has detected, after the despatch of the consignment, that a part of the consignment did not pass quality control and should therefore be destroyed. The consignment arrives. It faxes back that the low-quality soaps have been destroyed. But actually, full consignment is sent out in the market, and the distributor and the factory owner divide between themselves the sale proceeds from the 'destroyed' soaps.

Here is another case. A company releases its unaudited annual profits. The figures show a 60 per cent rise in turnover and 110 per cent rise in profits. The news is sent to stock market and to friends. The stock market price rises by 20 per cent in two days. That is when 10,000 shares are sold which were purchased only a few days ago. Then the actual figures are released which show that the company's turnover has grown only by 10 per cent and profits have dipped by 7 per cent.

This is how white-collar (or occupational) crime is committed and it is difficult to detect it. The cheat here is often a highly intelligent, educated and sophisticated criminal who uses the most ingenious ways. He is familiar with the loopholes and the lacunae in the system in which he operates. Sharebrokers in the share scam in Bombay in 1992 who committed fraud on many banks and earned crores of rupees belonged to this type of white-collar criminals. Here, it is the 'grow-rich quick' mentality which meshes with blind ambition, quest for power, and confidence in the ability to hoodwink the system. There is no readily discernible victim. White-collar (or occupational) crime is a sleeper who may lie unnoticed under managerial noses for years. Detection comes only when a certain bank collapses or a certain bank is defrauded of millions of rupees.

One concern (KPMG Peat Marwick) conducted the first ever survey into the extent of fraud in the largest businesses in corporate India. In all, 72 business houses responded to the survey. More than half said that they had experienced fraud during the last financial year. The total loss reported by these companies was Rs. 45 crore. What is significant is that 87 per cent of managers felt that the incidence of fraud will either increase or stay the same in their concerns. As businesses are being globalised or as businesses are becoming transnational and too big to be monitored effectively from the top, economic crime in the form of fraud is bound to increase.

The most common forms of fraud are padded-up expense accounts (billing by employees) and inventory theft (pilferage). It is said that in any big concern, 20 per cent employees are most unlikely to commit a fraud, 20 per cent are prone to commit a fraud, and 60 per cent are susceptible to it, depending on the four ingredients of fraud, termed 'GONE' which stands for greed, opportunity, need, and expectation of going scott-free.

The pilferage is found today even among engineers and technical staff in computer business, which is often most difficult to detect. Computer parts (like motherboards, floppy drives, and memory modules) are easily smuggled out. There is also the practice that at the time of upgrading a machine, local spares are most easily substituted for branded ones and this is done routinely. This is one way to keep the margins high. This is white-collar crime.

Some types of external frauds in business are false invoices, secret commissions, patent infringement, product substitution and so on.

How can white-collar crime (frauds) in business be checked? This is possible by keeping an eye on the 'red flags', i.e., on employees with a lavish lifestyle beyond their salary, or sales or income decreasing while accounts payable and receivable are on the rise.

Factors which increase white-collar crime in business may be identified as: the weakening of society's values, presence of most sophisticated criminals, economic pressures, lack of emphasis on prevention and detection, and lack of government intervention.

All economic offences (other than bribes) are investigated by specific departments of Government of India. Normally, the Central Bureau of Investigation (CBI) can take up the investigation of only those cases of economic offences which are referred to it for investigation by the department concerned. The CBI investigation on its own is rare. Another distinguishing feature of most of the economic offences is that for prosecuting the accused, complaints have to be filed by the designated authorities. The police or the CBI cannot file charge-sheets.

Some people may ask: Is occupational/white-collar crime really a crime? The answer is an emphatic 'yes' because it has serious effect on the economic fabric of our society, even far more devastating than all thefts, burglaries, robberies and dacoities put together. In fact, a single crime of the type committed in a city like Mumbai may involve an amount exceeding the amount involved in all property crimes in India for a decade. If one considers the securities scam alone of 1992 in Mumbai, the economic loss involved will equal the loss suffered by India in decades together.

Features of White-Collar Crime in India

The white-collar/occupational-economic crimes/criminals in our country have some important features (*see*, K. Madhavan, *Frontline*, July 30, 1993: 124):

1. The crimes result in social injuries far greater than conventional crimes where only individuals are affected. However, these crimes/criminals have generally been regarded by criminologists as a class apart because the administrative, investigative and judicial procedures for many of them have been different from the procedures for other violations of criminal laws.
2. A large number of these offenders are recidivists, though repetition is not necessarily of the same type of crime.
3. The illegal activities (or white-collar crimes) follow more or less the same *modus operandi*.
4. A white-collar criminal does not lose his status among associates because it is not considered a violation of the 'business code'. In fact, many successful criminals of this category are hailed as dynamic and innovative leaders of industry/society.
5. White-collar criminals feel and express contempt for law, for government, and! for government officials. In this respect, they are similar to many professional criminals.
6. While ordinary criminals are afraid of enforcement agencies, white-collar criminals are rarely so, because they think that on being detected, they may only be transferred or fined or given a short-term simple imprisonment.

In spite of the fact that a large number of occupational scams/economic offences have been unearthed in our country in the last few years---like securities scam, hawala scam, sugar scam, banking scam, telecommunication scam, fodder scam, urea scam, etc.—in which thousands of crores of rupees were involved, surprisingly no offenders have been convicted so far. The accused persons against whom the cases are pending in the courts are yet to be prosecuted and punished. We read in the newspapers of the systematic raids conducted by the Income Tax Department and the Enforcement Directorate against business tycoons but we never read anything about their prosecution. Politicians support them for the funds they receive from them for elections and for filling up their personal coffers. Policemen do not take them into custody for the fear that they (businessmen) might retaliate with court actions or might get them transferred by seeking help from the politicians. The courts also do not impose serious punishment on these economic offenders. In case of big capitalists (like Kirloskar), the judges grant bail by hearing the case in their houses even at night. In a majority of economic crimes, sentences imposed by the courts are ridiculously mild. Generally, some ground for the benefit of the doubt is brought into play and the accused is acquitted. Many white-collar offenders bribe the enforcement personnel and thus get out of the clutches of the law.

With such attitudes of politicians, the police and the courts, the recent enactments and amendments in statutes prescribing deterrent punishment to economic offenders have come as a pleasant surprise. The amendment in the Consumer Protection Act is a step in the right direction. People are becoming increasingly conscious of the fact that economic progress is possible only if business is made to behave. The recent liberalisation of the economy aims to rid business and industry of the permit licence raj. What is urgently required is the strengthening of enforcement agencies such as the Central Bureau of Investigation, the Enforcement Investigation, the Enforcement Directorate, the Directorate of Revenue Intelligence, the Income Tax Department, the Customs Department, and all other agencies concerned with the enforcement of fiscal laws.

K. Madhavan (*Frontline*, July 30, 1993: 129) is of the opinion that what further needs to be stopped is selective prosecution and the malafides of the government. Suppose there are twenty industries in a particular line, out of which ten are known to be committing a certain type of fraud, such as showing non-existing stocks to banks in their cash credit accounts. Of these, two industries are found having contributed funds to opposition political parties. Only these two cases will be registered. This is selective victimisation by the government which needs to be stopped with the help of the media.

One change that is being observed in India against occupational (white-collar) crime is that while earlier victims suffered losses silently, many consumer councils have now come into existence to fight for consumers. The victims of occupational crime are scattered, unorganised and lack adequate information. Most important of all, no single victim suffers a loss in a particular transaction which would justify his taking recourse to legal action. The trouble and the expense involved in legal action would be far too large in relation to the injury suffered. This aspect is now gradually undergoing a change. The National Consumer Redressal Commission and similar organisations at the state and district levels are rendering yeoman service to the consumers.

PROCESS OF BECOMING A CRIMINAL: DIFFERENTIAL ASSOCIATIONS

Sutherland has explained the process of becoming a white-collar criminal through 'differential associations'. An individual learns the techniques of crime, the general attitudes towards criminality, and of protection against crime through interaction with law-violators. However, the process of becoming a white-collar criminal is different from that of becoming an ordinary criminal. A white-collar criminal is mature in relation to chronological age but he makes no provision for immunity in case of detection and has no philosophy to support him in his trial and punishment. His character is not integrated; in this respect he is immature. According to Sutherland, the process in the life history of white-collar criminal may be explained as follows (*ibid.*, 220-22): First, persons with reputation, for honesty, uprighteousness and straightforward behaviour accept positions of financial responsibility in corporations, companies and organisations with no intention of indulging in illegal activities. Later on, they become embezzlers, frauds, cheats, pilferers (i.e., white-collar criminals) by ignoring their positions of trust. These persons are seldom psychopathic, feeble-minded or personally or situationally pathological. Usually, these people (occupying positions of financial responsibility and indulging in illegal activities) are not recent recruits but have held positions for many years. Initially, they acquire small sums over a long period of time but ultimately they 'snatch' large sums of money. *First*, the law-violator defines a financial problem which confronts him as 'non-shareable', i.e., one which cannot be shared with other persons (who could help in its solution). In many cases, these 'non-shareable' financial problems arise from obligations incurred in gambling, extravagant living, maintaining an extra-marital relationship, fulfilling the responsibility of marrying a daughter or sending son for professional training, etc. *Second*, the potential violator realises that he has the ability and opportunity to solve the 'non-shareable' problem by violating the position of trust, i.e., by using the same 'technical skills' which he had been using in the legitimate aspects of his position. *Third*, he defines activity (embezzlement, fraud, cheating) in such terms which enable him to look upon the activity as essentially non-criminal, as justified, or only as part of a 'general irresponsibility' for which he is not completely accountable. For example, he might say, he is only 'borrowing' money but not 'stealing'. Such rationalisation enables him to take initially relatively small amounts of money over a period of time, with the intention of repaying it. In some cases, he actually repays the 'borrowed' money and his fraud/embezzlement/cheating goes undetected. Later on, he takes a considerable amount of money which he is never able to 'repay'. He is, thus, forced to abandon the notion that he is 'borrowing'. He then goes on committing more and more frauds till he is detected and arrested. During all this period, he remains in contact with his associates who condemn crime. But when he finds himself in 'too deep a situation' and becomes tense, nervous, emotionally upset, he describes old values and ideals as useless and undesirable. This exposes him and he comes to be looked at with suspicion. Gradually, he even comes to adopt the attitudes of new category of persons (criminals) with whom he now finds himself identified. He is then apprehended and prosecuted. These crimes are generally committed individually, but occasionally two or more persons may be in collusion.

Similarly, the processes in the life histories of other types of white-collar criminals might also be described. Some organisations gradually learn from other organisations that there is nothing wrong in showing a sample of a particular quality of goods but despatching a slightly inferior quality of goods and thus earning a few extra thousands of rupees; or there is nothing wrong in filing false sales or income-tax returns; or, there is nothing wrong in actually packing less quantity than the one printed on packets. This is learning through 'differential associations'.

The behaviour system in ordinary crime is described by Sutherland (*ibid.*, 230-39) in terms of three principal characteristics: *First*, a behaviour system is not merely an aggregation of individual criminal acts but it is an integrated unit which includes, in addition to the individual acts, the codes, traditions, etc. of the criminal participants. It is, thus, essentially a group way of life. *Second*, the behaviour of a criminal is not unique to any particular individual but it is common behaviour shared with other offenders. *Third*, all criminals share common interests and standards. On the other hand, the bahaviour system of white-collar criminals is different. A white-collar criminal does not identify himself with other criminals, nor does he share the interests and sentiments of other criminals.

Robert Lane (1953: 151) has said that in some occupations, a man may actually learn the techniques by which the law can be violated, building up such rationalisations as "business is business" or "good business demands it". This diffusion of illegal practice originates and spreads from a person already in the occupation to new persons, and from one business establishment to another. Unethical and illegal practices are circulated in the trade as part of a definition of the situation, and rationalisations to support these violations of law are transmitted by this differential association. Types of violations are picked up in conversations with businessmen and from descriptions of violations in trade journals and the press.

Clinard and Quinney (*op. cit.*: 135) have submitted that although many forms of occupational crime can be satisfactorily explained by a theory of differential association, yet this theory, as an explanation for all cases, has several limitations. Many individuals do not engage in these practices although they are familiar with the techniques and rationalisations of violation and frequently associate with persons similarly familiar. In fact, all businessmen acquire knowledge of the illegalities involved in business. But persons accept or reject opportunities for occupational crime according to their orientations towards their roles and their attitudes towards general social values. People may have negative attitudes towards other persons yet they may have positive attitudes towards business reputations.

Some forms of occupational crime are related to the structure of the occupation in which the 'offender' is engaged and in the roles played by the 'offender' within the occupation. For example, a chemist does not mind mentioning certain medicines in the cash memo even if in place of these medicines some other medicines/goods are purchased which are not reimbursible according to government rules. The business-oriented pharmacists are interested in the general business goal of monetary gain. They subscribe to the popular belief in business that self-employment carries with it independence and freedom from control. Thus, 'differential orientation' of retail pharmacists is related to the roles within the occupation.

EFFECTS OF WHITE-COLLAR CRIME

Some important effects of white-collar crime may be described below:

1. Its economic effect or the financial loss to society is more serious than ordinary economic crimes committed by persons of the lower socio-economic class. The average loss per theft or burglary is less than Rs. 5,000 while theft/burglary which yields as much as Rs. 50,000 or so is rare, and one which yields a lakh rupees or more is still rarer. On the other hand, embezzlements and frauds of lakhs and millions of rupees committed by business organisations, corporations, trusts, and companies are reported in a single year.
2. While ordinary crimes cause some inconvenience to the victims and

serious crimes cause general community disturbance, white-collar crimes spread feelings of distress, lower public morale, and produce social disorganisation.

3. Though a very large number of white-collar crimes are committed in society yet only a few white-collar offenders are prosecuted and punished. A large number go scott free because of their economic and social influence. Even the criminal courts are lenient towards persons accused of white-collar crimes.
4. Protection to society against white-collar crime is too meagre because efforts to make the criminal law more effective in dealing with white-collar crime are often blocked by vested interests.
5. Absence of adequate knowledge regarding white-collar crime contributes to a distortion of the criminological theories of causation since criminologists to a great extent have restricted their data to cases dealt within criminal courts and prisons.

SOCIETAL REACTION

Why is societal reaction to white-collar criminal different from its reaction to a conventional criminal? This is because most of the laws violated by them are not part of the criminal code as the bulk of white-collar legislation regulates business and professional activities and administrative processes. Sutherland offers three explanations for laying emphasis on administrative rather than judicial agencies (*White-Collar Crime*: 46; *also see*, Barlow: 217): the status of the given occupation, the general trend away from punishment, and the relative lack of resentment of the public against white-collar crimes. Why is the labelling of criminal status—applied to conventional offenders—withheld from white-collar criminals? One, detection of white-collar criminals is highly problematic. Two, the public and the judges, are reluctant to prosecute the white-collar criminals because of the general repute of their occupation and because of the fear that prosecution for an offence embedded in the occupational system will have adverse effect on the vital services that the occupation provides to community. Lastly, it is believed that unlike conventional criminals of the lower class, the white-collar criminals of the middle and the upper classes are free of criminality. As such, even though theoretically equal justice calls for similar degrees of punishment for conventional and white-collar offenders alike yet a reduction in the intensity of punishment is a desirable policy.

Criticisms of White-Collar Crime

1. White-collar crime is a non-legal term which refers to certain criminal acts but it does not specifically name the criminal acts to which it has reference.
2. It refers to a certain type of person, namely, a member of the upper socioeconomic class but does not provide specific criteria by which to determine the social class of the person involved.
3. The criminal law in defining the acts that are usually referred to by the term 'white-collar crime' does not make any distinction regarding the social class of the offenders. Thus, there are no official sources of criminal statistics by which to estimate the incidence of white-collar crime.

There are imperfections in the criminal law and its procedure. The remedy for this is not to disregard the preventive devices it has created to shield the innocent. The correct approach to this crime lies in redefining occupational crime, in the improvement of the criminal law, in the stricter enforcement of its provisions, and in the vigorous but unbiased and impartial prosecution of the accused.

References

Barlow, Hugh D., *Introduction to Criminology*, Little Brown and Co., Boston, 1976.

Clinard, M.B. and Quinney, R., *Criminal Behaviour Systems: A Typology*, Holt, Rinehart & Winston, New York, 1967.

Madhavan, K., *Frontline*, July 30, 1993.

Sutherland, E.H. and Cressay, Donald R., *Principles of Criminology*, The Times of India Press, Bombay, 1965.

Chapter 8

Professional Crime

A professional crime is one in which crime is committed in a specialised way with prime motive of economic gain. According to Sutherland (1965: 232), the term 'professional', when applied to a criminal, refers to the following four things: the pursuit of crime as a regular normal occupation, the development of skilled techniques, careful planning, and status among criminals. It is on the basis of factors like these that the professional criminal is differentiated from the occasional criminal, the amateur criminal, and the unskilled criminal. Walter Reckless (*The crime Problem*, 1955: 148-50) has used the term 'career criminals' for professional criminals.

Professional criminals who commit crime as a regular business use techniques which have been developed over a long period of time and transmitted to them through personal association. With their codes of behaviour and consensus, they tend to look down upon amateur criminals as 'kids'. What is important in professional crimes like burglary, robbery, dacoity, picking people's pockets, etc. is the skill with which crime is committed. For example, committing robbery in a professional way involves finding a person carrying a good amount of money, ornaments, jewels, etc., locating a place for the holdup, planning the hold-up, and executing the job. Generally speaking, a professional crime is committed in a non-violent way, though sometimes it involves violence too.

Professionalisation extends beyond the execution of a crime. It involves prior location of spots and prior preparation for escaping punishment in case of the detection of crime. Arrangements are made in advance for bail, legal service, and fixing the case. It is in these advance arrangements, quite as much as in the technique of executing the crime, that professionalisation is found.

Similarity has been noticed in the behaviour patterns of professional criminals and businessmen engaged in legitimate activities. Both are engaged in a full-time pursuit; both are self-employed; both take their activities as the main means of earning their livelihood; both work for economic profit; both use specialised skills in their activities; both enjoy respect and reputation in their own worlds; and both have their own philosophy of life pertaining to their profession.

CHARACTERISTICS OF PROFESSIONAL CRIME AND CRIMINALS

Sutherland (1965: 240) has given the following six characteristics of professional crime:

1. *Regularity*, i.e., continuity in work as crime.
2. *Technical skill*, i.e., use of complex techniques for committing crime which have been used in crime over a long period of time.
3. *Status*, i.e., enjoying a position of high prestige in the world of crime.
4. *Consensus*, i.e., sharing of common values, beliefs, and attitudes with other criminals.
5. *Organisation*, i.e., pursuing activities through an informal information and assistance system.
6. *Differential association*, i.e., association with other professional criminals to the exclusion of ordinary criminals as well as law-abiding persons.

Caldwell (1956: 57) has given the following characteristics of a professional criminal:

1. *Crime is his main source of livelihood*: He devotes his full working time and energy to it and constantly attempts to improve his skills. He tries to specialise in one or two crimes. He normally obeys the law, except when it interferes with his crime.
2. *Crime is his way of life*: The professional criminal develops a philosophy of his own and organises his life and activities around new values, attitudes, and beliefs.
3. *He operates with proficiency and carefully plans his activities*: He takes calculated risks and dislikes those who bungle and fail. He differs

from the habitual criminal in the sense that the latter commits crime regularly but without specialised skills.

4. *He is a product of a process of development*: He acquires his specialised knowledge, attitudes, and skills gradually. Usually, he acquires skills under instruction from and guidance of somebody who has already achieved proficiency and status in his criminal speciality. However, no formal process of recruitment and training is involved in the development. Some professional criminals begin their careers as juvenile delinquents, some as adolescent criminals, some as youth criminals and some take the first step only after achieving adulthood and move from legitimate means of earning their livelihood to a life of criminality.
5. *He identifies himself with the world of crime and criminals*: His friends, security, affection, recognition, sympathy, and respect, etc. all come from the underworld. This does not mean that he totally cuts himself apart and becomes isolated from the conventional world. He continues to have friends and acquaintances in the law-abiding world also.

TYPES OF PROFESSIONAL CRIMINALS

The nature of crime in which the professional criminal specialises determines the type of criminal he comes to be identified with. On this basis, he is called a burglar (who breaks into shops, residences, offices, and buildings and steals money, goods and merchandise. He has his own techniques of picking locks and opening doors), a sneak (who steals from shops, offices, and parked automobiles), a purse-snatcher (who snatches hand-bags from women), a pick-pocket (who picks pockets with his nimble fingers), an auto-thief (who specialises in thefts of cars, scooters, motor-cycles, etc.), a forger (who specialises in forging cheques), a merchandise thief (who acts as a member of an organised gang which specialises in stealing merchandise in transit, i.e., stealing from goods-trains, trucks, etc.), a receiver of stolen property (who provides opportunity to the thief/robber for the disposal of the loot), a confidence man (who gains the confidence of the victim and then cheats him), and so forth.

MATURATION PROCESS OR DEVELOPING CRIMINAL CAREER AND PROFESSIONAL PHILOSOPHY

As discussed earlier, a criminal does not become a professional all of a sudden but learns techniques and skills in an educational process, involving habituation to a life of crime. Caldwell has also said: "Gradually he participates more and more in criminal activities and progressively shifts his loyalty from the world of law and law-abiding citizens to the underworld of crime and criminals." It is, however, not only the learning of skills but also developing a new philosophy of his own which makes him a professional criminal. Not only he considers himself a criminal but others also accept him as one, and thus he achieves status in the world of crime. Ruth Cavan (*Criminology*, 1962: 134) has said: "The process of becoming a professional criminal may be described as a gradual alienation from loyalty to and participation in agencies that conform to the community mores, such as family, neighbourhood, peer group, and occupational group. For a time, he may be a member of both the conventional world and the criminal world but when he arrives at the point of complete severance with the conventional groups and organises his life in terms of the criminal group, he has become a full-fledged professional criminal."

According to Frank Tennenbaum (*Crime and Criminality*, 1938: 177), "the new philosophy that the professional criminal develops is the philosophy of beliefs that are acquired in a process of adjustment over a period of time, organised into a system of principles and hardened and crystallised in terms of experience". This philosophy gives meaning to his life, determines his attitudes towards life and his work fixes his views, gives him insights, binds him to prejudices, and pushes him towards bias. He develops values quite contrary to those acceptable to organised society. For him, pockets are made to be picked, purses to be snatched, and ventilators for not getting clean and fresh air but for entering the house. Further, he holds that all politicians have a price, all policemen are corrupt, all businessmen are cheats, all traders are eager to make an easy and dishonest buck, and all victims are naive and stupid. If he is caught by the police, he blames himself for not being careful enough and vows to be more cautious next time. He says: "Everybody runs into tough luck once in a while and he too will get his chance some day: in the meantime, he must lie low." He knows that if he has failed to 'fix' his case, it is because he did not contact the 'right' person. Like a normal person, he too seeks love, affection, sympathy, recognition, and security but he finds them only in the world of crime. Small wonder then that he tends to be loyal to this world of crime. Just as a businessman may not like some businessmen, a professional criminal also may not like some professional criminals. However, in the face of danger, all criminals tend to unite.

Some criminals live together but many prefer to live alone. They live in socially disorganised areas, cheap hotels, rented rooms, and favourite lodging places where social control is not so effective. Many of them remain constantly on the move. They do not have stable family life nor any dependents. A few professional criminals think of retirement even when they strike it rich.

Some professional criminals display 'toughness' in dealing with their victims. This is in part based on segregation of criminals from criminal behaviour. Just as businessmen act on the principle, "business is business", so also professional criminals act on the principle, "crime is crime". There is no place for sentiment in either case.

The sexual life of professional criminals is usually loose. They generally have relations with prostitutes and mistresses. They meet other criminals and middle-men in cheap restaurants and gambling dens, etc. They also use their own codes to interact with other criminals. It may, however, be remembered that very few professional criminals are ever arrested, brought to trial, convicted or made to serve time in prison.

The Criminal Code

All professional criminals follow code of the underworld. According to this code, a criminal should be honest with other criminals, particularly with the members of his own gang (if he belongs to a gang he should divide his loot with them; he should be loyal to the underworld; he should avoid violence; he should not leak out his secrets to others, and so forth). The codes are not the same for all types of crimes or all types of criminals. According to Sutherland (1965: 232), professional criminals have two general rules. One is not to inform on another criminal, the other is to make an honest division of the loot with companions or partners in crime. "Do not squeal' i.e., do not cry indicating pain or terror", and "Do not burn your partner" are the basic commandments of professional criminals. Unquestionably, the criminal code is violated frequently.

ARGOT

Professional criminals have their own argot, i.e., distinctive language which grows out of the specialised activity of the criminals. The words and terms used by them have developed over a considerable period of time and reflect the attitudes of the professional criminals towards the law, the police, the magistrate, the victim, the other criminals, and towards society in general. All professionals speak the language associated with their particular crime.

The argot serves several functions: (i) it consolidates the criminal subculture and develops group solidarity; (ii) it helps criminals to solve problems with certain known techniques unknown to ordinary people; (iii) many concepts exist for professional criminals for which there are no terms in the vocabulary of the ordinary citizen. It is necessary that professional criminals create, borrow, or adapt words to meet their unique needs; and (iv) it helps criminals to confuse and deceive victims. Most professionals speak argot only among themselves and not in the presence of outsiders. Clinard and Quinney (1967: 433) have said: "The specialised language serves as a means of social support for the way of life of the professional criminal."

SAFETY

Professional criminals try to attain security before, during, and after committing crimes. According to Sutherland (1965: 240-44), security is attained broadly in three ways:

1. *Selecting crimes that involve a minimum of danger*, say, confidence game, theft, shoplifting, picking people's pockets, burglary, etc. These crimes are relatively safe. In confidence game, the victim generally agrees to participate in a dishonest transaction and when he finds that he is the victim, he cannot make complaint without disgracing himself. In the world of picking people's pockets, the criminal can escape through the crowded area without being recognised. Further, because the legal rules of evidence require direct evidence that the thief put his hand in the victim's pocket and withdrew the money, such evidence can seldom be secured. Thefts on the other hand, are generally committed when occupants are sleeping or are not present in the house; robberies are committed in isolated places where there is nobody to protect the victims; shoplifting is relatively safe because the shopkeepers do not wish to run the risk of accusing legitimate customers of stealing, and the professional shoplifter makes it a point to look and act like a respectable customer.
2. *Developing clever and skilled techniques for executing crimes*: Cleverness and skill may mean dexterity, brashness, using another person to manoeuvre the victim so that he (the criminal) can commit the crime, and many other ingenious devices.
3. *Making arrangements to fix those cases in which he may be caught*: The

professional criminal sometimes 'fixes' the case himself and sometimes through others. In large cities, the 'fixing' work for the criminals is generally done by the professional 'fixers'. The fixing work is accomplished by direct or indirect payment of money. A promise is usually made to the victim that his stolen property will be returned with 'bonus' if he refused to push the prosecution or if he testified in a way that would not damage the criminal. Some victims accept such offers, particularly those who are more interested in receiving back the stolen property than in attending the police stations and the courts and facing lawyers and the risk of 'vengeance' from other professional criminals. If the victim refuses to cooperate, the bribe is given to policemen, prosecution, judges, etc.

DIFFERENCE BETWEEN PROFESSIONAL AND ORDINARY CRIMINALS

Professional criminals differ from ordinary or conventional criminals. The difference may be discussed at several levels: (1) Professional criminals are skilled in their criminal activity but not the conventional criminals. (2) Professional criminals depend on crime as a main source of earning their livelihood but not the ordinary criminals. (3) Professional criminals are habitual criminals but not ordinary criminals. (4) Professional criminals not only regard themselves as criminals but are also known to others as criminals, while many ordinary criminals think that they are not criminals but are the victims of circumstances. Others also may or may not regard them as criminals. (5) Professional criminals get status and recognition only in the underworld while the ordinary criminals have status in the conventional world too. (6) Professional criminals avoid other types of criminals and associate primarily with one another but ordinary criminals associate with other criminals too. (7) Professional criminals have their own philosophy of life but this is not true of ordinary criminals. (8) Professional criminals tend to come from better economic backgrounds than do ordinary criminals. (9) Professional criminals begin their career in crime at a relatively late age as compared to ordinary criminals. (10) Professional criminals tend to continue in crime for most part of their lives but not ordinary criminals.

SOCIETAL REACTION

How does society react to professional criminals? How do the policemen, the lawyers, and others react to them? Public officials allow them to escape arrest and prosecution because of their favoured position in crime.

The law enforcement officers sometimes work for them because they get money for the services rendered. Some politicians use them for their vested political interests. A professional criminal is also able to escape arrest by regular payments to certain officials, by seeking help of influential people to 'fix' case for him and by maintaining contacts with the power elite. According to Sutherland (*op. cit.*: 128), professional criminals maintain that "there is no one who cannot be influenced if you go at it right and have sufficient backing, financially and politically. It may be difficult with some victims, some officials in some places but it can practically always be done. It is just a question of using head in the right way."

Public toleration of professional crime results from public apathy towards law-violation which does not affect each person directly and concretely. David Maurer (1964: 129) has suggested that public toleration of professional crime results from a combination of factors, including the involvement of the public as victims in illegal arrangements, public indifference towards crimes, naiveness about crime, and relationship between criminals and officials of law-enforcement agencies.

References

Caldwell, Robert G., *Criminology*, Ronald Press Company, New York, 1956.

Cavan, Ruth Shonle, *Criminology* (3rd edn.), Thomas Y. Crowell Company, New York, 1962.

Clinard, M.B. and Quinney, R., *Criminal Behaviour Systems: A Typology*, Holt, Rinehart & Winston, New York, 1967.

Reckless, Walter, *The Crime Problem*, (2nd edn.), Appleton Century Crofts Inc., New York, 1955.

Sutherland, E.H. and Cressay, D.R., *Principles of Criminology* (6th edn.), The Times of India Press, Bombay, 1956.

Chapter 9

Political Crime

Political crime may be perceived at two levels: (i) law-violation by politicians (people holding political posts) for their vested interests, and (ii) violation of law by people attempting to express their opinion on the political structure of the state, with a possible attempt to bring about change in the existing political system. We will discuss these two types of political crime separately. First, we take up corruption among the politicians.

POLITICAL CORRUPTION AS CRIME

What types of acts of politicians can be called corrupt? Though the term 'corruption' has wide connotations but the following patterns of behaviour can be described as corrupt within the provisions of law (Malhotra, 1992: 251-56): (i) acceptance of gratification as reward for work done in an official capacity, e.g., granting licence, assigning a project, etc., (ii) obtaining any object (car, house, fridge, etc.) or pecuniary advantage illegally, (iii) fraudulent misappropriation of public money/property, (iv) being in possession of financial resources, or property disproportionate to one's known sources of income, (v) misuse or abuse of official position, (vi) 'borrowing' money for purchasing a costly article from someone with whom one has official dealings, and (vii) accepting gifts from persons.

There are at least four ministries in the Union Government which are regarded as gold mines for making money by politicians in power. These are defence, petroleum, power and communication. The Defence Ministry spends about Rs. 25,000 crore on defence every year out of which a good percentage is spent on purchase and repairs. It is alleged that commissions from 15 to 40 per cent are not uncommon on purchase of weapons, ammunition, spare parts, and the overhauling of planes, mirages, etc. The Petroleum Ministry spends about Rs. 20,000 crore every year, including money on import of oil and natural gas. Barrels of oil imported yield kickbacks to concerned political decision-makers. A lot of money is also spent on giving drilling rights, installing pipelines, the opening of petrol pumps, and so forth. The Ministry of Power has a budget of about Rs. 900 crore every year. The budget of the Ministry of Communication also runs in thousands of crores every year. Kickbacks are common in both above-mentioned ministries. The three other departments where corruption is fairly common are the railways, excise, and revenue. It is not only the politicians at the top who accept bribes but also others all along the line in these ministries and departments. The scope of corruption is greater where substantial decisions are taken. In recent years, so many scams involving prime ministers, chief ministers, union and state ministers, members of parliament and vidhan sabhas, and leaders of political parties have come to light that an attitude of weary resignation on the part of the people has allowed an astonishing complacency to develop over the magnitude of corruption in the country. The size/quantum of kickbacks keeps on shooting up every few years. The Preparatory Committee for Alternative Economic Policies—a collection of largely left-wing economists—has done some research on the kickbacks. It estimates that the kickbacks shot up from Rs. 3,036 crore in 1980-81 to an astonishing Rs. 19,414 crore in 1990-91, i.e., the amount involved increased by more than six times in one decade.

Honest politicians are a rare breed today. Corrupt politicians not only go scot-free but they also manage to strut about on the political stage as honourable leaders. Examples of political leaders like Lal Bahadur Shastri are rare indeed who had very little bank balance to his credit at the time of his death. In this land of ours, while a person who commits a theft to feed his hungry children after remaining unemployed for a long time, is promptly put behind bars, while those who plunder the country go about as honourable citizens, basking in unwarranted glory, merely because they happen to be political bigwigs.

Before analysing major political scandals involving top politicians and thousands of crores of rupees, it would be of interest to refer here to a case, reported about two years ago (July 1994), in which large quantities of gold and cash were found in the Raj Bhawan of a state whose governor had died in an air crash along with eight members of his family. Initially, it was stated that cash and gold worth Rs. 44 crore had been found, but, after a few days figures reached Rs. 150 crore. After, a fortnight these figures escalated to Rs. 800 crore, which included the cost of the late governor's palatial houses, farm-houses, and agricultural land. It was later reported that a union minister had taken the cash, gold, diamonds, and relevant papers in huge trunks to Delhi. A public-interest litigation case was filed, inquiries were demanded but the case was suppressed, even though many businessmen, jewellers, and engineers had confessed to giving gifts and presents of diamonds and gold worth lakhs of rupees to the late governor and the members of his family. Even if the most conservative estimate regarding cash, gold, gems and property worth Rs. 30 crore is accepted, the question arises: how could the governor, who was an ex-police officer, amass such a vast fortune?

THE SCANDALS

In the last two decades or so, several scandals or financial irregularities, including the paying of massive commissions, pay-offs and kickbacks, have been reported in our country. Mostly it is chief ministers, central and state ministers, and leaders of political parties who are reported to be involved in these scams. But hardly anything has been done to uncover, trace, apprehend, prosecute, and punish the culprits on the plea of 'lack of evidence'. From among the more notorious scandals like Hawala, Bofors, stockmarket securities, sugar, fodder scam, etc. mentioned below, we will analyse only a few more recent ones involving political corruption and pertaining to years 1985 and 1996.

Bofors Pay-off Scandal in 1987 involved a total amount of Rs.1,750 crore in the purchase of guns from the Swedish firm for the armed forces. It was alleged that a sum of Rs.64 crore had been paid as kickbacks, though one estimate puts the figure of Rs. 160 crore and another estimate at as high a figure as Rs. 204 crore. High-ranking politicians, including the former prime minister were alleged to be involved in the scandal. A Joint Parliamentary Committee (JPC) was appointed in 1987 to find out the nexus between politicians and recipients of kickbacks. It submitted its report in April 1988 that Bofors had not used any middlemen to win the contract, nor had it paid any bribes. But a south Indian newspaper (*The Hindu*) pointing out the hollowness of these conclusions made many disclosures of commission paid to middlemen, including politicians. Following the publication of these documents, an inquiry was ordered by the Central Bureau of Investigation (CBI) and the Directorate of Enforcement. However, no action has been taken against anybody till May 2000.

The *Hawala Scandal*, which surfaced in 1991, not only rocked political circles but also the whole country. It was a case of a person (Surendra Kumar Jain) influencing the country's top politicians and bureaucrats by paying money to them. In fact, this was the only case in which the Supreme Court of India directed the CBI, on a public interest litigation filed by two journalists in October 1993, to unravel the scandal sincerely. In this case, the leaders of all political parties—except the left party—were accused of receiving money from Jain brothers.

The nefarious activities of the Hawala racket came to light in March 1991 following the arrest of two persons which led to a search of S.K. Jain's house and the discovery of a diary which contained names of 111 politicians, bureaucrats, public servants, and others having received payments from the Jain brothers between April 1988 and March 1990. The diary and the files were seized on May 3, 1991 along with cash, bearer bonds and foreign money. The diary languished for four years and it was only on November 28, 1995 that the CBI filed charge-sheets in the court against thirteen public sector bureaucrats, and on January 16, 1996 against ten politicians, and on February 22, 1996 against fourteen more politicians. It was said that the former Central Energy and Civil Aviation Minister received Rs. 7.5 crore, late Prime Minister received Rs. 2 crore, the Chief Minister of a northern state Rs. 1 crore, and another Chief Minister Rs. 1.9 crore, the Central Agriculture Minister Rs. 6.1 million, former Deputy Prime Minister Rs. 5 million, the President of Hindu-oriented political party Rs. 6 million, and the President of another political party Rs. 1 crore, the Union Minister of Parliament Affairs Rs. 6.6 million, the Central Energy Minister Rs. 5.4 million, former private secretary to the Prime Minister Rs. 5 million, and five central ministers who were given below Rs. 2 million each (*Frontline*, March 22, 1996: 9).

The money was paid for various favours received. The Jains had received 241 contracts during the period 1988 and 1993 mainly in the fields of power, steel, and coal. The total amount of the Hawala transactions by the Jain group was estimated at 65 crore rupees. Some recipients of money from the Jains have lost political power, some have died and some are said to have fled the country. The case against the politicians involved was tried by the especially designated CBI court of Additional Sessions Judge, Delhi, which ultimately discharged all cases for want of evidence in 1999.

The *Animal Husbandry Scam* involved a large number of public officials of animal husbandry department and politicians in South Bihar. They were accused of purchasing fodder beyond the sanctioned amount and of illegally withdrawing about 600 crore rupees from government

Reported Scandals Between 1987 and 1996

Name of Scandal	*Year*	*Amount Involved (in crore)*	*Person(s) Involved*	*Nature of Scam*
Bofors Scandal	1987	64	High-rank politicians	Purchase of guns from a Swedish firm for the armed forces.
Plots Scandal	1988-89	Hundreds of crores	CM (Maharashtra)	Allotment of plots of land to builders
Brown Neyvei locomotive deal	1993	Crores of rupees	Central Railway Minister	Amend a big contract for locomotives
Contract in Communication Ministry Scandal	1995	500	Central Communication Minister	Contracts to friends
Securities Scandal	1992	4,183	Several Central Ministers (also share-brokers, bank officials, etc.)	Fraudulent transactions in Govt. securities and using public (bank) funds
Pay-off Scandal	1993	1	Prime Minister	Receiving a suitcase full of money from a share-broker
Sugar Scandal	1994	650	Central Minister of State for Food	Receiving money and permitting import of sugar
Hawala Scandal	1995	65	A large number of central ministers and leaders of political parties	Receiving money for personal gain and for fighting elections
Animal Hus-bandry or Fodder Scam (Bihar)	1996	500-700	Public Officials of Animal Husbandry Dept.in collution with political figures including chief minister	Large-scale misappropriation and fraudulent transactions in dealing with public funds by officials of Animal Husbandry Dept.
Textile or Dhoti-Sari Scam (Tamil Nadu)	1996	35	Public officials of Handloom Dept. and P.S. to Handloom and Social Welfare Minister	Purchase of yarn from non-existing firms and supplying it to govt. handloom cooperatives which did not even own looms for producing saris and dhotis for distribution to the poor.

Contd...

Contd...

Name of Scandal	*Year*	*Amount Involved (in crore)*	*Person(s) Involved*	*Nature of Scam*
Letter of Credit Scam (Assam)	1995	200	Public officials	Misuse of letters of credit in state's veterinary Dept. since 1985 and money fraudulently withdrawn from govt. treasuries.
Balarpur Scam (Orissa)	1996	7	CM (Orissa)	Misusing official position and granting concessions on bamboo royalty in 1992 to paper mills in which chief minister's son and wife had business interests.
Rice Scam (Madhya Pradesh)	1996	50	CM (MP)	Issuing levy-paid certificates to fictitious companies of rice traders and enabling them to export 100% rice-produce instead of premitted 60% produce.
Urea Scam	1996	133	Former PM's son, former central Fertiliser Minister's son, Managing & Executive Directors of NFL and a person related to former PM's son.	Paying crores of rupees in advance for 2 lakh tonnes of urea to a Turkish firm. The urea has not reached NFL till date and thus the Indian govt. has been defrauded. Kickbacks of US dollars 4 million are alleged to have been paid.
Colour television case, coal import case, disproportionate assets case, granite case and Meena advertising case.	Between 1990 and 1996	Coal import: 3.5 crore; TV purchase: 10 crore	Former Chief Minister of Tamil Nadu.	In 1993, the CM had imported coal from Indonesia which was high-priced and of substandard quality. She possessed disproportionate assets of more than her income. She had purchased 45,000 coloured televisions at a very high price which had caused a loss of Rs. 10 crore to the state. She spent 7-8 days in jail also for this case. She had received a cheque of about 2 crore from one NRI. The last two cases are yet to be started. In TV case, she was discharged in May 2000 though five IAS officers and one former minister got five year imprisonment.

treasuries in South Bihar between 1990 and 1995. It is said that many bureaucrats and several political leaders in power were aware of these withdrawals but consciously covered up the misappropriation by misusing the civil deposit and public ledger accounts in order to balance state finances from time to time. It is alleged that many government officials were in league with the animal husbandry mafia in siphoning off money. The allegation was that the state government did not spend much on 'centrally aided' projects against which the state government was expected to put up matching grants. The money to be contributed by the state government was shown as 'released' by a government order but was superseded by another immediate directive to the concerned departments to surrender the 'released' amount in its entirety in the state chest or the civil deposit account. In this way, funds for the project were actually deposited in the state chest till central funds were again released on the basis of work stated to have been expedited. While in many departments, a proper check was maintained on such 'orders' and 'deposits', in the animal husbandry department, the 'expenditure' was allowed to be shown as 'genuine expenditure'. There were huge withdrawals from treasuries and the 'loot' was shared by the officials. The finance officials consciously misquoted the actual expenditure from grant-in-aid for development projects. The officials of the state government thus misinformed the central government with the backing of bureaucrats and some political brokers. The financial officials denied being a party to such misappropriation and fraudulent transactions. They only described the 'order' for diverting the money to the civil deposit or public ledger account to save state funds from the 'March loot' when during the closing stages of the financial year, excess withdrawals are regularly noted. Probably, this is the reason why in spite of the Patna High Court's directive to the CBI to investigate the whole case, and the Supreme Court's rejection of the state government's appeal, the state government continued to resist CBI inquiry and insisted on an inquiry by a judicial commission to be set up by the state government. The case started in the court in 1998 and the former CM has been sent to jail twice for a short period. At present he is on bail.

The *Pay-off Scandal* involved the former Congress Prime Minister who was alleged to have received a suitcase containing one crore rupees from a share-broker who was the main accused in the securities scandal in 1992. This former Prime Minister was also declared as co-accused along with Chandra Swami in July 1996 by the chief metropolitan magistrate, New Delhi, in one Lakhubhai Pathak cheating case involving one lakh dollars. The former Prime Minister has been accused and chargesheeted in another case in the matter relating to the bribing of Jharkhand Mukti Morcha MPs. He was also named by one Jain brother (of Hawala case) as one of the largest beneficiaries of receiving several crore rupees. The CBI officer who obtained this confession from Jain brother was moved out by the CBI Director who was alleged to be very close to the former Prime Minister. No wonder that Bureau's conduct is now described by the Indian media as a national scandal.

The *Urea Scam* is the scam of the century. It is a scandal that makes Bofors scam look like a teddy bear's picnic; a deal that makes the sugar scam seem puny in comparison; and a deal in which the corruption is of a magnitude that is unprecedented in the history of Independent India. The urea scandal is different not because of the size of the kickbacks (Rs. 133 crore) but because the transaction was essentially fraudulent. The deal was made in October 1995 by National Fertilizers Limited (NFL), a public sector undertaking operating under the Fertilizer Ministry with an unknown small Turkish firm to purchase two lakh metric tonnes of urea—a raw material used for the manufacture of fertiliser. The entire amount was to be paid in advance to the firm. Though the total amount was paid to the firm within a week of signing the deed but the urea which was to be supplied by March 1996 was not supplied till August 1996. The kickbacks of US dollars 4 million are alleged to have been paid by the Turkish company's agent to the son of former Prime Minister, son of former Central Fertiliser Minister, Managing and Executive Directors of NFL, and a person related to former Prime Minister's son. The judgment of the case is likely to be announced in May, 2000.

The *Rice Scam* in Madhya Pradesh was reported in the media in February 1996. According to the state's levy scheme, 40 per cent rice produced was to be sold to district administration and the remaining produce can be exported. But in most cases, almost 100 per cent of the total produce was palmed off by the traders to rice-buying companies that existed only on paper. The fictitious companies were issued levy-paid certificates for as many as six lakh tonnes of rice in the last few years when only two lakh tonnes were actually sold. The top politicians were alleged to be involved in the fraudulent dealings involving fifty crore rupees.

In the *Balarpur Scam*, the former chief minister of Orissa is alleged to have abused his official position by granting concessions on bamboo royalty in 1992 to the Thapar-group (owned) Ballarpur Paper Mills in which the chief minister's son and wife had business interests. The state incurred a loss of seven crore rupees.

In the *Textile* or *Dhoti-Sari Scam* of Tamil Nadu, detected in mid-February, 1996, public officials of the Handloom Department, Handloom and Social Welfare Minister, her private secretary and his brother, and an AIADMK activist were alleged to be involved. This was when the Tansi and the Coal-Import Scams in which the chief minister was alleged to be involved remained unsolved upto May, 2000. In the textile scam, the strategy was to effect purchase of yarn (from non-existing firms) by Tamil Nadu Textiles Corporation (TNTC) and then show it as consumed by supplying it to government handloom cooperatives (which did not even own looms). These cooperatives were supposed to be weaving saris and dhotis from the yarn so received and then to distribute these to the poor under the government "clothing for the poor" scheme in operation from 1978. In the year 1994-95 alone, close to 200 lakh bundles of yarn were shown to have been bought. The saris, dhotis and children's dresses actually distributed on the Pongal day were bought from the open market in Tamil Nadu and Andhra Pradesh and sold to the Handloom Department at highly-inflated prices. The bungling by the state's Social Welfare Department was not a major embarrassment for the chief minister who was alleged to have spent about Rs. 70 crore in her adopted son's marriage in 1995.

It will not be out of place to recall here the public reaction to corruption amongst politicians and the failing standards of integrity in public life on the basis of a survey commissioned by *India Today* (magazine) and conducted by MARG. The survey was conducted in ten constituencies of ten politicians involved in the Hawala scam. In all, 3,901 registered voters scattered in 630 localities (i.e., rural and urban areas) in six different states (Nandiyad in Andhra Pradesh, Gandhinagar in Gujarat, Satna, Gwalior and Raipur in Madhya Pradesh, Ghosi and Bahraich in Uttar Pradesh, Ranchi and Madhepara in Bihar, and Sikar in Rajasthan) were interviewed. The survey was carried out in the second and third weeks of February 1996.

It was found (*India Today*, March 15, 1996: 52-59) that 75 per cent of the voters believed that the level of political corruption in India is worse today than it was five years ago. Further, 52 per cent respondents agreed (against 27% who disagreed) that politicians are more corrupt than people in other fields; 35 per cent agreed (against 51% who disagreed) that one has to be corrupt in order to survive in politics today; and 45 per cent agreed (against 40% who disagreed) that they preferred leaders who are corrupt but efficient to those who are honest but inefficient. In 9 out of 10 cases of politicians involved in the Hawala case, 35 to 80 per cent of the respondents believed that their leaders had taken the money (from Jain brothers) and 45 to 75 per cent voters said that they were unwilling to re-elect the politicians involved from their constituencies in April 1996 elections (though surprisingly a good number of these accused politicians were actually elected). All this points out the premium placed by people on honesty in politics today.

The money received by politicians as bribes and kickbacks is mostly spent on contesting elections, seeking political support for advancing their political prospects, ensuring splits in opposition political parties (Congress is said to have spent 70-100 million rupees to ensure a split in the Janata Dal in 1991), constructing bungalows, purchasing farm-houses and agricultural land, buying diamonds and jewellery, investing in shares, bonds, and certificates, sending children to foreign countries for education, maintaining accounts in foreign banks, and setting up their children in business. An average politician spends Rs. 10 lakh on contesting a Vidhan Sabha seat (against the permissible amount of Rs. 1.5 lakh) and Rs. 30-40 lakh on a Lok Sabha seat (against the permissible figure of Rs. 4 lakh in big cities). Without accepting pay-offs, it is impossible for politicians to arrange for such huge amounts. One Prime Minister (Indira Gandhi) had banned corporate contributions to political parties in 1983 but another Prime Minister (Rajiv Gandhi) reversed that policy in 1985. Politicians now receive cash contributions from fat cats. Consequently, politicians remain obliged to businessmen because of which the prices of sugar, oil, cement, and many other commodities suddenly rise during/after elections. Who supports the politicians who are not in power but continue to travel by planes for addressing rallies and attending meetings of their supporters? The money is probably dished out by business concerns who consider it an 'investment' with an eye on future profits. Such a thing happened in Gujarat in October 1995 when fifty lakh rupees were supposed to have been spent merely on transporting and accommodating, in a five-star hotel for one week in Khajuraho, about 60 dissident legislators of one faction of the ruling political party. All this analysis demonstrates not only the nature and extent of corruption within our political system but also how it has become embedded in the national consciousness.

If we take only mega scams in a period of ten years between 1986 and 1996, the country lost about Rs. 15,000 crore, or Rs. 1,500 crore a year. If we take various other 'questionable deals' in which colossal sums of money were received by the politicians and bureaucrats, India has been losing about twenty crore rupees every single day. This is surely a big threat to the very survival of democracy in our country.

Different scholars have pointed out different causes of political corruption. My contention is that the main factor is the emergence of political elite who believe in self-oriented rather than nation-oriented programmes and policies. Not surprisingly, the post-British Raj (rule) has been described as the "Raj of Ministers and Bureaucrats". The political elite in the first two decades after independence were honest, dedicated and nation-oriented to the extent that they always worked for the country's progress. In the fourth general elections in 1967, such persons came to hold political power—both at the centre and in the states—who worked only on the basis of some vested interest, say interest of self, family, region, party, and so forth. Their policies and programmes incidentally might have been nation-oriented but mainly they were self interest-based. They encouraged bureaucrats too to follow suit. A majority of bureaucrats (subelites in politics) in our country are 'ritualists' and remain concerned more with perks and privileges than with development-oriented policies for society. The politicians and bureaucrats thus started using their power and position for illegal benefits. The emergence of new business leaders who wanted to make quick profits, and who did not mind sharing them with people in power, was equally responsible for growing political corruption.

Political corruption also ensues from the vast powers enjoyed by position-holders and having no sense of accountability to people. Politicians have powers of taking decisions, say, issuing licences, sanctioning contracts for projects, enacting laws for the chosen minorities who can give them votes for winning elections, and so forth. It is not the rules but the interpretation of the rules which enables power-holders to receive kickbacks and pocket bribes. The point is that political corruption exists in our country---it is all-pervasive and this fact is undeniable. This is so not because we are a congenitally corrupt people, but because we are living in a system that is flawed. How do we set about tackling it? Is simply reporting cases in the newspapers or filing chargesheets in the courts or appointing commissions of enquiry enough? Has any politician in India ever been punished? So many commissions have been appointed against so many chief ministers and ministers, and on occasions even the charges levelled against them were proved but what action was taken against them? They were asked to resign from their political posts. We may not expect our rulers to be too honest but we surely expect them to work for the development of the community and society. Let the amount of money transferred to politicians by industrialists be accepted as a corporate payment—a donation that is accounted for. Let not unreasonable limits be placed on the amount of money a campaigner needs to spend on elections. Let there be fewer rules. At the moment, numerous rules achieve nothing except their violation.

What we expect from our politicians is honesty in their dealings, not the amassing of wealth. People expect them to think only of the country's development. Political corruption, let it be emphatically stated, will only ruin our country.

POLITICAL ACTIVITIES AS CRIMES

We now take the second type of political crime, namely, violation of laws with a political motive.

Every political organisation creates rules of conduct for controlling the behaviour of individuals, groups and institutions. These rules are binding on all persons in the country. Criminal law thus not only prohibits certain kinds of conduct and determines the nature of the sanctions attached but it also initiates a process of formulating and administering public policy. Further more, the political nature of criminal law affects the administration of the law as well as its content, i.e., the decision as to who is a criminal is also made in the enforcement and interpretation of the criminal law. In other words, the values and actions of the groups holding political power can establish criminality of an individual. Thus, political crime refers to that behaviour which is defined as criminal because it is regarded as an apparent threat and danger to the state. Violation of curfew, or of section 144, or a ban on holding political meetings—all these are regarded by political authorities as detrimental to the state. Suppression of such behaviour is considered necessary for political reasons. Included in this definition of 'political is a wide range of behaviour like: treason, espionage, sabotage, political assassination, war collaboration, violation of military draft regulations, youth protests, and violation of certain laws because of radical beliefs.

Horton and Leslie have included in the definition of political crimes actions of political office-holders against 'legalistic criminals' who hold unpopular political ideas. Many political radicals are often convicted of conventional crime on flimsy evidence. These 'legalistic criminals' have nothing in common with conventional criminals. They lack criminal intent and criminal orientation, and need no special treatment. George Vold (*Theoretical Criminology*, 1958: 299-300) has outlined several criminal sub-types that exist because persons pursue certain activities which are not favoured by the political majority. Among these criminals are: (1) political offenders whose views are regarded as subversive by the government, (2) religious or philosophical sectarians whose behaviour is contrary to the law, and (3) non-conformist intellectuals who because of their convictions persist in outlawed behaviour.

Merton (Cf. Merton, "Social Problems and Sociological Theory" in Merton and Nisbet's *Contemporary Social Problems*, 1966: 808-11) has distinguished between 'non-conforming' and 'aberrant' behaviour to understand the career of the political criminal. According to him, the non-conformer, in contrast to the aberrant: (a) announces his dissent publicly, (b) challenges the legitimacy of the norms and laws he violates, (c) aims at changing the norms he is denying in practice, (d) is acknowledged by conventional members of the society to depart from prevailing norms for disinterested purposes and not for what he personally can get out of it, and (e) lays claim to a higher morality and to ultimate values rather than to the particular norms of the society. Criminologists have concentrated their attention on the career of the aberrant to the almost total neglect of the non-conformer.

Clinard and Quinney (*op. cit.*, 1967: 279) have maintained that political crime as a behaviour system consists of a number of sub-types but all these (sub-types) share certain characteristics. These are: (1) political offenders usually do not engage in criminal activities as a full-time career; (2) persons who commit political crimes do not conceive of themselves as criminals and do not identify with crime or criminal bahaviour; (3) they violate the law only when such behaviour seems to be the most appropriate means for achieving certain ends which are not personal but are deemed desirable for the larger society; (4) the action taken by the offender is usually public rather than private. The criminal behaviour is regarded by the offender as symbolic of a higher purpose; and (5) political offenders carry on their illegal activities in pursuit of an ideal.

What are the characteristics of persons who engage in political crimes? Political offenders differ not only from non-criminals but also from one another according to the type of political crime they commit. For example, in regard to social class, some political offenders are from the middle class but some are from the lower class too. Likewise, in respect to religion, there are political offenders who are Hindus, Muslims, Christians, as well as members of scheduled castes and scheduled tribes. The political 'offenders' of Jharkhand movement arrested in Bihar in 1993 and 1994 were mainly scheduled tribes people. Quinney (*op. cit.*, 180) too has said: "It appears that the crucial factors in the career of the political offender are not personal and social characteristics *per se* but the values of the offender and the value systems to which he is actively responding."

Political criminals usually violate law because they want a social order different from the existing one. Clinard and Quinney are of the view that the social order to which political offenders are committed may be a modification of the one that exists or may be an entirely new order. Traitors and spies are examples of political criminals who are not necessarily committed to a new social order but indulge in political crimes purely for economic reasons, i.e., the huge amounts of money they get from the countries for which they spy. The scientists' scam in 1994 in which several scientists (and also non-scientists) were arrested may be cited in this context. Their entire career is not devoted to passing on secret information, generally of a valuable military nature, to a foreign power. They are committed to their own country but are carried away by their self-interest and the lure of financial gains. Thus, it may be said that the vast majority of political offenders are conscientious followers of the political philosophy of their own government. There are some persons without integrity who yield to the temptation of extensive bribes offered by foreign powers or by local groups. However, Kashmiri political criminals who get money from foreign powers cannot be included in this category because their objective is not financial gain but overthrowing the existing government and politically acceding to another country or establishing an independent Kashmir. The Sikh militants who had raised the political slogan of 'Azad Khalistan' may also be included in this category of political criminals. Political offenders, thus, present a paradox for they are criminals who carry on their illegal activities in pursuit of their ideals as well as for selfish financial interest. In other words, there are political criminals who are not motivated by the sordid desire of extracting money, but, are idealists, and, are devoted to a cause, while there are political criminals who are interested only in money.

SELF-IMAGE OF POLITICAL CRIMINALS

What is the image that political offenders have of themselves? How do they react to being labelled as 'political offenders?' By and large, pursuit of illegal (political) behaviour is not regarded by political offenders as a serious matter. After all, they obey most of the laws of the country. The violation of some criminal laws only represents their political ideology and a desire for establishing a new type of political system. Political offenders do not consider themselves as persons who are 'disloyal' to their country; they consider themselves loyal to a social order or a political system which they regard as more worthy of allegiance. In fact, they believe that their political crime has 'group support'. The participants in the Nagaland movement, the Bodo movement (Assam), the Gorkhaland movement, the Jharkhand movement, and the Uttarakhand movement were persons all of whom were committed to a certain political ideology but who never regarded themselves as 'traitors'.

GROUP SUPPORT TO POLITICAL CRIMINALS

Clinard and Quinney (*op. cit.*, 182-83) have pointed out that the group nature of political crime varies from one kind of political crime to another. Some political criminals receive less group support than others. Also, the groups to which political offenders may belong differ greatly in their ideologies. In addition, the social organisation of groups supporting political crime varies with the size of the group, cohesiveness of the group, formality of organisation, duration of the group, geographical dispersion of its members and patterns of leadership. Also, groups differ in the techniques and tactics used by members in the course of committing offences. Some political criminals support violence as a political tactic but not all encourage it. The obvious examples of the first type are Kashmiri and Khalistani political criminals who advocate the use of violence, while the agitators of Uttarakhand, who believe in passive methods only, belong to the second category. Both are arrested as political law-violators but both have different ideologies and use different tactics. Khalistan supporters killed thousands of Hindus and Sikhs in Punjab. Kashmiri militants too have killed hundreds of Kashmiris, looted banks and kidnapped persons. Many of them have been arrested as 'political criminals' under TADA because they had used force and violence.

SOCIETAL REACTION

Political criminals may be classified in two groups: one, who are considered a threat and danger to society, and two, who are considered only as corrupt persons who misuse their political positions to get more money either for themselves or for their political parties. The involvement of more than sixty politicians in the Hawala case in India in which thousands of crores of rupees are believed to have been given to political persons points to a scam in which the second type of political criminals are involved, while the militants in Punjab, Kashmir, Nagaland, Assam, and Mizoram may be included in the first category. Political criminals of this type are not dealt with lightly. Reaction to their crimes is harsh and severe because the criminals' loyalty to nation is in question. Public reaction to an activity regarded as a threat to political authority is hat these criminals should be punished so that similar political behaviour does not occur. The official reaction to political crime of this type is equally severe.

It may be concluded that both types of political criminals are a nuisance to society. The sooner society gets rid of them, the better for the country.

References

Caldwell, Robert G., *Criminology*, Ronald Press Company, New York, 1956.

Clinard, Marshall B. and Quinney Richard, *Criminal Behaviour Systems: A Typology*, Rinehart, Holt and Winston, Inc., New York, 1967.

Malhotra, K.L, *Facets of Vigilance* (2nd edn.), Malhotra Publications, Delhi, 1992.

Nye, J, *Corruption and Political Development: A Cost-benefit Analysis*, *American Political Review*, 1967.

India Today, New Delhi, March 15, 1996.

Frontline, Madras, March 22, 1996.

Chapter 10

Crime Against Women

HARASSMENT AND HUMILIATION OF WOMEN

Humiliation, harassment, torture and exploitation of women is as old as is the history of family life. In India, women are way ahead of women elsewhere in the matter of social legislation but the implementation of laws granting rights to women has been so slow, lopsided and haphazard that socially, economically and politically women lag far behind men. They are discriminated against at work and are denied their due in every field. At home, they are often even worse off, reduced to being slavish drudges and maltreated in a hundred different ways. Constantly derided, frequently bullied, sometimes assaulted and occasionally burnt to death, they remain victims in every role. Surprisingly, female victims of crime and violence have not been given much attention in books on social problems or in literature on criminal violence. The attitude of indifference and negligence is primarily the result of general acceptance of man's superiority over woman because of which violent acts against women have not been viewed as violent acts. It is also the result of denial of violence by women themselves due to their religious values and social attitudes. It is only recently that the issue of crime against women has been transformed from a private issue into a public problem.

CONCEPT OF CRIME AGAINST WOMEN

Although, women may be victims of all kinds of crime, be it cheating, murder, robbery, etc., yet the crimes in which *only women* are victims and which are directed specifically against them are characterised as "crime against women". Broadly, crimes against women are classified under two categories:

(1) *Crimes under the Indian Penal Code* (IPC), which include seven crimes: (i) rape, (ii) kidnapping and abduction, (iii) dowry deaths, (iv) torture---physical and mental (including wife battering), (v) molestation, and (vi) sexual harassment, and (vii) importation of girls.

(2) *Crimes under Special and Local Laws* (SLL), which include seventeen crimes, of which the important ones are: (i) immoral traffic (1956 and 1978 Act), (ii) dowry prohibition (1961 Act), (iii) committing Sati (1987 Act), and (iv) indecent representation of women (1986 Act).

It is equally important to clarify the concept of 'violence' against women. If we take 'violence' as "conduct which incurs the formal pronouncements of the moral condemnation of the community," or "deviation from conduct norms of the normative groups", the scope of cases of 'violence against women' becomes too broad. Narrowly, the term 'violence' has been applied to "physically striking an individual and causing injury" (Kempe, 1982; Gil, 1970), to "the act of striking a person with the intent of causing harm or injury but not actually causing it" (Gelles and Strauss, 1979), to "acts where there is the high potential of causing injury" (Strauss, 1980), and to "acts which may not involve actual hitting but may involve verbal abuse or psychological stress and suffering". Megargee (1982: 85) has defined violence as the "overtly threatened or overtly accomplished application of force which results in the injury or destruction of persons or their reputation."

While understanding the concept of 'violence' and distinguishing it from concepts like 'aggression', 'force', and 'coercion', is both necessary and desirable, there is always the fear of getting bogged down in controversies relating to these concepts raised by various scholars. As a result, one may miss the very purpose of understanding broader aspects of the problem of "crime and violence against women". 'Violence' must be recognised as a human phenomenon inasmuch as it consists of an act of one person which encroaches upon the freedom of another (Domenach, 1981: 30). Here, we consider the operational definition of violence as "force, whether overt or covert, used to wrest from the individual (the woman) something that she does not want to give of her own free will and which causes her either physical injury or emotional trauma or both". Thus, rape, abduction, kidnapping, murder (all cases of criminal violence), dowry death, wife battering, sexual abuse, maltreatment of a widow and/or an elderly woman (all cases of domestic violence) and eve-teasing, forcing wife/daughter-in-law to go for foeticide, forcing a young widow to commit *sati*, etc. (all cases of social violence), are issues which affect a large section of society. In the analysis of the problem of 'crime against women', we may focus on important issues like nature and extent of female crime in India, on identifying women who are generally victims of crime and violence, on those who are the perpetrators of crime and violence, on what motivates criminals to commit crimes or victimisers to use violence, and on measures which could contain the depersonalisation trauma of the victims.

INCIDENCE OF CRIME

The figures pertaining to seven types of crimes against women in India in the three years, between 1996 and 1998, indicate that these crimes have been constantly increasing every year. Broadly speaking, every year about 15,000 rapes, 30,000 cases of molestation, 15,500 cases of kidnapping, 4,000 cases of torture, 6,500 cases of sexual harassment and 6,000 cases of dowry-deaths take place. Of the total crimes against women under the Indian Penal Code (IPC) in three years between 1996 and 1998 (1,22,760), 30.7 per cent are torture cases, 24.7 per cent are molestation cases, 5.3 per cent are eve-teasing cases, 12.7 per cent are kidnapping and abduction cases, 12.3 per cent are rape cases, and 5 per cent are dowry deaths, 6.7 per cant are immoral traffic cases, 0.1 per cent are importation of girls cases, 0.1 per cent are indecent representation cases and 2.4 per cent are cases under Dowry Prohibition Act (*Crime in India*, 1998: 156).

The proportion of IPC crimes committed against women towards total IPC crimes remained around 6 per cent during 1996 to 1998. The number of crimes against women per one lakh population worked out to be 13.5 during 1998. With reference to female population, this comes to 28.1 per cent per one lakh female population. Uttar Pradesh reported highest incidence of these crimes (13.3%), followed by Madhya Pradesh (12.1%) and Maharashtra (10.9), Rajasthan (12.1%) and Maharashtra (10.9%), Rajasthan (9.3%), Andhra Pradesh (8%) and Tamil Nadu (6.5%) (*ibid.*: 150).

Statewise it is seen that the high level of incidence of rape is found in Madhya Pradesh (22.3%), Mizoram, Arunachal Pradesh, Uttar Pradesh, and Maharashtra. The level of kidnapping is high in Delhi, Uttar Pradesh, Rajasthan and Jammu & Kashmir. Dowry-deaths are high in Uttar Pradesh, Andhra Pradesh, Haryana, Maharashtra, Orissa and Rajasthan.

Torture (cruelty by husband and other relatives) is recorded high in Maharashtra, Uttar Pradesh, West Bengal, Andhra Pradesh and Rajasthan. The crime level of molestation is high in Andamans and Nicobar Islands, Madhya Pradesh, Maharashtra, Uttar Pradesh, Andhra Pradesh and Mizoram. Lastly, eve-teasing cases are found high in the union territory of Pondicherry, Delhi, Chandigarh, Uttar Pradesh, Andhra Pradesh and Maharashtra (*Crime in India*, 1998: 159-160).

There are 10 molestation cases every three hours and five rapes every three hours in our country. Though in comparison to the West, the annual rate of rapes per one lakh of population may not be very high (it being 0.5 per one lakh of population in India in comparison to 26 in the United States, 8 in Canada, 5.4 in England). In view of the fact that a very large percentage of rape cases goes unreported either because the victim does not have the courage to face shame and humiliation poured on her by society, or because of the disgrace reporting will bring to her family, or because of police harassment, or threats of retaliation by the rapists, and considering the fact that molestations and rapes constitute the highest percentage (37) among crimes against women, rape should be viewed as a serious problem that causes personality disorders in victims, attracts social stigmatisation of their children, and social disgrace to their families.

Like molestation and rape, the incidence of kidnapping and abduction has also been increasing in our society. The incidence in 1973 increased by 8.7 per cent over 1972; in 1978, the incidence increased by 11.1 per cent over 1977; in 1982 the incidence increased by 14.1 per cent over 1981, and in 1998 the incidence increased by 4.9 per cent over 1997. It could be said that 5 girls/women are kidnapped/abducted every three hours. The rate per one lakh of population is 2 in our country (*ibid.*: 156).

Dowry-deaths too have been increasing every year. At a rough estimate, the figure for deaths in India that occur owing to non-payment or partial payment of dowry could be placed around 17 in one day. Delhi police recorded 421 cases of bride-burning in 1980,568 in 1981, 619 in 1982, 423 in 1987, and 647 in 1994. In Andhra Pradesh, against 14 cases registered in 1983, there were 27 cases in 1984, 160 cases in 1985, and 172 cases in 1994. The Andhra Pradesh Mahila Federation, however, claims that there are more than 300 cases of dowry-oriented suicides and murders every year. Of the total dowry deaths every year in the country, the highest percentage (32.2) is reported in Uttar Pradesh, followed by Bihar (15.0), Madhya Pradesh (8.6), Andhra Pradesh (7.2), Rajasthan (6.2) and Maharashtra (6.1) (*Crime in India*, 1998: 164).

As regards female murders, though the figures pertaining to victims of murder on the basis of sex are not available in India, it is well known that the number of female victims of homicide in comparison to male victims is low. Whereas in the United States, female victims constitute between 20 and 25 per cent of the total victims of homicide (about 25 to 30 thousand every year), in India, of about 38,700 murders committed every year, women constitute about 10 to 15 per cent of the total victims, i.e., about 4,000 to 6,000 per year.

Lastly, though cases of torture (wife battering and cruelty by relatives) are seldom reported to the police in our society, yet it may not be unreasonable to believe that the numbers involved are high as more than one woman in every 500 to 1,000 women is battered.

Adding cases of sexual harassment and molestation, we get a rough idea of the incidence of cases of crimes against women and various forms of subjugation of women by men in our country.

THE VICTIMS

What types of women are the victims of various types of crimes? Who are the criminals or the victimisers? What motivates males to commit crimes against women? I would like to mention here some of the findings from my empirical study on 'crimes against women' conducted in 1985-86 in Rajasthan. In this research, I had studied 189 crimes of rape, abduction, dowry death, wife-battering, and murder. I will mention here only a few important findings in each of the five types of crimes (against women).

The findings in respect of *rape* or *criminal assault* cases are:

1. About 56 per cent rape victims are in the age group of 16-30 years, 23 per cent in the age group of 10-16 years, 4 per cent are below 10 years and 17 per cent are above 30 years. Thus 8 out of 10 victims are adolescents and young girls.
2. Criminal assault does not always occur between total strangers. In about half of criminal assault cases, the assault victim is known to her assailant (as a relative, neighbour, family friend, co-worker, boss, teacher, acquaintance).
3. Though criminal assault is generally a situational act but in four out of every ten cases criminal assault is a fully or partially planned event
4. Pair and group assault cases or multiple offender victimisation accounts for one fourth of the total assault cases.

5. Criminal assault is victim-precipitated only in a very small number of cases. In a majority cases, victims are not responsible for their victimisation.
6. While in a large number of cases, temptation and verbal coercion are used to subdue the victim, in some cases physical violence too is used to coerce her.

The findings in *kidnapping* and *abduction* cases are:

1. Unmarried girls are victims of kidnapping/abduction more than married women.
2. Both abductors and victims are generally young in age. A little less than three-fourths victims belong to the age-group of 16-21 years and about one-fourth to the age group of 22-25 years. Against this, 80 per cent of the abductors belong to the age group of 18-29 years.
3. Abductors and the abducted victims are slightly acquainted with one another rather than being total strangers.
4. The initial contact between the abductor and his victim frequently occurs in their own homes and neighbourhoods rather than in public places.
5. As motivating factors, sex and marriage are more important in abduction than economic gain.
6. There is a significant association between victims of abduction and the social class to which the abductors belong.

The findings in *dowry-deaths* are:

1. Middle-class women have a higher rate of victimisation than lower-class or upper-class women.
2. Almost all girls, who are killed over the dowry issue, belong to the age group (21-24) in which they can be considered rather mature not only psychologically but socially and emotionally too.
3. Households headed by dominant mothers-in-law and uncompromising husbands have higher victimisation rates.
4. Before actual murder, several forms of harassment and humiliation are perpetrated against the young brides which show the chaotic patterns of social adaptation of the members of the victim's family of procreation.
5. Killers in dowry deaths are brutal and authoritarian and the murder of the victim is only one expression of the offender's personality maladjustment and abnormality.

The findings pertaining to *wife-battering* are:

1. Young wives (below 25) have higher victimisation rates than middle-aged or older women.
2. Though illiterate wives are more vulnerable to beating by husbands than educated wives, there is no significant relationship between beating and the educational level of the victims.
3. Women in the low-income families (below Rs. 500 per month) are more likely to be victimised, though family income is difficult to associate with victimisation.
4. Most of the husbands beat their wives not in a state of drunkenness but when sober.
5. Wife-battering rates are directly related to stress situations in families. The stress situations could be: financial problems, unemployment or part-time employment of husband, ill-treatment of wife by in-laws, and having an incompatible partner.

Lastly, the findings pertaining to *female murders* are:

1. In a large majority of cases, murderers and victims are members of the same family, and a large number of murders by men are wife murders.
2. About half of the murder victims are women with long-standing relationships with the male murderers.
3. The ratio of malicious female murders with or without an explicit intention to kill to non-malicious emotional or accidental murders is 4:6.
4. Familial maladjustment in general and marital relations in particular are very crucial in female homicides. Arguments and altercations precipitating homicides generally related to money, treatment of in-laws, care of children, and illicit relations.
5. Only one-fifth of the murders tend to be victim-precipitated.

Taking all five types of crime cases together, it may be generalised that the victims of violence are generally women:

- Who have the feelings of helplessness, depression, poor self-image, and suffer from self-devaluation or self-deprecation; or who are 'emotionally consumed' by the perpetrators of violence or violators of law; or who suffer from 'altruistic powerlessness'.
- Who live in stressful family situation and are economically dependent on others.

- Who lack social inter-personal skills because of which they face behavioural problems.
- Whose husbands/in-laws have pathological personalities; and
- Whose husbands are frequent alcohol-users.

MALE CRIMINALS OR EXPLOITERS OR PERPETRATORS OF VIOLENCE

The male criminals or women's exploiters or the perpetrators of violence are generally those who:

- are victims of violence in childhood;
- face stressful situations in family;
- have depressions, inferiority complex, and low self-esteem;
- lack resources—skills, talents—and are sociopathic;
- have personality disorders and are psychopaths;
- have possessive, suspicious and dominant nature; and
- are frequent users of alcohol.

Types of Crimes or Exploitations

If we were to develop the typology of crimes against or exploitation of women, we can give five types of crime and exploitation:

- Crime which is the result of stressful family situations.
- Crime which aims at pleasure-seeking.
- Crime which is the result of criminal's pathology.
- Crime which is victim-precipitated.
- Crime which is alcohol influenced.

INTRA-FAMILIAL SEXUAL VIOLENCE

Just as cases of beating by husband or in-laws are rarely reported to the police, cases of sexual attacks by family members like brother-in-law, father-in-law, and sometimes even by father are also never brought to the notice of the law-enforcement agencies. A study conducted in 1993 in Jaipur by Mukesh Ahuja *Widows: Role Adjustment and Violence* (1996) on widows reveals that more than 10 per cent widows (out of 193 widows studied) were victims of sexual abuse. We read of cases in which sisters-in-law are seduced by their brothers-in-law or daughters-in-law are sexually assaulted by their fathers-in-law. The women in these cases are silenced either by threats or promises. The 'assaultor' capitalises on being 'special' and leaves the victim with the heavy price of guilt. Following Mukesh Ahuja's study, it may be pointed out that: (1) A high proportion of women who become victims of sexual attack by the family members are those who are economically dependent on others. (2) There is rarely an application of physical force or threat of bodily harm. More often, the women are psychologically enticed by affection for and dependence upon the assaultors. (3) In a large number of cases, the attempt at seduction and molestation is not repeated over a period of time. It is only in a very few cases that the attempt is repeated for a period ranging from weeks to months and in rare cases to years. (4) The cases of sexual attacks are found more in low and lower-middle classes with illiterate or less educated women. This, however, does not mean that cases of upper class women being molested by their close family members never occur; only their number is very small. (5) The attackers are generally married, indicating that the object of sexual attack is purely biological pleasure and not intention of marriage. (6) Victims and attackers' age distribution is not always homogeneous (young and early middle-aged), i.e., there does not appear to be a positive correlation between the victim's age and the attacker's age.

What are the etiological factors in intra-familial sexual assault? Three factors may be identified as important in this context: (i) personality traits of both victims and victimisers (victim's feeling of helplessness, inadequacy, dependence, etc. and victimiser's traits of dominance, and his feeling that he is not accountable to anybody); (ii) family structure and family environment; and (iii) situational factors like isolation, etc. These factors are to be taken together rather than in isolation, i.e., sexual attacks within the family should be seen as occurring in a context consisting of family living patterns and work situation that offer an opportunity for such behaviour.

MOTIVATION IN CRIME

What causes men to be criminal, violent, abusive and cruel towards women? Three theoretical schools on criminal violence are: *Psychopathological* school (which focuses on personality traits of offenders and victims), *socio-psychological* school (which focuses on effect of external factors on individual's everyday action), and *socio-cultural* or *sociological* school (which focuses on pressures of social systems and social structures on individual). Five important theoretical propositions of socio-psychological school are: (1) innate aggressive drive is directed to source of frustration (*Frustration-Aggression Theory*); (2) deviant act is the result of infantile instincts, distorted feelings, and split ego of the deviants (*Perversion Theory*); (3) persons of low esteem seek to improve their image in the eyes of others and themselves through deviant or violent acts (*Self-Attitude Theory*); (4) deviance is a normal response to provocation (*Provocation Theory*); and (5) individuals indulge in deviant behaviour when their resentment escalates on attributing malevolent intent/mo ivations to the actions of other individuals (*Motive Attribution Theory*).

Four important theoretical propositions of sociological school are: (1) cultural values and norms support and facilitate crime (*Theory of Subculture of Violence*); (2) crime is the result of strains caused by gap between goals and means (*Anomie Theory*); (3) crime is used as an instrument when an individual lacks resources for achieving his interests and yet wants to be a dominant person (*Resource Theory*); and (4) crime is conduct which is learnt through direct experience by observing others' behaviour and imitating it. Individuals raised in abusing homes learn that violence can and should be used against the weak (*Social Learning Theory*).

My contention is that causes of crime against women are found to be related mainly to five factors: (1) structure of the situation in which crime is committed, (2) situational 'facilities' which enable the committing of crime, (3) precipitating factor(s) that lead to crime, (4) strains experienced by the offender, i.e., his individual problems; and (5) victim's behaviour with the offender much before the crime is committed against her. A holistic approach to the combination of these factors alone will give us the correct causes of crime against women.

Specifically, three factors seem to play a major role in prompting a man to commit crime against a woman: (1) offender's history of abuse as a child (like unhappy upbringing, physical beating by parents and emotional rejection); (2) stressful situations in the family; and (3) status frustrations. The first factor points out that the offender's deviant behaviour is mostly learnt from childhood and adolescent experiences of emotional distresses. This posits the thesis of the 'Generational Theory' that growing up in a violent home increases the likelihood of an individual becoming violent/deviant as an adult. The fact that a very large number of offenders in my study (78%) were the victims of violence in childhood shows that my data supports this theory. The data also supports the 'Social Learning Theory' according to which indulging in deviant behaviour as a method of conflict resolution or as a coping mechanism is learnt behaviour. Women's tolerance of violence is explained in terms of 'Learned Helplessness Theory' and 'Traditional Socialisation Theory'. The latter theory refers to woman's imbibing traditional values and 'sex-role ideology' through socialisation process that man is superior to woman and that woman has no right to protest. The former theory maintains that some events occur in a woman's life with sufficient regularity because of which she acquires feelings of depression, helplessness and poor self-image and comes to believe that she cannot escape abuse.

Some of the theories mentioned above overemphasise personality, others underestimate the role of environment, and yet others focus on a single factor as the cause of crime. Most of the social scientists today consider holistic approach as a scientific approach in explaining deviant behaviour.

Besides the above theoretical explanations, three other theoretical approaches have also been used for explaining miseries heaped on women and/or the victimisation of women: (i) patriarchy approach, (ii) interpersonal power approach, and (iii) context-specific approach. (*see*, Mukesh Ahuja, 1996).

Patriarchy Approach

According to this approach, exploitation, ill-treatment and humiliation of an individual woman by an individual man is not an individual problem. It is simply one manifestation of the system of male domination of women. Societal tolerance of pitiable condition of women is also a reflection of patriarchal norms which, more generally, support male dominance in family and society. Del Martin [*Battered Wives*, 1976, quoted by Yllo Kersti in Finkelhor and Gelles (ed.), *The Dark Side of Families*, 1983], a noted feminist, has said:

> The historical roots of patriarchal family models are ancient and deep. Unless new norms of marriage and family are created, the victimisation of women will grow naturally out of ancient and time-honoured traditions.

Dobash and Dobash (1983) have also emphasised this factor in explaining violence against women. They assert that "men who use violence against women are actually living up to cultural prescriptions that are cherished in society—aggressiveness, male dominance, and female subordination—and they are using force as a means to enforce that dominance".

Patriarchy creates structural and institutional conditions whereby residence, lineage, authority and property rights tend to be the prerogative of males. Thus, male dominance is an obvious consequence of a structural milieu which conditions men for power and women for subordination, defines male domain as public and female domain as domestic.

Interpersonal Power Approach

This approach focuses not on "structured inequality on the societal level" but on "inequality and the balance of power" within the family and society. Those men who believe in "equality of power" respect women both in and outside the family, while those who believe in non-egalitarian power structure, ill-treat and even humiliate them.

Context-Specific Approach

This approach in explaining exploitation of women focuses on three specific factors: family structure, victimiser's traits, and victim's stresses. The family structure includes not merely the dimension of relationship and roles but also the pattern of interaction. The victimiser's traits refer to traits like lust, greed, dominance, selfishness, etc. Victim's stresses refer to victim's docile nature and passivity because of which she conceals her agonising desire to protest. This may be the result of her lack of resources, economic dependence and lack of husband's, parents', and in-laws' support.

A NEW THEORETICAL MODEL

Using such holistic approach, I propose a new theoretical model for understanding crime against women or women's exploitation. My model focuses on the linkage between women's (victim's) personality traits and social environment in which she lives and functions. It assumes that woman's exploitation (rape, molestation, beating, harassment for dowry, [eve] teasing, kidnapping for leading a life of a prostitute) is the result of interaction between a woman's personality (including imbibed feelings of helplessness, timidity, etc.) and her environment. Each woman lives in an environment composed of different persons with varied perceptions and expectations. A woman's perception of her own exploitation will depend on her own will and efforts to challenge it with courage.

Diagram 1

Model of Relationships between Personality Traits, Social Environment, and Woman's Exploitation by a Male

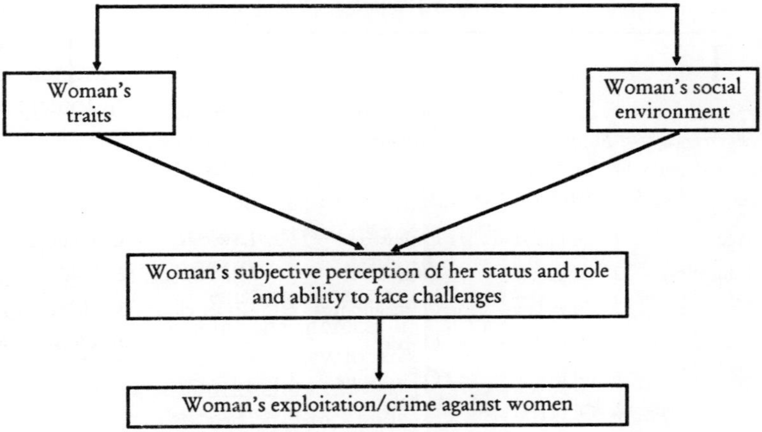

In this theoretical model, it is assumed that a woman's exploitation (or crime against women) is dependent on five things: (i) social background (which refers to her age, educational level and her training), (ii) level of support (which depends on the support of her parents, in-laws, peers and others), (iii) expectations of others (including her husband, parents, in-laws, children, kin, working colleagues, peers, etc.), (iv) economic base (i.e., whether she belongs to low, middle or upper income group), (v) self-image (whether she considers herself timid, bold, helpless, weak, strong, etc.).

My model explains crime against women in terms of *social structural conditions* (like family crises, role frustrations, inappropriate upbringing, and unfortunate incidents in life), *that create anxieties and stresses which affect the adjustment, attachment, and commitment of man.* (Adjustment is a smooth switch-over from one status to other; attachment is the bond of affection between an individual and other persons; and commitment is a feeling of obligation to seek a particular goal or to follow a particular course of action.) *The resultant maladjustment, unattachment, and non-commitment lead to frustrations and relative deprivation, which in turn determine man's attitude towards others, including the weaker sex or women.* (Relative deprivation is perceived discrepancy between capabilities and achievements. Here, the important factor is 'perceived' by an individual offender; hence, variations in behaviour). *Depending on his personality*

Diagram 2

Factors Affecting a Woman's Exploitation

A Woman's

Social Background:	*Level of Support or Support System:*	*Expectations of others:*	*Economic Base of Class Level:*	*Self-Image:*
1. Age	1. Of husband	1. Of husband	1. Low class	1. Timid
2. Education	2. Of parents	2. Of in-laws	2. Middle class	2. Bold
3. Training	3. Of in-laws	3. Of neighbours	3. Upper class	3. Helpless
	4. Of children	4. Of peers		4. Weak
	5. Of kin	5. Of working colleagues		
	6. Of peers			

traits and the resistance potential of the victim, a man commits crime against a woman.

Frustrated and relatively deprived individuals indulge in crime by being influenced by (i) women against whom crime is to be committed, i.e., victims have to be those who lack 'resistance potential' towards deviant/aggressive behaviour, and (ii) by the idea of justification of their act (criminal) before and after its commission. Thus, crime is committed by these frustrated individuals when they view *certain* females as appropriate victims and *certain* situations as suggestive of, even opportune for, committing crime, i.e., in *specific* circumstances and not in *all* circumstances.

My theory is, thus, based on a conjunctive approach which takes into account social factors like stressful situations endogenous and exogenous to family, personality traits of criminals and victims, and cultural milieu, like normative pressures and ambiguities.

POLICE AND JUDICIAL REACTIONS

How does the police react to those who commit crimes against women? What is the attitude of judicial officials to female victims? The police generally hold an image of a set of characteristics that would comprise a 'real victim' as well as a 'fake victim'. It is, therefore, not surprising that a

Diagram 3

New Theoretical Model Explaining Crime Against Women

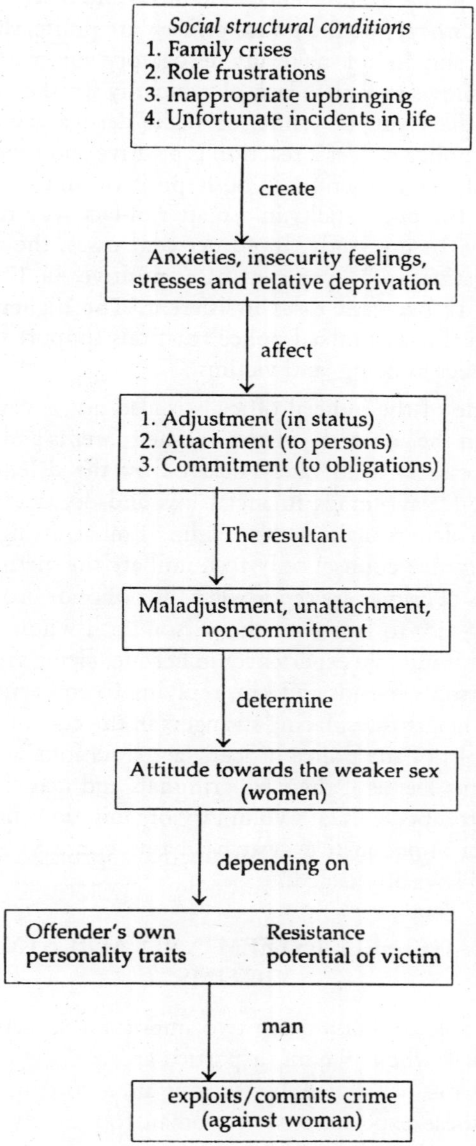

sorting process may occur in the police force in case of female victims of male crime. Victims in my study indicated such a sorting. On the basis of the reactions of the respondents and their parents in my study, the reactions of the police against female victims could be classified into four categories: (1) *positive*, i.e., the police officers are polite, show sympathy, listen seriously, and do not make any derogatory comments, (2) *negative*, i.e., the police shows complete lack of sympathy for the victim, does not take seriously the claim of crime, or make derogatory comments, (3) *mixed*, i.e., one police officer's reaction is positive and other's is negative, or the same officer's reaction is both positive and negative, and (4) *indifferent*, i.e., the police talks in a matter-of-fact way rather than in a derogatory way. In my study, in 40 per cent cases, the reaction of the police was negative, in 31 per cent cases positive, in 17 per cent cases mixed, and in 12 per cent cases indifferent. The higher percentage of negative, indifferent and mixed police reactions support the stereotyped image of the police as being 'anti-victims'.

The attitude of the judicial officials is also not always sympathetic. Once a case is in the court, the victim and her parents and kin are greatly harassed. The case is deliberately delayed by the defence lawyer as a pressure tactic. Delay entails financial loss and degradation. The court encounter also depersonalises the victim. Embarrassing questions are asked by the defence counsel only to humiliate the victim. No wonder, only a few cases of crimes are reported to the police or brought before the courts. Coming face to face with the person with whom the victim had one of the most traumatic experiences in her life, facing sarcastic smiles of the accused person's friends and kin, replying to embarrassing questions of lawyers and magistrates, facing strangers in the court-room, observing threatening looks of the police officers, are situations which sometimes make the victims feel as if they are criminals and it is they who are on trial. All this prompts women's voluntary organisations in the country to demand that criminal justice system in our country be changed and victim-oriented laws be enacted.

SELF-IMAGE, SELF-ESTEEM AND ADJUSTMENT OF VICTIMS

Self-image and role evaluation are two important aspects of behaviour. Every individual when playing a particular role according to certain social expectations is judged by society in accordance with his/her fulfilment of these expectations. A woman too, as a victim of crime/violence, evaluates herself which in turn helps/hinders her in performing the expected roles. Mukesh Ahuja studied self-image and self-esteem of 193 women (widows), victims of violence in 1993, by asking them ten questions each on self-image and self-esteem. The questions on self-image included questions on ill-treatment, humiliation, being ignored, on the feeling of being a burden, feeling rebellious, feeling like running away from home, and on leading a life of one's choice, etc. He found that about one-third (31%) victims had high self-image, about two-fifths (41%) had moderate self-image, and about one-fourth (28%) had low self-image. Making allowance for variables like education, income, age and working status, he concluded that self-image of victims is affected by age, (youth) high education and high income but not by working status.

As regards *self-esteem*, generally it is believed that women victims of crime/exploitation/violence develop a negative view of themselves. What Engeland (1983) has called "low self-esteem", Elwer (1987) has described as "self-devaluation", Kinard (1980) as "poor self concept" and Hjorth and Ostrow (1982) as "poor self-image". Mukesh Ahuja put ten questions to female victims (questions on success/failure in life, high/low status in family and society, feeling happy/unhappy, confidence in self, considering oneself strong/weak, and so forth). He found that a little less than one-third victims (30%) had high self-esteem, about two-fifths (40%) had moderate self-esteem, and a little less than one-third (30%) had low self-esteem. It was also found that like self-image, self-esteem of the victims too depended upon emotional support they get from different sources. Self-image and self-esteem were also found to be correlated with adjustment in family and society. High self-esteem is positive personality dimension and reduces dependency syndrome despite the socio-cultural stigma attached to being sexually assaulted, kidnapped, battered, and humiliated. It leads to adequate familial adjustment owing to equalitarian mode of relationship.

Following Mukesh Ahuja's empirical study (on widows), the following important sociological facts may be pointed out about the female victims of crime:

1. *Structures as source of problems*: The problems of females who are victims of crime arise from the functioning of social structures in which they live and work, and the stresses caused by family interactions and support systems.
2. *Tradition of barriers to assertion*: The involvement of victims in social roles and relationships after being victimised is dependent less on their own initiative and self-confidence and more on the will of heads of families (of procreation and orientation) and social pressures, i.e., traditional culture discourages female victims from taking up

assertive social engagements outside the home.

3. *Resource deprivation and suffering of self*: Resources like higher education and work with wages increase victim's self-image and self-esteem which considerably change her relations with others, and also enable her to face the strain of transition to life and 'recovery' and adjust herself in family and society.
4. *Attachment*: A large number of victims of crime overcome their feelings of being isolated and condemned by attaching themselves to some love object, social service, religious commitments, etc.
5. *Structural suffocation*: Factors which prevent victims (of crime) from renewing, redeeming, restoring, reviving and revitalising their lives lie more in social structures than in their personalities.
6. *Negation of revolt*: A few young and independent victims have a secret desire of rebelling and adopting modern methods of adjustment but they fail to rebel for the fear that their husbands, in-laws, and parents might severe ties with them. They are also scared of being shunned and ostracised by their kin and friends.
7. *Self-esteem situation*: Victims with soppy emotions lead a suppressed life but victims with courage of conviction, character, and consciousness chart their own course in their (working) life.

Adjustment Phases

The adjustment of victims after being stigmatised (i.e., raped, molested, kidnapped, beaten, harassed) to new life and their taking up new roles involve several phases, although there is much intermeshing of these phases. The phases seem to follow a sequence. Bowlby (*see*, *Journal of Social Issues*, Vol. 44, No. 3, 1988: 45-46) has identified four phases of 'recovery': shock, protest, despair and a long interval of adaptation. Following Bowlby and Mukesh Ahuja (1996), we may identify following four phases in female victims adjustment to life after stigmatisation: (i) shock and pain, (ii) removing pain, (iii) avoidance and humiliation, and (iv) adaptation.

All victims, however, do not experience the same level of shock and pain, the same level of humiliation and avoidance, and the same problems of finding substitute sources of adjustment.

Theoretical Explanation of Adjustment

After being molested, raped, frequently battered by husband, constantly

Diagram 4

Phases of Adjustment to New Life by Female Victims of Crime

Phase I

Shock and pain (depends on):
nature of crime committed against her and also on factors like:
1. Age
2. Education
3. Employment
4. Emotional attachment

Phase II

Removing pain (depends on) :
1. Support
2. Security

Phase III

Avoidance/Humiliation (by):
1. Family members
2. Kin
3. Friends
4. Acquaintances

Phase IV

Adaptation (through):
1. Religious consolation
2. Accepting social challenge
3. Neutralisation
4. Attachment and identity change

mocked at/harassed by eve-teasers, on being recovered after kidnapping, and/or after living in Rescue Home for weeks/months, how do women adjust themselves? How do they face social stigma, disgrace, shame, and grief? Disgrace and stigma are intense pain-generating emotions. Emotions are constituted in part through their relation to social systems and in part through their relation to personality systems. Pain-suffering is thus faced in the social context in which it occurs and adjustment is made possible in the context of social relationships and culture.

Two theories may broadly be referred to in providing a perspective on suffering humiliation and pain after exploitation, on adjustment after facing crime/disgrace/stigma: the Symbolic Interaction Theory and the

Family Systems Theory. The former has been explained by scholars like Berger and Kellner (1964), Marris (1974), Lofland (1985) and Rosenblatt and Wright (1984) (*see*, Rosenblatt, P.C., "Grief: The Social Context of Private Feelings" in *Journal of Social Issues*, 1988, 44 (3): 68-69), while the latter is explained by Berkwitz (1977), Kreil and Rabkin (1979), and Rosenblatt (1983). We will try to understand the pain, suffering and the attempts at adjustment of (women) victims of crime in terms of both these theories.

The Symbolic Interaction Theory lays emphasis on: (a) the loss of respect due to humiliation, and (b) how others are important (helpful/barriers) in defining humiliation, feeling humiliation, and coming to terms with humiliation. The Family Systems Theory places stress on: (a) how family norms and patterns affect humiliation experiences, and (b) how much humiliation affects family/kinship/social relationships.

Symbolic Interaction Theory

Applying this theory to victim's loss of respect, the facing of stigma, and her attempts at readjusting herself after experiencing humiliation, it may be said that part of the 'social context' in which she developed her self-image and determined her actions is removed when she is raped, battered by her husband, constantly humiliated by her in-laws, or recovered after kidnapping or after spending some time in a Rescue Home. That part of the social context which used to define, organise, and provide meaning to her life is no longer present. The loss of respect which was so important to the woman (victim) in defining self and situation provides character to her pain/suffering/humiliation. It gives 'pain' qualities of searching for meaning, of uncertainty about one's self, uncertainty about what to make of what has happened—confusion, non-confidence, etc. The loss of social relationships for defining her feelings compels her to search for alternative bases for defining self and situation. It may lead her to turn to religion, to some person (child, younger brother), to social work, etc. The processes involved in locating the person, the object, etc. to whom the victim (of crime) may 'attach' herself, are complex, and involve social activities that may be 'constructionist' or 'negotiational', i.e., passive acceptance of definitions offered by others and concentrating on days before the 'event' (rape, kidnapping, severe beating, etc.).

Culture also affects the grief, the prestige and the effort to readjust. For example, the belief system in the culture/subculture that says "do not

Diagram 5

Suffering Humiliation and Attempting Readjustment

Suffering humiliation and attempting readjustment
(i) has a social context
(ii) occurs in the context of social relations and subculture

explained in terms of

- **Theory of Symbolic Interaction** — emphasis on
  - Loss of respect due to humiliation ↓ The victim loses social context for defining self and situation and feels sad/depressed. She therefore searches new persons/objects to whom to attach herself or concentrates on suffered humiliation.
  - How others are important (helpful/barriers) in defining humiliation, feeling humiliation, and coming to terms with humiliation. Others perceive of cultural norms, own values and emotional control used by the victim to face humiliation. If suffering/pain/grief appears to them bizarre, they shy away from helping her. The victim, thus, has also to be concerned with others' reactions to her suffering.
- **Theory of Family Systems** — emphasis on
  - How family norms and patterns affect humiliation experiences. Along with the victim, the victim's family members too suffer loss of respect. In an attempt of readjustment, they turn to one another for softening the loss. If they fail, they suffer not only the loss of prestige but also the dysfunctioning of the social system that has failed to help them.
  - How much humilitation affects social relations in the family, kin group and society.

grieve because you were not a willing party to the event, rather you were the victim of circumstances" may reduce the grief of the victim. It has been said, not without reason, that there is never just a single human response to pain/suffering/humiliation, but there always is a substantial range of responses, each of which expresses feelings of grief/loss of respect.

The victim who suffers lacks flexibility to deal easily with relationship issues. The 'others' around her perceive her grief/suffering/loss of respect in the context of existing cultural norms and the emotional control used by the victim to face the 'event' (rape, molestation, assault, etc.). Victims of eve-teasing, molestation and husbands' beating may face one type of reaction but victims of rape, or kidnapping with a few day's stay in a kidnapper's house may face totally different reactions of their family members and kin. If the victim is found to be a 'willing partner' in the crime, they make themselves less available to her. Thus, besides suffering loss of prestige, the victim also faces the problem of symbolic reactions of others to her grief. The anticipation of reactions of family members, kin, neighbours, peers, working colleagues, etc. to her actions and activities necessitates paying attention to possible reactions to her behaviour and lifestyle. Her subjectivity is socially-induced which, in turn, leads to conformity to societal expectations.

Theory of Family Systems

The Family Systems Theory touches on individual psychology as it affects the relationship system. The theory helps us to understand how the family maintains itself after the crime is committed and a (woman) member becomes its victim. On the one hand, the (woman) victim suffers humiliation and on the other hand, the family members too suffer loss of prestige. But they may differ in their suffering. Sometimes, when the family members fail to help the victim, the victim realises that the whole system (family) has become inadequate to meet her needs. Family affects the victim's efforts at readjustment in terms of social relationships too. Interaction with others or even mere awareness of their existence may be experienced as painful or helpful. Victims who are more isolated make slower progress towards dealing with loss of prestige.

Measures Taken by Government Courts

Three government measures taken with regard to crimes against women are worth mentioning.

First, a bill entitled "The Prevention of Barbarous and Beastly Cruelty Against Women Bill, 1995" was introduced in the Rajya Sabha on December 1, 1995, seeking capital punishment against those who perpetrate barbarous and beastly cruelties on women. The Bill states that such offences be declared cognisable and non-bailable and should be tried in special courts. While introducing the Bill, Mrs. Saroj Khaparde hoped that deterrent punishment for such crimes would reduce the number of atrocities against women. Some of the acts listed as being beastly and cruel include killing a woman by battering, strangulating, or by other means after committing rape on her, killing a woman and disposing of her body by burning or by other means, burning of a woman alive leading to her death, killing a woman by gang-rape, and committing rape on a pregnant woman resulting in her death. This bill, however could not be passed.

Secondly, the Supreme Court gave a decision on 17 January, 1996 that rape cases be tried as a rule in camera to protect victims from facing humiliation in the witness box during trial. Trial in camera would not only protect the self-respect of the victim of crime but it is also likely to improve the quality of evidence of a prosecution because she would not be so hesitant or bashful to depose frankly, as she might be in an open court under the gaze of the public. The judges declared that an open hearing in such cases should only be held in exceptional cases. It was also declared that it would not be lawful to print or publish any matter in relation to the proceedings in the case, except with the previous permission of the courts. This would spare embarrassment caused to the victim of sex crime. It was also suggested that as far as possible, sexual assault cases be tried by lady judges. Lastly, the courts should avoid disclosing the name of the prosecution in their orders to save embarrassment to the victim.

Thirdly, Mahila Courts have been established in Delhi to try cases of crimes against women. Four such courts were set up in 1994. The atmosphere in Mahila Courts is not aggressive or charged as in other courts where women victims have to face a volley of questions from the defence counsel. Normally, it takes years to impart justice to a victim in ordinary courts, but a Mahila Court takes only a few months.

The rationale behind the setting up of these court is: (i) to lend a sympathetic ear by female judges to women victims who are unable to depose truthfully and fearlessly before male judges; (ii) to deliver speedy trials to women as Mahila Courts are to deal with cases pertaining to women only.

The important characteristics of Mahila Courts are: (1) These courts take up cases of women only. (2) The judges are women. (3) These courts try cases of Indian Penal Code (IPC) only of (a) outraging the modesty of a woman (Section 359), (b) kidnapping (Section 363), (c) criminal breach of trust pertaining to not returning *streedhan* (Section 406), and (d) cruelty of any sort inflicted by the husband or his relatives (Section 498). (4) These courts have predominantly all women teams, including women prosecutors. Only the accused and the lawyers are likely to be men.

However, the Mahila Courts have been criticised on the following grounds: (1) These courts are unconstitutional and unwarranted. Even the President of the All India Lawyers Forum for Civil Liberties (AILFCL) has described the very nomenclature of these courts as misleading and violative of the constitution. (2) The courts would be biased in favour of women and the accused would inevitably be treated severely by the female judges and the prosecutors. (3) The courts are not Mahila Courts in the real sense of the term. Public prosecutors, stenographers, and readers are still male employees. (4) The number of Mahila Courts is not adequate enough. Three-fourths of cases involving women victims are still tried by male judges. (5) Keeping in view the large number of cases, the strength of judges is quite insufficient.

The counter-arguments against the above criticisms are: (1) Allegation of gender bias against women judges is baseless. Mahila Courts are not partial. There is no question of taking sides. A judge is a judge. It hardly matters whether the judge is a man or a woman. (2) Women judges in fact create a sense of confidence in the victim to come out openly against the accused and his/her counterparts. (3) The disposal of cases is more speedy. In many cases, women judges have given less severe punishments to the old accused on the ground that there is no point in giving a ten-year sentence to someone who is between 70 and 80 years of age as he might not survive the entire sentence.

What is needed along with Mahila Courts is: (1) curbing loopholes in the trial process; (2) curbing corruption; (3) providing for speedy disposal of cases; and (4) interrogation of a female victim by a woman police officer, preferably in the presence of her relatives and under camera surveillance.

NEED FOR CHANGE: A HUMANISTIC APPROACH

Besides need for change in the attitude of law-enforcement officials, there is also a need for change in the attitudes of victims' parents. When we focus our attention on the cases of domestic violence (wife beating, the committing of sex offences by family members, compelling daughter-in-law to commit suicide) an important question arises: why should parents be not blamed for the plight of their daughters? Why do they seek matches for their girls where to solemnise marriage they even have to borrow money or spend all their life savings? Why do they decide to marry their daughters in dowry-greedy families? Why do they not ask their daughters to leave their husbands—'in-laws' house when they come to know of their daughter's harassment? Why are they so concerned about social stigma and decide to send back their daughters to their husbands/in-laws whenever their daughters are beaten and tortured by their husbands and parents-in-law? Why do they acquiesce in the demands of their daughters' in-laws? Why do they sacrifice their daughters at the altar of (the legality of) a bad marriage?

There is also the question as to why girls submit to oppression? Why do they not realise that a divorce is better than continuing with a marriage where money is the be-all and end-all of all relations. Why do they not walk out of their marriage and try to stand on their own feet? Why do they not realise that by committing suicide, they are creating problems for their children and an emotional trauma for their younger sisters and parents? Marriage is not the ultimate end in life but happiness certainly is.

Suffering violence is so deep-rooted in our cultural milieu that not only illiterate, less educated and economically dependent women but even sophisticated, highly educated and economically independent women do not seek legal or police protection. This fact is necessary to keep in view while pondering over measures to control woman's abuse in our society and for dealing with female depersonalisation trauma.

Five measures need our attention in this direction: (1) creating awareness among males for changing their traditional outlook towards women, (2) strengthening voluntary women's organisations, (3) focusing on education and training programmes for women, (4) opening women's hostels, and (5) changing criminal justice system.

1. *Creating awareness among males for necessity of change in their traditional outlook towards women*: Within the family, what a woman requires from a man is a touch of concern and sympathy. She does not want complete authority; what she wants is that she should be consulted in decision-making processes. Her husband and her in-laws should have some confidence in her. They should speak soft words of encouragement instead of taunting and teasing her, and make her feel that she is wanted in the family. Outside the family, she wants to get freedom and opportunity of taking her own decisions. She may not want to do everything on her own, but she surely does not want always to lean on a man's shoulder.

2. *Strengthening women's voluntary organisations*: Women have now to say things publicly which they dared not say before. The voice of an individual woman carries no weight. In fact, a woman is accused of being outspoken if she expresses her radical views. However, if a group of

women of like-minded views join together, form an organisation (*sangathan*) to articulate their resentment about women's oppression and suffering, they can easily do so and make appropriate impact. It is through these organisations alone that women can attack the outdated social norms and values which need to be overhauled. It is, therefore, necessary to activate vigorously a larger number of women's organisations. These organisations can undertake following activities regarding women's oppression: (1) hold demonstrations and public meetings and create public pressure, (2) help victims economically, emotionally and socially, (3) create awakening among women by setting up '*Parishads*' on specific issues. (4) make reconciliatory efforts with the victim's husband/in-laws wherever needed, (5) pressurise the police to act speedily, (6) file writ petitions in the courts against assaulter, deviant police officials and magistrates, etc. and demand a review of cases whenever necessary, (7) organise press conferences for highlighting specific cases of torture and cruelty.

3. *Focusing on education and training programmes for women*: So long women are dependent on their husbands economically, socially and psychologically, they will continue to be harassed and humiliated in our society. It is only by educating them (through adult education classes and by laying emphasis on female education from childhood) and giving them training in skills and crafts that they can be made to become independent. It is this independence which will enable our women to liberate themselves from their antiquated sex role ideology (the solution implied by Traditional Socialisation Theory), become assertive and self-accepting (Learned Helplessness Theory) and stop goading their husbands/in-laws into ill-treating them (Provocation Theory).

4. *Opening women hostels*: The victims of violence who want to take up a job to escape torture face the problem of finding accommodation in new places. Constructing more women's hostels by government, voluntary agencies, philanthropists, employers, or by trusts, etc. will provide shelter to victims who have no place to go to. Fortunately, there is already a trend in this direction but these hostels are being created only in big cities. Similar efforts in smaller cities and towns will prove to be a great boon to the needy victims of violence.

5. *Changing criminal justice system*: What is suggested in this context is: (a) a change in attitudes and values of judicial officials, (b) a change in police attitude, and (c) the strengthening of family courts. Change in the rigid and traditional values of magistrates can be brought about through orientation courses where findings of empirical works undertaken by

scholars in different social sciences could be discussed and analysed. Before the public loses faith in the courts (it has already partially lost faith in the police) before the courts' judgments have a dampening and demoralising effect on people, judges have to learn to depend more on the sociological interpretation of law rather than rigidly sticking to technical formalities and precedents. Similar change is required in the police attitude too.

In brief, the following measures may be suggested for reducing women's depersonalisation trauma: (1) Legal literacy of women, or creating awareness of rights among women through media, published literature and voluntary agencies. (2) Judicial activism, i.e., giving liberal and creative interpretation of law than literal or technical interpretation. (3) Constant monitoring of justice and examining impact of legislation. (4) Monitoring rescue homes. (5) Strengthening free legal aid societies. (6) Effective functioning of Family Courts and Family Counselling Services.

References

Ahuja, Ram, *Crime Against Women*. Rawat Publications, Jaipur, 1987.

Ahuja, Mukesh, *Widows: Role Adjustment and Violence*, Wishwa Prakashan, New Delhi, 1996.

Bowlby, B., *Journal of Social Issues*, Vol. 44, No. 3, 1988.

Chapman, Jane Roberts and Gates Margaret (eds.), *The Victimisation of Women*, Sage Publications, Beverly Hills, 1978.

Finkelhor, David, Gelles Richard, Hotaling Gerald, Straus Murraya, *The Dark Side of Families*, Sage Publications, Beverly Hills, 1983.

Gelles, R.J., *Intimate Violence in Families*, Sage Publications, Beverly Hills, 1985.

Chapter 11

Youth and Crime

The thinking and behaviour of the youth today has been affected by a number of factors. Some of these are: expansion of education, increasing unemployment, reservation policy of the government ignoring merit of a section of the youth, lack of adequate attention and guidance by the parents, tremendous and not very wholesome influence of the mass media, the newly acquired affluence of some young people, failure of educational institutions in imparting value-oriented education, questionable influence of the peer group at an intermediate stage between leaving the protection of the family with its distinctive patterns of behaviour, and entering the increasingly impersonal and competitive wider society. With the emergence of these changes, it is imperative to study why the youth deviate from legal and social norms, to identify the type of young people who indulge in criminal behaviour, and, above all, to determine whether or not deviant youth can be resocialised.

But before analysing these issues, it would be profitable to understand the concept of youth. Who are the youth? Is the concept of 'youth' age-linked or age-graded? A person below 12 years of age is called a child, one between 12 and 18 years is regarded as an adolescent, one between 18 and 30 years is viewed as a young person, and one between 30 and 50 years is described as a middle-aged person. Before the enactment of the Juvenile Justice Act on December 1, 1986, a child between 7 and 18 or 21 years of age (age prescribed differently in the Children Acts in different states) violating the law was considered a juvenile delinquent. However, the Juvenile Justice Act, 1986 defined a 'juvenile' as "a male below 16 years of age and a female below 18 years of age". For the purposes of analysing the problem of 'youth crime', a person who is between 16 and 25 years, i.e., one who is in his late adolescence and early adulthood, and one who has still a 'dependency status', has been regarded as 'youth'.

In present-day India, a person normally marries in the age group of 20-25 years. After marriage, his responsibilities and experiences with different persons gradually make him more prudent, more mature, and more responsible. Before marriage, a person is less mature socially and is more dependent on others. We have, therefore, termed the age-group of 16-25 years as 'youth'.

In the total population (1991 figures) of our country, 12.85 per cent persons belong to the age-group of 0-4 years, 23.15 per cent to 5-14 years, 19.17 per cent to 15-24 years, 38.33 per cent to 25-59 years, and 6.50 per cent to 60 plus years. (*see*, *India*: 1992, 19). If we take only male population of 439.2 million (out of total population of 846.3 million or 51.9%) in 1991, 25.8 per cent belong to 0-9 age group, 11.9 per cent to 10-14 age group, 9.9 per cent to 15-19 age group, 8.6 per cent to 20-24 age group, 7.8 per cent to 25-29 age group and 36 per cent are above 30 years. (*Manpower Profile, India, 1998*: 16-17). Thus, only 18.5 per cent males (of 15-24 years) are youth. Thus, there are nearly 16 million persons in India in the age-group of 16-25 years, or it may be said that nearly one-fifth of the country's population constitutes the 'youth'.

The youth (16-25 years) are distinct from juveniles (7-16 years) and adults (25+ years) because of the following factors:

- While juveniles are totally immature socially and mentally, youth are comparatively more mature.
- While juveniles function more on the basis of imitation and suggestibility, youth tend to function more on the basis of rationality and reasoning.
- While juveniles have no aspirations, youth have quite a few aspirations—occupational, economic, marital and career.
- While adults have marital and familial responsibilities, youth are usually free from such liabilities and duties.
- While adults are comparatively free from family dominance, youth continue to remain under family control.
- The attitudes of the youth are not so rigid, stern and strict; these are comparatively flexible.
- The youth are full of greater energy and enthusiasm and are more adventurous.

On the above basis, a youth offender needs to be separated from a juvenile delinquent and an adult criminal on the following three grounds:

1. *Age*: Since a youth offender is above 16 years of age, he cannot be treated as a juvenile delinquent. Nevertheless, he belongs to an age-group, unlike an adult criminal, where he cannot be considered a person who is *totally* responsible for his criminality.

2. *Accountability*: Though a youth has the capacity to understand the consequences of his act, yet being dependent on his family and many others for his need gratification and not being obliged to discharge any responsibilities to his family, he cannot be held guilty "in will". Because of his 'young' age, his parents and other family members shoulder the main responsibility of ensuring his social obedience and conformity to social norms.

3. *Social philosophy*: In recent philosophical trends in sociology and criminology, while dealing with immature youth offenders, the focus is on three things: (a) *Emphasis on environmental influences*: A youth's crime is explained as a result of the influence of social environment on his behaviour. His individual responsibility is thus minimised in all areas. His crime is interpreted as symptomatic of a failure of social systems to protect him and to provide him security. (b) *Emphasis on resocialisation*: The emphasis on social environment has led to a greater faith in his correction, resocialisation and rehabilitation. Care and protection rather than punishment or mere custody are stressed. (c) *Emphasis on prevention*: A further development consonant with modern social philosophy is the conviction that the state has greater responsibility than the family of adopting measures to prevent youths from criminal activities.

CRIME TRENDS AMONG THE YOUTH

Before assessing different patterns of crime committed by the youth, a clarification is warranted. If we take the different age groups of persons arrested in three years (1996 to 1998), we find that on an average 2.6 per cent were below 18 years, 51.6 per cent belonged to 18-30 years age group, 38.4 per cent belonged to 30-50 years age group and 7.4 per cent were above 50 years of age (*Crime in India*, 1998: 266). Thus about half of the offenders were young (18-30 years). The data on age structure of offenders as given in *Crime in India* are incongruent to youth offenders, i.e., offenders in 16-25 years age group. Therefore, we interpolated the percentage of offenders in the age groups of 16-21 years, 21-25 years, and 25-50 years. The calculated figures are given in Tables 11.1, 11.2 and 11.3.

TABLE 11.1

Crimes Committed by Offenders in India in Different Years and in Different Age Groups under the IPC and SLL

(calculated by interpolation)

Year	*7-16 (0.55%)*	*16-21 (12.16%)*	*21-25 (28.96%)*	*25-50 (50.77%)*	*50+ (7.56%)*	*Total crimes (in lakhs)*
1986	0.24	5.34	12.71	22.29	3.32	43.90
1987	0.27	6.08	14.47	25.36	3.78	49.96
1988	0.29	6.33	15.08	26.43	3.93	52.06
1989	0.30	6.54	15.57	27.30	4.06	53.77
1990	0.27	5.96	14.18	24.87	3.70	48.98
1991	0.28	6.14	14.62	25.63	3.82	50.49
1992	0.29	6.38	15.20	26.64	3.96	52.47
1993	0.30	6.61	15.73	27.58	4.11	54.33
1994	0.30	6.70	15.96	27.99	4.17	55.12
1995	0.32	7.29	17.36	30.43	4.53	59.93
1996	0.34	7.66	18.23	31.97	4.76	62.96
1997	0.35	7.80	18.57	32.55	4.84	64.11
1998	0.34	7.51	17.90	31.38	4.67	61.80

Source: Crime in India, 1998: 42.

Table 11.2

Percentage of Different Types of Crimes under the IPC Committed by Criminals of Different Age Groups (including youths (i.e., between 16-25 years) in India in 1998

(calculated by interpolation)

Crime	*All age groups*	*% of total crime in India*	*16-*	*16-21*	*21-25*	*25-50*	*50+*
Theft	2,87,792	16.18	0.1	2.4	5.7	10.0	1.5
Burglary	1,19,130	6.70	0.04	0.9	2.2	3.8	0.6
Murder & attempt to murder	69,360	3.90	0.02	0.5	1.2	2.2	0.3
Riots	91,201	5.12	0.03	0.7	1.7	2.9	0.5
Cheating	38,173	2.14	0.01	0.2	0.6	1.0	0.1
Robbery	23,565	1.32	0.00	0.2	0.4	0.8	0.1
Kidnapping & abduction	23,504	1.32	0.00	0.2	0.3	0.6	0.1
Rape	15,031	0.84	0.00	0.1	0.2	0.4	0.05
Criminal breach of trust	16,186	0.90	0.00	0.1	0.3	0.5	0.1
Dacoity	8,064	0.45	0.00	0.1	0.2	0.3	0.04
Others	10,87,105	61.13	0.3	6.8	16.2	28.4	4.2
Total	17,79,111	100.00	9785	216340	515231	9032543	134501

Source: Crime in India, 1998: 44.

Table 11.3

Percentage of Different Crimes Under the Local and Special Laws Committed by Criminals in All Age Groups (including youths, i.e., between 16-25 years) in India in 1998

(Calculated by interpolation)

Crime	Total LSL Crime in India in 1998		Percentage of Crimes by Youth (16-25 years)	
	No.	Percentage	Percentage 16-21 (12.16%)	Percentage 21-25 (28.96%)
Prohibition Act	5,40,157	12.3	1.9	4.6
Gambling Act	1,12,311	2.6	0.5	1.3
Excise Act	1,11,625	2.5	0.3	0.7
Arms Act	63,518	1.4	0.2	0.5
Railways Act	40,123	0.9	0.1	0.2
Narcotic Drugs and Substances Act	18,273	0.4	0.1	0.2
Immoral Traffic Act	3,695	0.1	0.04	0.09
SC/ST Atrocities Act	14,578	0.3		
Others	34,97,605	79.5	9.0	21.5
Total	44,01,885	100.0	N=462522	N=1101534

Source: Crime in India, 1998: 96.

The above figures point out the following characteristics of crime by youth (i.e., between 16-25 years age group):

1. Crime by youth in India is serious inasmuch as the youth commit about 40 per cent (41.1% in 1998) of the total crime (under the IPC and LSL together). This comes to about 6,962 crimes a day or about 290 crimes per hour.
2. The ratio of crimes by the youth under the Indian Penal Code to crimes under the Local and Special Laws is 1: 2.8, establishing the fact that the youth crime is not so serious in its nature.
3. The ratio of felonies (murder, rape, kidnapping, burglary, dacoity) to misdemeanours is 1: 2.3.
4. The volume of crimes against persons is about three times the crimes committed against property (1: 3.09).
5. The volume of crimes by 'adults' (in 25-50 years age group) is about 20 per cent more than those committed by the 'youth' (in 16-25 years age group).

CHARACTERISTICS OF YOUTH CRIME AND YOUTH CRIMINALS

This author conducted a study of youth offenders in 1994-95 in Rajasthan in which 272 offenders in three central jails in the state were studied. Of the total offenders studied, at the time of interview, 24 per cent belonged to the age group of 16-18 years, 47 per cent to the age group of 18-21 years and 29 per cent to the age group of 21-25 years. However, at the time of committing crime, 44 per cent belonged to the age group of 16-18 years, 39 per cent to the age group of 18-21 years, and 17 per cent to the age group of 21-25 years. Further, 62 per cent of the respondents were convicted and 38 per cent were undertrials. Eighty-eight per cent were convicted under the Indian Penal Code and 12 per cent under the Local and Special Laws. In the former group, 42 per cent were convicted for murder,17 per cent for theft, 15 per cent for vagrancy, 9 per cent for assault, 4 per cent for rape, and fewer than 1 per cent for dowry-deaths. In the latter group, 6 per cent were convicted under the Excise Act, 3 per cent under the Railways Act, 2 per cent under the Possession of Arms Act and 1 per cent under the Gambling Act. Of the convicted offenders, 58 per cent were awarded life imprisonment, 7 per cent were imprisoned for 10-13 years, 8 per cent for 7-10 years, 4 per cent for 5-7 years, 2 per cent for 2-5 years, 6 per cent for 1-2 years, and 15 per cent for less than one year.

On the basis of our empirical study, several characteristics of youth crimes and youth criminals may be pointed out as below:

- Crimes requiring lesser physical strength and alertness (like theft, etc.) are more characteristic of younger persons (16-21 years) while crimes requiring greater physical energy, skill and risk (like murder, rape, assault, dowry death) are more commonly found among youths between 21 and 25 years of age.
- The young adolescent group of 16-18 years makes up little more than two-fifths (44%) of the offenders; the group of 18-21 years makes up little less than two-fifths (39%) of the offenders and the older youth group of 21-25 years makes up little less than one-fifth (17%) of the offenders. Thus, the large segment of offenders belongs to the young adolescent group of 16-21 years.
- More than half of the offenders (55%) come from the lower-middle economic class (with an income between Rs. 1,500 and Rs. 2,500 per

month) while about two-fifths (40%) come from the lower economic class (income of less than Rs. 1,500 per month).

- About three-fifths youth criminals (62%) hail from the urban areas and little less than two-fifths (38%) from the rural areas.
- Youth criminals have a lower marriage rate. About four-fifths of the offenders (77%) are unmarried and have no liability.
- Though the educational background of the youth criminals varies from illiteracy to graduation, a majority is illiterate (39%) or educated below secondary level (41%).

Our findings, thus, indicate that in the case of the youth criminals:

(a) there remain some important common areas like distinctive illiteracy or low level of education, lower and lower-middle class membership, and absence of or very little marital obligations.

(b) that youth criminals seem to be those who do not widely follow specifically middle-class social norms or customary patterns of behaviour, nor are middle-class lifestyles consciously emulated by them;

(c) that youth criminals seem to have no powerful motivation to gain higher material standards of living, nor do they strive for higher social status, i.e., their social horizons are not free from traditional limitations;

(d) that assimilation of these youth into middle-class society is neither in process nor is it a desired objective; and

(e) that they have no particular desire to develop 'social' relationships, and in general tend to follow a family-centred and relatively privatised pattern of social life.

GENESIS OF YOUTH CRIME

Youth criminals are not altogether a different kind of people for the law abiding youths. The motives and satisfactions sought by criminals are the same as those that influence normal young men. For example, a young person engaged in financial crime (embezzlement, cheating) is motivated by a desire for wealth, recognition, social status and achievement in the same way as is the businessman. The only difference is that the latter (businessman) operates within the framework of legal definitions, while the former (criminal), using many of the same techniques, operates outside legal definitions. In sex assault and rape, a criminal's motive is almost always the same as that of a normal man. The only difference is that the force of the criminal is outside the accepted social definitions. The point that is to be recognised is that the roots of crime lie in the social system. Criminality is only a difference in behaviour patterns, in philosophies of life, in responses to the prevailing system of social control, and in varying reactions to legal control devices.

How do causative factors actually work in crimes committed by youth? What are the social situations in which the learning of criminality and development of the criminal personality operate? What are the conditions that make it more likely for these causative factors to prevail and thereby increase the risk of youth criminality to be widespread? One thing that needs to be emphatically stated is that in the area of criminal behaviour, we are not likely to find situations in which crime always follows a particular event or characteristic. Criminal behaviour does not always exist among people living in poverty, although it may often exist in impoverishment. Thus, in crime, there are only factors which may be 'necessary' to produce crime in conjunction with other factors. Neither crime in general nor any specific crime can ever be the outcome of one single factor which would invariably produce this result.

I selected six causal factors as suggested by some scholars to examine to what extent their importance is indicated in an empirical study. These factors were: (a) the family, (b) companionship and associations, (c) deprivations, frustrations and stresses in life aspirations, (d) the mass media, (e) personality disposition, and (t) reckless spirit of adventure.

The Family

The most direct source of youth criminality has been identified as family's failure to gratify needs and provide necessary emotional support to maintain social control, and to effectively transmit the dominant values of society. A young person of 16-25 years of age is still so dependent on his family that he requires love, affection and sympathy of both parents. Emotional deprivation comes from father's and mother's lack of interest in the welfare of the young person. However, if the young person is married, his adjustment with his partner can provide him the necessary emotional security, though the failure of marriage can also create new stresses.

With change in family structure, family ties have presumably got loosened, with the consequent weakening of the family's ability to transmit moral values. The absence or decline of cohesiveness in the family and its resultant weakness as a control factor are easily discernible in the behaviour of the family members, particularly young persons.

Some youths are so ill-treated, beaten, harassed, humiliated or neglected by their parents that their life becomes miserable. When this kind of treatment goes on for a long time, they begin to resist. This resistance makes their parents even more tyrannical and they resort to chastising them mercilessly even for trivial reasons. With bitter spirit, the youths decide to leave their homes, and are occasionally forced to adopt a violent way of life as a direct result of the violence of their parents.

My study, however, did not reveal many cases of this type of family situation in the youth criminals. About 70 per cent respondents described their relations with their parents as harmonious, 14 per cent as conflicting, while 17 per cent described their parents' attitude towards them as indifferent or negligent. These figures point out that family control and discipline in a large number of cases in my study were effective. I also did not come across cases in my study in which the youth offenders had acquired their attitude towards or technique of criminality from the family. No respondent described his father, mother or siblings or any other family member as having a criminal record. This fact too points to the absence of role of the family in youth's criminality. Taking all these three factors in their totality, namely, emotional deprivation factor, control or discipline factor, and learning factor, it may be said that family situation is only made a scapegoat for youth criminality, while, in truth a youth does not necessarily become a criminal because of his family. He becomes a criminal of his own volition; or it may be said that the youth's own demoralisation and lack of self-discipline appear to be more decisive factors in his criminality.

Companionship and Associations

Companionship of and association with persons having anti-social tendencies formed in post-adolescence years lead some youths to deviant life. But my study revealed that youth crime is not necessarily a group operation. In my study, 64 per cent respondents had committed crime all by themselves, 19 per cent had a companion(s), while 17 per cent avered that they had committed no crime but had been falsely implicated. Of the 19 per cent respondents who had an accomplice(s) in crime, 10 per cent had a single companion, 3 per cent had two companions, 4 per cent had three companions, and the remaining 2 per cent had four or more companions. Further, of the criminals who had some accomplice in crime, 50 per cent had a friend as their accomplice, one-tenth had a kin as accomplice, one-tenth had an acquaintance as accomplice and about five per cent had a colleague as accomplice. This shows that youth criminals do not acquire any learning experience in criminality from persons of their own age group; nor do they always wish to conform to the ways of their peers. The young criminals also do not use the anti-social channels provided by their peers for charging their energies or for satisfying their special personality needs; nor do they depend upon their peers for security, recognition, affection and new experiences. We thus hold that there is an indication that in a large number of cases (about 95%) peer groups are not the cause of youth criminality.

Deprivations and Frustrations

Deprivations, particularly economic deprivation, breed criminality. Criminality rates among youths are closely correlated with low income. Nevertheless, the argument that poverty is a direct cause of youth criminality is not being put forth. According to Landis (1956: 55), there are three important ways in which economic deprivation enters as a risk factor in youth criminality: (a) when material success is highly prized, economic deprivation breeds demoralisation and apathy; (b) economic deprivation hampers integration into society. Those who are unemployed or who receive low wages have no secure place in the community of work and their ties to the larger society are extremely tenuous, (c) economic deprivation makes housing conditions for the young so intolerable that they feel encouraged to develop a 'street society'. This means that their lifestyle becomes street-centred. In the streets, the young people are exposed to influences from which law-abiding youths are often isolated.

In my study, it was found that 72 per cent respondents were gainfully employed, 16 per cent were engaged in cultivation, and 11 per cent were studying. Only one per cent were unemployed. Further, it was found that the income of about two-fifths working respondents (38%) was below Rs.1,000 per month, while about a half (52%) were earning between Rs.1,000 and Rs.2,000 per month and one-tenth (10%) were earning over Rs.2,000 per month. About three-fourths (77%) respondents being unmarried had no marital liabilities. In two-fifths (40%) cases, the income of youth's families was less than Rs. 1,500 per month, in little less than three-fifths (55%) cases between Rs.1,500 and Rs. 2,500 and in five per cent cases above Rs. 2,500 per month. Thus, economic deprivation could be considered a significant factor in youth criminality.

Mass Media

Some of the present-day movies, various TV programmes and serials whet and sharpen the appetite of the young people for excitement and violence, as also for indulging in undue risk and adventure. Moreover, these movies and TV programmes also glorify deviant activities, impart knowledge of criminal techniques, and exaggerate the extent and spread of criminality in society. Thus, television programmes and motion pictures have now come to be blamed for many youth crimes. Quite a few movies depict scenes of adventure, kidnapping, rape, assault, murder which offer new examples of behaviour to today's youth, who tend to emulate them in their real life. Songs and movies shown on various satellite channels carry pictures, scenes and visuals that are in awfully poor taste and tend to emotionally disturb and unhinge the young minds. They often depict techniques of committing a crime. Sex and violence seem to have become two of the major television themes. Motion pictures too have their own share of violence and some of them are much too preoccupied with sex. This fact is borne out by the lurid advertisements for these motion pictures in well-known magazines. Some thinkers are of the opinion that the aggression built up by frustrations which youths encounter may be drained off by these movies and TV serials. The youths project themselves into the stories and release their aggressions in the field of fantasy rather than in overt aggressive behaviour. However, there is no gainsaying the fact that these movies and TV programmes do really cause, or at least facilitate, deviant behaviour among the youth.

In my research, however, I did not come across any case where the mischief could be attributed to motion pictures or TV programmes; yet it can be held that mass media in general, and movies in particular, are a factor, at least a secondary factor, aggravating, if not causing, already existing dispositions to criminality.

Personality Dispositions

Some scholars have pointed out that youth criminals have certain personality traits which make them more susceptible to criminal behaviour. These youth criminals could be described as follows: they are less submissive and more aggressive to authority; they do not have as great a fear of failure and defeat; they are less self-controlled and less masochistic; they are less cooperative with others; they show less dependency on others; they are more impulsive and extroverted; they are more resentful of others who try to dominate them; they are more defiant towards persons in power; they are hostile and destructive

(Sheldon and Glueck, 1959: 124-26). In the opinion of these scholars, it is the personality traits which determine a person's integration in social groups, and his conformity to or deviation from social norms. However, it will not be wrong to hold that the youths who take to crime are unadaptable, non-alert, complex, and are rear-stumblers. Such youths feel within themselves the strain and division which lead to the emotional tensions of anxiety and conflict. In sociological terms, it leads to disorganisation.

While these traits may point out differences between youth criminals and non-criminals, they cannot be considered as causes of crime. Personality traits cannot explain why some youths with serious personality problems become criminals and others do not; nor can they explain the converse. Many psychologists, therefore, do not accept the validity of the thesis linking personality traits with crime. Youths with 'sociopathic personality' may be frequently callous and hedonistic, show marked emotional immaturity, lack of sense of responsibility, lack of judgement, but these characteristics cannot be considered as a 'cause' of their crimes. Some of the characteristics of a sociopathic youth—like, emotional immaturity, egocentricism, excessive dependency on others, sexual immaturity—may indicate the type of person a criminal is, which may be helpful in treating him, but these characteristics may only be advanced in an attempt to explain the causes of sociopathy, like childhood deprivations, etc. They cannot be identified as causes of criminal behaviour. There are many criminal youths who do not show marked personality traits of criminal kind, just as there are many non-criminal youths who do. The criminal personality approach is valuable in individual treatment and in giving causative analysis, but it does not explain the rise or fall of criminality rate among the youth.

Reckless Spirit of Adventure

Some youths have vagrant, roving, and itinerant dispositions and tastes and a reckless spirit of adventure that emboldens them to embrace anti-social behaviour. The feeling of restlessness, the unrestrained indulgence of licentious passions make them run away even from comfortable homes. The most remarkable characteristic of these youths is their extraordinary licentiousness. Nothing can well exceed the extreme animal fondness for the opposite sex which prevails amongst them. To my mind, among the propensities of the criminal youth, pugnacity is a predominant element. Gambling and alcoholism may also be rife among a few of them. But these factors help us understand a given youth criminal rather than explaining the problem of youth criminality. It is the social control factor—the effective transmission of dominant values—that normally prevents youth with various emotional problems and aggressive tendencies from becoming criminals or from succumbing to criminal influences to which they are exposed.

After analysing the six factors, broadly speaking, it may now be stated that the factors which appear to play an important role in making youth criminals are: (i) failure to gratify needs, (ii) parental neglect of immature youth, (iii) criminal associations, (iv) deviant dispositions and tastes on the part of the youth, (v) general want of employment and the bleak employment environment, and (vi) police harassment. All these factors operate on different levels. We do accept the thesis that youth's crime is learnt and that it is conditioned by the environment but we do not accept the view that youths' crime can be explained only on the basis of these factors. We will be committing dualistic fallacy by assuming that there are two distinct groups of youths—criminals and non-criminals—and that these mutually exclusive groups indulge in behaviour that is readily distinguishable. While one commits criminal acts, the other, simply acts. Since criminal behaviour is just like any other kind of behaviour in its instrinsic elements or components, no one factor that causes such behaviour can successfully explain youth crime. Even if we assume that these factors play a role in youths' criminality, predicting criminal behaviour on the basis of these factors, in our opinion, would not be feasible. These will have marginal utility in crime control programmes.

Deciding a *proximate cause* by the courts may be necessary to assign liability to an act by a person but it is surely not *sufficient* in social sciences. Ideally, sociologists and criminologists would like to know the variables which *produce* crime. What is it that must exist before crime occurs? Since determination of such causes has thus far been not found to be possible, sociologists try to feel satisfied with the search for *critical* and *recurrent* factors in human relationships. Although we have referred to some *key* and *critical* factors, we must adequately emphasise the fact that the factors associated with youth crime must be understood in the perspective of *the total experience* of the youth concerned. That is, these factors alone cannot be analysed; they must be seen within a total theoretical framework. One such theoretical paradigm has been presented in the following pages.

THEORETICAL EXPLANATION

The need to move away from the existing theoretical approaches which seek to explain crime and take a fresh look at etiology of criminality has been acknowledged at all hands. I believe it is possible to develop an altogether new approach to the problem. If we were to portray a typical criminal youth, he would in all probability be a young person, in the age group of 18-25 years, a first offender charged with vagrancy, theft or some petty offence, and his likely destiny would be a custodial sentence of two to three years. There are, of course, some criminal youth who deviate from this description. These are those who commit serious crimes, such as murder and are imprisoned for a long duration. But their number is rather small. Gangsters, smugglers, professional thieves or pickpockets are scarcely found amongst the ranks of criminal youth. There is also little evidence of criminal youth indulging in gang activity which may excite the interest of sociologists and criminologists. It is in this context that I have attempted to present a new theoretical model. My approach is neither functionalist nor interactionist nor purely structural. It is *holistic* in the sense that it partly derives from social strains and partly from 'personality structures'.

My thesis is that youth crime is caused by frustrations and deprivations arising from a failure to achieve goals, desires and aspirations. These frustrations break or weaken the youths' social bonds with groups which control their social behaviour. However, the breaking/weakening of social bonds depends upon youth's personality structure. One who is *committed* to social norms, continues to remain *attached* to the family, and since he has the ability to *adjust* to a situation, he is not likely to break his bonds with his social groups. Thus, the breaking or weakening of the social bonds becomes the cause of a youth's criminal behaviour.

Since the growth of personality traits largely depends upon cultural background, I maintain that *situation* and *personality together* are responsible for youth's crime. While Merton holds that frustrations are eliminated by the individual either by dropping the goals or relinquishing the means, my contention is that the degree of *adjustment, commitment* and *attachment* holds or weakens an individual's social bonds. Emancipation from social bonds leads to deviance. The central fact in my thesis, however, is that deviance is created not by an individual youth but by society. By this I do not mean that the causes of youth's deviance are to be located only in the social situation of the youth or in 'social factors' which prompt his action. When a youth faces a 'complex' situation in his post-adolescence period, he finds it difficult to harmonise with the external surroundings. He faces several problems, like finding himself in a subculture where conflicting goals abound and the compulsions towards the attainment of these goals are so overwhelming that he is tempted to resort to anti-social means of attaining them, or facing the task of adjusting himself in varied groups with diverse standards, or being unable to regulate his impulses and bring them in line with systems of control accepted by his immediate group. The youth under the influence of new stimuli finds himself without a rudder to steer his course. Because of all these factors, he faces stresses and frustrations which sometimes come to be translated in crime.

Some youth encounter problem after problem and become distraught by repeated strains or by the piling up of the situations which exhaust their capacity in adjustment. Disagreements in the family, failure to get a job, social rejection by peers or kin, and a great number of similar crises, any of which coming alone may have been endured. Coming together, they cannot be endured. Can we identify the youth who fail to adjust themselves in their new surroundings? It appears these youth are mainly those: (1) who are unsure of their place in the social system; (2) who consider the existing social norms of behaviour too rigid; (3) who regard the social milieu in which they function as too complex; and (4) who have wrapped, distorted personalities. Could it then be said that since personality factors and life situation largely account for deviance, the deviants (youth) constitute a *homogeneous* category? My answer is a clear 'yes'. But for this homogeneity, development of a theory pertaining to youth's deviance would not have been feasible. In my theoretical paradigm, I have centred around three ideas in the analysis of crime; (i) weakening of social bonds, (ii) relative deprivation, and (iii) marginalisation of the youth owing to certain personality traits.

INVERTED U-CURVE ADJUSTMENT PHENOMENON IN YOUTH BEHAVIOUR

The deviant behaviour of a youth, as stated earlier, is the result of his maladjustment and the breaking or weakening of social bonds with family and other groups. The adjustment pattern of a youth in 16-25 years age group may be described as "Inverted U-Curve Phenomenon". When a youth considers himself ready to take up a job, ready to settle in life, ready to undertake responsibilities of life, and ready for enjoying material advantages of society, it (his situation) is the top of the "Inverted U-Curve". When his situation is suddenly affected by a failure to get a

Inverted U-Curve Adjustment Phenomenon in Youth Behaviour

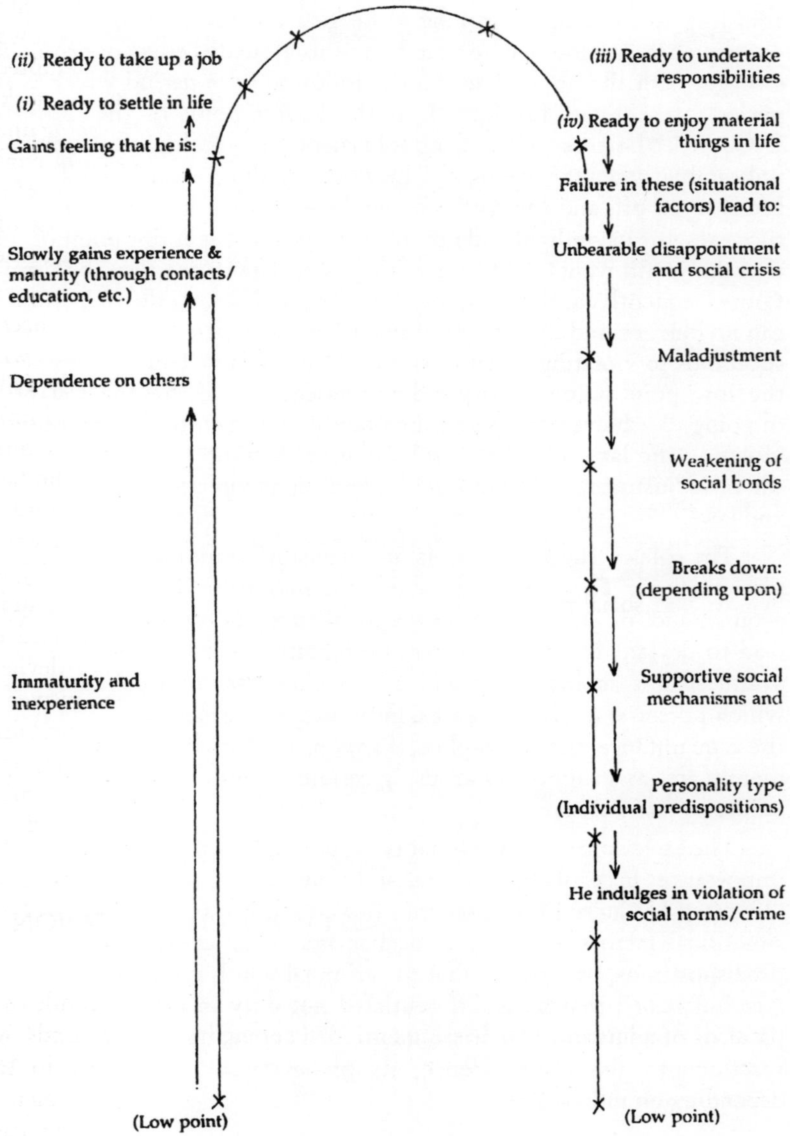

job, by being falsely implicated and accused of some action not committed, by a sudden jolt in life, or by the many practical problems of adjusting to existing environment, he gets the shock of his life. As a consequence, he feels that he is under the accumulated effect of protracted struggle with the unfamiliar. This is followed by a period which is the period of acid test for him. It is the lowest point of the "Inverted U-Curve", the time when disappointments in youth's life seem most unbearable, when the feeling of achieving something special/significant in life is worn off, and the past is remembered for its dreams of imminent successes, for its sunlight and not for its shadows. It is at this point of time that the youth wants to 'do something', not 'after some time' but 'now'. Quite frequently, at this point of time, the youth breaks down because he can no longer stand the 'disappointment' or 'false accusation' or crisis. He succumbs to violating social norms or even the law. Thus, starting from the 'low' point of immaturity and inexperience, he reaches the 'top' point of going to achieve success and then falls down again to the low point of violating the law. The "Inverted U-Curve Phenomenon" thus explains the maladjustment of a youth in life resulting in violation of social norms and laws.

The role of 'supporting social mechanisms' cannot be ignored in this phenomenon. The support at crisis time may come from a peer or an acquaintance or merely from a situational opportunity which may finally lead to deviant behaviour. It may be repeated here that the delinquent youth acts as an individual and not as a member of a cohesive group which possesses a subculture of significance for its members. The friend, the acquaintance, the accomplice, if any, or the 'situational' opportunity merely acts as a support in arousing certain feelings which result from a failure to face a crisis.

The relevance of 'personality type' has also to be given due importance in explaining criminal behaviour of the youth through "Inverted U-Curve Phenomenon". If we look for an interplay between situational factors, supportive mechanism, social crisis, and individual predispositions, we observe that the criminal youth is not *one personality type* but *many*; that he is differentiated not only in regard to different patterns of adjustment to crisis, mentioned above, but also in individual reactions to the crisis. Hence, its phases occur at different times depending on individuals.

TYPOLOGY OF YOUTH CRIMINALS

Youth criminality is an umbrella term covering a variety of criminal phenomena. It includes all those youths who have been legally adjudged criminals. On the basis of the causes of youth crime identified earlier, we may point out six types of youth criminals:

1. *Emotional*: Those youths who are at times so much carried away by their emotions of anger, hatred, fear, etc. that they totally lose control on reason and logic and indulge in anti-social behaviour of which they repent later on.
2. *Victims of police harassment*: Poor and unemployed/underemployed youths who are on the lookout for jobs and in this attempt become victims of police harassment and exploitation and are brought to courts for conviction.
3. *Perverts*: Those youths who violate ethical and moral standards, break laws and harm individuals and groups because they have identity problems.
4. *Accidental*: Those youths who want to help their friends and inadvertently become entrapped in criminal activity.
5. *Media products*: Those youths who are the creation of the mass media, i.e., who become criminals by watching and adopting techniques of committing crimes shown in movies and TV serials.
6. *Situational*: Those poor youths who failing to find legitimate means of earning a livelihood take-to illegitimate means of earning money to help their families. Their number is, of course, very small.

Youth criminals can also be classified in the following four categories on the basis of the type of crime committed:

1. Those who commit crimes which have no relation to material gain.
2. Those who commit criminal acts for financial gain.
3. Those who do not commit any unlawful act but having been falsely implicated by the police or by some kin, friend, etc. are labelled by the courts as criminals.
4. Those who violate not the criminal laws but the civil rules of conduct. Since civil laws are also enforceable by the courts, these violations carry some penalty.

On the basis of their personality type, criminal youths may be classified as under:

1. *Pseudo criminals*: Those who may commit a criminal act but are not seriously out of social control. Their criminality is only incidental to the central problem they represent, namely, failure of society at large.

2. *Amoral criminals*: Those who have somehow failed to internalise and fully accept the moral principles of their socially-oriented families and subculture.
3. *Real criminals*: Those who have imbibed criminal values and do not suffer from any guilt-feeling when violating the law.

Lastly, youth criminals may also be categorised in terms of relationship between their personality type and adjustment, i.e., their adjustment experience under impact of facing a crisis of whatever dimensions. Three types of youths may be identified in this context: the *non-idealist*, who does not embrace the experience of enthusiastic young people and therefore becomes progressively disillusioned; the *rigid*, *biased* with a *constricted* outlook, determined never to listen to others' advice but considers his own opinion as rational; and the *non-adjuster*, who lacks the will to understand tradition and innovation.

Youth Subculture and Crime

There exists a school of thought which holds that a number of factors in the last few decades have given rise to youth subculture. Does youth subculture exist? Does a social value system exist among youth that is "apart from and a part of" a larger, more central or general value system? Is this youth subculture responsible for crime among youth? Scholars like Alfred McClung Lee, Milton Gordon, Albert Cohen and Milton Yinger accept the existence of youth subculture. Marvin Wolfgang (1963: 8) refers to it as "a system of ideals, norms and institutions developed and followed by youthful generation, that is different from those of the larger adult society". Assuming that a separate system of youth values exists, do these values vary from class to class? Do the values of lower-class youth differ from those of middle-class or upper-class youth? Do we have separate lower-class, middle-class and upper-class youth subcultures? Are values unevenly developed among different classes by existing socialising agencies?

There exist different sociological perspectives on youth culture and their subcultural style. One such perspective refers to their distinct manner of dress and behaviour. The general view is that the youth of today lack civility of the youth of earlier generations. This view relies on evidence from newspapers and magazines. However, this view is criticised on the basis that "things aren't what they used to be" syndrome is found in every age and that the supposed good behaviour of the youth in the past is and always has been a myth. At the time of 'moral panic' in the 1950s and the 1960s, people looked back to the 1910s and the 1920s.

However, a study of the press of *that* time reveals a 'moral panic' then about the behaviour of the young people.

There is a school of thought led by Pearson (1983: 92) which holds that a number of factors in the last few decades have given rise to youth subculture. Following this school, a few factors may be identified in the Indian context. These are: decreasing employment opportunities, lack of proper guidance to the young from their overbusy parents, lack of training skills and values for entering the increasingly impersonal and competitive wider society, break-up of the joint family system, deteriorating educational system and diminishing dedication on the part of teachers, increasing political interference in educational institutions, support to the wards of the powerful and the affluent by their influential parents, widespread corruption and callousness of the elite in solving youth problems, and increasing influence of the mass media. It would not be an exaggeration to aver that a new society has come into existence in which our youth have to struggle hard to fit in.

In the new society that has emerged, it appears that the search of the youth for the adult to be emulated is often a desperate and a futile quest. Youths have a different character structure, different goals, different aspirations, different values, and a radically different tempo of life. They have competitive and aggressive attitudes towards life and possess courage, guilt-free morality and settled self-judgements. On experiencing frustrations when their ego is attacked and traumatised, they project hostilities. They find it quite difficult to perform the expected roles. Many youth feel alienated, detached, isolated and relatively deprived. Society offers them very little that is stable, relevant and meaningful. They often look in vain for values, goals, means and institutions to which they can be committed because their thrust for commitment is strong.

Parents are often accused of not understanding their children. In this context, what is really important to remember is the fact that either a large number of parents could not care less about not understanding their children or that it is increasingly impossible for them to understand them. Perhaps then, it is not that parents are poor models for the kind of lives that the youths lead in their mature years; parents become simply irrelevant models for their children. The result is that the youth of today have difficulty in projecting a concept of themselves as adults.

In view of this emerging situation, could it be said that studying youth crime is really studying it as a manifestation of youth subculture? Though it is true that adults transmit a value system and a life pattern to youth, yet, not all of the ideals, conduct norms, and ways of life are respected, accepted and followed by the youth. Reacting to most of the adult values, they develop their own which are not only different from those of the larger adult society but may also be in open conflict with its values. Sellin (1952: 8) is of the opinion that such a cultural conflict of the youth with the adult society is often expressed in crime of other forms of deviant behaviour (say, drug abuse, alcoholism, etc.)

My own contention is that the thesis that something like youth subculture exists and that crime among youths is the result of this subculture is not based on any logical arguments. This viewpoint needs to be further debated and researched. Why do youths accept some values of the adult society and reject others? What type of youth rejects the adult values? Do rejection of adult values and the forming of new values necessarily lead to crime? Should western scholars' view routinely apply to the Indian society also? Unlike the youth in the Western society, the youth in India tolerate the authority of the patriarch and the control of the parents over them, even if they disagree with them. Even when the conduct norms of the children are not tolerated by the dominant power in the family or outside it, it does not necessarily prompt the children to indulge in deviant behaviour. Since most of the crimes committed by youths in India are not committed in groups, in spite of some shared values, but in isolation, it is difficult to accept association between youth crime and youth subculture. Furthermore, as long as the parameters of youth subculture are not identified, and the measurement of these parameters is not done on scientific basis, we cannot justify any correlation between subculture and crime.

Humanising the Deviant Youth

We have presented our arguments against the theoretical perspectives which explain crime in terms of man's physical nature and/or personality traits. Logically, we do not accept the approach towards the treatment of criminals which works through a typology of behavioural styles grounded in physiology or the psychiatric framework of the offenders, or in factors like impulsiveness, depression, obsession, personality disorders, etc. Inevitably, we find fault with the idea of 'transforming' human personality by punishment.

It has also been pointed out that a large number of young criminals are victims of situations and they do not have disorganised personalities. As such, the question arises: how to deal with these criminals after their conviction by the courts? Should they be sent to prisons or kept in specially created reformatories or released on probation? Our view is that different methods need to be used for different categories of young criminals. The three effective methods appear to be: (i) creation of special Corrective Homes for them on the lines of Borstal Schools for the adolescent and young offenders, (ii) release on probation, and (iii) imprisonment. This involves developing a typology of criminals for the purposes of correction. We classify the youth criminals in five categories:

1. *Minor perverts*: Those who are involved in petty offences and have economic and/or personal problems and for whom imprisonment would serve no purpose.
2. *Victims of harassment*: Those who participate only to a small degree, if at all, in crime and who identify mainly with social norms, and who generally subordinate personal interests to group goals.
3. *Toughs and defiants*: Those who participate to a higher degree in crime and identify with illegitimate standards.
4. *Integrated*: Those who deviate from norms under specific circumstances and who, when arrested, interrogated and imprisoned, maintain dignity while enduring the problems of humiliations and tribulations.
5. *Manipulators*: Those who manipulate the powers that be not through skill and wit but with high deceit and dishonest tricks and manage to get some facilities and privileges illegitimately.

Our thinking is that criminals of the first type should be released on probation, those of the second, fourth and fifth types should be kept in special Corrective Homes, and those of the third type should be kept in prisons.

To conclude, the following measures may be suggested for dealing with the youth criminals:

- Separate Corrective Homes may be established for such criminal youths as are not considered a threat to society.
- Indeterminate sentence system may be introduced for young criminals sent to prisons or Correctional Homes.
- Reshaping of police subculture, through police organisation, and the professionalisation of the police force are necessary for winning confidence and cooperation of the young criminals.
- Legal aid may be provided to poor youths and legal-aid organisations may be expanded.

- Judicial officials may be given powers of summary trial with regard to certain petty offences of young criminals (under 25 years of age) so as to avoid the moral dangers of detaining them in prison for long periods without trial.
- The courts may be restructured for providing appellant facilities.
- Class-bias may be contained as far as possible in trials.
- New work programmes may be introduced in prisons for training youths to help them in economic rehabilitation.
- There should be a greater concern for effective after-care of the young criminals released from prison and Corrective Homes, for without this vital support most of these offenders would return to a life of petty crime. The important thing is that on their discharge from prison/Corrective Home, they should be separated from their former associates and weaned away from their former habits.
- Stress has also to be laid on prevention of crime along with correction and rehabilitation. If as much effort is expended on crime prevention among the youth as is expended on apprehension, conviction, imprisonment and after-care homes, the incidence of crime would probably be considerably lower. Some factors in crimes committed by youths are clear—role of the family and the peer group (though our empirical study did not support such factors), lack of employment opportunities, harassment by the police, and callousness of the judiciary. If measures pertaining to these sources of crime are pursued, they by themselves may not eliminate youth crime but they at least would reduce the incidence of crime.

Policies, attitudes and actions change with the wisdom acquired over the years. The criminal youths who are only in early and mid-twenties of their life have a feeling that the best is "yet to be". Opportunities have, therefore, to be provided to them for social functioning. They have to remain active participants in family and community affairs. Without such participation, youth will lack a meaningful social place and may even withdraw from life which may prove to be detrimental to society.

References

Ahuja, Ram, *Youth and Crime*, Rawat Publishers, Jaipur, 1996.

Crime in India, 1993, National Crime Records Bureau, Government of India, New Delhi.

Landis, Paul, *Social Problems*, J.R. Lippincott Company, Chicago, 1959.

Trowler, Paul, *Active Sociology*, 1987.

Wilkins, Leslie T., *Social Deviance: Social Policy, Action and Research*, Englewood Cliffs, New Jersey, 1965.

Chapter 12

Punishment

SOCIETY AND SOCIAL CONTROL

Social control on the behaviour of individuals in a society is necessary for maintaining social order and stability. The means of social control vary from society to society and period to period. Individuals' conformity to society's expectations or to social norms is achieved by socialising them through which they internalise values, norms and taboos, which shape their habits, wishes as well as actions. The violation of social norms is prevented either by one's own conscience or by the fear of punishment. Social pressures also prevent violation of conduct norms when friends begin to avoid the violators and give them a feeling that they are 'outsiders'. Such pressures bring the violators back into a comfortable conformity. It is not only the formal controls but also the secondary group controls that compel people to conform to social expectations. Informal controls like ridicule, laughter, gossip, and ostracism operate in secondary group settings, but generally with a reduced impact. However, no system of social control works perfectly. Some persons fail to conform to social expectations, i.e., they deviate from social norms. Deviation, thus, is behaviour marked by violation of the norms of a group or society. Violation of the laws of the land is described as crime. Pain or suffering is inflicted upon a person who is adjudged guilty of committing a wrong, violating a law or indulging in crime.

CONCEPT OF PUNISHMENT

Punishment involves pain or suffering produced by design and justified by some value that the sufferer is assumed to have violated. Accidental pain or suffering is not punishment.

Jerome Hall (*The Aims of the Criminal Law*, 1958) has described punishment in the following terms: First, punishment is inflicting pain. Second, it is coercive. Third, it is inflicted in the name of the State, i.e., it is 'authorised'. Fourth, it presupposes rules, their violation, and a formal determination of that (violation) expressed in a judgment. Fifth, it is inflicted upon an offender who has caused/committed a harm. Sixth, the extent or type of punishment is in some defended way related to causing commission of the harm, and aggravated or mitigated by reference to the personality of the offender, his motive, and temptation.

Benn and Flew (Cr. Hart, H.L.A. in Radzinowicz and Wolfgang [ed.] *Crime and Justice*, Vol. II, 1971: 21) have given some elements of punishment: (1) It must involve pain and its consequences must normally be considered unpleasant. (2) It must be for an offence against legal rules. (3) It must be given to the actual offender who has committed the offence. (4) It must be imposed by an authority constituted by the legal system. Referring to these elements as the 'central case' of punishment, Hart has also pointed out four 'secondary cases' of punishment: (a) punishment for breaches of legal rules imposed or administered otherwise than by officials; (b) punishment for breaches of non-legal rules or orders (e.g., punishment in family or school); (c) collective punishment of some member of a social group for actions done by others without the former's authorisation; and (d) punishment of persons other than under (c) who neither are in fact nor supposed to be offenders. However, in criminology we talk of 'punishment' of only those persons who violate the law for which the state imposes some pain/suffering on them.

Why are certain kinds of action forbidden by law described as crimes and made punishable? It is to discourage certain types of conduct considered harmful to society. The nature of punishment or inflicting of pain upon those who violate laws depends upon attitude towards causation of crime, i.e., whether crime is viewed in terms of free will or determinism. Retributive and deterrent punishment is suggested if the society holds that individual himself is responsible for the crime he commits, while reforms are suggested if social structures and social systems are held responsible for criminality. The inflicted punishment may be physical, economic, psychological (causing mental suffering as in imprisonment) or social.

THEORIES (OR OBJECTIVES) OF PUNISHMENT

Broadly speaking, four theoretical explanations have been advanced as the basis upon which society acts in imposing penalty upon one who violates laws. These are: (i) to effect retribution or revenge or vengeance; (ii) to restrain offender physically so as to make it impossible for him to commit further crimes; (iii) to deter others from similarly violating the law; and (iv) to bring about reformation of the offender. These objectives are also described as bases for the origin of punishment.

Lowie (*Primitive Society*, 1920: 397-405) has described two more bases in the origin of punishment. One is the conflict of interests of different groups, as one group imposed its authority upon another; and the other is the fear of offended gods. Accepting the fact that tracing origin of punishment is not easy, it may be said that crime and punishment are functionally related to the culture in which crime occurs.

Reid (1976: 44-96) has referred to three objectives of punishment. These are:

1. *Incapacitation*: This aimed at making the offender physically incapable of committing offence again by giving him corporal punishment. This involved cutting of hands, making him blind, sexual castration for sexual perverts, branding an individual on the forehead with the letter indicating the type of crime committed (as was done with three women offenders in Punjab in 1994), and so on. Today, such practices are not endorsed.
2. *Reparation*: This is an act of compensating for loss or damage demanded from the criminal. The criminal is asked to restore the victim to his state prior to the crime. This method is prevalent more in civil cases where damages are paid to the victim out of the fine imposed on the offender. However, this philosophy is not applicable in criminal law. How can one repay for murder, rape or assault?
3. *Maintenance of social solidarity*: The justification for punishment is that (a) it prevents private revenge, and (b) it upholds the moves of society. Durkheim (*The Division of Labour in Society*, 1964: 108) has stated that "the true function of punishment is to maintain social cohesion intact". When people feel that state is not taking punitive action against an offender, they may take the law into their own hands. The criminal law should therefore meet the natural desire for vengeance.

It is said that many people repress their desires to commit offences. They therefore enjoy punishing others who have been caught committing them. This view not only lacks support of empirical evidence but also suffers from a basic flaw that there is no way to determine how much, if any, punishment is necessary to prevent private revenge.

Caldwell (1956: 390) has referred to three purposes of punishment: retribution, deterrence and reformation. *Expiation* as purpose of punishment is no longer given importance because it is chiefly used in a religious sense. Expiatory principle regards crime as a violation of the divine or moral order. The moral order can be restored, or the violation atoned for, only by inflicting pain upon the one guilty. Expiation thus refers to infliction of pain and suffering to make amends for an offence to appease the deity and to enable the wrong-doer to make amends or work for his inward moral development and spiritual regeneration after a sin/crime has been committed. We will, therefore, analyse in detail only three theories of purposes of punishment, viz., retributive, deterrent and reformative.

Retributive Theory

This theory is based on the idea of vindictive justice, or a tooth for a tooth and an eye for an eye. The principle is that if a man has caused the loss of a man's eye, his eye one shall cause to be lost; if he has shattered a man's limb, one shall shatter his limb; if a man has made the tooth of a man that is his equal fall out, one shall make his tooth fall out. This is to pay back the wrong-doer for his wrong-doing. It means that the wrong-doer has to be made to suffer by way of retaliation, even if no benefit results thereby to himself or to others. Historically, at first the instinct or the impulse of revenge was gratified by retaliatory measures on the part of the individual who suffered by the crime committed, or in the case of murder, by his relatives. Later, the state took away the right of retaliation from individuals because it was believed that since the criminal has broken the law and hurt someone, he deserves to suffer. It was also argued by those who were in favour of retribution that the victim of crime and/or his relatives and friends will refuse to cooperate with society if the offender is not brought to justice. Thus, assuming the function of revenge by the state really constituted the beginning of criminal law.

Morris Cohen (*see*, *Crime and Justice*, Vol. II, *op. cit.*, 1971: 27) has said that it is easy to dismiss the retributive theory with the remark that it is a remnant of the barbaric conception of vengeance. But the fact is that the early Greeks and many ancient spiritual books decried that one has an obligation to avenge the killing of a kinsman. The traditional code of honour still prevalent in many societies is that a gentleman must, at the risk of life, resent an insult to the extent of seeking to remove it with the blood of the offender. Even in the modern times, popular sentiment is that if a wife of a person is insulted or violated, he need not wait for a policeman; it is his duty to knock the offender down. Such a view prevails in almost all enlightened nations. But the problem with the retributive theory is that it fails to suggest an acceptable criterion whereby to discriminate between just and unjust punishment. Kant offers us the principle of equality between the crime and the penalty. This sounds simple in the case of murder—a life for a life. But it is obviously not capable of being extended. Morris Cohen (*ibid*.: 28) asks: can crime and punishment really be equated? What penalty can equal the crime of rape, kidnapping, forgery, dishonesty and so on? For the state to exercise the same amount of brutality against the criminal that the criminal exercised against his victim would be demoralising to any community. This theory of vengeance was, however, rejected with the ingress of the idea of refinement and the humanising of society. It came to be argued that the passion of revenge cannot be allowed to drive out reason. The feeling of retaliation will create demand for making punishment as severe as possible. It will only array man against man. The idea of treatment of criminals on the other hand will place a premium upon violence against criminals. Besides, in modern society, neither the victims of crime support the idea of physical torture of criminals nor the public opinion would tolerate sanguinary methods of punishment. In fact, now the popular demand is to eliminate all methods of punishment that cause physical suffering. The idea of doing away with *severe punishment* for taking revenge does not mean that the offender will escape all pain. Punishment will be awarded to the criminal but it would be devoid of the idea of vengeance.

The argument is that if a criminal is not punished, the public would feel frustrated and its obedience of the law would appear meaningless. Punishment of criminals would help to unify society against crime and criminals and also maintain respect for law. If law-violators and law-conformists receive the same treatment, there would be no reason to abide by the law. Thus, punishment of the criminal will make people rally in support of law enforcement, encourage them in their fight against crime, and help the authorities to maintain the public sense of justice.

Today, not only the idea of revenge in punishment is rejected but even the idea of punishing the offenders is criticised by many scholars. The argument that is most accepted is that we should hate the crime but not the criminal. There are many ways for achieving social solidarity. What is needed is the measures designed to prevent crime. The idea of retribution is to be totally rejected. Further arguments against retribution are:

1. It is now scientifically established through various empirical studies that the functioning of social systems and social structures is more responsible for crime than individual himself. As such, would it be logical to give retributive punishment to those who commit crimes due to force of circumstances rather than their personality traits?
2. Protecting the interests of criminals is as important today as protecting the interests of society or the victims. The punishment should therefore be proportional to the loss incurred.
3. The present society stresses humanitarianism and scientific progress. The movement in such a society should be to prevent crime rather than make criminal suffer, which is largely repressive.
4. Since almost all prisoners return to society, it is necessary that they must not be so stigmatised that they cannot take up lawful pursuits upon their release. Retributive punishment only makes criminals confirmed enemy of society.
5. Religious conscience and moral and ethical principles have always emphasised the importance of forgiveness, pity, mercy, charity, and considered these values as supreme values. It is, therefore, only moral and proper to pardon the criminal.
6. Holding that if society fails to punish the offender, the victim and his relatives may take the law in their own hands is not correct. Today, the victims of crime tend to shrink from the idea of subjecting criminals to physical torture. In fact, the victim feels satisfied if his loss is restored or he is properly compensated. He disregards the causes that produce a criminal or the measures adopted for dealing with criminals.
7. Resorting to the argument that a person can be prevented from indulging in crime by awarding him retributive punishment is invalid. Mackenzie has stated that it is only when an offender sees the punishment of his crime to be the natural or logical outcome of his act that he is likely to be led to any real repentance and it is only this recognition that is likely to lead others to genuine abhorrence of crime.

In spite of these arguments, it may be pointed out that though reformation and in some cases deterrence receive more attention, yet retribution too continues to remain one of the purposes of punishment. There are cases where retributive punishment is still considered necessary. The retributive punishment of imposing death penalty on offenders like Ranga and Billa in Delhi who had killed Chopr children was not condemned by society, nor the retributive punishment to the terrorists of Punjab and Kashmir who had killed a large number of innocent persons of all religions—Hindus, Sikhs, and Muslims—has been described as severe and unjustified. Rather, people look forward to having such offenders punished severely. It is in such cases of crime that retribution stands out distinctly as a purpose of punishment.

Deterrence Theory

Deterrence has two purposes: (i) to restrain the wrong-doer from repeatedly indulging in crime, and (ii) to set an example for others to deter and prevent them from committing crimes or violating laws. Just as a wild animal cannot be allowed to range at will in the city streets, similarly assuming that there is a danger that the criminal may again commit crime, the penalty of law is imposed upon him and his liberty is restrained until the danger of his giving indulgence to his criminal propensities be past. In certain cases, imprisonment may not be sufficient for the protection of society, or restraint by imprisonment may not be wholly effectual, therefore, if it is reasonably considered necessary to terminate criminal's life, even that is done for the purposes of deterrence. This requires going into the history of the criminal and investigating the circumstances in which crime was committed. If it is found that he is indeed a dangerous criminal, or that he is a man of uncontrollable violence or of homicidal tendency, or that he habitually commits serious crimes, or that he has a savage nature, or that he has committed crime with inhuman brutality, or that he is likely to escape from prison if imprisoned and may again make innocent people his prey, or that his existence is a danger to community, then the sentence of death is justifiable and advisable. If death penalty is considered not necessary, a long term of imprisonment or imprisonment for the remainder of his life may be awarded to protect society from any further depredations on his part.

Deterrent punishment may also aim at frightening others from violating law. Where crime is committed in a planned way and not under impulse or emotion, or where murder is deliberately planned with a motive of vengeance, the extreme penalty works a deterrent effect. Typical examples for deterrent punishment could be terrorism, bank or highway robberies, and murders committed and the bodies cut into pieces either to get rid of persons or to attain monetary benefits. In cases where crimes are not the result of reasoning or of weighing considerations for or against the intended crime, punishment with the intent of setting an example may not serve any purpose.

Deterrent punishment is in fact based on the doctrine of freedom of the will, according to which a person is free to do as he pleases. Society should, therefore, try to discipline him and to bring his behaviour into conformity with generally accepted standards by giving him deterrent punishment for violating laws. Not only must he be taught a lesson but others may also be frightened through his punishment to obey the law. The believers in the doctrine of freedom of the will are known as 'libertarians'.

There are, however, scholars who reject this doctrine and argue against deterrence in punishment. Their arguments are:

1. In spite of the fact that capital punishment is awarded mainly for murder yet hundreds of murders are committed every year. This points out that punishment is not always deterrent.
2. To say that "man is free to do as he pleases" is not correct because his behaviour is determined by values which he derives from his culture. What is considered right by one may be considered wrong by other, or what pleases one may be disagreeable to other. How can, therefore, one be expected to imitate others, particularly when one accepts the values of his culture and is also susceptible to a wide range of educational programmes. Denying the role of education as well as the role of one's experiences in determining one's 'choice' of action/behaviour would be placing man beyond the influence of education and send him bounding through life like an utterly unpredictable person. Assuredly, this is not correct.
3. It is empirically established today that criminal behaviour, like all human behaviour is the result of heredity and environmental causes, i.e., an individual does not have a single choice for determining his behaviour but it is determined by various factors. In such a situation, fear of law and punishment alone cannot deter a person from indulging in what is considered as anti-social behaviour. The policy of detection and apprehension is given little thought by many violators of the law, and often the penalty is not even thought of, assuming it is known to him. Most normal persons do not order their lives by thoughts of the future.
4. Man does not live by fear alone. Economic insecurity, loyalty to family and friends, and ambition, anger, and resentment many a time compel him to face the greatest dangers in violating the law. No wonder many people defy the law and risk arrest and imprisonment in order to satisfy their desires.

Moreover, it cannot be denied that if punishment is quickly, uniformly, publicly, and severely inflicted, it undoubtedly would prevent many crimes that are being committed by those who pay no heed to the punishment that they may receive for their acts.

Reformative Theory

The reform theory is the most popular theory today. It holds that the proper aim of criminal procedure is to reform the criminal so that he may become adjusted to the social order. This theory is in fact a mixture of sentimental and utilitarian motives. With the fading of faith in inflicting pain and with the spread of humane thought, belief in re-educating the criminal to enable him to become a useful member of society developed. Even from the most strict economic point of view, individual men and women are considered to be the most valuable assets of any society. It is therefore better to save them for a life of usefulness rather than punish them by imprisonment.

Punishment has its limitations: (1) It may produce harmful effects in the criminals who are punished. There remains the possibility of serious damage to the personality of the offender. With bitterness in his heart, he may seek an opportunity to strike back at society. (2) It may label the offender not only a criminal in his own eyes but also in the eyes of the community. Thus stigmatised, a man may be psychologically isolated from law-abiding groups and again be driven into the association of criminals upon his release from prison. (3) Punishment may also cause a person to develop caution and unusual skills, so that he could protect himself from apprehension, conviction and imprisonment.

It is, therefore, necessary that punishment is replaced by some alternative so that an offender might preserve his self-respect and renew loyalties for group standards. Criminologists have, as a result, started talking of reformation and rehabilitation of offenders. Reformation must involve change of environment which makes a person criminal reducing his personality adjustments, and create barriers in the inculcation of the principles of good citizenship. Such a programme may even require restriction of liberty and curtailment of rights and privileges. In other words, the reformative procedure must not be so pleasant as to encourage further criminal activities but it must be so designed as to produce desirable changes in the personalities of offenders.

The propounders of reformative theory like Bentham (*Rationale of Punishment*, 1830: 21), Ewing (*The Morality of Punishment*, 1929: 5), and Hart (*Punishment and Responsibility*, 1968: 10) rejected the retributive and deterrent theories of punishment in the nineteenth and twentieth centuries and sought to take the anger out of punishment. According to Bentham, "punishment is not an act of wrath or vengeance but is an act of calculation, disciplined by considerations of the social good and the offenders' needs. The reformative and utilitarian justification of punishment was that it would persuade the offender to accept his sufferings and face his own guilt. Reformative theory thus presented punishment to offenders as being in their best interests, while utilitarian theory cast it as an impartial act of social necessity (Fitzgerald *et al.*, *Crime and Society*, 1981: 52). In other words, the reformers' task was to make punishment self-evidently rational. On this question, Jeremy Bentham's views on whipping are important. In the early nineteenth century, the severity of whipping in Britain, France, the US etc. depended on the strength of the person who inflicted it and the degree of indignation that the offender aroused in the crowd. It struck Bentham as unjust and irrational that punishment should vary according to the emotions of those who inflicted it and those who watched it. In his view, its severity should depend only on the gravity of the offence. In his conception of pain, what was rational was impersonal and what was impersonal was humane. He, therefore, held that punishment should not be scattered by a monarch's wrathful hand but apportioned to each crime as precisely as the market allocated prices to commodities. Punishment would then become a science, an objective use of pain by the state for the regulation of the egoistic calculus of individuals.

It may thus be said that: (i) the reformative theory gives importance not to crime but to criminal; (ii) it considers defective functioning of social systems and social structures, defective environment, and lack of opportunities to achieve one's goals as the causes of crime.

There are, however, a number of highly questionable assumptions at the back of this which need to be critically examined. Morris Cohen (*ibid.*, 30-31) has raised the question whether crime is curable and if so, at what cost to society. Many social reformers and social scientists are apt to ignore calculating shrewdness found among criminals. Some hot-blooded criminals may even respond to emotional appeal but they are also likely to backslide when they get an opportunity or when they are exposed to temptation. Most criminals are also religious-minded but religious education does not eliminate crime nor does education minimise crime. Even the records of special reformatories for young offenders show that it is fully possible to reform delinquents and criminals so that they will stay reformed for any length of time. The analogy of the criminal law to medicine breaks down. The surgeon can determine with a fair degree of accuracy when there is an inflamed appendix or cancerous growth so that by cutting it out he can remove a definite cause of distress. There is no such physician in our complex social system who can readily point out one cause of crime on the basis of similarly verifiable knowledge which can be easily removed. Ignoring this question, we may ask another question: to what extent can criminals be re-educated or re-socialised so that they can live useful lives? Do we not know our limitations with regard to answering this question? Can we really deal with that group which determines the morals of its members which ultimately provokes some to commit crimes? And here we must not neglect the question of cost. If poverty and unemployment are the main causes of many crimes, can we afford the cost of removing these causes? (The expense in punishment on the other hand is not unlimited.) Suppose a correctional institute gets success in reforming deviants and criminals. Will people provide funds for such correctional institutes when honest law-abiding people cannot get adequate hospital facilities? Suppose a prison submits a plan that it requires several lakhs of rupees on a concurrent basis every year to provide specific type of vocational education to prisoners which will help them in economic rehabilitation after release from prison. Would our community stand for such expense when so many promising young people remain unemployed? Will people be satisfied to see a criminal convicted of a dangerous crime simply reformed and not express a feeling of resentment against such criminal?

On all these grounds, should we accept the reformative ideal and totally forget the punitive aspect of crime? It is, however, not easy to give a clear-cut opinion on how to deal with criminals. Perhaps, punishment policy for some and reformative policy for some other criminals would be a pragmatic path. It is, thus, clear that punishment cannot be abolished and correction cannot be ignored in dealing with delinquents of differential types.

THEORIES OF VARIATIONS IN PUNISHMENT

Sutherland (*op. cit.*, 1965: 256-29) has given three main explanations for variations in punitive reaction to law-breaking, i.e., why do some societies punish some acts severely and others mildly, and why do some societies not punish at all? Why do punishments vary from time to time within the same society?

Some crimes and acts regarded as wrong upset the equilibrium of society as well as the interests of its individual members and various punitive reactions partially restore this equilibrium. However, it is to be remembered that the punitive reaction is only one of the many reactions to law-breaking, and it was not at all important among reactions to offences in the preliterate life. According to Sutherland, reactions depended on the type of wrongs in the preliterate societies. These wrongs/offences were classified as: (i) wrongs consisting of injuries to the tribe (like treason, witchcraft, etc.), (ii) wrongs consisting of injuries to private individuals (like assault, murder, theft, etc.), and (iii) wrongs consisting of injuries to members of the same family. Reaction against the first type of offence was annihilation of the offender, against the second type of offence was vengeance and severe suffering, and against the third type of offence was disgust but not punishment.

For change in penal reactions in complex societies, Sutherland (*ibid.*, 298-307) has given three explanations:

(1) *Cultural consistency theory*: According to this theory, the methods and severity of punishment are consistent with other developments within the culture at a given time. Severe punishment to offenders was imposed when physical suffering was regarded as the natural lot of man, while severity of punishment was reduced and uniformity in sentencing was introduced when the dignity of the individual and the importance of equality of all citizens was recognised. When the system of fair price in relation to a commodity was introduced, the system of prescribing punishment commensurate with crime was practised. Individualisation in the treatment of criminals occurred when individualisation became important in medical treatment. Thus, change in penalties varies with change in different values gaining or losing importance. Today, imprisonment is considered a severe form of punishment because: (a) an individual's freedom is considered to be very important and imprisonment deprives a person of that freedom; (b) institutions for imprisonment have been constructed on extensive scale for large numbers of people; (c) labour power has been appreciated only in the recent times, therefore, it was thought necessary to conserve labour; and (d) decrease in the social distance between those who imposed punishment and those who suffered enabled a larger proportion of the population to appreciate the situation of those who committed offences, so that the imposition of severe pain or suffering was not considered necessary.

(2) *Psychoanalytic or scapegoat theory*: This theory explains punishment in terms of man's need to satisfy aggressive impulses, especially the sex drive. When sexual behaviour is not severely repressed, punishment of criminals is not so severe. Similarly, if man has other ways to express his aggression (e.g., in time of war), he does not take his

aggression out on criminals. As outlets of sexual expression and release of aggressive tendencies vary, there is variation in punishment also. Caldwell (*op. cit.*, 505) has described this explanation as vague and elusive.

(3) *Sociological or social structure theories*: According to one social structural theory, punishment is related to the characteristics of the social structure. For example, when labour is needed, punishment will be light since prisoners are required for labour supply. When labour is in great supply, offenders are punished severely. If this theory is accepted, punishment should become more severe as unemployment rises. But there is no evidence to support this proposition.

According to another social structural theory, there is relationship between power of the middle class and punishment. When the lower middle class, in which persons most frequently repress their natural desires, is in control of punishment, they inflict severe and frequent punishment. When the lower-middle class is absent in a society, severe punishment is non-existent.

Third social structural explanation of punishment is found in Durkheim's writings. His proposition is that punishment varies with the complexity of the division of labour in a society. In societies characterised by mechanical solidarity (where society is cohesive and deviation is a serious threat) punishment is repressive so that deviant behaviour could be repressed. But in societies characterised by complex division of labour, i.e., by organic solidarity, the emphasis is on restitution, i.e., punishments are not severe.

The fourth social structural explanation associates punishment with the degree of social disorganisation. When a society is basically homogeneous, few people deviate and therefore non-punitive reactions prevail in society. But as heterogeneity increases, often increasing social disorganisation, severe punishments are invoked. Sutherland cites the example of severe punishment to deviants during periods of revolution when there is increase in social disorganisation.

All these theories have, however, been criticised for the lack of empirical evidence.

KINDS OF PUNISHMENT

Specific techniques for punishing offenders have varied from time to time and place to place. Six methods have generally been used in the history of mankind for punishing law-breakers: death penalty, exilement, corporal punishment (physical torture), imprisonment, imposition of fine, and social degradation. Of these, exilement and physical torture have fallen into disuse, capital punishment is given in the rarest of rare cases, and social degradation method is used not by the courts but by castes and communities. Thus, imprisonment and financial loss are the two methods which are in vogue today. Since death penalty is analysed in detail in a separate chapter, we will briefly discuss here the remaining five methods of punishment.

Corporal Punishment

This punishment includes flogging, branding, mutilating, and confinement in the pillory. *Branding* is inscribing letters on forehead, hands, etc. indicating the type of crime committed. *Mutilation* is cutting off of hands, ears and legs or piercing the tongue with a hot iron. It was based on the doctrine of retribution. The idea was to socially disgrace the offender and deter him from repeating crime and also to deter other potential offenders. Herbert Bloch and Glibert Geis (*Man, Crime and Society*, 1962) have reported that in Denmark,600 sex offenders were castrated in 20 years---between 1935 and 1956. *Pillory confinement* is fastening hands and feet in a wooden frame. The pillory was driven through towns accompanied by minstrels to entertain the citizens as they watched the offender suffer humiliation. The observers threw rotten vegetables and occasionally stones at the offenders which sometimes resulted in their death. *Ducking* in water is a technique in which the culprit is made to sit on a chair attached to a long lever. The operator ducks the chair into water and thereby submerges the culprit. The crowds watch and jeer. All these types of punishment aim at inflicting physical pain upon the offender. While flogging is still practised in countries like Pakistan, Iran, etc., all other methods have been abolished all over the world. Though legally these methods have been abolished, yet in practice, the police still use some of them against criminals. In India, the blinding of criminals in Bihar in the 1980s and the branding of three women in one case in Punjab in the early 1990s and five Sansi women in another case in 1994 are two recent examples reported in the newspapers.

Transportation

This refers to removal of a criminal from his country to some other country or to a penal colony. This method was employed to a great extent in Europe, Latin America, Australia, France, England, Russia and many other countries. It was reported that in Australia, between 1787 and 1867 as many as 1,35,000 criminals were sent to England's penal colonies (Ives: 123, Caldwell, 424). Russia transferred their criminals to Siberia, and France to Africa. In India, during the British period, many criminals were transported to Andaman and Nicobar Islands. Ghastly tales of brutality, sordidness, desperation, and depravity were often reported from these colonies. Today, these islands are no more used as penal islands. Many people are settled there and are engaged in agriculture and other occupations.

Banishment and Exile

Banishment is somewhat like transportation in that a criminal is compelled to leave a city or country for a specified period of time. While transportation deprives the criminal of liberty after he arrives at the place to which he is transported, banishment merely forbids the banished criminal from returning before the expiry of the sentence.

Fines

Imposing financial penalty is considered to be a minor penalty. Sometimes a fine is imposed along with imprisonment, i.e., sometimes it is used as a supplement to imprisonment and sometimes as a substitute for it. Arguments in favour of fines are: these cost little to administer; these provide a source of revenue to the state; these do not impose any stigma on the offender; these do not interfere with the occupation of the offender; these do not expose the individual to the corrupting influence of hardened criminals; these are the only penalties that are completely revocable in cases where mistakes are made; and these can be utilised to compensate the victim of the crime.

Arguments against fines are: these are paid by the parents and relatives of the criminal and thus the practice becomes a punishment for criminal's parents than for the criminal himself; these bear more heavily on the poor; and these do not exert any reformative influence on the offender. However, if fines are imposed with discrimination and understanding, these can play an important role in law enforcement, particularly in violation of traffic and licensing regulations.

Imprisonment

This method which originally was a means of detention till the trial was completed or a debt was paid is now more frequently used for all crimes except light misdemeanours. However, the horrors of imprisonment are so well-known that no one ventures to say much in defence of the system.

Still it maintains itself as it has no practical alternative. This method is discussed in detail in a separate chapter.

To conclude, we have struggled a great deal to get rid of the cruelty of the old forms of torture in the criminal law. We have now become quite sensitive to pain and are quite anxious to deal with humans in a humane way. Imprisonment and the imposition of fine do have a purpose in some legitimate cases. Though we do not support the idea that for protecting society, a person should be incarcerated for a long period, yet we do support imprisonment in particular and punishment in general for certain categories of offenders. Welfare of criminals is equally an important issue. Society can never be truly protected by any procedure that does not deal justly and wisely with individual criminals. The philosophy that is considered ideal today is that offenders must, in the first place, see that their punishment is 'just' before that punishment is seen to be effective in rehabilitation. They should not feel that they are being victimised by the system. They should not consider 'justice' as hypocrisy. Thus, punishment should not be an obstacle to correction, and rehabilitation ideal should not totally be oblivious of the fact that some offenders do need to suffer for their vicious actions.

CHANGES IN PUNITIVE PHILOSOPHY

Changing attitudes towards punishment may be analysed on the basis of five theoretical paradigms: classicism, positivism, conservatism, strain theory and new deviancy theory.

Classicists believe in proportionate punishment, i.e., (i) punishment should not be greater than what is 'deserved' by the criminal, (ii) amount of punishment should depend upon achieving defined social purposes, and (iii) punishment should not be imposed merely by assuming that the criminal is dangerous to society. Thus, criminal act and not the criminal should be the basis of punishment and law should be applied uniformly to all offenders. Punishment must bear down directly on the responsibilities and calculations of the individual. Since the purpose of punishment is not to inflict pain or to take vengeance but to make men obey the law, punishment must be made proportional to the actual social harm it causes, and limited to only that required to deter further criminal acts (Fitzgerald *et al.*, *Crime and Society*, 1981: 260-61). In short, the classicist theory of punishment permits neither inappropriate leniency nor undue harshness. Incarceration is to be conceptualised as a time during which we try to reorient a prisoner to the lawful use of power.

Positivists have rejected punitive action as advocated by classicists and conservativists. They believe that if a criminal is not responsible for his actions, it makes no sense to punish crime. Instead, we must replace punishment by treatment. A panel of experts (and not laymen as in jury system) should diagnose the condition of the *individual* and prescribe appropriate treatment. Diagnosis of the criminal should be based not so much on what he or she did (the *act*), not on who he or she is (the *actor*) but on his or her background (the *antecedents*). The thief may cause damage worth five rupees or five thousand rupees but to sentence him proportionately to the impact of the act (as the classicists would) is meaningless. What is necessary is to see if the vandalism sprang from a deep-seated malaise of socialisation or if it was a mere experimentation of a normal youth. And once diagnosis is made, the criminal must be treated for as long as is necessary. Sentences should therefore be indeterminate, just as one's stay in hospital is indeterminate and based on satisfactory treatment or 'cure' rather than on the fixed sentences of the classicists. Rehabilitation rather than punishment must be our priority.

Conservatives are mainly interested in the maintenance of order. To achieve this aim, coercion is a necessity. They believe that laxity in the exertion of authority undermines social control. Crime will never be eliminated either by the propagation of Reason or by the socialisation process. A more pragmatic approach is therefore desirable, which means adopting the 'dual track' system of punishment. This means that an offender is first judged strictly on his or her offence—as in the classicist theory—but such a proportional punishment is then added to or substracted from by a series of criteria whose concern is order. This refers to three factors: ascriptive criteria, dangerousness and deterrence. In 'ascriptive criteria', the focus is: who is the offender? Is he a person in a position of responsibility—say a police officer or a bureaucrat or a politician—or an ordinary worker? The severity of punishment should be determined in accordance with his position. In 'dangerousness', the focus is whether a person is a first offender or a recidivist, a habitual or a professional criminal, one who commits crime all alone or as a member of an organised gang. This will determine danger from him to society. A more dangerous criminal has to be incarcerated longer than strict justice requires. In 'deterrence', the focus is whether punishment to the offender is likely to deter similar offenders. Thus, in maintaining order, proportionate justice may be added to or subtracted from, preferably at the point of sentencing. The judge's discretionary role is central here. We thus find that while classicism insists on focusing on the *act* of crime and positivism on the *antecedents* of the criminal, conservatism stresses the *actor* himself or herself. Similarly, while classicism talks of deterrence to inhibit the *individual's* future transgressions, conservatism insists upon a *general* deterrence, i.e., deterrence of all others. The conservatives, therefore, want that punishment should be expressed as publicly as possible; the classicists want the punishment to be meted out in the privacy of a prison where the offenders might rationally dwell upon the consequences of their crime; and the positivists want the culprit to be treated in the atmosphere of a therapeutic unit.

The *strain theorists* want to alleviate the disjunction between aspiration and opportunities, institutional means and structural goals. They are more interested in changing the social structure which causes crime than the punishment of the offender. In other words, they are interested in piecemeal social engineering to provide opportunities to lessen the 'strain'. Coercion should be minimal. Punishment is obviously irreconcilable with this approach. What is necessary is to teach the offenders skills that will allow them most profitably to use their opportunities and demonstrate that many subcultural 'solutions' are of limited use.

New deviance theorists talk of *social control* giving rise to deviance. For much social control is seen to be irrational and dysfunctional. The prisons do not work; they have a high recidivism rate. The stigmatisation of the delinquent leads to his becoming a hardened criminal. The over-reaction of the people in power creates more deviance which further raises the level of coercive strategies necessary to maintain control. The key to controlling the crime problem, therefore, lies in the control of reaction against deviance, rather than in structural change. What is needed is reconstructing the foundations of laws and legal procedures in the society in order to increase the safety of the people and their property, while at the same time increasing the sense of social justice and the degree of social order. Our laws and legal practices cause most of the problems of crime and injustice. Therefore, instead of talking of socioeconomic reordering of our society, we should focus on the responsibilities and failures of legislators and legal authorities to create and administer just laws and legal procedures.

Marxists have altogether a different philosophy. While New Deviancy theorists consider crime as behaviour which violates the interests of the powerful, Marxists have a different viewpoint. They stand for the ideals of equality, justice and liberty for both the working class as well as the ruling class. Only when the laws will stand for equality and security of the whole society can the society fulfil the 'moderating' function and keep the class conflicts within the bounds of 'order'.

According to Marxists, the cause of crime is "disparity between effort and reward", or "unequal reality of a class society", or "stress on individual competition". Thus, a society which increases its wealth without decreasing its misery will face increasing crimes. As such, what is needed is removing the conditions in society that give rise to miseries and problems. The solution is not opening up more opportunities but abolishing the class system altogether, or establishing a classless society, i.e., to create a world where formal and substantive inequalities would disappear.

HUMANITARIAN THEORY OF PUNISHMENT

According to this theory (Radzinowicz and Wolfgang, *Crime and Justice*, Vol. II, 1971: 43-48), punishment should be therapeutic. To punish a criminal because he deserves it, and as much as he deserves, is mere revenge and, therefore, barbarous and immoral. It is maintained that the only legitimate motives for punishing are to mend the criminal and the need to deter others by example. This doctrine accepts the view that all crime is more or less pathological and a criminal needs to be healed and cured. The theory appears to be logical but then the question, as already pointed out in earlier pages, is: how to cure? Will the 'cure' process for the criminal be as compulsory as punishment was considered earlier? Is depriving a criminal the rights of a human being a correct cure? The humanitarian theory talks of 'justice'. But how to decide what is just or unjust? Furthermore, can the question of justice ignore the questions whether the 'course of cure' adopted will really reform the criminal and whether it is likely to deter others? We talk of a deterrent method, not of whether it is just, but of whether it will deter. Similarly, we talk of treatment method not of whether it is just or not, but of whether it will correct and resocialise the criminal. Who will fix the 'right' sentence? A judge who at present awards punishment is a person who is trained in what is law and deciding whether a law has been violated or not; if yes, what is the punishment prescribed for that violation? He is surely not a 'social doctor' or a 'social engineer' to know that the 'punishment' awarded by him will definitely cure the criminal. Can a penologist judge that? How is a penologist trained? Is he a psychiatrist or a psychotherapist or a sociologist or a jurist? The fact is that he is not an expert. We all may say as men "this punishment is unjust; it is disproportionate to the criminal's crime", but it will be only our subjective opinion.

The humanitarian theory talks of the 'use' of the criminal. This means that if a criminal is put in jail, he should not be released till it is felt that he has been 'cured'. On the other hand, if his term of imprisonment is long and it is felt that he has been 'cured' in a short period, he should not be kept in prison any more. This in simple words means substituting 'definite sentence' system by "indeterminate or indefinite sentence" system. And who is to judge the 'cure'? It is not the experts in moral theology nor even in psychotherapy but only those ordinary judges who inflicted sentence. Will this be logical? Where lies the difference between 'cure' and 'punishment' then? Let us not be deceived by a name. Who cares whether this is called 'punishment' or not? The 'cure' includes most of the elements in 'punishment'---shame, deprivation of freedom, bondage, work imposed by others, and so forth. This is not criticising humanitarian philosophy. It is only the logic of position. To be punished for an action which others think 'wrong' is to be 'cured' against one's will. Even if the 'treatment' is painful, even if it is life-long, even if it is fatal, it cannot be called 'punishment'; it has to be described as 'therapeutic'. The humanitarian theory of punishment, therefore, cannot be called precise, specific or a new approach to crime and criminals. Lewis (*see*, Radzonowicz, *Crime and Justice*, Vol. II: 47) has, therefore, suggested that it is essential to oppose the humanitarian theory of punishment, root and branch. It carries on its front a semblance of mercy which is wholly false.

CURRENT DEBATE ON PUNISHMENT

The current discussion among philosophers on punishment is concerned with three aspects: object, justification, and methods of punishment. Some philosophers describe the object of punishment as 'coercive conformity'. Suppose a boy of fifteen is charged with using abusive language and holding out threats in anonymous phone calls to a girl. The lower court finds him guilty but releases him on probation for 'treatment'. The case is then referred to the High Court which adjudges him 'criminal' and awards him rigorous imprisonment for two years. Here the object of 'punishment' is surely "coercive conformity to rules" which is a legal consequence of declaring him a criminal, because his conduct is viewed as a threat to the community. For achieving conformity to social norms, the methods of punishment are no longer traditional (like flogging, mutilation, etc.) but "a wide variety of deprivations", including the trial process itself. This indicates change in public sentiment, change in punitive philosophy, progress in science, and the advent of law-enforcement agencies (the police and the courts).

In the recent past, we have witnessed divergence of opinion among the political rulers and the judges on the issue of violation of social norms. What was considered by the political rulers as 'aberration' is considered a 'serious law violation' by the courts for which they have started giving radical judgments for the benefit/welfare/interests of the people. The recent judgments of the Supreme Court and the High Courts with regard to vacating government bungalows after the persons concerned had ceased to occupy political/official positions, imprisonment of senior bureaucrats (as in Karnataka) and even police officers (as in Haryana) for disregarding the judgments of the courts, keeping control on the behaviour of the police and other officials at public functions (as in Punjab), pulling up Central Bureau of Investigation for deliberately dragging investigations in some cases and allowing vital evidence to disappear (as in Chandra Swami's St. Kitts probe), making university authorities accountable for failing to ensure students' attendance in classes and teachers' failure to engage classes (Rajasthan High Court) indicate change in the interpretation of rules and laws. The courts are 'rationalising' the penal code chaos. One notes happily that the judges have made this choice consciously.

Some of the judgments of the courts on 'punishment' are, however, criticised by the legislators as attempts to deprive the ruling elites of the privileges they enjoy. Some people connected with the correction of criminals also find in these adjudications a veiled threat to the rehabilitative ideal. A concern for responsibility in criminal law and for the principles of legality make it vital that clear objectives of punishment be prescribed by legislators. If there is no punishment for the violation of social norms and if punishment is not accompanied with some moral responsibility, the general preventive goal will fall outside the definition of punishment.

As regards the methods of punishment, perhaps Jerome Hall's definition of punishment is too narrow by reason of its inclusion of 'pain'. Today, there are many explicitly punitive sanctions which are neither painful nor disvaluing. For example, some correctional institutions run a series of rehabilitative programmes for inmates which are in part or whole required of them. Could such activities be properly classified under the criteria of traditionally given definition of punishment by scholars like Hall? It would seem not. The definition of punishment has, therefore, to be broad enough to include even new methods of correction and reformation, if at all 'reformation' aims at seeking conformity to norms in future.

It is at this point in the debate that we discover that one's definition and methods of punishment depend on one's approach to the goals and objects justifying punishment. Rudolph Gerber and Patrick McAnany (*see*, Radzinowicz, *op. cit.*, 127) have rightly said that if one justifies punishment solely on grounds of individual's (criminal's) rehabilitation, it is evident that criticising the essential characteristics as involving pain or even deprivation is hardly sensible. No wonder, we have not been able to formulate a broader definition of punishment which may satisfy new aspirations and goals of punishment. No doubt the goal has shifted from pain-infliction to humanitarianism to the reform of the criminal. Science today has become the means, replacing religion and moral exhortations, whereby anti-social men are turned into social men. But the figures on recidivism indicate that not even science is able to meet the need of reformation.

We may thus point out that the present debate on goals and methods of punishment continues to be an on-going process. One school totally rejects the traditional goals of retribution and deterrence as the goals of penal system and opts for a rehabilitatiortist approach to punishment. On the other hand, there is a rejuvenation of retribution and deterrence as ideals of punishment. At one time, utilitarianism appears to be a popular approach while at other time, retributive need and concern for morality are given importance in criminal punishment. The discussion thus talks of the need for multiple purposes in penal system.

DESIRABLE PENAL SYSTEM

We may now conclude our views on the desirable aims of penal system in the present age. Nigel Walker has suggested five aims (*see*, Radzinowicz, *Crime and Justice*, Vol. II: 48-50):

1. *Humanitarianism*: The penal system should be such as to cause the minimum of suffering to offenders or others.
2. *Reductivism*: The penal system should reduce the types of behaviour prohibited by the criminal law.
3. *Retributivism*: The penal system should protect offenders and suspected offenders against unofficial retaliation.
4. *Expiation/Atonement*: The penal system should be designed to ensure that offenders atone by suffering for their offences.
5. *Denunciation*: Punishment should show society's abhorrence of crime.

We may also add the following three aims to the above-mentioned five aims:

(a) *Consistency*: Instead of dealing with similar acts by similar measures, punishment should be "individualised", i.e., it should fit offender's culpability and his prospects of reform. This should depend upon the interpretation of 'individualisation' by one who is imposing punishment.

(b) *Legal nominalism*: All acts (offences) which have the same legal name are considered equally culpable. The offences should, therefore, be 're-classified' to make variation in punishment possible.

(c) *Harm*: The sentence should be related to the intentions of the offender committing crime, i.e., the severity of punishment should depend upon the harm done by the offence and not upon the retributive motive.

References

Barlow, Hugh D., *Introduction to Criminology*, Chapter 13, Little Brown and Company, Boston, 1978.

Caldwell, Robert G., *Criminology*, Chapters 18 and 19, Ronald Press Company, New York, 1956.

Radzinowicz Leon and Wolfgang Marvin, *Crime and Justice*, Vol. II, Basic Books Publishers, New York, 1971, pp. 21-113.

Reid, Sue Titus, *Crime and Criminology*, Chapter 14, The Dryden Press, Illinois, 1976.

Reckless, Walter C., *The Crime Problem* (2nd edn.), Chapters 19 and 20, Appleton Century Crofts Inc., New York, 1955.

Sutherland, E.H. and Cressay, D.R., *Principles of Criminology* (6th edn.), Chapters 14 and 15, The Times of India Press, Bombay, 1965.

Chapter 13

Capital Punishment

AGGRAVATED DEATH

Punitive ideology is not typical in criminal justice. Physical cruelty was systematically practised in earlier ages. Death was used as penalty for a wide range of offences. Inflicting death penalty upon a person convicted of a serious crime is called 'capital punishment'. For centuries, death penalty was used without much thought for justification. It was simply accepted as an efficient method for handling a difficult person. There was total lack of respect for human life. The methods used for killing a condemned criminal were also inhuman. In India, for example, forcing an offender to fight lions and ferocious animals, trampling him under an elephant's feet, dragging him by a running horse, burning him in fire, putting him in boiling oil, and other similarly cruel and torturous methods were used for putting offenders to death. In Japan, only a few generations ago, a gruesome form of execution was practised. The condemned persons were tied to a cross by rope and then transfixed by light spears by the executioner. The spear was not directly transfixed in the heart but spears were passed slowly through the body, missing the vital parts. The persons thus passed through excruciating agony before death released them. In France and Germany, during the medieval period, persons convicted of heinous crimes were killed on the wheel. This method involved tying the condemned person to the spokes of a large wheel by breaking his limbs to conform to a wheel's rim. The person was then left to die of exhaustion. In some Muslim countries, killing by stones and flogging is quite common.

Besides, executions were generally public. People gathered as if visiting a fair. The idea behind executing in public was deterrence and moral education and reinforcing the belief in the people that the acts for which the condemned suffered were wrong, sinful, and damnable. Today, these torturous methods of execution are no longer used. Most of the countries use painless methods of execution, generally hanging by the neck and electrocution.

TRENDS IN THE USE OF CAPITAL PUNISHMENT

Several trends could be observed with regard to capital punishment during the past few decades. These may be described as under:

The *first* trend is towards the abolition of death penalty. In about 25 countries, it has already been abolished by law or tradition, while in many other countries, movements to abolish it are very strong. In quite a few Islamic countries, however, there are no signs yet to do away with it.

Secondly, the overall number of capital crimes in being steadily reduced. For example, in England in the eighteenth century, there were more than 200 capital crimes for which capital punishment was awarded but in 1952 there were only 4 such crimes. Today, it has been totally abolished. In India, there are seven crimes for which capital punishment is prescribed, but, in practice it is awarded only in murder cases. In the Unites States, capital punishment is prescribed for eight crimes but most of the states award it only for one or two crimes.

Thirdly, torturous methods are not used for giving effect to death penalty. Swift and painless methods are generally used in execution.

Fourthly, capital punishment is not given in public. The number and type of persons to be present at the time of execution has been restricted by law and administrative regulations.

Fifthly, some safeguard measures have been provided for miscarriage of justice.

Sixthly, certain types of persons are totally excluded from getting capital punishment, like children below a certain specified age, old persons above a certain age, pregnant women, and insane persons.

Lastly, the trend is towards reduction in the number of executions. In India, for example, the number of persons actually hanged has come down from about 200 in the early 1960s to less than 50 in the early 1990s. In the United States, while 155 persons were executed in 1930, only 62 persons were given death penalty in 1953 (Caldwell: 413). Between 1916 and March 1994, only 237 executions were carried out in America (*The Hindustan Times*, August 5, 1994).

HISTORICAL OVERVIEW OF ABOLITION EFFORTS

The abolition movement of death penalty started with Beccaria in Italy in the 1700s. The increasing emphasis on humanitarianism resulted in the mitigation of harsh punishments. The utilitarian philosophy was that "punishment should be no more than just, nor more than necessary". This led people in Italy and other countries to question the need for capital punishment. Death penalty was thus gradually eliminated in most European countries during the last half of the nineteenth century. However, by the turn of the twentieth century, a counter-movement began as crimes increased. Garofalo wrote about socially dangerous criminals in 1885, Lombroso wrote about born criminals in 1911, Healy wrote about personality disorders of criminals in 1915, and Hooton wrote about feeble-mindedness of criminals in 1939. These ideas led some people to conclude that capital punishment was a necessary eugenic measure.

In America, death penalty was abolished in 1967 but restored in 1976. In June 1972, three persons who had received death sentences appealed to the American Supreme Court arguing that the imposition on death penalty constituted crude punishment and was, therefore, unconstitutional. But the court did not rule that capital punishment *per se* is cruel and unusual punishment and, therefore, unconstitutional. The court, thus, left open the door for new legislation for capital punishment in those states, which had retained death penalty.

In England, King Henry VIII executed 72,000 thieves and vagabonds during his regime. We may never know if this figure is accurate since complete records have not survived; but it is certainly true that death penalty was awarded even for petty offences. In 1500, England had only seven major crimes (treason, murder, larceny, robbery, burglary, rape and arson) for capital punishment but by 1800, there were over 200 crimes, including crime against public peace, for death penalty. (Reid, 1976: 474) Capital punishment has now been abolished in England.

Those countries which have abolished capital punishment may be classified in three groups:

1. Those in which it has been abolished through legislative or constitutional provision (*Abolitionist de jure*). About 22 countries fall in this group which include Portugal (1867), the Netherlands (1870), Switzerland (1874---however, out of 22 cantons, 7 have reintroduced it), Norway (1905), Sweden (1921), Denmark (1933), and England (1969). In Austria, capital punishment was abolished in 1949 but was reintroduced in 1952. In Rumania, it was abolished in 1865 but was

reintroduced in 1939. In West Germany, it was abolished in 1949 but was restored in 1932.

2. Those where law makes provision for death penalty but death sentences are never awarded/carried out by virtue of an established custom (*Abolitionist de facto*). About four countries, including Belgium, fall in this group.
3. Those in which death penalty is laid down only for offences which are never committed (*Almost abolitionist*). This category includes two states in Australia and three states in America (*Social Defence*, January, 1964).

Capital punishment, however, is still prevalent in India, China, Russia, France, Japan, Indonesia, Iran, Iraq, Burma, Pakistan, in 13 states of the USA, and so on.

Amongst those countries which permit capital punishment, death penalty is awarded for murder in 58 countries, for revolution in 24 countries, for arson in 21 countries, for spying against the country in 20 countries, for kidnapping in five countries, for rape in five countries, for black marketing in four countries, for drug trafficking in three countries, and for counterfeiting currency in two countries.

Some countries have provided reasonable safeguards against miscarriage of justice. Four such safeguards may be identified as: (i) appeals (retrial by higher courts), (ii) review (re-opening of cases after new facts come to light disclosing miscarriage of justice), (iii) confirming by some non judicial authority, as in Iran, the Philippines and Thailand, and (iv) confirmation by the Council of Ministers or by the Ministry of Justice, as in the Sudan and Somalia. Islamic law offers three choices to a victim's kin: (i) to pardon the murderer, (ii) to accept money in compensation, or (iii) to kill the murderer in the same way he killed his victim. For instance, in March 1991 in Pakistan, a person convicted of murder was executed by his victim's brother, who was permitted to use the same gun that was used by the criminal in his brother's murder. In Sudan, a Palestinian terrorist killed seven people in 1988 including a Britisher, his wife and their two children. When he was arrested, the Sudanese government asked the Britisher's parents to decide if the suspect should live or die. North Carolina law in the United States of America allows a prisoner to be hanged to invite guests to his execution. When murderer Gary Gilmore, sentenced to death in Utah (in the USA) in 1976, was granted his last request by the judge that he be executed by a firing squad, citizens actually volunteered to pull the trigger.

CAPITAL PUNISHMENT IN INDIA

In India, in 1814, there were three cases of boys of eight, nine, and eleven years who were hanged. In the Mughal period, torturous methods were used in the execution of condemned criminals. However, today there are a very few crimes for which death penalty is imposed. Four characteristics of capital punishment may be pointed out in our country: (1) Capital punishment is given only for (selected) seven crimes. (2) Hanging in the presence of public is totally abolished. (3) No painful methods are used in executing death sentence. (4) Capital punishment is awarded only by a governing authority.

The Indian Penal Code recognises capital punishment under eight sections (121, 132, 194, 302, 303, 305, 307, and 396) for different offences. Article 21 of the Indian Constitution provides that "no person shall be deprived of his life and personal liberty except according to the procedure established by law." On the basis of this article, the constitutional validity of capital punishment has been accepted by our Supreme Court on several occasions, if the procedure adopted is "just, fair, and reasonable" and is not "fanciful, oppressive, or arbitrary". There was a proposal in mid 1999 from some sources that capital punishment should be awarded to rapists. However, this view has not been accepted by many. Even the National Commission for Women in its recommendation made in April 2000 *did not* recommend capital punishment for rape. This recommendation was made on the basis of opinions expressed by social workers, victims of rape, counsellors, psychiatrists, NGOs, etc., in 16 workshops organised by State Women's Commissions in different parts of the country. Only four workshops recommended capital punishment, 10 were against it and two did not express any specific opinion.

The first successful effort for abolishing capital punishment in India was made in Travancore in 1944 but it was reintroduced in 1950. The number of persons awarded capital punishment by the courts in Travancore was 159 in 1950,168 in 1951 and 170 in 1952. In 1956, a bill was introduced in the Lok Sabha by one Agrawal for abolishing capital punishment but it was rejected by Parliament in 1961. The then Deputy Minister for Home Affairs (Mrs. Violet Alva) intervening in the debate on the resolution had said:

> A correct assessment of the situation in the country rather than sentiment should guide our approach to this question. Since the crime situation continues to be serious, the time was not ripe to do away with capital punishment, though principles underlying the demand for its abolition may be accepted (*The Hindustan Times*, September 10, 1961).

In 1963, the Law Commission was asked to look into the question of abolishing capital punishment. It gave its recommendations in November 1971 and turned down the idea of abolition. In 1980, five judges of the Supreme Court of India discussed its justification. Of these, four were in favour of retaining it, while one was in favour of abolishing it.

At present, capital punishment in India is given for seven crimes. These are: murder, dacoity coupled with murder, war against the state, false evidence which results in capital punishment to an innocent person, instigating a minor or an insane person to commit suicide, and leaking out secrets to other countries. Though capital punishment is still sanctioned in our country, yet four types of persons are exempted from it: (i) children below 15 years of age, (ii) pregnant women, (iii) mentally deranged persons, and (iv) persons above 70 years of age. There is also a provision for appealing to the President for mercy after the Supreme Court rejects appeals.

The Indian Constitution provides for altering the death sentence into life imprisonment if there was prolonged delay in the execution of death sentence. Such cases occurred in 1944 (in the case of one Piare Dusadh when he awaited the execution of death sentence for over a year), in 1974 in Andhra Pradesh (in the case of Edigo Anamma who awaited execution for two years), in 1978 in Uttar Pradesh (in the case of Bhagan Bux Singh who awaited execution for two and a half years), in 1978 in Uttar Pradesh (in the case of Sadhu Singh who awaited execution for three and a half years), in 1983 in Tamil Nadu (in the case of S.M. Fazal Ali who awaited execution for eight years) (Cf. Jaswal and Jaswal, *Social Defence*, January 1986, 30-35). However, the Supreme Court also said in one case in 1983 that in every case in which there is a long delay in execution of death sentence, the sentence need not be substituted by sentence of life imprisonment. Because of two different rulings of the Supreme Court, confusion prevailed for two years in the courts but in 1985 it was again ruled by the Supreme Court that if there was a prolonged delay of two years or more in the execution of death sentence, the accused could invoke the law (Article 21) and get the sentence substituted.

The number of persons admitted with death sentence in India was 843 (830 males and 13 females) in 1959 and 791 (785 males and 6 females) in 1960. However, the actual number of persons executed was 190 (188 males and 2 females) in 1959 and 210 (all males) in 1960. In 1982,56.4 thousand persons were arrested for 23,339 murders (*Crime in India*, 1993). Of these cases, trial was completed only in 14,000 (28%) cases, of which 6,335 (i.e., 45%) were convicted, 200 (i.e., 37%) were given death penalty but only 64 (i.e., 0.3%) were actually hanged.

In 1998, 81,093 persons were arrested (77,649 or 95.8% males and 3,444 or 4.2% females) for 38,653 murders (*ibid.*, 1998: 271). Of these, trial was completed in 63,974 cases (including pending cases), of which 20,396 were convicted and 134 were awarded capital punishment. But hardly 20 were hanged. Thus, in the last two-three decades, the number of persons actually executed has sharply come down.

Table 13.1

Capital Punishment in India in Different Years

Year	*Total Murders*	*Persons Actually Convicted*	*Persons Awarded Capital Punishment*	*Persons Actually Hanged*
1959	10,712	7,992	843	190
1960	10,910	4,992	791	210
1970	15,708	8,508	576	13
1976	16,673	13,039	312	82
1978	19,314	14,347	329	80
1982	23,339	6,335	203	64
1993	38,240	11,200	316	<50
1998	38,653	20,396	134	<50

Source: Crime in India, 1982, 1993, 1998.

A study was conducted in America in 1958 by Elma Rober on attitudes towards capital punishment. He found that 50 per cent respondents were opposed to death penalty, 42 per cent were in favour of death penalty, and 8 per cent expressed no opinion. In 1972, the Supreme Court of America declared death penalty unconstitutional but in 1976, the Supreme Court heard new arguments and ruled that death penalty was not unconstitutional *per se*. Between 1967 and 1976, there were no legal executions at all in the country. Today, only thirteen states in the United States have retained capital punishment while all others have abolished it.

Since capital punishment is usually associated with the crime of murder, the questions criminologists ask are: why do people commit murder and what type of persons actually kill? David Abrahamsen (1952: 184) is of the opinion that murder is caused by frustration which is caused by financial inadequacy, social inadequacy (long accumulated bitterness), sexual inadequacy, and intellectual inadequacy. The reasons for committing murders in India are analysed as: personal vendetta or enmity

(14.5%), property disputes (10.6%), love affairs (6.9%), dowry (2.8%), gain (4.7%), sexual causes (6.0%), communalism (31.9%) and other motives (22.6%) (1998: 122). Explaining the type of persons who kill, Barnes and Teeters (1943: 317) have classified murderers into three groups: (i) those who suffer from serious physical, mental, and cultural deficiencies that make it possible for them to contemplate murder as a more or less natural form of conduct. Their point of view is so defective, judged by socially approved standards, that the hatred against taking human life, which exists in the normal individual, is more or less absent in their case; (ii) those who are relatively normal—physically, mentally, culturally—but are subjected to difficult or inciting emotional situations which lead them to commit murder, whereas under normal circumstances, they would lead a law-abiding existence; (iii) the professional gunmen in the matter of taking life bear close resemblance in their mental habits to army personnel. Their attitude towards the taking of human life is very much like that of the soldier on the battlefield, namely, it is taken as a matter of course not involving any personal responsibility.

ARGUMENTS OF ABOLITIONISTS AND RETENTIONISTS

Although capital crimes are few as compared with the total crimes committed in our country, they arouse heated value conflicts between those who advocate death penalty as the supreme protection for society and those who see it as making the state a calculated violator of the sanctity of human life. Elmer Jhonson (1964: 257) holds that the controversy is of great significance because the ultimate question is whether or not punitive ideology will continue to characterise criminal justice system in general.

Arguments about death penalty stir emotions more than the reason. In the last 200 years, arguments have not changed much except one that society has a basic right to kill its citizens, a right given to the state by the citizens. Some Italian and French scholars in the last quarter of the eighteenth century argued that this right was part of the social contract. But scholars like Beccaria did not accept it on the basis that since man did not have the right to take his own life, he could not give that right to the state. In the twentieth century also, this argument has been totally rejected. We summarise here important arguments advanced for and against capital punishment.

Arguments of Retentionists in Favour of Capital Punishment

1. *Retribution*: The main argument is that retribution is the chief basis

for capital punishment, and murderers, traitors, and rapists deserve to die for committing terrible crimes. Only death will satisfy the public and keep it from taking the law into its own hands.

2. *Deterrence*: The threat of death penalty deters people from committing capital offences. Persons like Ranga and Billa who had killed two children in Delhi, murderer Auto Shankar who had killed seventy persons with a stone, Nagaraj who killed dozens of people in Karnataka and Andhra Pradesh, a typical psychopath Maya Dolas of Mumbai, the psychopath called the 'VIP Serial Killer' of Lucknow, the four persons in Punjab who dragged out a large number of men and women from a bus and killed them, and many such more killers deserved death penalty. It is necessary to protect society against acts of this kind, and to keep other people from committing similar crimes.
3. *Protection*: It protects society from dangerous and ravaging criminals who would otherwise prey upon people.
4. *Social solidarity*: Execution unifies society against crime. It also avoids private vengeance.
5. *Cost*: Capital punishment is less expensive than keeping a man in prison for life.

Arguments of Abolitionists Against Capital Punishment

1. The retributive philosophy of eye for eye and tooth for tooth cannot be accepted in civilised and advanced society of today. No wonder, the number of capital crimes is being reduced and the methods of execution are becoming more painless. The approach to offenders is more humanitarian than punitive.

2. The argument of deterring people by setting an example through fear of capital punishment is also not based on any hard evidence. Three methods may be used for determining the deterrent value of death penalty: One, by comparing the homicide rates in countries which have abolished death penalty with the countries which retain it; two, by comparing homicide rates in the countries which have abolished death penalty before and after the abolition; and three, by comparing homicide rates in a country/state before abolition, during the abolition period, and again after the reintroduction of death penalty (as in Travancore State in India or in Italy which abolished capital punishment in 1890, reintroduced it in 1930 and again abolished it in 1947). We do find differences in homicide rates. For example, in the United States, homicide

rate in the states which have abolished capital punishment is 30 to 50 per cent higher than those states which continue to have capital punishment (Sutherland, 1965: 292). In Travancore, the number of murders reduced during the abolition period (between 1944 and 1950) but increased after its reintroduction from 159 in 1950 to 170 in 1952. Italy also showed the same pattern between 1930 and 1947. Norway and Sweden which have abolished death penalty have homicide rates about one-half as high as England which had retained it till 1969. In Australia, the homicide rate was slightly higher after abolition than before abolition. The difference in the rate of homicides is due to things other than death penalty. The composition of the population and the general culture of the country is much more important than the presence or absence of death penalty in determining homicide rates. All this data do not justify an absolute conclusion regarding the value of death penalty as a deterrent. It is true that human behaviour is influenced through fear but it is not always true that all individuals think of death penalty before committing murder. In India, it is estimated that three-fourths of murders are emotional and only one-fourth are premeditated. Selling (1932: 12) has stated: "Death penalty can never be made deterrent. Its very life seems to depend on its rarity and therefore on its ineffectiveness as a deterrent."

John Lawrence writes in his book, *A History of Capital Punishment*: "Executions in the times when they were universally public were occasions for rioting, revelry and ribaldry (using indecent language) and seldom was the demeanor of the crowd decorous in the face of death. and seldom too did a public execution act as a deterrent."

Further challenging the view whether capital punishment really has deterrent value, references are made to people's reactions to persons being executed in some countries. In Saudi Arabia, even today huge crowds gather at public beheading. In Afghanistan also, thousands of people are encouraged to witness executions. In America, there is a scramble among media persons to witness executions. In April 1990, when Robert Harris, the prisoner who got reprieve three days before his execution in California, the press people, for whom sixteen spectators' seats were reserved out of a total of forty-two seats, were reported to be very disappointed. Balconies overlooking the prison were rented to reporters. One resident even asked for 250 dollars for the use of his lawns by television crews. A woman sold space in her front window for 400 dollars (*The Hindustan Times*, August 5, 1994). Do such instances indicate that people do not want capital punishment or that people really abhor it?

3. The object of protecting society from dangerous offenders can be

achieved by long imprisonment and also by improving conditions in prisons. Besides, it is now scientifically established that crime is not the result of personality deficiencies but is caused by unfavourable environment and interaction of many factors.

4. The argument that capital punishment unifies society against crime is not supported by evidence. Offenders today are not executed in the presence of the public and no efforts are made to give publicity to executions. Besides, social relationships have become impersonal today and people pay little attention to the punishment of offenders. At most, the victims remain interested in compensation for the loss suffered by them.

5. Savings to be achieved by awarding death penalty to murderers instead of putting them in jail for life are paltry indeed. If we take the case of our country, assuming that we hang 100 persons a year, and also assuming that we spend Rs. 500 per month at present (in 1996) on each prisoner and that a murderer will live in prison for 14 years, we save hardly 84 lakh rupees a year. This is surely not a significant amount. More importantly is it logical and sane to link economy with hanging human beings? Is it proper and civilised to argue that since it would be cheaper to kill mentally and physically ill persons than to treat them, we should hang all such persons. Besides, the introduction of wage system in prisons will make it possible for prisoners to earn money and support their families. Some of the open jails in India permit prisoners to live with their families in prison, take loans from banks and establish themselves in business.

6. Owing to defects in the judicial system, sometimes innocent persons are given death penalty for crimes which they did not commit and the truth comes to be revealed after the persons are hanged. Who will compensate the families of such persons? A learned judge has observed: "Our 'beyond-a-reasonable doubt' burden of proof in criminal cases is intended to protect the innocent, but we know, it is not foolproof. Various studies have shown that people whose innocence is later convincingly established are convicted and sentenced to death." Some criminals whose death penalty was converted into life imprisonment later blossomed into eminent writers, botanists, wrestlers, etc. In some cases, thus, replacing capital punishment by incarceration can prove to be beneficial.

7. Capital punishment lessens people's respect for human life. Law is expected to present the finest model of justice and reason to people but if laws spill human blood, then these very laws alter the idea of justice and

injustice in the hearts of citizens. Capital punishment causes anger and revenge among the citizens. Brutal public executions have demoralising effects on people.

8. Capital punishment has a negative effect on the system of criminal justice. On the one hand, judges take a lot of time in deciding cases which deserve capital punishment, and, on the other hand, the convicted offenders go in appeal to the higher courts, and finally to the highest court to avoid the imposition of death penalty. The possibility of death penalty also sensationalises the entire trial and sentencing process. Many judges are not able to decide the vague distinction between first and second degree murder. If capital punishment is abolished, the system of criminal justice is likely to improve.

Another consequence of the existence of capital punishment is 'panic' legislation to include spectacular crimes not already covered by capital punishment in the existing list of capital crimes. For example, in India, at the time when terrorists tried to damage railway lines for causing derailment of trains, and, thus, create panic in the public mind, the government seriously thought of providing death penalty for this offence. Similar public and official reaction arose with regard to kidnapping for political reasons, rape, and forcing a woman to commit *sati*. Public emotionalism reaches such high level that rational debate on the issue becomes difficult. Enacting legislation and prescribing capital punishment for 'fatal' offences needs to be considered coolly and carefully.

In our opinion, the most important argument in favour of the abolition of capital punishment is the admission of the fact that human judgement is fallible. No system can ever be devised, given the limitations of human condition/existence, that would be infallible. Infallibility is not a human trait---it is divine. Let not human beings abrogate to themselves the powers that are rightfully not theirs. Let us render to Caesar things that are Caesar's, and, to god, things that are His.

It may be relevant here to recall the viewpoints of some judges and other eminent persons. Justice Krishna Iyer, former judge of the Supreme Court, is of the opinion that capital punishment must be abolished because it is a crime against criminals. He has said: "The flag of human justice should be hung half-mast everyday a human being is hanged." Justice Anand, former judge of the Supreme Court, has said: "Capital punishment is a legal injustice because justice is imparted on the basis of considerations other than moral or ethical." He thinks, murder is the result of sick mind of a criminal. If a criminal, not in his senses, commits a crime, he is mad, but if a judge who is in his senses, awards death penalty to a criminal, he is more mad. Justice P. Bhagwati, former Chief Justice of the Supreme Court, is of the opinion that capital punishment must be abolished because it gives arbitrary discretionary powers to the courts.

Mahatma Gandhi, the spiritual leader of India, was of the opinion (*Harijan*, March 19,1937): "I do regard death sentence as contrary to *Ahimsa*. Only HE takes life who gives it. All punishment is repugnant to *Ahimsa*. Under a state governed according to the principles of *Ahimsa*, therefore, a murderer would be sent to the penitentiary and there given the chance of reforming himself. All crime is a disease and should be treated as such." Beccaria has maintained: "The state has no right to put an individual to death because the life of an individual was not surrendered to it as part of consideration for the control."

On the other hand, Justice Luthra justifies capital punishment. Justice A.P. Sen also says that capital punishment must be retained. When a person kills an innocent person in a pre-planned and cold-blooded manner, he has no right to live. The United Nations Organisation in its Declaration of Human Rights on 10 December, 1948, declared: "Everyone has a right to life, liberty and security." On 16 December, 1966, it adopted civil and political rights resolution and maintained that all persons who are given capital punishment must be given the right of pardon and sentence commutation.

Professor Gillin (1958) has said: "There seems very little reason why the state should keep the murderers alive in the face of the social resentment which their deed excites. No matter how well they work or how well they behave themselves in prison, they can never repay society for the damages they cause, not only to the family of the victim but to the humanitarian sentiments which lie at the basis of our society." Clarence Darrow is of the opinion: "God gave life and only God should take it away." Prof. Hentig has said: "I see in capital punishment a means of punishment whose advantages can be obtained by other means and whose disadvantages can be prevented in no other way than by abolishing it. It is socially insufficient means of punishment to which must be added the possibility of a judicial error which we cannot exclude."

It may, thus, be concluded that opinion on capital punishment is divided. There are people who want to retain it for serious crimes, to be awarded in exceptional cases. On the contrary there are people who want it to be abolished altogether. Legislative bodies and the courts talk of its need in the legal framework while liberal-minded people who talk of humanitarianism in punishment want to do away with it in the broader social context.

References

Caldwell, Robert, G., *Criminology*, Chapter 19, pp. 408-18, Ronald Press Company, New York, 1956.

Johnson, Elmer., H., *Crime, Correction and Society* (4th edn.), Chapter 12, The Dorsey Press, Illinois, 1978.

Social Defence, National Institute of Social Defence, New Delhi, January 1986.

Sutherland, E.H. and Cressay, D.R., *Principles of Criminology* (6th edn.), Chapter 14, p. 262, The Times of India Press, Bombay, 1965.

Chapter 14

Prisons

Changes in a society demand changes in the way of maintaining social order. The techniques of social control are also adjusted to changed situations, as no system of social control works perfectly. People often deviate from social and legal norms, although non-conformity varies greatly in form and frequency. Though deviation is perceived as a threat to social stability yet attitude towards deviants keeps on changing with change in beliefs in the causes of deviant behaviour in general and crime in particular. There was a time when crime was attributed to the possession of an individual by evil spirits. Then, it came to be believed that crime was the result of biological defect, mental illness, defective social environment, or of conflicting sets of norms and values, and so forth. With such changes in attitude towards crime, general attitude towards criminals and particularly with regard to punishing criminals, has also kept on changing.

With this change over time, the functions of prisons have also changed from custodial, to coercive, to corrective. In early India, jails functioned on the principle of custodial care. With the assertion that a jail is for confinement and not for punishment, prisons were concerned simply with holding prisoners while they waited for trial. During the medieval and early British periods, emphasis came to be laid on retributive and deterrent aspects of punishment. Physical torture, social degradation and restrictions on freedom were among the programmes used for inflicting pain on criminals. Prisons were primarily used as penal institutions. No attention was paid to differences in age, sex, nature of crime, criminal background or mental status of the offenders. It was only after the recommendations of the Jail Reforms Committee of 1919 were accepted that conditions in prisons gradually improved and prisons came to be used for corrective purposes, i.e., for bringing offenders round to becoming good citizens through discipline of work, education, and moral instructions.

The basic functions of prisons today are as follows:

- *Social isolation and confinement*, i.e., to isolate an offender from society because he has proved to be a threat to its organisation, stability, and cohesion, and to keep him out of circulation and so securely confined that his deviation from law does not disturb the peace of mind of the man in the street.
- *Repentance*, i.e., to keep an offender in an isolated place where he could ponder over the consequences of his wrong deeds.
- *Punishment and deterrence*, i.e., to inflict some pain and suffering, on an offender (i.e., some punishment) for violating legal norms, so that criminals should be worse off than the poorest of honest citizens; law-abiding individuals must be satisfied that law-breakers are penalised and they are being protected against the threat of recidivism; and members of society may be deterred from committing crimes.
- *Protection*, i.e., protecting community from criminals by marking out persons who violate laws and stigmatising them so that others are warned against them.

  Criminal = Deviance + Prosecution + Stigma
- *Reformation*, i.e., to change offender's values, motivations, attitudes and perceptions and to resocialise him and restore him to community.

But are these functions shared by the prison personnel with the law-framers? If yes, what means do they adopt to accomplish these purposes? Why is there split between the managing and the managed groups, i.e., between the inmates and the prison staff? It is because of the stereotyped hostile and antagonistic attitude towards each other, or because of the inefficiency and incompetence of the staff, or because the staff has to function within a structure of limited freedom and formally prescribed framework of social distance which restricts their initiative for new programmes of reformation?

PRISON STRUCTURE AND PRISON MANAGEMENT

There were three types of prisons in India till two decades ago: maximum security prisons, medium security prisons, and minimum security prisons. The *medium security prisons* were called *Model Jails*. Of two such prisons in India, one was located at Lucknow and the other at Ajmer. But both have now been converted in central jails. The three important characteristics of model jails which distinguished them from the maximum security prisons were: *panchayati-raj* system (in which the management of the jails is vested in the inmates), the wage system (in which the inmates were paid wages for the work assigned to them) and the canteen system (in which the jail canteen---run by the inmates on no profit no loss basis---provided essential things of daily use, like tea, oil, soap, bidis, etc. to the inmates within the jail itself). These jails had introduced some new training programmes also for the inmates. The jails were supposed to function as models for central jails in the states. However, the panchayat system created many administrative problems in these jails and the canteens also incurred losses. This forced the authorities to convert the model jails in central jails.

The *minimum security jails* are called *open jails* or wall-less prisons. They still function in many states. The detailed description of these jails is given elsewhere in this chapter.

The *maximum security jails* in India are of four types: central jails, district jails, subjails, and special jails. The central jails are meant for the offenders imprisoned for more than one year, district jails for offenders imprisoned for three to six months and subjails for offenders sentenced to less than three months' imprisonment. Special jails are meant for juveniles, females and political prisoners. Central jails function as correctional institutions while the district and the subjails function as punitive institutions. The number of central jails in every state in India varies from one to six. The district jails are located at the headquarters of districts or subdivisions, and are classified as 'A' category, 'B' category, and 'C' category district jails.

Inspector General or Director General of Prisons (IGP or DGP) is the overall incharge of all jails in a state. He is assisted by Deputy Inspector General of Prisons (DIGP). A central jail is in the charge of an officer of superintendent rank and a district jail of deputy superintendent rank. Each jail has jailors and wardens. In central jails, some inmates are promoted as convict officers (COs). The minimum conditions for appointing a CO are more than one year's imprisonment and completion of at least one-fourth of the total term of sentence. Such prisoners who are convicted of excise offence, poisoning, forgery, vagrancy, unnatural offence, and counterfeiting of currency notes are not eligible for the post of a CO. The COs are further categorised as convict watchmen (CW), convict overseers (CO), and convict wardens (CW). A convict watchman is promoted as convict overseer if he has served as watchman for at least three months and has completed one-third of the total imprisonment. The convict overseer is promoted as convict warden if he has served as convict overseer at least for four months. The COs are assigned supervisory work in jail. They also get special remission (5 days per month as CW, 6 days per month as CO, and 7 days per month as CW). Since most of the corruption in jails is attributed to COs, some jail reforms committees have recommended abolition of these posts. However, in practice, these COs continue to operate in jails. A central jail is divided in wards and a ward into barracks. The number of wards in each prison varies from 8 to 15 and the number of barracks in each ward varies from 3 to 4. Each barrack accommodates 30 to 50 prisoners. In an emergency, this number increases to even a hundred. There are cells (*kothris*) for the condemned offenders.

The total number of jails in India in 1986 was about 1,100 while at present (in 2000), it could be between 1,200 and 1,400 (*see*, Report of National Expert Committee on Women Prisoners, 1986: 135-36). Of these, about 98 pre cent are maximum security jails and 2 per cent (1.6% exactly) are minimum security jails. Of the total maximum security jails in the country, about 7 per cent are central jails, 20 per cent district jails, 53 per cent subjails, 1 per cent (0.6%) women jails, 1 per cent (0.7%) juvenile jails, and 18 per cent other jails. The total number of offenders admitted to prisons every year is about 4 lakh, but excluding those who are released every year, the total annual prison population remains at about 2.3 lakh. Of these, 30 per cent are convicts and 70 per cent are undertrials. In Uttar Pradesh, for example, the ratio of convicts vis-a-vis under trials which was 1:2 in 1947 became 1:5 in 1991 and 1:7 in 1997 (*The Hindustan Times*, April 25, 1998). According to a survey conducted in the second half of the 1990s by 'Worldwatch' organisation, the highest number of prisoners in the world is found in America, followed by China, Russia and India. The number of prisoners in jails in 1998 in America was described as 17 lakhs, in China: 14.10 lakh and in India 2,31,325. The number of prisoners per one lakh population was 687 in Russia, 645 in USA, 39 in Japan, 37 in Bangladesh, 29 in Nepal, 24 in India and 20 in Indonesia. (*Rajasthan Patrika*, May 28, 2000). Of the convicted offenders in India, 80 per cent get less than six months' imprisonment, 13 per cent six months to two years, and 7 per cent more than two years. In other words, more than 90 per cent are short-termers, and less than 10 per cent long-termers.

Of the total prisoners (including undertrials), about 1 per cent are below 16 years of age, 12 per cent are between 16 and 21 years age, and 87 per cent are above 21 years of age (*see*, National Expert Committee Report on Women Prisoners, 1986: 141-43). The break-up of those above 21 years (i.e., 87%) is found to be as follows: 42 per cent are between 21 and 30 years of age, 30 per cent are between 30 and 40 years, 13 per cent between 40 and 60 years, and 2 per cent above 60 years. Thus, about two-thirds prisoners (72%) belong to 2140 years age group, or are young offenders. About 45 per cent have agricultural background and about 33 per cent are literate.

Of the undertrials in jails, about 75 per cent remain under trial for less than six months, about 15 per cent for 6-12 months, about 7 per cent for 1-2 years, about 2 per cent for 2-3 years, and about 1 per cent for more than three years (*ibid.*: 144-45).

PRISON REFORMS

The first committee on prisons, called the Indian Jails Committee, was appointed in 1836. It gave its report in 1838. It drew attention to the existing horrible conditions and corruption prevalent in the lower staff, but, it did not give any suggestions for the improvement of conditions. It rejected education, moral lectures, and rewards to inmates and laid stress on hard and monotonous life in jail, i.e., on retributive punishment. The first central jail was established at Agra in 1846, while the first superintendent, jails was appointed in 1850. On the recommendations of the 1864 Committee, two significant changes were made: one, Jail Manual was framed in 1870, and two, segregation system was introduced in prisons, segregating males from females, adults from children, and 'civil' offenders from 'criminal' offenders. On the recommendations of the 1889 Committee, the under-trials were segregated from the convicted criminals and the habitual offenders from the casual offenders. The 1892 Committee recommended nine hours work in jail. But, the most significant recommendations were given by the 1919 Jails Committee and their implementation in 1920 completely overhauled the prison system in India. The important recommendations implemented were: segregating offenders on the basis of sex, age, conviction, and type of offender; introducing classification system for residence and work-assignment purposes, giving training to inmates in various crafts, giving education to offenders below 25 years of age, adopting recreation measures like indoor games, music competitions, etc., permitting offenders to maintain social contacts with the outside world by writing and receiving letters and meeting relatives and friends in jails on prior appointment basis, arranging moral and religious lectures, introducing remission system, and giving economic aid to offenders on their release from prison. The two important recommendations made by the 1919 committee which could not be accepted by the government immediately but which were implemented after a few years were: introducing the probation system (i.e., suspending sentence and releasing offenders by courts on certain conditions without sending them to jails) and establishing Borstal Schools for the adolescent offenders. The last committee—called Mulla Committee or All India Jail Reform Committee—was appointed by the Government of India in 1980 which submitted its report in 1983. The recommendations of this committee were not considered by the government to be revolutionary in any way.

Some provincial (state) governments had also appointed committees for introducing reforms in prisons in their states: Punjab appointed such a committee in 1925, Uttar Pradesh in 1946, Rajasthan in 1962, Bihar in 1972, Tamil Nadu in 1978, and Kerala in 1991. The Central Government appointed one UNO Expert (Walter Reckless) in 1951 for studying conditions in Indian jails and for suggesting reforms. Reckless's main suggestion was to make changes in the old jail manual.

ADJUSTMENT OF INMATES IN PRISONS

When an offender enters prison, he leaves behind one world and enters a new one where he is not only stripped of the social status he enjoyed in the community but is also deprived of many rights and privileges.

Deprivations

According to Sykes (1958), on being imprisoned, a criminal faces the problem of: (a) deprivation of liberty, (b) deprivation of privileges, (c) deprivation of emotional security, and (d) deprivation of heterosexual relations. Donald Clemmer (1940) has described prison as a community of persons of one sex, a community where all persons have been stigmatised for violation of law by the broad society. The people here have no privacy and no consensus for common goal. It is a world of individuals whose daily relationships are impersonalised and who hold attitudes which are predatory or assaultive or sexually unconventional in nature. It is a world of 'I', 'me', and 'mine', rather than 'ours', 'theirs', and 'his'. Its people are bitter, revengeful and socially illiterate. There is monotony and dis-interest in work. There is desire for love and hunger for sex. On the one hand, the inmates have to operate in accordance with a fixed autocratic routine, and on the other hand, they are expected to develop individual initiative. While they are refused voice in self-administration, they are expected to become thinking individuals in a democratic society.

The main features that distinguish prison life from home life are: (i) in prison, various activities of life (like working, eating, sleeping and playing) are conducted in the same place and under the same single authority; (ii) each activity is carried on in the immediate company of 'strangers', all of whom are required to do the same thing together; (iii) all activities are tightly scheduled; and (iv) all activities are imposed from above through a system of explicit formal rules.

Do these features of prison life help prisoners to become 'reformed persons' when they return to community? One view is that the organisation of prisons is so defective that instead of being *decriminalised*, the inmates become prisonised. The other view (of inmates who reject prison values and inculcate anti-prison values) is that prison life has no discernible effect on subsequent criminality and non-criminality of prison inmates.

The problem of adjustment of inmates in prisons has been studied by scholars from two viewpoints: psychological and sociological. From the psychological viewpoint, adjustment has been studied—by Barbash (1950), Lebo (1955), etc.—in terms of change in personality traits like being aggressive, emotional, impatient, intolerant, introvert, suspicious, and so forth. From the sociological angle, adjustment has been studied—by Clemmer, Wolfgang, Sykes, Caldwell, McCorkle, Ahuja, etc.—in terms of social relationships within and outside the jail.

How does social system in a prison function? The inmates compete and cooperate with each other, love and hate each other, and vie with each other for privileges, power and prestige. In this way, a prison is a microcosm of society at large. When an offender stays for long in a jail, a process—what is termed by Robert Sommer as *disculturation* or what is called by some others as *desocialisation*—occurs. This is the process of 'unlearning' which renders a prisoner temporarily incapable of managing certain features of daily life in the outside world, if and when he gets back to it.

Inmate System

Inmates in jails use certain processes of mortification to preserve their civilian selves because of various barriers placed by the jail establishment. Prisoners develop a set of norms and procedures for controlling conduct within their organisation. Their directives make up *prisoners' code*, or *inmate code*, or *inmate system*. Some examples of the inmate code are: always cooperate with other inmates, don't criticise or argue or quarrel with other inmates, don't interfere with the interests of other inmates, don't exploit other inmates, always share eatables with other inmates, don't have any confidence in officials, don't reveal secrets to officials, do least work, always express dissatisfaction with the food, clothes, etc. given in prison, and so forth.

The inmate code serves four main functions: (i) it maintains cohesion among inmates; (ii) it creates self-confidence in inmates; (iii) it enables inmates to face jail officials; and (iv) it lessens the problems of imprisonment. The process of internalising the inmate code has been termed as the process of deculturation or the process of *fraternalisation*. This is the process through which socially distant persons find themselves developing mutual support and common counter-moves in opposition to a system that has forced them into a single and equalitarian community.

The process of socialisation in correctional institutions has been studied by several western scholars like Donald Clemmer (1940), Gresham Sykes (1958), Peter Garabedian (1963), Wellord (1967), and Stanton Wheeler (1969), etc.

Donald Clemmer has studied causes of inmate system in prison, nature of adjustment in prison community, and corrupting effects of a penal institution. Gresham Sykes has discussed major deprivations experienced by prisoners and cause of social code of inmates. He has claimed that inmates develop their own social code in direct response to these deprivations, i.e., to reassert their autonomy, to control their reactions against opposition to the staff and the values upheld by the institution, and to develop loyalty to each other. Stanton Wheeler has studied socialisation in correctional institutions, prison culture, and role conflict in correctional communities. He has concluded that the nature of prison culture varies from prison to prison; that prisons are dominated by criminal elements among prisoners; prison culture cannot be explained simply in terms of response to deprivations that imprisonment brings; structure of society from which prisoners come also affects the cohesion and values of inmate society; and some prisoners adopt themselves superficially and temporarily to the standards of the prison subculture while others absorb prison subculture permanently. Peter Garabedian has studied social roles and processes of socialisation in the prison community. He has analysed the patterns of individual involvement during sentence with the values of prison staff on the one hand and of the prison subculture on the other. Wellord has studied the normative socialisation of inmates in prison, i.e., factors associated with adoption of the inmate code.

Prisonisation

This is a concept developed by Donald Clemmer in 1940. According to Clemmer, prisonisation is a process of assimilating prison culture or a process of taking on in a greater or a lesser degree the folkways, mores, customs and general culture of a prison in integrative steps. The main elements of prisonisation are:

- Every prisoner is prisonised.
- Prisonisation takes place in stages.
- Degree of prisonisation may be low, medium or high.
- Prisonisation depends upon several factors like age, cell-inmates, nature of crime, term of imprisonment, type of relationships before imprisonment, and relations with the outside world.
- There could be deprisonisation and reprisonisation also.

The integrative steps in prisonisation are:

- Acceptance of an inferior role by wearing jail clothes and becoming an anonymous figure.
- Accumulation of facts concerning the structure, organisation and the norms of prison, i.e., learning about ranks, titles and authority of various officials.
- Development of somewhat new habits of eating, dressing, working and sleeping.
- Learning and adopting local language and nicknames, i.e., jail argot.
- Recognition that he is not obliged to anybody for the food, clothes, etc. he gets in jail.
- Demands more facilities and desires a good job.

Wheeler (1961), Wolfgang (1961), Caldwell (1956), Sykes and Howard Jones (1977) empirically verified Donald Clemmer's concept of prisonisation and adjustment of prisoners in prison culture. Wheeler studied 237 prisoners in a close-custody prison in the United States and found that the degree of prisonisation varies with the length of time served. Wolfgang found that: (a) young prisoners (below 35 years) adjust less than the middle-aged prisoners; (b) felons adjust less than misdemeanours; (c) short-termers (imprisoned for less than six months and between six months and two years) indicate high conformity to jail norms than long-termers (imprisoned for more than two years), and (d) marital status has no effect on prisonisation.

Evaluation of Clemmer's Prisonisation Process

I conducted one study about fifteen years ago (between 1977 and 1980) with the main objective of examining the effectiveness and the effects of imprisonment (Ahuja, *The Prison System*, 1981) and also to test Donald Clemmer's theory of prisonisation, studying different temporal aspects of prison culture and evaluating decriminalisation process in a prison. In this study, 252 prisoners were interviewed in three Central Jails in Rajasthan. These prisons receive prisoners of 16+ years of age and at the time of my study had the capacity of accommodating up to 800 inmates (it has now been increased to 1,600 inmates).

The prisoners in each prison were grouped into six categories on the basis of the term of imprisonment: prisoners with less than 6 months imprisonment, 6 to 12 months imprisonment, 1 to 2 years imprisonment, 2 to 5 years imprisonment, 5 to 10 years imprisonment, and more than 10 years imprisonment. On the stratified random sample basis,15 per cent of the total convicted inmates from each category in prison 'A', 20 per cent from each category in prison 'B', and 10 per cent from each category in prison 'C' were selected for the interview. The prisoners were further classified on the basis of crime characteristics and personal characteristics. On the former basis, they were classified according to the type of offence, term of total sentence, term served in jail, term yet to be spent in jail, and earlier conviction. On the latter basis, they were classified according to age, education, marital status, occupation, monthly income, and rural-urban background. The sample was so chosen that it represented all categories of inmates with respect to the above characteristics. In addition to prisoners, two categories of prison staff—custodial officers and treatment/training officers—were also interviewed.

The acceptance and/or rejection of prison and/or inmate norms by the inmates in our study was analysed by classifying inmates into four groups on the basis of attachment to prison norms and inmate norms. On this basis, the following four types of inmates were identified: (i) *conformists*, who identified only with conventional prison norms and rejected outright inmate norms; were bound by loyalty to staff; and had great contacts with those inmates who rejected inmate norms. (ii) *Partial Conformists*, who partially accepted prison norms and partially inmate norms; were bound by loyalty sometimes to inmates and sometimes to staff according to promptings of their own advantage; and had a wide range of contacts with both prison officials and inmates. (iii) *Non-conformists*, who identified with inmate norms; were bound by loyalty to inmates; and had great contacts with inmates who rejected prison norms and were relatively isolated from staff contacts. (iv) *Isolationists*, who rejected both prison and inmate norms; were bound by no loyalty either to staff or to inmates; and avoided contacts with both prison officials and inmates.

This typology was considered significant because it explained not only the personal orientation of the inmates but also their attitudes towards self and others. The four types of inmates were identified in our study on the basis of their responses to eight questions included in the questionnaire, of which three reflected inmates' loyalty to staff or inmates, three reflected inmates' identification with prison or inmate norms, and two reflected inmates' contacts with officials or inmates.

These questions were: Would you accept punishment for any inmate if the need arises? What would you do if you were to choose between siding with inmates and the prison officials? What is the necessity of inmate solidarity in jail? Do you subscribe to the idea of self-sacrifice for maintaining inmate solidarity? How do you spend most of your spare time? Do you talk to all or only to selected inmates? Do you subscribe to values always/or sometimes/ or never acceptable to administration? Do you consider yourself bound by loyalty to inmates or to prison officials or sometimes to inmates and sometimes to officials?

The responses revealed that about one-third respondents (36.8%) identified with prison norms, about one-third (30.7%) with inmatenorms, and about one-third (32.5%) with both prison and inmate norms. One-fifth respondents (19.6%) were loyal to staff, a little less than half (46.3%) to inmates and about one-third (34.1%) to both staff and inmates. One-fifth respondents (18.3%) had contacts with only officials, a little less than half (45.2%) only with inmates, and about one-third (36.5%) with both officials and inmates. Taking the three types of responses together, one-fourth inmates (24.1%) can be categorised as *conformists*, two-fifths (41.8%) as *non-conformists*, one-fourth (27.3%) as *partial conformists*, and one-fifteenth (6.8%) as *isolationists*. It may be inferred from this that *prisons decriminalise only about one-fourth of the prisoners, or that prisons do not function as correctional institutions for more than half of the inmates.*

For studying the nature and extent of absorption or rejection of prison or inmate code, or for studying conformity to staff role expectations, the respondents were asked to evaluate a series of fifteen questions in two different hypothetical situations. Five questions referred to one situation of life *outside* prison while ten questions were related to another situation or behaviour in prison. Two different types of situations were taken to compare the inmates' support for law-abiding values in prison with their values in civilian roles outside prison. This was based on the assumption that those who supported law-abiding values before imprisonment must support prison values after the imprisonment too. If there is a difference between the two types of values, it is because of the impact of the inmate system and the internalisation of the inmate values, or it is the result of the phenomenon referred to as 'prisonisation' by Clemmer.

The inmates were asked to indicate their reactions for each situation by tick-marking the appropriate number on a five-category justified-unjustified continuum. A five-point scale was used and weights of +2, +1, 0, -1, and -2 were assigned to the strongly justified, justified, neutral, unjustified, and strongly unjustified categories respectively. The scores were summed over the total items (pertaining to behaviour inside and outside jail) with possible scores ranging from positive to negative. The positive scores indicated adjustment by conformity to the inmate norms while negative scores indicated adjustment by conformity to staff role expectations.

Forty-eight per cent respondents obtained positive scores (i.e., conformed to inmate norms), 45 per cent secured negative scores (i.e., conformed to staff role expectations), and 7 per cent got zero score (i.e., remained neutral) in the ten statements pertaining to behaviour in jail; while 40.5 per cent secured positive scores, 57.5 per cent negative scores, and 2 per cent zero score in the five statements pertaining to values related to civilian roles before coming to jail. *The above results do not strongly support Donald Clemmer's proposition that every man who enters the penitentiary undergoes prisonisation to some extent.* Only about half of the inmates adjust themselves in a prison by adopting the inmate culture. This, however, does not mean that the inmates who do not adopt the norms and codes of the inmate world do not remain criminalistic. Such inmates may continue to be much more criminalistic than the inmates who become socialised to inmate culture.

Taking only ten statements pertaining to the behaviour of the respondents in prison and assigning scores to their responses, our study showed that amongst 121 inmates who secured 'plus' scores (i.e., who conformed to inmate norms), the degree of conformity to inmate norms was low in 52 per cent cases, medium in 44.6 per cent cases and high in 3.4 per cent cases. On the negative side, amongst the 131 inmates who secured 'minus' scores (i.e., who conformed to official norms), the degree of conformity to prison norms was low in 44.2 per cent cases, medium in 40.8 per cent cases, and high in 15 per cent cases.

Several observations can be made on the basis of this data: *First*, the rate of absorption of inmate norms (48%) appeared to be about the same as that of absorption of the prison norms (45%). *Secondly*, almost all those inmates who accepted law-abiding values pertaining to behaviour in civilian roles before coming to prison also accepted prison norms after coming to prison. *Thirdly*, since the degree of conformity to inmate norms was low in 52 per cent cases and high in only 3.4 per cent cases, and similarly since the degree of conformity to prison norms was low in 44.2 per cent cases and high in only 15 per cent cases, *it could be inferred that in reality, most of the inmates remain in an ambiguous position insofar as accepting or rejecting prison and/or inmate norms* is concerned. *Finally*, the processes operating within a prison produced a pattern of adjustment that did not appear to be much consistent with Clemmer's observations on inmate socialisation: (that) when new entrants in prison mix with the old inmates, slowly and gradually they come to share their folkways, mores, dogmas, sentiments, and traditions more or less unconsciously, ultimately leading to their integration into the inmate scheme of life. But this also does not mean that the culture and social organisation of prisons is necessarily conducive to the process of resocialisation of prisoners.

We also analysed the absorption of inmate/prison code or the internalisation of prison culture in terms of certain selected factors to test the validity of Clemmer's and Wheeler's hypotheses. We concentrated on five factors, namely, length of time served, phase of prison career, age, nature of crime, and involvement in informal group life. Conclusions pertaining to all these aspects of adaptive pattern were as follows:

- Conformity to inmate code and to prison norms in the first five years of prison life was about the same. However, after spending five years in prison, conformity to inmate code decreased. Thus, Clemmer's hypothesis that longer the duration of stay of a prisoner in a prison, higher the degree of his prisonisation (*see*, Johnson, *op. cit.*, 1962: 113) was not supported.
- The percentage of inmates who conformed to the inmate norms in the last phase of six months, when they were about to be released, was very low (6.4%) showing thereby that inmates appeared to shed prison culture before they left prison.

- Wheeler's finding (*see*, Johnson, *op. cit.*, 1962: 159) that a large percentage of inmates is strongly opposed to staff norms during the last stage of their confinement than during the first stage was not supported (8.2% in late phase against 21.8% in early phase). When conformity to prison norms in the three phases (early, middle, and late) was represented graphically, we got "inverted V-shaped" trend. This did not support Wheeler's finding (*ibid.*: 159) that a "U-shaped" distribution of high conformity responses exists over the three time periods.
- The number of middle-aged persons accepting inmate norms (58.1%) was about the same as that of young persons (59.1%). It, therefore, cannot be hypothesised that the young are more maladjusted than the middle-aged. This rejects Wolfgang's hypothesis that a significantly higher proportion of adjusted prisoners is found in the group of young prisoners (17-35 years) than in the middle-aged group (35-60 years).
- Persons committing felonies do not necessarily internalise more fully a value system built upon the rejection of prison norms.
- The higher the informal involvement with the inmates rejecting prison norms, the higher will be the internalisation of inmate values and vice versa. This supports Clemmer's proposition (1940: 302) that higher degree of prisonisation is related to higher degree of involvement in the informal life of the inmate community. It also supports Wheeler's hypothesis that both the speed and degree of prisonisation are a function of informal inmate involvement.

Taking together the above-mentioned five temporal aspects of adjustment of inmates to prison subculture, it could be concluded that all hypotheses of Clemmer and Wheeler pertaining to determinants of prisonisation are not fully correct, though Clemmer's prisonisation theory stands supported. For example, age and serious nature of crime do not appear to have significant relationship with prisonisation; length of time served has partial relationship; while prison-career phase and informal group life do affect acceptance and/or rejection of inmate norms.

Self-Image Model of Socialisation within Prison Walls

Through prisonisation model, we are not in a position to answer important questions like: what types of inmates follow the pattern of prisonisation, or what type of inmates attach themselves more to prison norms, or what conditions lead to one process rather than to the other, or can prison authorities exert control over the processes by policy decisions? Thus, since prisonisation model is inadequate in explaining adjustment and reformation pattern in prison, we have to search for some new model which may adequately explain socialisation within prison-walls. We present a new 'self-image model' in this context.

Borrowing from Talcott Parsons' view, we hold that reformation has to be understood in terms of prisoners' personality system, social structure of prisons, and the normative system of inmates. The self-image model not only leans heavily on these three subsystems but it also takes into consideration the recent dominant theory of deviant behaviour, namely, Naturalistic Theory of Deviance which views deviant acts as 'interactional productions'.

The self-image model is based on the assumption that reformation in prisons can be studied by analysing and assessing: (i) social structure of prison, (ii) inmates' personalities, (iii) inmates' normative system. This model has four elements: (a) self-image of a prisoner, (b) value conformity which deals with a prisoner's detachment from inmate value system and attachment to prison value system and which doesn't have any overt manifestations, (c) actual conformity to norms, and (d) prisoner's social prestige among other inmates, jail officials and in the outside community. With these four elements, the model could be described as:

Reformation = Self-image + value for conformity to norms + actual conformity to norms + social prestige.

In this model, self-image, value conformity, actual conformity and social prestige are interrelated to one another and are linked to reformation in a descending order of significance. We may briefly try to understand each of these four components of the model separately.

(i) *Self-image*: Self-image is the inherent ontological conception of self which is gained by an individual through his interaction with his surroundings, especially with 'relevant' others around him. The self-image of an inmate in prison as a conformist or a deviant, as a good man or a bad man, as one who has harmed society or has been harmed by society, is crucial in his reformation. Besides this self-image of being guilty or innocent, he also develops an image of self on the basis of the treatment he receives from others in prison and the attention he gets from his relatives and friends outside prison. He tries to find out reasons why he was praised by his friends and relatives before committing crime and why the same people avoid him today. He tries to find out why some inmates shun him and others seek him and why prison officials regard him as a bad person or a good person. When the reasons prove to be puzzling or evasive, the ontological introspection may make him a confused person. This confusion may result in 'role strain' which may ultimately force him to deviate from the 'expected role' in the prison which in turn may prove to be a barrier in his reformation.

(ii) *Value conformity*: Desire to conform to prison norms and reject the norms of the 'inmate world' depends upon internalisation of non-delinquent values and conformity to the expectations of 'significant' others. It also reflects one's religious and moral beliefs. If a person has an egocentric faith in his religious values, if he regards his deviant actions as sins, he will take no time repenting of his wrong deeds. The simple and logical inference is that the feeling of being wronged and the desire for revenge have to be destroyed/erased to make way for reformation.

(iii) *Actual conformity*: Actual conformity to norms may be inwardly directed or outwardly directed. The latter is one which is directed to groups and social institutions in society, while the former is one which is directed to the individual himself. The inwardly-directed conformity may arise because the inmate is either a moralist or a traditionalist wh[illegible] outwardly-directed conformity may arise because he is a pragmatist and [illegible] tied to reality.

(iv) *Prestige*: The labelling, condemnation, derogatory stigma, praise, cooperation and sympathetic and tolerant attitudes are also crucial factors in changing a prisoner's values and in making him accept or reject formal and informal values in prison. The environment in which a jailor or a warden abuses or assaults an inmate, other inmates jeer at him or stand by watching passively, or in which jail officials are crucial disciplinarians, would not succeed in changing the values and behaviour of a prisoner. If an inmate comes to the conclusion that his existence is neglected and treatment by the staff is devoid of reality and meaning, he may assert his existence by negative acts, such as openly criticising prison officials, demanding more facilities, and instigating other inmates to revolt. 'Counter role' here, which he assumes as a cover to protect himself from the penalties associated with his actual role, is an act of self-definition. Add to this the indifferent attitude of family, kinship group, caste, and community members of the prisoner, the possibility of his reformation becomes even more dim.

The above self-image model points out that inmates who make good institutional adjustment and conform to prison norms create within the prison community a dissenting minority. This minority resists, at least to some extent, the dominant influence of inmate groups who reject prison norms. Therefore, an effective programme segregating the minority group from the majority group, and also breaking the majority groups (who conform to inmate norms) by segregating them in such a way so as to minimise social contacts between them, will considerably diminish the influence of 'inmate culture' on inmates and check the kinds of anti-social influence an inmate encounters in prison life. This idea clearly challenges the present structuring of prisons and indicates the necessity and desirability of establishing prisons where a heterogeneous criminal population may be protected from the hazards of 'inmate culture'.

PRISON LABOUR

Assigning work to inmates in correctional institutions is considered today a major issue. Work is necessary for keeping inmates engaged to contain their idleness and reduce their unrest and disciplinary problems, for removing their monotony and improving their morale, for assigning such hard labour to them which may deter them from repeatedly indulging in crime, for teaching them some useful trade which may help them to become self-supporting after release from prison, for enabling them to earn and get some extra facilities for themselves in jails and also for sending some money to their families to support their children, and for reducing the operating cost of maintaining jails. Thus, the basic objective of prison labour is neither to be punitive nor to make jails self-sufficient but to keep prisoners engaged.

The tasks assigned to prison inmates till a few decade back were generally unproductive. Besides, a large number of inmates remained entirely unemployed. Even today, no work is assigned to the undertrials and prisoners of 'A' class.

In all, six systems of prison labour have been identified which prevailed/prevail in different parts of the world. These systems are: the lease system, the contract system, the piece price system, the state use system, the state account system and the public works system. The first three are *private* systems while the last three are *public* systems. In India, only the last three public systems of prison labour are prevalent at present.

Under the *lease* system, prisoners were turned over to a lessee who agreed to house, clothe, feed, and guard them and pay to the state a stipulated amount of money for each prisoner received. In return, he had the right to assign work of his choice to prisoners and to keep the products of their labour. Tales of ruthless exploitation and cruel treatment of prisoners aroused public indignation to such an extent that government was forced to abolish the lease system.

Under the *contract* system, a private individual or a company entered into a contract with the penal institution for the labour of prisoners at a stipulated amount per prisoner per day. The contractor/industrialist/merchant furnished raw materials, tools and machinery and inspectors to guide the production. In return, the penal institution supplies food and clothes to prisoners and also disciplined them. In this system, the industrialist found cheap labour, the state, a source of easy revenue, and the public low-priced articles. However, this system was also open to such serious abuses and corrupt practices among prison officials that strong public opinion was organised against it and it was totally abolished.

The *piece price* system was almost the same as the contract system, with the difference that in this system the contractor, instead of paying a stipulated amount per prisoner per day, furnished raw material, machinery and tools and paid a specified price per piece for the finished product. This system thus gave the state complete control over prisoners and their employment. It also did not permit the contractor to come into direct contact with prisoners and use their labour entirely for his own selfish interests. However, this system also did not escape public debate/controversy against it because of possible collusion between the contractor and the prison authorities. As such, this system was also abolished.

Under the *state account* (or also called the public account) system, inmates manufacture various commodities in the institution and the products are sold in the open market in competition with the goods produced by free labour. The state thus earns profit (or incurs loss) and exercises complete control over the inmates as well as the entire business. This system is prevalent in India even today and things like carpets, niwar, furniture, durries, flower-pots, cane baskets, etc. are sold by prisons in the open market. But the system has not picked up much owing to small demand for prison-made goods, poor quality of the goods produced, introduction of machinery in private industry, and lack of capital and transportation facilities.

Under the *state use* system, the state supplies products of prisoners to public institutions and agencies (like the police, schools, post-offices, government offices, and so forth). This practice of restricting the market avoids direct competition with private enterprise and free labour while utilising prison labour for the benefit of the public.

Under the *public works* system, the services of prisoners are used for constructing dams, digging canals, cultivating land, and so forth. The prisoners are paid the same wages as are paid to free labour. However, the prisoners have to arrange for their own food out of the wages earned by them.

The state account and the state use systems are the two systems which are usually adopted by prisons in India. The training given and the work assigned to inmates in prisons can be classified into *five* major groups: textiles and subsidiary, carpentry, leather work, blacksmithy, and producing soap, rope, etc. It is estimated that no more than 30 to 35 per cent of prisoners are engaged in productive work. Of these, more than 50 per cent are engaged in durrie-making, 25 per cent in handloom textiles, and the remaining 25 per cent in other tasks (like carpentry, tailoring, black-smithy, etc.). A majority of the workers (about 80%) feel dissatisfied with the work assigned to them. It is, therefore, necessary that before assigning work to prisoners, the authorities concerned must examine: (i) the effect of work on the health of prisoners, (ii) effect of work on reformation and value-changes, (iii) economic benefit to the state, (iv) effect on administration's efficiency, (v) competition with market, and (vi) market demand. Besides these considerations, other factors which can be given importance in assigning work could be term of prisoner's imprisonment, his age, education and previous training, the nature of crime, economic benefit to the prisoner, and the rehabilitative value of the work assigned.

Following Caldwell (1956:606), the five measures may be outlined for prison employment programme:

1. *Diversification of work*: Making penal institutions self-supporting is neither feasible nor desirable. The system of assigning age-old works like niwar-making or durrie-making is also to be discouraged. The keynote of modern prison employment programme must be diversification which will not only provide an opportunity for meeting the individual needs of prisoners but will also prevent intense competition with private industry. The employment programmes have also to vary in accordance with the available raw materials in the region, the size and the nature of the institution (viz., central or district prison), types of prisoners, availability of trainers, potential markets, and such other considerations.
2. *Emphasis on state use system of employment*: The state account system lends itself not only to competition but also to many abuses. Consequently, while this system may not be totally abolished, it should be used only in a limited way. The state use system has to be

supported more vigorously. With the active cooperation of government and semi-government institutions, this system can provide a well-balanced prison employment programme.

3. *Assigning work on the basis of the social background of prisoners*: Employment to prisoners should be carefully assigned on the basis of age, education, abilities, training needs, term of imprisonment, nature of crime and trustworthiness. Individual interests can be ascertained by keeping the newly-admitted offenders in the reception centres for a few weeks. The prisoners may then be classified in terms of being assignable to industrial work, agricultural work, public works, trade work and so on.
4. *Introducing wage system*: Prisoners will not work with efficiency without a wage or some other incentive. The wage system may, therefore, be introduced in prisons keeping in mind that food, clothing, etc. are to be provided by the prison administration free. If a daily wage earner can earn Rs. 40 to Rs. 50, a working prisoner can be given Rs. 10 to Rs. 15 per day depending upon the nature of work in which he is engaged. The spare time in the evening can be utilised for imparting education to illiterates, giving educational facilities to those who are interested in taking examinations and getting degrees, or for increasing the skills and abilities of prisoners and for improving their attitude towards their work. The educational programme should be carefully coordinated with the wage scheme.
5. *Appointing trained staff*: The employment programme should be organised, staffed and equipped in accordance with the highest standards. Prison industries must be provided with an adequate number of fully qualified persons who can handle the technical problems of training, production, and quality maintenance.

We also believe that creating a Bureau of Prison Industries in each state will be very helpful. At present, different government official and semi-government agencies in a state do not know what things are being manufactured in different jails and how they can be useful to them. If such a bureau comes into existence, all orders from different departments will be directed to this Bureau located at a central place. The bureau will receive manufactured goods from all prisons in the state and supply them to the departments concerned. The bureau will also suggest introduction of new training programmes in jails useful for manufacturing essential goods or for providing necessary services in specific fields. If a policy is framed that at least half of the prison population will be given industrial assignments, and if the practices of outside industries are emulated in as many aspects as possible, the bureau can create a wide market for the goods manufactured in prisons and also compete with private business. The goal of the bureau will be not only to turn out jail products that compare favourably in quality with those made by private interests but also to teach prisoners to work under conditions which provide a real transfer value to civilian life.

OPEN PRISONS

An open prison, also called minimum-security prison, open camp, or prison without bars, is a prison which is open in four respects: (i) open to prisoners, i.e., inmates can go to market at sweet will during the day but have to come back in the evening; (ii) open in security, i.e., there is absence of precautions against escape, such as walls, bars, locks and armed guards; (iii) open in organisation, i.e., working is based on inmates' sense of self-responsibility, self-discipline, and self-confidence; and (iv) open to public, i.e., people can visit the prison and meet prisoners. It is the kind of authority and the nature of management transferred to the inmates and the degree of freedom from physical restraints (to escape) that should be the real measure of openness of an open prison.

The main objectives of establishing open prisons are: to reduce overcrowding in jails, to reward good behaviour, to give training in self-reliance, to provide dependable permanent labour for public works, to prevent frustrations and create hope among long-termers, to provide training in agriculture and industry, to examine the suitability of releasing offenders from prisons, and to enable prisoners to live with their family members (in some states).

The first open prison was established in Switzerland in 1891, in the United States in 1916, in Britain in 1930, and in the Netherlands in 1950. By 1975, there were 13 open prisons in England, 25 in the United States, four each in Sri Lanka and the Australia, three in Hong Kong, two each in New Zealand, China, Japan, Malaysia, Pakistan, Philippines and Thailand, and 23 in India (Ghosh, 1992: 9-10).

In India, the first open prison was started in 1905 in Bombay Presidency. The prisoners were selected from the special class prisoners of Thane Central Jail, Bombay. However, this open prison was closed in 1910. The state of Uttar Pradesh established the first open prison camp in 1953 for the construction of a dam over Chandraprabha river near Benaras (now Varanasi). After completing this darn, the prisoners of the open camp were shifted to a nearby place of constructing the dam over Karamnasa river. The third camp was organised at Shahbad for digging a canal. Encouraged by the success of these temporary camps, a permanent camp was started on March 15, 1956 at Mirzapur with a view to employing prisoners on the work of quarrying stones for Uttar Pradesh government cement factory at Churk, Mirzapur. The initial strength of prisoners in this camp was 150 which went up to 1,700 but has now come down to 800. Another permanent camp—called Sampurnanad Shivir—was established in 1960 at Sitarganj in Nainital district in Uttar Pradesh. At the time of its establishment, Sampurnanand camp had 5,965 acres of land but later on 2,000 acres of reclaimed land were handed over to the Uttar Pradesh government for the rehabilitation of displaced persons. At present, thus, the Sitarganj camp has 3,837 acres of land and is one of the largest open prisons in the world. Prisoners selected for the camp from different jails of the state are transferred to district jail, Bareilly, from where they are shifted to the camp. The camp staff at present consists of one superintendent, five jailors, 12 deputy jailors, 16 assistant jailors, three assistant medical officers, six pharmacists, 126 warders and accountants, etc. The camp has capacity to accommodate 1,000 prisoners. However, on an average about 650 prisoners live in the camp during the year.

Uttar Pradesh was followed by many other states in establishing open prisons. In 1996, there were 24 open prisons (excluding semi-open camps) found in 12 states in India. Of these, three prisons are located in Maharashtra [Yeravada (1955), Paithan (1968) and Chandrapur (1972)], three in Rajasthan [Durgapur (1955), Sanganer (1963), and Suratgarh (1964)], two in Karnataka [Sanmdathi (1968) and Koramangala (1971)], two in Uttar Pradesh [Mirzapur (1956) and Sitarganj (1960)], two in Tamil Nadu [Singanallar (1956) and Salem (1966)], two in Gujarat [Amreli (1968) and Ahmedabad (1972)], two in Andhra Pradesh [Hyderabad (1954) and Anantapur (1955)], two in Bihar, two in Punjab, one in Kerala [Nettukeltheri (1962)], one in Assam [Jorhat (1964)], and one in Himachal Pradesh [Bilaspur (1960)].

The area of open prisons in different states varies from 10 to 50 acres except in Andhra Pradesh (which has 1,427 acres), and Sitarganj camp, Nainital, Uttar Pradesh (which has 3,837 acres). The open prisons, usually located on the outskirts of a town fall within five kilometers of the nearest town, except in Kerala and Uttar Pradesh where they are situated 15 to 35 kilometres from the nearest towns. The capacity of prisons varies from less than 100 to 1,000 prisoners. The nature of accommodation also differs from place to place. Assam, Kerala, and Himachal Pradesh prisons have permanent barracks; Mysore prison has pre-fabricated structure, and Andhra Pradesh and Maharashtra prisons provide dormitories with asbestos roofs. Some of these prisons provide work only in agriculture, some in industries, and some both in agriculture and industries.

Eligibility conditions for admission to open prisons vary from state to state. The main conditions are: (1) prisoners should be willing to abide by the rules of open prisons; (2) they should be physically and mentally fit to work; (3) they should have been sentenced for terms of one year or more and must have spent at least one-fourth of the total term of imprisonment in jail; (4) they should have record of good behaviour in prisons; (5) they should not be below 21 years or above 50 years as prescribed by the state; (6) they should not have been convicted for certain types of crimes (like dacoity, forgery, counterfeiting, etc.); (7) they should not have any case pending in the courts; (8) they should not be habitual offenders; and (9) they should not be class I (one) prisoners or women prisoners.

The procedure for selection of prisoners for open prisons is simple. The superintendents of prisons prepare lists of prisoners to be sent to open prisons on the basis of the eligibility conditions (as described above). These lists are sent to the selection committees which examine each case-history and make the final selection. About 60 per cent of prisoners in open prisons are those who have been sentenced for more than 10 years, while about 85 per cent are those who have been imprisoned for more then 5 years. The average stay in the prison varies from two to three years. The wage system also varies from prison to prison.

It may thus be maintained that open prisons differ from the ordinary prisons in four respects: in structure (affecting organisation and administration), in role systems (affecting work and interaction in everyday life), in normative systems (affecting social restrictions and expectations guiding behaviour), and in value orientations (affecting conduct and training). While inmate system in ordinary jails is dominated by a set of values and norms which are largely anti-social and anti-administration, the inmate system in open prisons is pro-administration. Open prisons are characterised more by consensus among inmates.

Ghosh (1993) studied 200 prisoners from two open prisons (Sitarganj and Mirzapur) in Uttar Pradesh in 1991 for analysing attitudes, personality traits, and reformation of prisoners in open jails. For a comparative study (control group), she selected 200 prisoners from two central jails of Banaras (Varanasi) and Bareilly in the same state. She focused on two aspects: personality variables and adjustment level. In personality variables, she studied three aspects: (a) self-esteem, (b) guilt-feeling, anxiety and insecurity, and (c) extroversion, neuroticism, and psychoticism. She found that:

- More prisoners in open prisons indicate a high level of adjustment to personal problems as well as to co-inmates and the staff than those in closed prisons. The high adjustment is the result of better facilities and free environment.
- Inmates in open prisons exhibit more positive self-esteem and positive attitude towards co-inmates than those in closed prisons.
- Anxiety, insecurity and guilt-feelings are found more among the inmates of closed jails than open camps.
- Attitude towards authorities is more cooperative among prisoners in open camps than those in closed jails.
- Psychoheism, neuroticism and extroversion among convicts are found to be much less in open prisons than in closed prisons.
- Inmates of open prisons show more positive attitude towards society than those in closed prisons.

These findings thus point out the positive use of open prisons in the reformation and rehabilitation of criminals. It may, however, be noted that open prisons need to be restructured and reorganised. What really needed is:

1. Establishing open prisons in all those states where they do not exist at present.
2. Framing common rules of eligibility for admission and providing facilities for offenders in open prisons in all states.
3. Laying down common rules of remission for inmates. For instance, a prisoner in Sitarganj camp, Nainital (Uttar Pradesh) and Sanganer prison, Jaipur (Rajasthan) earns remission at the rate of one day for one day stay. In addition, he is entitled to fifteen days' remission for good conduct every year. Besides, the superintendent and Inspector General of Prisons are also empowered to grant special remission. The prisoners are also permitted to keep their families with them, if they so desire.
4. Checking biases, pressures and corruption in preparing lists of prisoners to be sent to open prisons by superintendents.
5. Assigning powers to the courts for sending certain types of offenders directly to open prisons.

RESTRUCTURING PRISONS: A NEW APPROACH

Before giving my own viewpoint, it will be relevant to survey briefly what the Supreme Court of India has recommended from time to time for improving prison conditions, and what the recommendations as given by the Amnesty International in 1955 on standard minimum rules for the treatment of prisoners are.

Suggestions of the Supreme Court

The Supreme Court has given the following suggestions in the last 15 years or so in different cases from states like Andhra Pradesh (Giasuddin, 1977; Patnaik, 1974), Maharashtra (Sheela Barse, 1983), Delhi (Sunil Batra and Prem Sankar, 1980), Kerala (1983) and Bihar (Rakesh Chand, 1986) (*see*, National Expert Committee Report on Women Prisoners, 1989: 30-40).

1. *Assigning congenial work*: A prisoner should be assigned congenial work which gives job satisfaction. We (Supreme Court judges) direct the State Government to see that within the framework of the jail rules, the prisoner is assigned work not of a monotonous, mechanical, degrading type but of a mental, intellectual or like type mixed with a little manual labour.
2. *Remuneration*: A prisoner must be paid a reasonable fraction of remuneration by way of wages for the work done, since unpaid work is bonded labour and humiliating.
3. *Meditation and sports and games*: Self-expression and self-realisation have a curative effect. Therefore, any sports and games, artistic activity and/or meditational course will stimulate prisoner's creativity and sensitivity.
4. *Parole release*: We have given thought to another humanising strategy, namely, a guarded parole release every three months for at least a week, punctuating the total prison term. The jail authorities should periodically check whether the prisoner is making progress.
5. *Therapeutic outlook*: Severity in jails is self-defeating. The emphasis has to be on man as well as on the system, on the inner balance as on the outer tensions. We consider a therapeutic rather than a punitive outlook should prevail in our prisons since brutal incarceration of the person merely produces laceration of criminal's mind. The direction of prison reform is not towards dehumanisation but humanisation, not maim and mayhem and vulgar callousness but man-making experiments designed to restore the dignity of the individual and the worth of the human person. This strategy involves orientation courses for the prison personnel. It is now time to revolutionise the conditions inside that grim little world (prison). We

make these observations only to drive home the imperative of freedom—that its deprivation by the state is validated only by a plant to make the sentence more worthy of that birthright.

6. *Legal assistance*: Legal assistance to a poor accused is a constitutional imperative. It is a necessary sine qua non of justice and where it is not provided, injustice is likely to result. Nothing rankles more in the human heart than a feeling of injustice and those who suffer and cannot get justice because they are priced out of the legal system, lose faith in the legal process and a feeling begins to overtake them that rule of law is merely a slogan or myth intended to perpetuate the domination of the rich and the powerful and to protect the establishment and the vested interests. Imagine the helpless condition of a prisoner who is lodged in a jail who does not know to whom he can turn for help in order to vindicate his innocence or defend his constitutional or legal rights or to protect himself against torture and ill-treatment or oppression and harassment at the hands of his custodians. It is also possible that his family may have problems and may not be able to arrange legal assistance. It is, therefore, absolutely essential that legal assistance must be made available to prisoners in jails, whether they be under trial or convicted prisoners.

7. *Human treatment and protection of fundamental rights*: If a person is incarcerated, it does not mean that inhuman treatment may be meted out to him and he be deprived of his fundamental rights. He cannot be segregated in a 'quarantine' as if he is an inmate of a 'fascist concentration camp'. Prison officials cannot resort to oppressive measures to curb the political beliefs of their opponents. The government cannot prevent a *detenu* from publishing a book. A prisoner also has a right to acquire, hold and dispose of property. Incarceration cannot be an impediment to it. The term 'life' means something more than mere animal existence and the inhibition against its deprivation extends to all those limits and faculties by which life is enjoyed.

8. *Handcuffs*: A prisoner in transit between prison and court should not be handcuffed, except under special conditions which have to be justified before or after. Handcuffs are rrimn facie inhuman and repugnant. It is brutalising to handcuff a person in public.

   The Supreme Court in one of its judgments in a case (of Prem Sankar) from Punjab in 1980 observed: "We share the concern and anxiety (of our learned brother Krishna Iyer) for reorientation of the outlook towards prisoners and the need to take early and effective steps for prison reforms. Jail manuals are largely a hangover of the past, still retaining anachronistic provisions like whipping. Barbaric treatment of a prisoner from the point of view of his rehabilitation and acceptance and retention in the mainstream of social life becomes counter-productive in the long run.

9. *Grievance boxes*: Grievance deposit boxes shall be maintained in the prisons which will be opened as is deemed fit, and suitable action taken on complaints made. Access to such boxes shall be accorded to all prisoners.
10. *Visits by magistrates*: District magistrates and session judges shall personally or through surrogates, visit prisons in their jurisdiction and afford effective opportunities for ventilating legal grievances. They shall make necessary enquiries there into and take suitable remedial action. In appropriate cases, reports shall be made to the High Court for the latter to initiate, if found necessary habeas action.

Amnesty International Rules

The Amnesty International adopted certain rules in 1955 for the treatment of prisoners. Some of these rules are (*see*, National Expert Committee Report on Women Prisoners, 1989: 100-102):

1. *No discrimination*: There shall be no discrimination among prisoners on grounds of sex, religion, political or other opinion, national or social origin, and birth or other status. Prison authorities are supposed to respect the religious beliefs and moral precepts of the community to which a prisoner belongs.
2. *Separation*: Different categories of prisoners shall be kept in separate institutions or part of the institutions on the basis of their age, sex, criminal record and other circumstances.
3. *Corporal punishment*: Corporal punishment by placing in dark cell, and all cruel, inhuman, degrading punishments shall be completely prohibited.
4. *Hygienic conditions*: Due consideration to hygienic conditions for living should be made. The food served must be of nutritional value. Services of qualified medical officers having some knowledge of psychiatry should also be made available.
5. *Undertrials*: Undertrials should be separated from the convicts. Young untried prisoners should also be kept separate from untried adults.

6. *Social relations and aftercare*: Before the completion of the sentence, it is desirable that necessary steps should be taken to ensure for the prisoner a gradual return to normal life in society. He should be permitted to correspond with and meet relatives from time to time.

Constitutional/Statutory Rights of Prisoners

The Constitution of India incorporates certain rights to prisoners. Besides, statutes like Prisons Act 1894, Prisoners' Act 1900, and Prisoners' Attendance in Courts Act 1955 also confer some rights on prisoners. Some of these constitutional/statutory rights are:

1. *Double jeopardy*: No person shall be punished/prosecuted for the same offence more than once.
2. *Testimony*: Jail authorities cannot compel prisoners to give testimony which is likely to expose them to criminal consequences.
3. *Physical protection*: It is the duty of prison authorities (on behalf of the state) to protect the person physically. The prisoners cannot be kept in prison in the open, exposed to sun, rain or cold. The authorities will provide accommodation in prisons. In case of overcrowding or outbreak of an epidemic, the authorities shall provide temporary accommodation. The medical officer shall be responsible for sanitary conditions. The medical officer is also required to examine the new inmates and shall advise the jailor regarding the nature of work to be carried out by the prisoner.
4. *Separation*: Male and female prisoners shall be kept in separate prisons or separate parts of the same building.
5. *Solitary confinement*: Solitary confinement is used to ensure the safe custody of other prisoners or is inflicted as a punishment. Prisoners in solitary cells must be examined by medical officer at least once a day if confined for a period of more than twenty-four hours.
6. *Under-trials*: Under-trials may be permitted to have their own clothing, food and other accessories from their own sources and are entitled to be permitted to contact these sources at reasonable hours.
7. *Civil prisoners*: Civil prisoners are also to be treated like the under-trials. They are allowed to work in jail according to their will.
8. *Work*: A criminal who is sentenced to labour shall not be allowed to work for more than nine hours a day. The medical officer shall examine such prisoners every fortnight to record the effect of work on their health.

A NEW PERSPECTIVE

How to restructure prisons so that they may resocialise offenders? Should we shift towards more liberal regimes or towards more custodial control? This author's contention is that there should be reconciliation between the goals of custody and reform. The following measures may significantly contribute to the adjustment of offenders in prisons, and prisons functioning as correctional institutions rather than as 'factories of crime':

- Short-term offenders (getting less than six months' imprisonment) should not be kept in prisons. In India, at present about four-fifths prisoners are those who are awarded less than six months' imprisonment. Short-term imprisonment only stigmatises persons. Such offenders can easily be released on probation. At present, only 8 to 10 per cent of offenders, eligible to be released on probation, are getting the benefit of probation services in our country, whereas in the United States these services are used to the extent of 60 to 65 per cent. Why can't probation system in India be extensively used by the courts to deal with these offenders? This will also reduce overcrowding in prisons.
- Many prisons are overcrowded, i.e., the strength of inmates is much more than the sanctioned strength. For example, in Uttar Pradesh against the sanctioned strength of about 33,000 inmates in 67 jails in the state, there were 45,000 inmates in 1998 out of whom about 6,000 were convicts and 39,000 were undertrials. The Tihar Jail, Delhi which has a capacity of 2,000 inmates, had 8,000 inmates in 1999 (*The Hindustan Times*, April 25, 2000).
- The most important problem is that of classification of prisoners. The main objectives of classifying prisoners till recently were: to segregate different types of offenders, to categorise prisoners for security purposes, to prevent moral contamination, to control inmate-inmate relations, and to maintain discipline. Thus, classification was done primarily for administrative purposes. Now what is needed is classification for training and reformative purposes. It is, therefore, necessary that some rational and scientific methods may be introduced for classifying prisoners in jails.
- Effective social work services may be provided within prisons (say, through Prison Welfare Officers) to ease inmates' worries about their families.
- Legal services may be provided by voluntary organisations to

under-trial prisoners to help them with problems other than those for which they are being detained. This would not entail any extra financial expenditure but would require only organisation.

- Prisoners who want to continue their education and obtain university degrees may be provided the necessary facilities, including a quiet place for study.
- A programme of services for the under-trial prisoners may be instituted. Programmes may be designed to help them with their occupational, family, legal, medical, psychiatric, and other subproblems. Help of this kind would be of immense value to them when in jail with nothing much to do but to laze and be damned.
- The furlough system and some community resources for the convicted offenders could also be introduced.
- Prisons may provide the opportunity for discussion groups in which prisoners, assisted by professionals, or maybe ex-offenders, might discuss problems of mutual interest. For prisoners with problem of drugs, etc. special provision may be made for such assistance.
- More offenders may be released on parole.

There is too much corruption in jails. It is not difficult for rich and influential inmates to get good food, mobile phone, alcohol, drugs, TV, facility of meeting visitors at all times, and so forth. It is claimed that when ex-Chief Minister of Bihar was kept in Beur jail in Patna during April, 2000, he was getting all facilities which any rich and influential politician outside the jail enjoyed. Even other inmates were getting much better food because of this VVIP prisoner. It is reported that he even used jail superintendent's chair while meeting with important politician visitors. Homosexuality is also reported from a large number of jails in the country. A case was reported in April, 2000 from one jail where a young prisoner was killed by some adult inmates when he refused to cooperate for sexual relations. The Central Home Minister gave a statement in Rajya Sabha on June 14, 1998 that prison administration is the responsibility of the state governments and the Centre can give only some assistance for the modernisation of jails. If facilities as available in some jails in Uttar Pradesh, Bihar and Maharashtra are not stopped, jails will cease to be viewed as penal and correctional institutions.

Obviously, implementation of the above programmes to convert prisons into corrective centres cannot be accomplished without involving some extra expenditure. But until that is accomplished, prisons will continue to function as human warehouses. It is important to strengthen correctional centres because in the long run the result will be both real cost savings and a reduction in crime. Financial cost is, of course, not the only cost. Even more important is the cost to society and to jailed persons in terms of the devastating effect incarceration has on its victims. In view of the prevailing inefficiency and corruption, neglect and indifference and partisan politics and inhumanity to man in prisons, the time is ripe for fundamental changes.

Coulson and Riddel (1970) have said that there exists a structural dialectic of social structure and social consciousness. In other words, there is a complex two-way process in which goals, ideas and beliefs influence and are influenced by the social structure. Applying this to prison, it might be said that prison relations are patterned by structural determinants. Meanings and motives of prisoners are socially generated and sustained in ways of which prisoners themselves may be unaware. As such, along with structural changes, interpersonal relations in prisons should be so permitted to develop that prisoners' own motives and meanings may get importance in their behaviour.

References

Ahuja, Ram, *The Prison System: Effectiveness and Effects of Prison Custody*, Sahitya Bhawan, Agra, 1981.

---- "A Prisoner is a Human-Being." *The Times of India* (Times Weekly), Vol.3, No. 47, May 27, 1973.

--- "Effecting Reforms in Jails," *The Hindustan Times*, Sept. 11, 1981.

--- "Treatment of Convicts," *The Radical Humanist*, Feb. 1983.

---- "Inmates' Adjustment to Prison Subculture: A New Model and a New Perspective," *The Indian Journal of Social Work*, Vol. XLIV, No. 3, Oct. 1983.

Bhushan, Vidya, *Prison Administration in India*, S. Chand and Co., Delhi 1970.

Carter, Glaser Wilkins, *Correctional Institutions*, Lippincott, Philadelphia, 1977.

Caldwell, R.G., *Criminology*, Ronald Press Co., New York, 1956.

Chaddha, Kusum, *The Indian Jail*, Vikas Publishing House, Delhi, 1964.

Chandra, P., *Open Air Prisons*, Vohra Publishers, Allahabad, 1984.

Clemmer, Donald, *The Prison Community*, Christopher Publishing House Boston, 1940.

Datir, R.N., *Prison as a Social System*, Popular Press, Bombay, 1978.

Freedman, John C. (ed.), *Prisons: Past and Future*, Heinamann Educational Books, 1978.

Ghosh, S., *Open Prisons and the Inmates*, Mittal Publications, New Delhi, 1993.

Radzinowicz, L. and Wolfgang M., *Crime and Justice*, Vol. III, Basic Books, New York, 1971.

Reid, Sue Titus, *Crime and Criminology*, The Dryden Press, Illinois, 1976.

Singh, I.P., *Indian Prisons*, Concept Publishing Co., Delhi, 1979.

Singh, M.P., *Personality of Criminals*, Sri Ram Publishers, Agra, 1973.

Srivastava, S.P., *Indian Prison Community*, Pustak Kendra, Lucknow 1977.

Syker, Gresham M., *The Society of Captives*, Princeton University Press, Princeton, 1958.

Wheeler, Stanton, "A Study of Prisonisation" in *The Sociology of Punishment and Correction*, ed. by Jhonston, Savitz and Wolfgang, John Wiley and Sons, New York, 1, 1962.

Chapter 15

Probation and Parole

Probation is suspension of sentence of an offender on certain conditions with permission to remain in the community, subject to the control of the courts, and under the supervision and guidance of a probation officer. Thus, probation involves: (i) the withholding of imprisonment of the convicted offender, (ii) conditional release, (iii) permission to live in the community, and (iv) supervision of an agent of the court. This definition points out six elements of probation:

1. The offence has been proved in the courts and has been found worth punishment.
2. Imposition of punishment is postponed for a specific period.
3. The offender is given one more chance to prove that he can live as a law-abiding member of society.
4. Imposition of conditions by the courts indicates that he is still under their control.
5. The offender is generally kept under the supervision of a probation officer.
6. The measure aims at not punishing but reforming and rehabilitating the offender.

The suspension of sentence may involve either suspension of the *imposition* of sentence or suspension of the *execution* of sentence. In some countries, the 'execution' is suspended; however, in India, the 'imposition' itself is suspended, which means that on revoking probation (on violating the conditions of release), the court is in a position to impose any sentence on him (probationer) for the original offence he had committed (and not for violating the conditions). Many courts, after suspending sentence, release the offender without supervision in the community. Some scholars believe that release without supervision is not probation because the purpose of probation is to provide assistance to the offender in his efforts to adjust himself in the community, and that assistance can be provided only by a probation officer.

ORIGIN AND DEVELOPMENT

Credit for the introduction of probation and enacting the first law for placing offenders on probation goes to the state of Massachusetts in the United States of America in 1869. Earlier, an experiment under the leadership of one John Augustus—a showmaker of Boston—was successfully carried out for suspending sentence of the offenders and supervising their behaviour and helping them in rehabilitation in society. Augustus had assumed responsibility for assisting about 2,000 persons—1,152 males and 794 females—between 1841 and 1858 during the period of their suspended sentences (Cf. Sutherland, *Principles of Criminology*, 1965: 423). He was thus called the first probation officer. The official origin of probation as a legal system authorising the courts to place offenders on probation was made in 1878 when Massachusetts (US) passed a law authorising the appointment of a paid probation officer. By 1917, 21 states in America introduced probation system in their states. The Federal Court of the United States enacted such law in 1925. By 1953,45 states and the Federal Courts in the USA had been provided with some sort of legislation authorising probational release of the offenders.

In England, the parliament passed the Probation of First Offenders Act in 1887. It restricted probation to first offenders and did not authorise the appointment of probation officers. This limitation was removed in 1907 while the appointment of probation officers in all courts was permitted in 1925. France enacted such a law in 1891.

In India, the Probation of Offenders Act was enacted in 1958 which was gradually extended to all states except Jammu & Kashmir, Karnataka, Sikkim, Tripura, Arunachal Pradesh and Mizoram. Of these six states, Tripura enacted its own Act in 1960, Jammu & Kashmir and Karnataka in 1966, while Sikkim, Mizoram and Arunachal Pradesh have still to enact Probation Acts in their states (*Social Defence*, January 1990: 59). Before that, some states (provinces) were permitted to enact their own laws. Madras and Madhya Pradesh enacted such laws in 1936, Bombay and Uttar Pradesh in 1938, and Bengal in 1954. However, these Acts permitted release on probation only of juvenile delinquents and for offences with less than seven years imprisonment. There was also a provision (Section 562) in the 1898 Criminal Procedure Code (CrPC) and later on in CrPC 1973 (Section 360) which permitted release of offenders on probation. But the scope of provision in 1898 CrPC was very limited. It applied only to juvenile delinquents and male (but not female) first offenders. Besides, only first-class magistrates were authorised to release offenders on probation. There was no provision for supervision either. The Probation of Offenders Act, 1958 has a wider scope. It permits probational release of all offenders (irrespective of age and sex). It also permits supervision of probationers by probation officers. Besides, it has authorised all types of magistrates to release offenders on probation. The Probation of Offenders Act, 1958, thus, permits (a) probation to all offenders except those who are liable to be given capital punishment for murder, treason, etc. and to dacoits and professionals; (b) release on probation for a maximum period of three years; (c) social investigation by a probation officer; and (d) revocation or premature termination of probation. The Juvenile Justice Act, 1986 makes the release of all juvenile delinquents below 16 years (18 years for girls) on probation obligatory. If a certain juvenile is not given this benefit, reasons are to be specified for it. Release on probation is based on four factors: (i) circumstances of the case, (ii) nature of crime, (iii) age of the accused person, and (iv) character of the accused person.

ORGANISATION AND ADMINISTRATION

There is diversity in the administrative systems of probation in different states. In some states, the probation departments are under the control of the social welfare departments, in some others under the prison departments, in one state (Madhya Pradesh) under law department, and in one state (Karnataka) it functions as an independent department. The states in which probation is under the control of social welfare departments are: Rajasthan, Uttar Pradesh, Assam, Himachal Pradesh, and Delhi. The states in which it is under the control of the prison departments are: Andhra Pradesh, Tamil Nadu, Kerala, Bihar, Bengal and Punjab. In Maharashtra and Gujarat, probation department functions as a semi-government department.

The Director, Social Welfare Department or Inspector General, Prison Department is the administrative in-charge at the state level. He is assisted by Chief Probation Officer. Some states have appointed Regional Probation Officers also. Probation Officer functions at the district level. Some states have the system of appointing Assistant Probation Officers also, while a few have the practice of appointing part-time probation officers too.

Diversity in the administrative systems of probation has raised some crucial questions. Is it better to have probation controlled by a court or by a non-judicial agency? Experts on the subject have differing answers to this question. Some have argued that probation can be better protected from inefficiency when it is not managed by the social welfare departments but is controlled by the courts. Others have argued that the success of probation requires flexibility in approach and courts do not permit that kind of flexibility but are rather rigid. Besides, the judges have neither the time nor the training to enable them to assume responsibility for administering probation. The prison department being generally considered a corrupt department cannot be expected to contribute to its successful functioning. It may therefore be said that probation departments should function as independent departments. What is important for the success of the probation services is the appointment of really committed persons as probation officers who are willing to work as social workers. Equally necessary are programmes like: (a) training of probation officers from time to time, (b) holding periodical meetings of probation officers at the state level for discussing problems of mutual interest, (c) developing uniform standards for probation services, (d) investigating and evaluating the work of probation officers, (e) collecting, analysing and publishing statistical information and other facts regarding probation work in the state, and (f) furnishing special services like psychiatric examination in areas where probation officers are unable to arrange such services. Inter-state contacts regarding reciprocity in the supervision of probationers is equally important. Transfer of probationers from one state to another may be necessary in special cases. Rules may be framed to make such transfers possible.

PROBATION OFFICERS

A probation officer is the most important single element in the probation system. In fact, the success of the whole system depends on the efficiency and dedication of probation officers. Probation officers are charged with two responsibilities: social investigation and supervision.

Social Investigation

This involves investigating the social background of the accused person, his current situation, his personality qualities, and the forces which prompted him to commit crime. The investigation of social background includes the history of the accused person's family, inter-personal relations among his family members, his neighbourhood conditions, his relations with peers, nature of occupation in which he is engaged, economic factors in his life, description of his previous criminal record, employer's report, and the plan of treatment. The social investigation report also includes the probation officer's recommendation to the courts to enable them to determine whether or not probation is to be granted, and if so under what conditions specified by the statute. The judge's decision depends to a great extent upon the thoroughness and skill with which a probation officer performs this duty. And it is one which requires much time and efforts. It involves frequent attendance at the courts, many interviews and meetings, going through numerous records, and the preparation of analytical reports for the courts.

Supervision

The strategies adopted by a probation officer for supervision include his meeting the probationer in his own home without being constrained by the excessive inhibitions of bureaucracy. It also includes tactful interviews with employers and other interested parties, use of various resources in the community such as clinics, psychiatric centres, schools, etc. in order to supplement his own efforts and the keeping of detailed records. In the event of serious violation of conditions of probational release, he must be prepared to assume the role of a policeman and act promptly and fearlessly in the enforcement of the law. He thus strives to understand the 'street subculture' and to meet his 'client' on his terms. Court orders are also translated by him to the probationer. Experimental relationships, not structured to serve court's interests alone, complicate the management of a probation officer's role but role flexibility helps a probation officer to reach the probationer successfully.

A probation officer plays an important role in the rehabilitation of the offender. Rehabilitation theory assumes criminality to be primarily the result of a personality defect or emotional disorder in the offender. Is probation officer competent to remove this disorder? A survey of the attitudes of a large number of probation officers in regard to their proper tasks shows disagreement as to whether or not their work should entail psychotherapeutic coping with deep-seated emotional problems. But the officers generally agree that they are useful in referring probationers for vocational rehabilitation, job placement, marital counselling, welfare services, and legal assistance by some specialised agencies. They also consider appropriate the advisory and guidance tasks of explaining the disadvantages of continuing associations with disreputable persons, how to apply for a job, how to use spare time, and the wisdom of pursuing education. Their task of informing the courts about the performance of probationers is regarded as vital. Maximising the probationer's compliance of conditions laid down by the courts is also a crucial task of a probation officer. Probationers generally comply with the rules only if close surveillance is maintained by a probation officer and violations are not tolerated by him.

According to Caldwell (*Criminology*, 1956: 447), supervision is neither policing which is negative and repressive in nature, nor coddling which is misguided sentimentality and indulgence. Instead, supervision should be conceived of as case-work in an authoritarian setting. This is a process in which social services and counselling are used to help the probationer to help himself towards an acceptable adjustment in the community, and it is supported by the authority of the law. It must begin with the establishment of a relationship of trust an. understanding. This means that the probationer and his family members must be induced to believe that the officer is sympathetic to and interested in him as a person, that he respects his feelings, and that he sincerely wants to help. But on the other hand, the probationer must also clearly understand that the officer expects him to abide by the conditions imposed by the courts and to assume definite responsibilities in the modification of his own behaviour.

Caldwell (*ibid.* 448) has also pointed out a few generally accepted principles to which the probation officer can look for guidance:

1. He must be a leader, i.e., he must always be in command of the situation and that he, and not the probationer, should be the one to decide what techniques are needed and how and when they should be used.
2. The probation officer should set a model of behaviour for the probationer by his own conduct. He should not be inconsistent with the values he expects the probationer to accept.
3. The probation officer should focus on both the environment and the personality traits of the probationer, keeping in mind the fact that criminality is the product of interaction of pressures of both.
4. He should try to seek help from all the available resources in the community—an interested employer, a loyal friend, a helpful neighbour, understanding parents, cooperating relative, a skilful psychiatrist, a recreation centre, if any—for changing the attitudes of

the probationer.

5. He should avoid threatening, ordering, and preaching but should seek the participation of the probationer in the solution of his own problems.

David Dressler (1969) has suggested three techniques to be used by the probation officer in his probation work:

(i) *Manipulative techniques*: to modify both the situation and the personality traits of the probationer.

(ii) *Executive techniques*: to discover and use other resources—medical, legal, educational, social service—in the community to supplement his own efforts.

(iii) *Guidance, counselling and leadership techniques*: to reduce probationer's conflicts and modify his behaviour patterns.

Besides the above techniques, the following measures are also likely to contribute to the success of probation services.

1. Contact of a probation officer with the probationer in his office, no doubt is necessary, for the purposes of privacy that cannot be secured in the home of the probationer, but frequent contacts in the probationer's home, school, and work-place are likely to be more useful and expedient.
2. Calling a probationer to office (by the probation officer) and just asking him two or three formal questions after keeping him waiting for hours together makes probationer lose confidence in the probation officer. Unless the probation officer spends an hour or two with the probationer talking to him like a friend, he cannot create in the probationer a sense of participation in the correctional process.
3. The supervision of probationer cannot be conducted satisfactorily without the maintenance of case records and the preparation of regular and adequate reports. The results of pre-sentence investigations have to be carefully maintained and used in the process of controlling the probationer's environment and personality traits.
4. Excessive case loads seriously interfere with supervision, maintaining records, and planning the future strategies. If more full-time probation officers cannot be appointed, part-time probation officers may be appointed to have their help in supervision and community contacts. Voluntary workers cannot strengthen probation work.

The total number of probation officers in India is estimated to be about 615, of whom 17 per cent are females and 83 per cent are males, and

85 per cent are stipendary and 15 per cent are honorary (*Social Defence*, January 1990: 60). Out of 22 states having the probation system, the average work-load pertaining to social investigation per probation officer per year in three states varies between 200 and 250, in three states between 150 and 200, in four states between 100 and 150, in five states between 50 and 100, in three states between 20 and 50, and in four states it is below 20. The average number of supervision cases (including those under the 1958 Act, Children Act and other laws) per probation officer per year is more than 50 in three states, between 25 and 50 in six states, between 10 and 25 in seven states, and less than 10 in six states.

Rajasthan is one state in India where the probation system has totally deteriorated. In this state, the probation services were merged with the social welfare services in 1972. As a result, out of 26 probation officers in the state (at that time) except six, all other probation officers were redesignated as probation-cum-social welfare or probation-cum-prison welfare officers. The social welfare work assigned to probation officers was found be so 'lucrative' by the probation officers that they devoted 80 per cent of their time to social welfare work and hardly 20 per cent to probation work. This was bound to affect the functioning of the probation services. The number of cases investigated (under the 1958 Act, Children Act and other laws) and supervised per year started falling steeply from 1980 onwards.

The probation officers in India may be classified into five groups on the basis of the type of interest taken by them and the type of the report they submit to the courts: (1) *constable-type* probation officer, who is more concerned with offence than the conduct background; (2) *lawyer-type* probation officer, who uses a good deal of legal language; (3) *sociologist-type* probation officer, who focuses more on presenting facts about social environment in which the accused person is found living; (4) *psychiatrist-type* probation officer, who attempts to analyse personality traits without having the scientific knowledge of psychiatry, e.g., extrovert, emotional, risk-taking, and so forth; and (5) *journalist-type* probation officer, who is more interested in using 'decorative' language and phrases in the report than presenting actual facts.

PROBATIONERS

What type of offenders are released on probation? Every year between 15 and 16 thousand offenders are released on probation under supervision in our country. Of these, about 93 per cent are males and 7 per cent are females. In terms of age, about 14 per cent are under 16 years of age, 17 per cent belong to 16-20 years age group, 31 per cent belong to 21-30 years age group, 26 per cent belong to 31-40 years age group, 10 per cent belong to 41-60 years age group, and 2 per cent are above 60 years of age (*Social Defence*, January 1990: 62). Thus, since about half of the probationers belong to the age group of 1630 years, it may be inferred that young offenders benefit more by this system. Among the juvenile delinquents, though Juvenile Justice Act, 1986 suggests release on probation in as many eligible cases as possible, but the given figures point out that only two-third juveniles get the benefit of probation. For example, in 1998, 18,964 juveniles were arrested and sent to courts under IPC and SLL offences. Of these, 2,620 (13.8%) were sent to homes, 2,107 (11.1%) were acquitted and 6,860 (36.2%) cases remained pending. Thus, out of remaining 7,377 delinquents punished, 4,718 (64%) were given the benefit of probation (*Crime in India*, 1998: 255).

In terms of education, about 52 per cent probationers are illiterate and 48 per cent are literate. In terms of marital status, about 44 per cent are married, 54 per cent are unmarried, and 2 per cent are widowed/divorced/separated. As regards the nature of employment, about 42 per cent are engaged in agriculture, 35 per cent are daily wage-earners, 8 per cent are engaged in service or some occupation, and 15 per cent are not employed (*ibid.*: 64). Lastly, the term of 'probation' points out that about 60 per cent probationers are kept on probation up to one year, 35 per cent for one to two years, and 5 per cent for two to three years (*ibid.*: 63).

S.L. Tandon studied 80 probationers in Delhi in 1986. Of these, 79 per cent were adults and 21 per cent juveniles, 94 per cent were male and 6 per cent females, 46 per cent were unmarried and 54 per cent married, 59 per cent were illiterate and 41 per cent literate, 73 per cent were employed and 15 per cent were unemployed, and lastly 12 per cent were between 10 and 18 years of age, 14 per cent were between 19 and 24 years, 44 per cent were between 25 and 28 years, 23 per cent were between 29 and 33 years, 6 per cent were between 34 and 38 years, and 5 per cent were between 39 and 43 years (*Social Defence*, July 1987: 13). The nature of employment of the 73 per cent employed probationers showed that 54 per cent were self-employed (cobblers, cycle-repairers, auto-scooter-drivers, rickshaw-pullers, fruit-sellers, mechanics, painters, etc.), 18 per cent were daily wage-earners, and 1 per cent were in service.

In terms of crime, 26 per cent were convicted for theft, 20 per cent for pickpocketing, 16 per cent for fighting, 14 per cent for dealing in illicit liquor, 8 per cent for attempt to murder, 8 per cent for possessing weapons, 6 per cent for ticketless travelling, and 2 per cent for peddling in drugs (*ibid.*: 14).

The period of probation was one year in 67 per cent cases, two years in 30 per cent cases, and three years in 3 per cent cases. It was further found that 90 per cent probationers had their meetings with the probation officers every month, while 10 per cent met them fortnightly. Mostly, the meetings took place in the offices of the probation officers. The probationers' homes were visited by the probation officers rather rarely. Twenty-one per cent probationers revealed that probation officers had visited their homes only once, 16 per cent twice, and 63 per cent never. Further, 30 per cent considered probation supervision useful to them, while 70 per cent did not consider it useful, as the probation officers were not able to solve their problems or build up their confidence. No probationer considered probation officer as his friend or guide. Two-third (66%) probationers described their visits to the office of probation officers as a mere ritual and a formality. The probationers stated that the probation officers only asked casual questions like whether they faced any problems or whether they were harassed by the police; they never tried to establish personal rapport with them or gave them any personal affection. The probation officers hardly even gave them more than five to ten minutes on every visit. In spite of such perceptions about the probation officers, all probationers perceived probation as a good device for saving criminals from the ill-effects of imprisonment. They were all happy to be on probation, though very few of them considered supervision to be of much use and benefit. All this shows that though probation system is appreciated by the probationers yet they want changes in its implementation, particularly in the services rendered by the probation officers.

SUCCESS OF PROBATION SYSTEM

The number of probationers whose probation is revoked is extremely small (2-3% only) in India. It may, therefore, be said that probation system is a success in our country. In the United States, Lowell Carr described it successful in 1950 in 54 per cent cases, and Ralph described it successful in 1957 in 75 per cent cases. On the other hand, some studies of probation have not been so reassuring. Sheldon and Glueck (Cf. Caldwell: 453) examined 390 male probationers and found that only 2.4 per cent probationers always behaved satisfactorily, 0.8 per cent succeeded at first and later failed, 4 per cent failed at first and later succeeded, 0.4 per cent were erratic in their behaviour and 92.4 per cent always failed. In another study of 806 juvenile probationers, Glueck (Cf. Caldwell: 453) found that 20.3 per cent always succeeded in making a satisfactory adjustment,21.8 per cent sometimes succeeded, and 57.9 per cent always failed. In India, S.P. Srivastava's and Tandon's studies also pointed out the dissatisfaction of probationers with probation services. Although these studies raise some doubts about the way in which probation is being used, yet belief in its principles remains unshaken among criminologists. Criminologists everywhere contend that probation could be made much more effective if competent persons were appointed to handle these services. If probation system is compared with the system of commitment to prison or confinement in a correctional institution or any other method of dealing with the offenders, probation will surely be found more effective. However, such comparison will be difficult because offenders who are being handled by different methods do not have the same characteristics.

There is still another aspect of measuring the success of probation. The percentages of violation and revocation refer only to the behaviour of offenders during their period of probation. But how do probationers behave after completing the term of probation? What is the rate of recidivism amongst them? In other words, does probation have a lasting effect on their behaviour? In India, no studies have been made on this aspect, though several of such studies have been reported in the United States by Sutherland (*Principles of Criminology*, 1947: 403) which indicate that "the number of failure is not greatly increased after the end of the probation period". Caldwell (1956: 455-56) also made a similar study of 403 persons after their discharge from probation. He found that 83.6 per cent of them committed no offences during the post-release period of eleven and a half years and of the 16.4 per cent who again became offenders, only 2 per cent (8 in number) committed felonies. These studies thus point out the success and effectiveness of the probation system in the correction of criminals and juvenile delinquents.

But what is significant is that courts still regard it as a measure of leniency rather than as a corrective method. No wonder, of those offenders who are eligible to be released on probation, hardly 10 per cent get its benefit in our country. This percentage is very low compared to 60 per cent in the United States.

Sparks (Cf. Radzinowicz and Wolfgang, *Crime and Justice*, Vol. III, 1971: 211) has also held that virtually every study in England on the after-conduct of offenders placed on probation has found that the majority are not reconvicted within the chosen follow-up period. The

1958 Cambridge study found that 79 per cent adults and 73 per cent juveniles successfully completed their periods of probation. In the follow-up study after three years, 70 per cent adults and 58 per cent juveniles had not committed any crime. Similar results were reported from the United States by R.W. Engeland (1955). According to him, 82 per cent of 490 offenders placed on probation in Pennsylvania were not reconvicted within a period of 6-12 years after completion of probation. Even though studies by scholars like Glaser have shown that prisons also show success up to 65 per cent cases, it can be said that probation treatment is not less effective than prison treatment. Taking into account the cost of treatment by probation technique (in comparison to imprisonment technique), it would be reasonable to hold that placing on probation a larger proportion of offenders from among those now being sent to prisons or other institutions would be more justified and effective.

This, of course, raises the question of case-load size of a probation officer in India. How many offenders can a probation officer properly supervise at a given time along with work of social investigation and time required for attending the courts and in corresponding with his head office for supplying required information from time to time? Answers to this and similar questions are not easy to give because answering these questions not only depends on the social expectations from a probation officer but also on his efficiency, the geographical conditions in a given state, the type of treatment that needs to be given to a probationer, the finances available, and so forth. Broadly speaking, it may be said that along with pre-sentence investigation work and other duties expected of a probation officer, the standard case-load of supervision should not be more than ten at a time, including old and new probationers (because new ones require more attention than the old ones). In England, it is between 50 and 60 while in the United States, it is over 100 (Cf. Radzinowicz *et al.*, Vol. III, 1971: 213-14). In 1966 in California, the average case-load was 140 persons per probation officer along with the work of pre-sentence inquiry, though in other states, it was less (*ibid.*: 214). Taking the entire country (the US), the average probation case-load was 84 in 1960. In the Indian conditions, the work of one pre-sentence investigation is often equal to the supervision of at least five cases of probationers. Taking into consideration other administrative duties of a probation officer, suggested cases for supervision cannot be as high as in England or America. A probation officer with a load of 15-20 cases of supervision can spend an average of two to three hours or so per case per month. Carter (Radzinowicz, 1971: 224) no doubt has pointed out that the caseload of 50 was 'ideal'. This view may be alright for the United States, but, for India, this has no validity whatsoever. It requires an empirical research in various states to determine the 'ideal', 'normal', 'maximum', 'minimum' and 'intensive' allocation of supervision and pre-sentence cases to a probation officer.

The success and effectiveness of probation depends upon three things: (i) an adequate pre-sentence investigation, (ii) a careful decision by the court that there is a reasonable probability of the offender's making good on probation, and (iii) a systematic supervision of the probationer by a qualified person who is not burdened with excessive case-load and who takes real interest in the probationer's rehabilitation out of his commitment and dedication to duty.

ARGUMENTS IN FAVOUR OF PROBATION

Any analysis of the advantage of probation must begin with the recognition that it is a substitute for commitment to a correctional institution, and nearly all persons who are committed to correctional institutions return to the community—most of them within a short time. In fact, about 60 per cent of prisoners return to the community within six months and 25 per cent within two to three years. In cases where probation is used, it is not a substitute for permanent incarceration, but, in all probability, a substitute for a short-term in a correctional institution, where there is often little effort to rehabilitate the offender and from which he is often discharged without guidance or assistance into an unfriendly community.

With this background, we may consider the following advantages of probation:

1. The probationer leads a normal life in the community and continues to perform the social responsibilities expected of him by society.
2. The probationer is not a liability on the state like a prisoner but supports himself as well as his family members economically.
3. Probation mitigates the adverse consequences of imprisonment. The probationer is not exposed to prison environment and experiences which may leave him stigmatised, embittered and may even make him a serious criminal in association with other prisoners.
4. He is not alone in his efforts to reform himself but is assisted by a probation officer who guides and advises him from time to time. The probation officer also attempts to keep him away from the environment which produces crime and delinquency.

5. It costs the state less to keep an offender on probation than to confine him in a prison.
6. The prison population is rapidly increasing with increase in crime and in the number of offenders imprisoned every year. As a result, jail officials face serious problems in maintaining internal order and discipline. With a lower population in jails, it would be easier to pay individual attention to offenders.

OBJECTIONS TO PROBATION

Many of the objections raised against probation are with regard to procedure adopted rather than the system itself. The important objections are as follows:

1. Probation is not a form of correction but it is a form of leniency which pampers an offender.
2. Probation enables an offender to avoid punishment which is necessary not only as a deterrent to crime and delinquency but also for maintaining law and order.
3. After release on probation, the offender returns to the same family and community environment that contributed to his crime. He is therefore exposed to the same influences all over again.
4. Probation does not protect the community since the offender lives in the community and may repeat his crimes or delinquencies.
5. Since social investigation has not been made compulsory, the judge finds it difficult to decide whether or not the offender should be released on probation.
6. There is no provision for compulsory supervision, i.e., offenders are released under suspended sentences but without supervision. This needs to be criticised and looked into.
7. The probation officers do not supervise the probationers properly due to heavy case-loads. The number of trained personnel is also insufficient. The supervision thus remains both inadequate and questionable.

COUNTER-ARGUMENTS AGAINST CRITICISMS

1. Probation is neither leniency nor pampering the offender. He is selected for this kind of treatment only after the court decides that there is a reasonable probability that he will adjust successfully in

the community and that his living in the society will not be a threat to its security.

2. Imposition of conditions and curbing the freedom of the offender is in itself a punishment for him. Besides, if he does not abide by the conditions of the court, he can be committed to an institution. Probation thus does not eliminate all pain. The condition of reporting to the probation officer from time to time also involves inconvenience, embarrassment and disgrace.
3. It is not correct to say that since the offender lives in the community, he continues to be a threat to it and the society remains unprotected. Here it is overlooked that only selected offenders are released on probation and in a good number of cases, there is investigation of his background as well as supervision over his conduct during probation, both of which operate to prevent the exposure of the community to further law violations on the part of the offender.
4. Though there is some logic to the argument that on being released on probation, the offender returns to the same environment in which he committed crime yet in a large number of cases, there is supervision by a probation officer over him, who guides and advises him and thus seeks to modify the situation. If there is no supervision, the answer is to be found in improvement of the probation system and not in its elimination. It may also be pointed out that the imprisoned offender also returns to his family and community after he is discharged from prison and there is no one there to guide or assist him.
5. Social investigation is ordered by the courts wherever it is considered necessary. The number of cases dealt with by the courts every year are so large (about 16 lakh in our country) that social investigation in all cases would not be feasible.
6. Supervision is made compulsory in all such cases wherever it is considered essential. If supervision is ordered and the probation officer is not able to supervise all cases under him because of excessive workload, supervision will be only a mockery. Besides, since the alternative to probation is not permanent imprisonment, but, in all probability, a short term of confinement from which there is often release without supervision, probation even without supervision may actually institute a successful alternative to imprisonment.
7. The insufficient number of probation officers and/or their heavy workload are deficiencies in the implementation of the programme and not the failure of the probation system itself. In view of the great advantages of probation, the solution is not the abandonment of

probation but the elimination of the conditions which make its use difficult.

EFFECTIVENESS OF PROBATION

How to make probation more effective? We suggest the following six measures for it.

Change in Concept

The first thing is that it is necessary to change the underlying philosophy and the legal definition of 'probation'. Subsection 4 of Section 4 of the Probation Act, 1958, provides for releasing the offender on his entering into a bond to appear and receive sentence when called upon by the court for violating the probation conditions. Section 9 of the Act refers to the procedure to be adopted for dealing with the offenders failing to observe the conditions of the bond. According to this procedure, if the probationer fails to observe any of the conditions of the bond, the court may either issue warrants or summons requiring him to attend the court on a fixed day. When he appears, the court may remand him to custody until the case is concluded or may grant him bail. On hearing the case, it may sentence him for the original offence or impose penalty of not exceeding Rs. 50 and if he fails to pay the fine, the court may sentence him for the original offence. This shows that probation is legally viewed as 'suspension of sentence' or 'postponing punishment'. This author's contention is that, instead of viewing probation as suspended sentence, it should be considered as a 'substitute of imprisonment'. When probation is so viewed, the probationer will not have to face the threat of punishment by the court for the original offence for which imposition of punishment was temporarily deferred but has only to bear the threat of punishment by the probation officer for the breach of probation conditions. After release from the custodial institution, when a person commits a new offence, he is reconvicted for his new offence and not for the first one for which he has already undergone the penalty. If within prison, a prisoner violates prison rules, he is dealt with by the prison officials for this violation and not by the court. The same pattern should be adopted in the probation services too. Instead of reporting the violation of the conditions of probation to the courts, the probation officer should himself be authorised to deal with such cases of violation. The legal argument that threat of punishment for original offence is to give the probationer another chance to improve his behaviour in society and escape commitment and its stigma is not very sound because 'prescribing conditions' on which the offender is placed on probation is in itself a punishment since he loses his liberty. The effectiveness of treatment in probation system being based on the concept of manipulation of the offender into good behaviour by the use of psychosociological devices, the need for removing the 'threat of punishment' is very essential to make probation a more effective treatment system.

There are certain kinds of criminal acts which are very difficult to eliminate. Likewise, no serious action is desired against all criminals. A substantial shifting of our policy is needed for misdemeanants whose crime is not the result of inherent criminalistic tendencies, and who do not appear to threaten the societal norms or consensus. In dealing with such offenders, our policy needs a certain amount of modification to permit greater flexibility in personal dealings. The obvious case in point here is dealing with the probationers whose offences are unfortunate slips and not very harmful to society. The flexibility with probationers is possible only when probation officers are given more powers. In the present structure of probation services, the possibility of this flexibility is minimum. A rational crime policy would require us to rethink as to what is intended to be accomplished by employing 'conditional release' as a means of social control. If probation is not a punitive measure but a reformative process, why should a permanent threat hang over the head of the probationer, namely, of sending him back to the courts? Why should probation be an instrument of the courts? Section 4 of the Probation Act lays down the object of the Act as preventing the turning of youthful offenders into criminals by their association with habitual and hardened criminals of mature age within the walls of a prison. If this is the feeling at the time of imposing sentence on the offender, why should this feeling be forgotten when a probationer is found violating one or more conditions of the bond? It could, therefore, be maintained that the object of Probation Act would be achieved only by changing the legal definition of 'probation' and modifying Sections 4 and 9 of the Act.

Supervision

Our other concern is with Subsection 3 of Section 4 of the Act regarding placing probationers on supervision and the suggestions of some probation officers that no offender be placed on probation *without supervision* and that Section 4 of the Probation Act be amended. The above referred Subsection provides that the court *may* pass orders for the supervision of the offender by a probation officer in the interest of the offender and public, i.e., *all* probationers need not be kept under probation officers' supervision. Some probation officers hold the view that probation not involving supervision is no probation at all and as such *all* probationers must be placed under supervision. The crucial questions about supervision are: how much supervision do offenders on probation now receive, and how much do they need? What are the techniques of supervision now in use and what effects have they on different types of probationers? These questions must be answered before we are in a position to say that it is probation *with* supervision rather than probation *without* supervision which is responsible for the apparently high effectiveness of probation.

The fundamental purpose of supervision is to help the offender in creating within himself the will and ability to employ his capacities for achieving his goals without being in serious conflict with the interests of other persons and society. Here there is probably an assumption that earlier the person was not assisted by his parents, kith and kin and peers, etc., in developing this will. This assumption is surely not correct. All offenders do not commit crimes only because of socialisation defects. Many indulge in deviant acts due to force of circumstances. But assuming that offender's crime was due to lack of proper counselling, could it be said that probation officer will definitely give him the required counsel, supervision and guidance? Are all probation officers adequately trained to be counsellors and are they committed to their occupational roles? Assuming that they are, is it not known that with the present caseload, a probation officer hardly gets about two hours or less per month of personal counselling time with each client? Could it be definitely contended that according to the provisions of the Act, all probation officers regularly visit probationers in their home surroundings, and where appropriate, their occupational environment, in order to see that the progress made by the probationers and the difficulties, if any, are met with by them satisfactorily? The standard probation case-load of a probation officer in India is much less in comparison to that in England and the United States. In several states in India, the position is of course not satisfactory and probation officers have high work-load. The number of probation cases under supervision at any one time is not, however an accurate measure of the probation officer's workload since he has also to perform the duty of pre-sentence investigation of offenders' social background and submit report to the courts. Moreover, administrative duties of probation officers have also increased in recent years. The result is that in many cases, the supervision of offenders on probation occupies only a fraction of the probation officer's time. A probation officer, with high caseload, thus spends very little time per case per month; and, in many cases, the amount of contact between probationer and probation officer is minimal.

It is true that all probationers do not require equal attention and that some need more supervision than others. Nevertheless, keeping in mind the 'minimum' supervision needed by probationers, the success of probation and the development of non-criminal orientations can easily be attributed to 'intensive' supervision only. Without normal or even minimum supervision, the probation officer cannot act as a proper guide and counsellor for a probationer. Assuming that he does, it is known that a probation officer is supposed to secure for the probationer training facilities, employment opportunities and financial aid. In the present circumstances, is the probation officer really able to get him a job? Can he give him financial assistance? Those people who suggest that no offenders be released on probation without supervision are in fact advocates of 'get tough' approach to crime. These advocates seem to forget that overzealous enforcement methods could well signal a serious curtailment of the individual liberties that we so highly prize. This is not to express sympathy for an offender but simply to restate what should be a governing tenet of democratic justice. In a complex, heterogeneous, rapidly changing, urbanised and largely individualistic society in which individual's dependence on secondary groups is increasing day by day for the satisfaction and fulfilment of his varied needs, the traditional agencies of socialisation often find themselves hard put to maintaining influence on the young. At the same time, there is some confusion as to what is desirable and what is undesirable what are crime-encouraging values and what are crime-preventive values. In such a situation, to have a right attitude towards the violators of the so-called social values and recommend regular visits of probationers to probation officers' office at fixed intervals and function under their guidance for a period of not less than one year would definitely have deleterious effects on the probationers' efforts of adjusting themselves in society. From all this it appears that the majority of probationers could be dealt with effectively by measures not involving supervision. Some offenders definitely are able to benefit more from supervision but the majority probably do not need it. In, particular, offenders who are not 'risks' can well be dealt with by probation without supervision. Let us, therefore, not indulge in overlegislating because it has its own perils. Seen from an operational point of view, probation has to be quite different from its ideal conception. Subsection 3 of Section 4, thus, does not need any amendment.

Social Investigation

The third point pertains to social investigation. According to the existing provisions of the Probation Act, it is not mandatory for the courts to send each case for social investigation to the probation officer before releasing an offender on probation. The Act maintains that the courts *may* call for a report from a probation officer regarding the character of the accused. Subsection 3 of Section 4 and Subsection 2 of Section 6 provide for court's taking the probation officer's report into consideration, *if there is any*, before it makes an order for release on probation. In this connection, we assert that social investigation in all those cases should be made mandatory where the judges plan to release offenders on probation with or without supervision. According to the present Probation Act, the probation officer has to report to the court the character and personality of the offender, the circumstances in which the offender is living, his problems and needs, his relationships with people, factors that underlie his specific offences and such other matters as may, in the opinion of the probation officer, require to be taken into consideration by the court before making the probation order. This clearly points out the use of the pre-sentence investigation report to determine a treatment plan. The diagnostic report is not to assist the court in assessing whether a person accused of committing crime is to be actually convicted for that crime or not. This is evident from the fact that probation officer's sealed report is opened by the magistrate only *after* the offender is found guilty, to know the character of the offender before making an order of release. For utilising probation wisely, it is essential for a conscientious judge to have at the time of sentence of the offender complete, accurate, reliable and confidential information on which to base his decision. For a judge to merely guess whether the offender should be sent to jail or placed on probation with or without supervision is almost as futile as to expect a doctor to prescribe medicine without getting details of the disease from the patient. True, there are not enough probation officers and their case-loads are too high. But these are administrative problems which are not difficult to solve. The argument that the probation officer may not be completely objective and impartial in conducting investigation and in writing the pre-sentence report is irrational and ludicrous because the same argument can be applied to the possibility of non-objectivity of the judges too. Similarly, the fear that the probation officer may write the report without going to the field and meeting the parents, relatives, neighbours and friends etc., of the offender, merely points out defect in the process of selecting probation officers and not in the validity of the pre-sentence investigation report. As such, an amendment in Subsection 2 of Section 4 and 6 for compulsory pre-sentence investigation and asking for the probation officer's recommendation regarding probation or commitment is necessary and highly desirable and should be regarded as an ideal measure.

An Appeal against Trial Court by the Probation Officer

Let us now take up Sections 4 and 6 of the Probation Act regarding the release of certain offenders, particularly juvenile and adolescent delinquents on probation along with Section 14 of the duties of probation officers. The Juvenile Justice Act, 1986 imposes restrictions on imprisonment of offenders under 16 years of age, guilty of an offence not punishable with life imprisonment and necessarily releasing them on probation unless the court feels that the case is not within the purview of release on probation or such release will not be in the interest of justice. In spite of this provision, it is well known that all offenders—adults and juveniles—eligible to be released on probation are not actually so released by the courts. Judges use probation much less frequently than imprisonment when sentencing offenders. Evidence clearly indicates that our courts consider the type of offence and not the personality of the offender in assessing the risk and imposing sentences. A few years ago, this author had an opportunity of collecting data pertaining to convictions from some courts in two districts of Rajasthan. The collected information revealed that out of 1,836 persons tried by four courts in the two districts, 55.3 per cent were acquitted and 44.7 per cent (or 820 persons) were actually convicted. Out of 820 convicted offenders, 71 per cent were sent to prison, 14 per cent fined, 6 per cent committed to sessions, 3 per cent released after admonition, 4 per cent given probation without supervision and 2 per cent placed on probation with supervision. It is really strange that our judiciary has not shifted from age-old purely legalistic attitude to lego-sociological attitude in initiating trials and more liberally using probational treatment. There is a provision in the Probation Act for making an appeal against the trial court. It is not only the convicted person and the prosecution who can file appeal against court's decision of declining to deal with the offender under Sections 3, 4 and 6 of the Probation Act and passing the sentence of imprisonment against him, but even the probation officer has been conferred upon power by the legislature to feel aggrieved with regard to the propriety of the imprisonment order passed by the trial court and move the court by way of an appeal against the correctional treatment. But, how many such appeals have been made in the last 15 years? It is surprising that about four lakh offenders are imprisoned and only 35,000-40,000 are released on probation every year in our country when more than 60 per cent offenders are eligible for probational release. At present, after submitting investigation report to the court, the probation officer remains only a passive observer in trial proceedings when he ought to be very active because of his knowledge of offender's background. It could, therefore, be emphatically stated that it should be the probation officer's main responsibility to get that offender released on probation in whose case after thorough investigation he really feels the need of his release on probation. By this, no change is being suggested in any section of the Act but only the need of taking Section 11 of the Act more seriously by the probation officers is being emphasised.

Conditions of Release

The other problem for analysis is the conditions of release as provided in the bond under Section 4 of the Probation Act. In this connection, it could be submitted that some of the conditions provided in the bond are extremely superfluous. For example, take the conditions of dissociation with persons of bad character, abstention from intoxicants, abstention from anti-social acts not committing any offence punishable by law and endeavouring to earn an honest livelihood. In fact, these are the behaviour patterns which are expected of all law-abiding citizens in any society. When an offender is released on probation, the basic assumption is that he is being given one more opportunity to become a law-abiding citizen. When every citizen is expected to abstain from anti-social acts, when every citizen has to earn money by honest means, why should these conditions be specifically mentioned in the bond, particularly because even without specifying them, the offender can be penalised for not complying with them. What is needed is that only those conditions be prescribed which have a direct effect on the criminal value system of the probationer, which may enable the probation officer to manipulate both the formal and the informal institutional and group environment in which the probationer is to live during the probation period, and which are appropriate for individualised treatment of the probationer.

Indeterminate Term

The last point deals with Subsections 1 and 3 of Section 4 of the Probation Act which provides for prescribing the *fixed period* of probation and supervision by the court, ranging from one to three years. Subsection 1 says that the offender be released on probation of good conduct for a period not exceeding three years and Subsection 3 says that he be kept under supervision for a period of not less than one year. In this connection, it may be submitted that these provisions need a radical change. What is being suggested in their place is the system of *indeterminate* term which provides for fixing the minimum and the maximum period of probation by the court, the exact period being determined by only a Probation Board or a Committee. It may be argued that Subsection 1 of Section 8 of the Probation Act provides for variation of probation conditions, i.e., if a probation officer feels that the probationer need not necessarily be kept under supervision any longer, he can request the court for discharging the bond. It is also known that in several cases in India, the probation terms have been reduced on appeal by probation officers. But the contention here is, why should this power of reducing the term be given to the courts only? If indeterminate term system is accepted, this power will automatically be exercised by the Probation Boards, and it would save them the cumbersome practice of approaching the courts. Convincing the courts for revoking or reducing the probation term is not so easy today since it has already been pointed out that the present judiciary continues to be committed to the old concepts of free will and hedonism in the causation of crime and believes in protecting the interest of only society rather than those of both society and criminals. Knowing, therefore, that probation officers are definitely more concerned with criminals' welfare, it is suggested that subsections and sections pertaining to the term of probation be amended and the policy of indeterminate term be introduced in this country.

It may be reiterated that we should be more pragmatic and rational in making modifications in the various sections of the Probation Act. Only a critical philosophy and a new consciousness should be the basis of assessment, evaluation and amendment. The recourse to negative sanctions must be taken in as rational a manner as possible. We should have sane and humane crime policies and greater caution should be exercised in resorting to criminal legislation. The goal of 'protecting the community'—admittedly a commendable one—must not serve as an excuse to ignore and deny the legitimate and substantive rights of criminals as individuals. The newer approaches represented by casework and its socio-psychoanalytic foundations have to find unanimous approval of legislators, administrators and scholars.

PAROLE

Parole is "releasing a prisoner from the prison into the community under certain conditions for a specific period, after he has served a portion of the prison sentence." Conventionally, parole is described as the granting of a *privilege* of release for a short period rather than a right. Release on parole is granted in return for an offender's compliance with rules in the prison. After release on parole, the parolee continues to be subject to the threat of penal confinement, if official expectations are not fulfilled. The supervision by an agent of a correctional agency is supposed to serve the parolee's interests by offering guidance and assistance.

It may, thus, be said that the important characteristics of the parole system are:

- Release from prison after completing a specified portion of prison sentence.
- Imposition of certain conditions for behaviour.
- Remaining under the control of officials of prison/correctional institution, or supervision by a probation or a police officer.
- Returning to prison after completing the parole term.

The objectives of parole are: (i) to check frustrations and attitudes of bitterness and hopelessness among long-term prisoners; (ii) to enable an offender to live with his family members during emergencies, particularly at the time of marriage, death, harvesting, etc.; (iii) to help the offenders to gratify their varied needs; (iv) to help the prison administration to use the strategy of parole-release as the carrot to seek prisoners' conformity to prison rules, to preserve internal order in prison, and to motivate inmates to accept work assignments.

Parole is intended to mitigate the adverse consequences of imprisonment. It shortens confinement and conceivably balances its deterrent effects by releasing inmates at that point in their prison career when they are most prepared for constructive adjustment to the community. McGrath (*Canadian* prepared for constructive adjustment to the community. McGrath (*Canadian Journal of Criminology and Corrections*, 1972: 241) says that parole in practice is utilised primarily as an ameliorative device that preserves the equity of penalties. Here the Parole Board takes a hand in sentencing decisions which a judge may not be inclined to take. For example, the Parole Board may recognise meritorious behaviour during violent prison incidents, exemplary behaviour in prison, and dedication to work in prison industries.

In India, eligibility for parole entails: (i) serving at least one-third sentence of the total term of imprisonment; (ii) evaluation of the inmate's record of behaviour in prison; (iii) granting parole only to long-term prisoners; (iv) parole period varies from state to state. For example, in Rajasthan, first parole release may be granted for 20 days after eleven months stay in the prison, second may be granted for 30 days after 22 months prison-stay and third may be granted for 48 days after staying in jail for 33 months. After the third parole, the prisoner may be granted premature release. The Inspector/Director General, Prisons has the authority to grant fifteen days parole in emergencies while the superintendent of a central jail may grant seven days parole under similar (emergency) circumstances; (v) before release on parole, a prisoner has to sign an agreement with the prison authorities for conforming to set release conditions; and (vi) the district magistrate is informed of the prisoner's release on parole so that he may arrange either police surveillance or probation officer's supervision.

This analysis enables us to point out similarities as well as differences between probation and parole. The similarities are: (1) Both systems represent a break with the classical theory of punishment. (2) Both are meant for selected offenders. (3) Both involve supervision. (4) Both take into consideration the crime as well as the criminal. The differences between the two are: (1) In parole, some period is spent in jail but not in probation. (2) Parole is granted by prison authorities while probation is granted by the courts. (3) Parolees are considered to be in custody during the parole period but not probationers. (4) Influence of punitive reaction to crime is clearly present in parole but not in probation. Probation is 'pure' treatment.

A question is often raised as to who should decide the release of a prisoner on parole, or what should be a consistent and competent decision-making body? At one time, this authority was given to the district magistrate who depended on the police report for his decision. The police knew nothing of the offender's behaviour in prison. There was thus the possibility of use of corrupt methods in getting parole release. The system was therefore changed and the authority for parole release was given to the Inspector General, Prisons, who constitutes a small board which includes the superintendent of jail also. Now, it is suggested that to check the possibility of corruption in the new system as well as to check biases and high-handedness of the Inspector General, Prisons and the superintendent jail in denying parole release, there should be a separate Parole Board altogether consisting of prison officials, a representative of police department, probation officer, a social worker, a doctor and a psychiatrist sociologist. The Parole Board should meet twice a year. For taking decisions, the Parole Board should not depend only on the information supplied to it by the prison department but may consider the information collected through secondary sources for dispassionate review of the relevant facts. Instead of making parole an extension of organisational interest of a prison, it should be made a rehabilitatory measure in the correction of offenders. The Parole Board members of course have to share prison department concern regarding a public outcry against 'undue' leniency. The possibility of public protest against parole of prisoners with more than average risk of failure must be balanced against the probability that arbitrary denial of parole will make parole a sham. The Parole Boards have to function as autonomous decision-makers functioning as 'neutral and detached' bodies. The Parole Boards may be made accountable to public, especially in the matter of revocations, i.e., sending parolees back to prison for violation of parole conditions. Measures like this will make the parole system really effective in achieving its set objectives.

References

Ahuja, Ram, "Probation Act: A Sociological Appraisal", *Indian Journal of Social Work*, Bombay, Vol. XL, No. 2, July 1979.

Caldwell, R., *Criminology*, Ronald Press Company, New York, 1956.

Dressler, David, *Practice and Theory of Probation and Parole* (2nd edn.), Columbia University Press, New York, 1969.

Reid, S.T., *Crime and Criminology*: Chapter 18, the Dryden Press, Illionis, 1976.

Social Defence, National Institute of Social Defence, New Delhi, July 1987, and January 1990.

Sutherland, E.H. and Cressay, D.R., *Principles of Criminology* (6th edn.), The Times of India Press, 1965.

Chapter 16

The Police

THE POLICE AND THE SOCIETY

The police have two main roles to play: crime investigation and crime prevention. The policemen's job is thus to enforce laws that protect people and property. It is said that the police reacts *after* crime is committed but plays no part in the causes of criminality. No wonder, with this presupposition, traditional criminologists did not pay much attention to the analysis of the role of law enforcement agencies. In recent years, however, the police organisation is paid more attention. This is because of the new role expected of the police, their increasing work-load, and the increasing corruption in the police system. Whether or not the police acknowledges police corruption, harassment, and violence, the public now wants some plain answers to some plain questions. In a meeting on January 17, 1995 of senior police officers with school children in Ludhiana (Punjab) under the programme of "catch them young" to refurbish police image and create a close understanding with the public, the police officers were at a loss to answer quite a few embarrassing questions and explain their conduct in dealing with the day-to-day problems of the society. Among the questions asked were: why are the police officials corrupt? Why do the police stations not record First Information Reports (FIRs) promptly? Why do the police close their eyes to the crimes of sons and daughters of VIPs? Why do they nab ordinary citizens for the smallest failings? Why do they break the bones of suspects during investigations? Why do the cops not pay for the fruit and vegetables they buy, or for the rickshaw and the state transport buses they board? These questions not only made the officers realise that it was much easier to extort a confession than to answer straight questions, but also the fact that even small children had such a bad impression of the police and harboured many prejudices against them.

Though allegations of incompetence, corruption, brutalisation, violation of human rights, communalisation, unlawful conduct, partisan behaviour against the police have all been made before but what has lent a new edge to these allegations is some recent incidents like the firing and use of brutal force against people agitating for the creation of Uttrakhand on October 2, 1994, the handling of bloody communal riots in Maharashtra and other states which followed the demolition of Babri Masjid in 1993, butchery in Manipur, failure of the police to catch criminals like Veerapan and his gang members in Karnataka. The list of alleged police failures is indeed a long one.

How do some criminals fall into the hands of the police while a large number remain undetected? The fact is that the police is *reactive* rather than *proactive*. Most offences are not reported to the police at all either because they involve no victim or because the victims are afraid of harassment by the police. Moreover, police contacts with citizens are mostly in response to calls initiated by them rather than the result of police action through detection of offences. Further, the police arrest only those offenders who are poor and powerless. The rich and the influential manipulate to remain free. In addition, a large number of crimes fail to result in the apprehension of the law-violators largely because of the obstacles to police work caused by influential politicians and bureaucrats. Many crimes known to the police are handled in informal and discretionary ways by the policemen. No wonder, the police often become a target of public hostility and the police too promptly return these feelings.

Lastly, the police responds to the public outcry to reduce crime by not registering a large number of reported cases, or by registering crime under less heinous sections. In states like Uttar Pradesh and Bihar, non-registration and minimisation of crime is practised on such a large scale that the statistics have little relevance to the actual state of crime. Even a senior police officer like Ved Marwah has said: "Managing of statistics has taken the place of implementation of anti-crime measures." (*The Hindustan Times*, October 25, 1993). Such a response is, in fact, counter-productive because not enough gets known to the police about the actual state of crime to enable it to take counter measures for checking crime.

For these reasons, it is now considered essential by social scientists to understand the variables that influence the differential handling of cases by the police. The social scientists even today get cold reception in the police department for they are suspected of having a major interest in exposing the police to further public condemnation. Nevertheless, some scholars (like P.D. Sharma) have attempted to study police functioning and written books and articles on the police system. Some police officers too (like N.S. Saxena, Ved Marwah, K.S. Ghosh, K.S. Mathur, Rustom, Shankar Sarolia, etc.) have tried to study the internal working of the police system. Our analysis of the police in this chapter is not concerned with police administration or with police structures or police organisation; rather it deals with the police as they actually operate.

POLICE STRENGTH IN INDIA

In India, the police is classified as civil and armed police. The total sanctioned strength of police in the country is about 14 lakh (11.01 lakh civil and 2.98 lakh armed). Of this, 6 per cent posts were vacant in December 1998. Thus the total police force in 1998 comprised 13.15 lakh personnel. Of this, 10.2 lakh (77.5%) is civil police and 2.95 lakh (22.5%) is armed police (*Crime in India*, 1998: 347-48). Of the total civil police personnel, 86.9 per cent constitute constables and officers below the rank of assistant subinspectors (ASI), 12.2 per cent constitute assistant subinspectors, subinspectors (SI) and inspectors, 0.6 per cent constitute assistant superintendent police (ASP), and deputy superintendent police (DSP), and 0.3 per cent constitute superintendent police (SP), deputy inspector general police (DIG), and inspector-general (IG) and director general (DG) police (*ibid.*:347). The highest contingent of civil police (1.32 lakh or 12.95% of the total) is found in Uttar Pradesh, followed by Maharashtra (1.21 lakh or 11.9%). Among the union territories, Delhi has 41,491 civil police personnel (*ibid.*).

In the armed police, 94.6 per cent constitute constables and officers below ASI rank, 4.8 per cent constitute officers of ASI, SI and inspector rank, 0.4 per cent constitute officers of ASP and DSP rank, and 0.2 per cent are officers of SP, DIG, IG and DG ranks. Like the civil police, the maximum strength of the armed police (11.4%) is also found in Uttar Pradesh.

Women police force also has been created in the country. The total strength of the sanctioned women civil police is 20,229 whereas the actual strength in 1998 was 20,620 (*ibid.*: 349). Of the total women police force, 89.9 per cent are constables and head-constables, 9.8 per cent are ASI, SI and inspectors, 0.3 per cent are ASPs and DSPs, and 0.1 per cent are SPs and DIGs (*ibid.*: 349). The maximum strength of women police (18.7%) exists in Maharashtra. As regards women armed police, only Assam, Madhya Pradesh, Goa, Jammu & Kashmir and Delhi have such police. The total strength of women armed police in the country in 1998 was only 1,015.

An analysis of the adequacy of police personnel to the total population of India shows that there are 136 police personnel per one lakh people. While the police investigated 6.96 lakh cases in 1961, it investigated 23.04 lakh cases (including pending cases) in 1998 (*Crime in India*, 1998:14).

WORKING PERSONALITY OF POLICEMEN

Sociologists are familiar with the notion that a man's occupation influences his personality. The varied conditions under which men earn their livelihood heavily influence their general perspectives on life and their modes of social participation. Keeping this point in mind, some features of policemen's 'working personality' have been sketched. Jerome Skolnick (*Justice Without Trial*, 1966: 42-70) has given the following features of policemen's personality: suspiciousness, conservatism, cynicism, prejudices, defenders of status quo, lack of desire for rapid social change, and social isolation from others. However, Robert Balch (*Journal of Criminology, Criminal Law and Police Science*, March 1972: 106) is of the opinion that there is no empirical evidence that the police can be distinguished by a particular personality type. Actually, a policeman is no different from the rest of the population. Policemen are very ordinary people who happen to be extraordinarily visible. It is the elements of danger and authority which are central to police work that lead policemen to develop these characteristics. Police officers come to be especially attentive to unusual situations, for the unpredictable is also likely to be dangerous. The dangerous aspects of their work and their task of compelling others to obey laws, many of which are unpopular with citizens, give rise to police solidarity and policemen's remaining reserve in developing contacts with others. Mostly they are involved in interaction with one another rather than with most other occupational groups.

Why does the policeman become authoritarian? It is not as if only authoritarian types are recruited in the police system. The fact is, normal people, once in the system, tend to become authoritarian. It is the police system, not the personality of the candidates, that is the more powerful determinant of behaviour and ideology. It is common knowledge that police constables mainly come from the upper-lower class, lower-middle class, and the working class. They are young but have limited education. They have no background of the psychology and sociology of human behaviour. Their training may equip them with some legal knowledge but it does not make them socially mature persons. This is so because they come into contact with only a limited number of life-styles. Putting in long years of service, they gradually come to regard themselves as lower and middle class civil servants and bureaucrats. They usually work with problems. Their social world is small. They perceive the larger community as consisting of people who do not understand them, do not wish to help or cooperate with them, and hardly even praise them for the good work they do. Within the police, there is a feeling of social solidarity which helps them get the support of their colleagues and their superior officers in times of crises. The nature of their role does not give them the opportunity to strike friendships. As a result of this isolation, departmental social solidarity, and the role entrusted to them, the police develop a subculture of their own.

A policeman faces the problems of *role conflicts* because of his position in society. Rapidly increasing demands are being made on the police at a time when they have limited resources, money, personnel and training. They are supposed to suppress protestors of all types (youth, peasants, workers, women, tribals, government employees, doctors, advocates and what not) but they are not supposed to use force against them, to hurt them or to injure them. They are unequipped to cope with the social ills that trigger these people to action. If they succeed in their roles, politicians get the credit, but if they fail, they are blamed by the politicians.

A policeman cannot always act according to the law. He is authorised to shoot a criminal who is trying to run away from the police station but most likely he will not shoot him because society does not expect him to shoot anybody. He can assault a person who is trying to set a public building on fire but he will not do that because society expects him only to arrest him and leave the punishment part to the courts. During riots—whether it is communal riots or students' riots—in which the possibility of killing, looting and destroying is quite great, he is expected not to use force because he is bound to be criticised later for excess use of force.

He faces the criticism of the media, the wrath of the citizens, unwarranted outbursts of politicians, and irritation of high police officials. He cannot punish a husband who beats his wife. He cannot show his emotions when he arrives at the scene of an accident and finds people crying. He faces lack of public acceptance.

Policemen also face conflict between the policing role and the rule of the law or protecting individual rights of citizens. The role of policing emphasises initiative rather than disciplined adherence to rules and regulations. The rule of law emphasises the rights of individual citizens and imposes constraints upon the initiative of policemen. This conflict between the operational consequences of initiative and efficiency on the one hand and legality on the other, constitutes a serious problem for the police.

Policemen also face conflict between loyalty to colleagues and honesty. What should a policeman do when he comes to know that another policeman has taken a bribe, or has deliberately helped a criminal to escape, or has manipulated evidence and involved an innocent person, or has done something dishonest? If he reports this dishonesty, he is criticised by his colleagues and if he ignores the dishonesty his own conscience as an honest officer pricks him. It is these dilemmas which affect his role performance.

Lastly, the policeman often faces role conflict in the courts. The credibility of police who testify in court appears to have been eroded. There was a time when a cop who testified with assurance helped the prosecutor in presenting his case. But now even the prosecutor wants him to manipulate his evidence. The defendant shows respect to the judge and the lawyer but he looks at the policeman with scorn. The policemen today feel that like the public, the judge also supports the accused. The police now talk of 'judicial leniency' in the disposal of cases. They hold that they take lots of pains in collecting evidence but the judges dismiss the evidence as unreliable. In India, in 1998, about 23.04 lakh cases under the IPC, inclusive of the pending cases, were taken up for investigation by the police. Charge-sheets were submitted in 12.71 lakh cases. The courts took up only 8.95 lakh cases for trial. Of these only 37.4 per cent cases were convicted (1998: 14). The policemen thus feel that they already had been lenient inasmuch as they had arrested only those persons who deserved punishment but, the courts, by not prosecuting all the arrested persons, in fact, put the police on trial.

DISCRETIONARY ACTION

Although the police publicly asserts that all laws are enforced uniformly and universally and without any discrimination yet the fact is that the police goes in for selective enforcement of criminal laws. This discretionary and selective enforcement is of two kinds: one is based on the policy that the police do not enforce certain laws, even though the conditions these laws attempt to regulate do exist in the community. For example, the running of gambling dens and of hotels which provide call-girls. The police adopt *tolerant* policies that allow such laws to be violated with impunity. The other is the policy of differential application of laws to different individuals, that is, the police often apprehend some, but not all persons whom they observe violating some law, or as is more frequently the case, those who have been reported to them by some citizens.

One common complaint against the policemen is that they practise discrimination against persons who come from villages, are poor and illiterate, and belong to underprivileged groups. Cases of the police helping rich, educated, and influential persons involved in crimes in the matter of getting bail are numerous as compared to the arrested poor. Likewise, poor persons are arrested even on a slight suspicion while the arrest of well-to-do people is avoided. Even when an identification parade is arranged, witnesses are given prior hints against the poor accused before their coming to police station, while in the case of the rich accused, many obstacles are created for witnesses. The police, court, and prison records also show that the cases with regard to offences like vagrancy, petty thefts, excise offences, railway offences, and other such minor offences are significantly larger against the illiterate and the poor persons. Even if it is contended that the poor are really more involved in these offences, the police tend to treat similar types of offences committed by the upper-middle and upper-class people more leniently. Perhaps, the economic status of the offenders from upper groups helps them (the policemen) line their pockets. In any case, discrimination is seen to be practised when the police is informed of the crime from rich neighbourhoods. The police is slow in responding to calls from localities inhabited by poor persons. Thus, decisions taken against the poor create suspicions in the mind of the public and attract the charge of discrimination and existence of bias.

Many police officials defend their discretionary actions on the plea that if they strictly followed rules, the judicial machinery will come to a halt and prisons would overflow and people and the media would complain of police highhandedness. The argument is also advanced that judicious enforcement of laws is needed to keep petty offenders out of the legal machinery while serious offenders do receive intensive attention. No doubt such policy best serves the interests of society but the problem arises when the discretion of the police is a biased one in favour of the rich and the influential. If a son of a chief minister steals a car, he is admonished and released but if a son of a poor clerk or a teacher does the same thing, he is arrested and put behind bars. There should be some principles to guide the police in exercising discretionary powers. Instead of taking decisions purely on a subjective basis, the policemen should try to be a little more objective so that people who suffer at their (police) hands are compelled to concede that the police are morally right in their activity.

LIMITATIONS ON POWERS

While policemen have the responsibility of apprehending all law-violators, a significant fact is that the police functions under so many constraints.

First, the rule of law in a democratic society emphasises the rights of individual citizens and places constraints upon the initiative of legal officials. According to Sholnick, this conflict between the operational consequences of ideas of order and initiative on the one hand and legality on the other constitutes the practical problem of police. Herbert Packer has also talked of conflict between the Crime Control Model and the Due Process Model. The Crime Control Model expects disposition of persons suspected of crime as the central value to be served by the criminal process. The Due Process Model expects to respect and maintain the dignity and autonomy of the individual. The Crime Control Model is administrative and managerial and the Due Process Model is judicial. The Due Process Model thus acts as an obstacle.

Secondly, some persons would applaud the police for harassing gamblers, call-girls, pimps, known criminals with past records, anti-social elements, eve-teasers, etc. but all these individuals as well as many other individuals would contend that the police is unnecessarily harassing them. When the police suspect somebody as being involved in crime, they take him to the police station for interrogation. In such situations the main charge levelled against the policemen is that they use third-degree methods in getting a confession from the suspected person. Even when this is not true, the image of the policemen is such that people take it for granted that violence must have been used against the suspects/accused persons at the police stations.

Thirdly, the procedural rules laid down by the courts for the police for collecting evidence against the accused persons many a time act as obstacles that prevent the police officers from doing their job to the extent of their capabilities.

Fourthly, the constitution guarantees the protection of fundamental rights of all individuals. The rich, the influential and the people with some political and bureaucratic contacts raise objection against searches, against being issued summons for testifying in the courts, and so on. Sometimes, the police officers are compelled to search without warrant, interrogate suspects for unduly long periods of time, and employ a variety of other expedient techniques to make arrests. The ignoring of procedural rules by the policemen is often criticised and used for describing their activities as harassment of the innocent.

Fifthly, many a time politicians in power pressurise the police not to take any action against law violators only because they (the violators) help them (the politician) in elections. In such difficult situations, the police either accept—not infrequently-political orders of the rulers on administrative grounds or resort to emphasising 'due procedure'.

HUMILIATING BEHAVIOUR AND VIOLENCE

People who fall in the clutches of the police generally complain of brutal behaviour of the police towards them either at the time of arrest, during interrogation, or while in the police lock-up. Some of the common practices of policemen reportedly are: use of abusive language or degrading epithets, compelling suspects/accused/offenders to obey all orders, asking embarrassing questions in the street, carrying out bodily searches on false pretexts and appropriating offenders' money and belongings (wrist-watch, etc.), repeated prodding with a thick stick, delivering blows to the offenders with hands and fists as also kicking them, arresting individuals with intent to harass them, holding out threats of violence if not obeyed and the actual use of physical force and violence. People consider these practices degrading to their status and violative of their rights. Further, these obnoxious actions on the part of the police not only cause them harassment but also restrict their freedom.

Strangely enough, it is not the nature of offence committed by the accused that precipitates the use of force by the police, rather it is the accused person's behaviour which leads to the use of force. The behaviour which verges on open defiance of a particular policeman's authority rather than of the authority of the police organisation in general elicits the use of force. A policeman is rattled by a simple refusal to acquiesce in his authority. If the accused person, when told to sit down does not do so, he is beaten up. A person is slapped for his refusal to approach the policeman and identify himself. Policemen are more likely to respond with force when they perceive the situation as one in which the question as to who is 'in-charge' remains undefined.

People belonging to the poorer sections of society are the most likely targets of ill treatment, harassing orders, and abusive language. If one talks to rikshaw-pullers, auto-rikshaw-drivers, labourers, cyclists, and scooter-drivers, it may be found that in two to three out of every ten respondents, the police will have "talked down to them", or "called them a bad name", or unnecessarily searched them. Young persons returning home after watching a late night movie or when going out for a walk late in the night are found to be most vulnerable to harassment. The youths have a natural dislike for authority. Their antipathy towards the police is heightened when any situation of friction arises. Police feel an obligation to receive respectful behaviour from youths both to symbolise their law-abiding attitude and to attest their acceptance of the policeman's authority. The youths, however, feel an equal need to establish and maintain their autonomy. The youths hold that their behaviour is a strictly private affair while the police insist with equal conviction that behaviour of all people in the streets is their legitimate concern. Feeling themselves both demeaned and challenged, the youths react with more or less open defiance and hostility, slouching or smirking or answering the policeman in an off-hand or uncooperative manner, thereby challenging the policeman. In that situation, the policeman, fearful of losing face and sacrificing authority on future occasions, feels virtually forced either to arrest the youth for a vague or minor offence (loitering, suspicion of theft, attempting to pick someone's pocket, disturbing the peace) or to make it appear that he is being let off because of the goodness of the policeman's heart. This, thus, is the backdrop for conflicts and encounters between the police and the people which result in trips to police stations. These shape their views of each other.

In recent years, the police has come to be very much criticised for the use of force and violence. During the British period, the policemen used violence against the political leaders fighting for political independence of the country. Today, the police uses violence under the orders of these very political fighters. who have now become rulers and need protection from the people who elected them as their representatives to serve the country. The policemen thus serve the rulers more than common people in society. In the last few decades, criticism of the police over illegal use of violence has been most apparent in the areas of demonstrations, communal disturbances, political agitations and campus unrest. Although some charges may have been exaggerated, there is little doubt that policemen often do use force in their dealings with citizens in which violence clearly exceeds the demands of the situation.

Numerous cases of police torture, rape and custodial death have been appearing in the press at frequent intervals. On April, 9, 1994, the police in Delhi arrested and beat up the young son of a Secretary to the Union Government for objecting to the obstructive parking of the vehicle of a police SHO near a market. A retired professor was pulled up by his shirt and slapped by police SHO for hitting his jeep from the rear side. Amnesty International has given details of many such cases for several years. Its 1992 report said, "some of those who have died in police custody appear to have been innocent of any crime. Often they were detained illegally with no charge registered against them."

CUSTODIAL CRIMES

The studies of custodial crimes indicate that crimes in custody have shown an upward trend. Most prevalent crimes in police custody are: assaults of various types, rape and murder. These custodial crimes have drawn attention of public, media, legislatures and even Human Rights Commission. The data pertaining to custodial crimes way collected for the first time in 1995. The data for years indicate that while there were 31 custodial deaths in 1995, their number in 1996 was 49, in 1997 was 40 and in 1998 was 46 (*Crime in India*, 1998:311). The number of rapes each year was six. However, one study made in 1992 indicated 149 deaths in police custody in 1991 against 112 in 1990. Maharashtra accounted for the maximum number (23) followed by Andhra Pradesh (15), Uttar Pradesh (10), Rajasthan (11), Kerala (11), and Delhi (6) (*The Hindustan Times*, June 26, 1992).

The People's Union of Democratic Rights (PUDR) looked into custodial cases of violence between November 1989 and February 1994 and submitted its report in April 1994. It pointed out 12 incidents of custodial rape involving 24 policemen. Surprisingly, not even one was convicted. Seven cases were closed and in five cases, the victim women retracted their charge of rape despite overwhelming medical and circumstantial evidence to the contrary. Of the ten dismissed policemen, four were reinstated (*The Hindustan Times*, May 27, 1994) and the rest were accused in a case where the victim had already retracted.

COMPLAINTS AGAINST POLICE PERSONNEL

A good number of complaints were reported to the police authorities against police personnel. The number of complaints received in 1995 was

76, 954 (excluding Bihar, Gujarat and Meghalaya), in 1996 was 36,624, in 1997 was 1,23,523 and in 1998 was 88,628 (*Crime in India*, 1998:337). The inquiries instituted against these complaints were of three types: departmental, magisterial and judicial. In 1998, the total number of inquiries held (against 88,628 complaints) were 9,281, i.e., in 10.5 per cent of the reported complaints. Of these, 91.6 per cent were departmental inquiries, 2.4 per cent were magisterial ones and 6 per cent were judicial ones. Of these, the number of complaints declared false/unsubstantiated was 34.9 per cent while cases were registered in 3.6 per cent cases only. After inquiry, 65.4 per cent cases (out of 3,242 cases) were reported for departmental action and 34.6 per cent cases were sent for trial (*ibid.*: 337).

Mostly, it is the lower ranks of the police who indulge in torturing and roughing up the accused/suspects in police stations. Referring to custody violence, the Calcutta High Court gave a direction in one case in June 1992 for a continuous judicial monitoring of conditions in lock-ups. The Ministry of Home Affairs convened a meeting of Directors General of Police and Home Secretaries of various states in November 1992 to discuss the issue of custody deaths and find remedial measures for these barbaric acts. The outcome is still awaited after four years. It is well known that corruption, irresponsibility, groupism and snobbery are the building blocks of this crime (custody deaths). Enacting legislation for safe custody and medical examination of the accused, payment of fines by the accused police officers in the event of conviction (as was done by the Supreme Court in one case from Orissa in April 1993 by ordering to pay a compensation of Rs. 1.5 lakh to the petitioner), senior police officers visiting police stations from time to time to keep a watch on torture—all these may reduce police excesses.

How does a policeman permit himself to engage in physical brutality against the accused persons? At police stations, his use of force is supported by his colleagues. In riots, just as civilians remain unidentified, the policemen who torture cannot be easily singled out. The witnesses may cite their observation of seeing policemen beating the people severely, of hitting the young and the old who fell to the ground bleeding, and of dragging the people by their legs, but the witnesses do not recognise the particular policemen. The cloak of anonymity thus works well. Some researchers and commissions have described the police behaviour as so appalling and sadistic that it has become a burning issue for civilized men, but little has been done to improve the situation.

Some scholars have suggested that police violence is routine behaviour both statistically and in terms of police attitude towards the violence. The police do not see it as a dark sin of which they should be ashamed or about which they ought to feel guilty.

Some people have justified (some forms of) police violence because of the occupational problems policemen face. In arresting felons, getting confession from hardened criminals or sexual offenders, teaching a lesson to those who tease/molest women or to the exploiters of the weak, if force is used by the police, they need not be blamed. What may be criticised is the 'third degree' methods against the poor or violence used for personal gains which police thinks is necessary to protect the status of their profession.

Policemen themselves justify their use of violence on expedient grounds. Police values particularly uphold the use of force if it creates fear, disperses crowds, elicits required information, and teaches a lesson to the criminal. In those offences, where the police finds it difficult to get the offender sentenced by the court, police officers regard violence as particularly useful as it operates as a deterrent to future conduct. Besides, the policemen consider the use of force appropriate in those cases too where respect needs to be obtained from hostile or defiant persons. Some people feel that abuse, intimidation and brutality remain common features in many police stations, though others believe that abusive physical force is much less commonly encountered at police 'thanas' (stations) than is harassment of various forms and verbal abuse. Whether the level of violence is low or high, any abuse of citizens by the police should be a cause for concern, in that instances of undue force can touch off citizen protests and disorder as well as undermine public confidence in the police.

How are the police to be brought under control so that they refrain from abusive conduct directed at the citizens? What are the impediments to efforts to "police the police"? The major obstacles are the policemen themselves. The police use an arrest together with the necessary testimony, to cover almost all street-corner abuses. The testimony is usually effective in covering the abuse for perfectly natural reasons; for example, because there is no one in the courts to contradict it except another policeman, and he will not do so. The police solidarity is a good protection in such cases. Since all policemen share similar values and since they never care and dare to betray one another's mistakes, including the officers high up in the chain, all policemen are protected from criticism. Perhaps, creation of a specialised agency, independent of the police, to handle, investigate, and make recommendations on citizen complaints, may succeed in 'policing the police'.

INTERROGATION

The behaviour of the police personnel at the various police stations in a large majority of the cases is usually described as discourteous and based on excessive use of force. A police station is the first place where an accused person—whether innocent or a law-violator—comes into direct contact with the law-enforcers for the first time in his life. Naturally, the manner in which the policemen talk to a person determines his attitude towards law and law-maintainers. The use of verbal abuse, insulting behaviour, and physical violence on the part of the policemen arouses deep hostility against the police. Many accused persons complain that they were interrogated by the police without sufficient evidence for accusation. Perhaps the idea is that if a person is interrogated long enough, he might confess to a crime. Those who refuse to confess are often tortured or threatened with torture. A good number of accused persons claim in the courts that confessions from them were obtained not by use of physical brutality but by psychological cruelty, like holding out a threat to criminally assault the accused person's sister or daughter or wife, to arrest his old father or mother, to level additional charges of crime against him, and so forth. The accused are taken into custody and interrogated for hours together without telling them that they have a right to have a lawyer present. The police obtain written confessions from the accused, maintaining that these are voluntary and made with full knowledge that these could be used against them and that they fully understood their legal rights. These confessions are admitted into evidence at their trial. This is nothing but compelling the accused to be a "witness against himself".

Persons who are suspected or accused of crime/law-violation hold that they do not mind being interrogated provided it is made without using abusive language or derogatory remarks. Courtesy and politeness only build respect for the law and the law-enforcers.

It may not be out of place to suggest here a code of conduct for the policemen interrogating the accused at police stations: (1) The policemen should not show any bias against the accused, particularly those who are illiterate, who come from the villages, who behave like rustics and show little politeness during interrogation. (2) They should control their behaviour patterns, use polite language and conduct themselves in a dignified and courteous manner. Any genuine complaint against their rude behaviour should be given due consideration at the time of their postings, transfers and promotions. (3) They should not 'talk down' or physically assault any person or use derogatory terms against the accused person's parents and relatives which might arouse his anger. (4) They should try to maintain informal contacts with the accused in the lock-up and try to establish a rapport with them so that the stereotyped hostility of the wrong-doers gets diminished.

CORRUPTION

One accusation against the police is that it is not only brutal but also corrupt. Lawrence Sherman (*Police Corruption*, 1974) describing police corruption has said: "It is accepting money or money's worth for doing something that a policeman is under a duty to do or that he is under a duty not to do, or to exercise a legitimate discretion for improper reasons." Fabrication of evidence, sleeping on duty, avoiding assigned responsibilities are all forms of police 'misconduct' but not corruption. Corruption is mainly "taking bribes". Roebuck and Barker ("A Typology of Police Corruption", in *Social Problems*, No. 3, 1974: 324-37) have provided a typology of eight forms of police corruption: misuse of authority, kickbacks, opportunist theft, shakedowns, protection of illegal activities, the 'fix,' involvement in direct criminal activities and internal payoffs.

One view is that all policemen are not corrupt. It is only a few "rotten apples" who bring bad name to the whole department. The other view is that the majority are 'bad apples' and only a few are clean and honest.

Sherman (*Police Corruption*, 1974: 10) has talked of three forms of police corruption: one form of corruption is that in which only a few isolated policemen accept bribes. The second form of corruption is that in which a large number of officers (lower and higher ranks) take bribes but they are not joined together to form networks of corruption. Also, the bribes offered in this kind of situation are most frequently tendered by individual offenders and citizens rather than by organised criminal syndicates. The third form of police corruption is pervasive organised corruption. In this type, corruption is organised in a hierarchical authoritarian fashion. In fact, this type of corruption extends beyond the police department to the high criminal justice and political officials and revolves around the vice operations of a local crime syndicate.

What are the causes of police corruption? What factors encourage corruption? Many people do not agree that low salary of policemen is the main cause. A police constable in India begins his career in the grade of Rs. 850-1250 and gets about Rs. 2,300 per month, while subinspector, in the grade of Rs. 12501650 gets about Rs.3,200 per month. Though Rs

2,000 or Rs.3,000 a month in no case can be described a good salary but it is not so low as to compel a man to accept illegal gratification. The important factors which encourage corruption in police department can be enumerated as follows: (i) discretionary power of the police in deciding whether to arrest someone or not, (ii) low visibility of police work and the 'secret society' character of police organisation, (iii) certain laws designed to enforce morality also generate corruption. These laws prohibit services or goods that are in wide demand among members of the public. They, therefore, provide opportunities to the police to permit them by accepting bribes; for example, prostitution, liquor and gambling, and (iv) solidarity among policemen which provides them immunity from a high risk of being detected, apprehended and punished.

CRIMINALISATION OF POLICE

In the last three decades or so, different types of cases have been reported in newspapers which indicate the criminalisation of police. This is found in three forms: (1) policemen committing crimes themselves, (2) policemen helping criminals in committing crimes and getting a share out of it, (3) policemen resigning from the department and joining the militant groups engaged in killing, looting and abduction, etc. In these three types, we have not included police corruption which by itself is a crime.

Robberies, extortions, kidnappings for ransom, and rapes of innocent women are some of the crimes allegedly committed by men in uniform. On May 28, 1992, a head constable and two constables were among the five persons arrested for forcibly taking away an employee of a private firm ill Delhi and then extorting Rs. 1,100 from him. In June 1993, a constable of Delhi Armed Police allegedly kidnapped and raped a 16-year-old girl. A head constable and two constables were arrested in one state in July 1994 for allegedly extracting Rs. 40,000 from two youths after threatening to involve them in narcotic offences. In January 1996, four policemen were arrested in Delhi for following four passengers from the airport and trying to rob them of their gold and money. A few months earlier, a head constable posted at Indira Gandhi International Airport and a head constable working in the armed police battalion along with some others robbed a passenger and his friend of 66 gold biscuits worth more than Rs. 30 lakh. In March 1996, two constables in one city stopped an auto-rickshaw passenger, threatened him and took Rs. 4,000 from the complainant. These are some of the crimes reported in newspapers from time to time. A close scrutiny of the cases clearly indicates that in a large number of cases, it is the constables and head constables who are involved in crimes. Unless exemplary punishment is given to such undesirable elements, the image of men in uniform is bound to sink low.

Reacting to the non-tracing of a kidnapped girl by the Delhi Police, the Supreme Court observed on February 12, 1994: "This court is determined to show to this country what type of police force they are paying taxes for. If these police officers serve a sentence, then only they will learn lessons." A judge of the Allahabad High Court a few years earlier had observed that "the police was the most organised group of criminals".

Unlawful activity by a policeman has been described as a manifestation of personal moral weakness, a symptom of personality defects, or the recruitment of individuals unqualified for police work. Are the policemen themselves responsible for their criminality or is it the police system that patterns them in illegal practices? Should police crime be analysed through the individualistic approach or the group approach? The first approach assumes inherent personality characteristics to be the determinant which makes a policeman a criminal. Current literature on police personnel management reaffirms individualistic orientation towards police crime. This approach suggests that the quality of police service is dependent upon the individual policeman. A modified version of this (individualistic) approach is the view that perhaps the individual chosen had already become 'contaminated' prior to being recruited as a member of the police force, and when presented with chances for bribery or acquiring material things, the 'hard core guy' steps in. In contrast to this individualistic approach is the group approach. Scholars like McCorkle, Cloward and Merton see police crime as a natural consequence of societal demands for illegal services. When these desired services are not provided through legal structures, they are attained through illegal means. However, there is little empirical proof for this view. Some people suggest that "crime is a way of life of police". Large criminal gangs want police support in committing crimes. They, therefore, keep many police officers on their payrolls. The 'good' citizens also try to buy police favour whenever the occasion demands it. Once a policeman commits one 'crime', it becomes his 'norm' or 'informal standard' of his behaviour. Many policemen thus come to be 'socialised' in criminal behaviour 'permitted' in the police system. When the 'reference group' norms involving illegal activity become routinised with use, they become identifiable informal patterns of behaviour.

Some of the terms used to describe police deviancy have become popular. These are: *mufatkhori* (an act of receiving free 'gifts' like liquor, cigarettes, groceries, etc. For possible future acts of favouritism), *dadagiri* (police demand for free admission to picture houses and entertainment places, *shopping* (picking up small items from shops without payment), *vasooli* (demanding money for advertisements in police magazines or purchase of tickets to police functions), *bribery* (payment of cash), and *harapna* (appropriating expensive items for personal use). Amongst these activities, *vasooli*, bribery, shopping, and *harapna* are all clearly unlawful but the manner in which they are carried out contains a measure of safety to the policeman, should his presence or behaviour be questioned. A policeman's investigative powers allow him entry into houses, shops, etc. in which a 'suspected theft' has occurred or search a person who is 'suspected' to be involved in 'crime'. Hence, 'search' is not 'suspected', rather it is 'expected'. 'Shopping', *harapna* thus become easy. In one of the recent railway accidents, cases were reported in the newspapers in which villagers saw many policemen 'searching' the bodies, pockets and bags of the victims, later on reported as theft of ornaments, money and possessions. Criminalisation or "khaki-coat crime" is thus getting widespread in the police.

PUBLIC HOSTILITY

People perceive the police as intruders, exploiters, cynical, prejudiced, suspicious, and parasitical. The epithets used to describe the police—khaki drones, khaki mercenaries, *rakshasas*, etc.—reveal profound resentment against them.

Why have people antagonistic views of the police? Why are policemen targets of negative responses from citizens? Why do people say: "the less the police intrude into their affairs, the better." Why are people dissatisfied with law enforcement agencies?

One reason is that people believe that the police is frequently linked with organised criminals and corrupt officials in the operation of vice of various kinds. The police is often believed to be in collusion with gambling dens, drug traffickers, smugglers and with those who are engaged in illegal activities. They have a share in the illegal income of these criminals and/or their organisations.

Secondly, the police is believed to use various illegal and questionable methods in dealing with the accused, including the use of excessive physical force in effecting arrests. Anybody who dares to challenge a policeman's authority or his commands becomes a victim of police harassment. Even in dealing with a crowd of protesters, they use excessive lathi charge, tear gas and other gratuitous methods typical to the police force. Such incidents encourage the spread of public notions that the police department is a heaven for sadists. Whether or not these notions square with the facts, such images contribute to the low esteem in which policemen are held in society.

Third aspect of police hostility is the attitude of the police towards the citizens. The police adopts the posture that all people are suspicious criminals, all journalists are their enemies and all sources of mass media are interested only in belittling them. As a consequence, the police never give any information about their internal working. Whenever the police get a report against any policeman, they go out of their way to protect their fellow brothers even when they are the most deviant men in the force.

In spite of prevalent hatred, people do not articulate the resentment felt against the police because of the power it possesses and because they know that nobody would take their complaint seriously and effectively. Occasionally, the organised groups—say students in educational institutions, women's voluntary organisations, shop-keepers, etc.—may ask and agitate for drastic action against police harassment, but the criminals, as individuals, never raise their voice against police oppressions.

NEW ROLE

One way to control police abuse of power and misuse of discretion is for control to come from within the police department. This requires 'professionalisation'. Police must develop a professional orientation that is sensitive to individual rights. Efficient enforcement of the law is not the sole end of police function. The police are also responsible for a humane law enforcement policy. This includes conducting interrogations according to cannons of humane process of law, and desisting from dealing with an arrested suspect or with a person who challenges policeman's abuse of power, in a humiliating manner. Such professionalisation will go a long way in restoring credibility of the police in the courts which in recent years has been considerably eroded. Judges, prosecutors, lawyers and many educated witnesses in the courts fail to show proper deference to the policemen and often demean their status by treating them as less professional or even unprofessional. As such, it would be politic on the part of the police to become more judicious in dealing with the people. They should take a suspect into custody not merely for maintaining respect for the police system but for maintaining public morality.

In the tasks of crime detection and repression, police work is considered to be tedious and unglamorous. Much of the time of the police is wasted in providing security to the so-called VIPs. Little time is spent on patrolling to keep an eye on vagrants, pickpockets, and anti-social elements. Can the police be assigned the task of providing assistance or support on personal or interpersonal problems besides criminal matters? Although citizens may not always admire policemen, yet the police are the first persons who come to mind when people want someone to help/rescue them from the complexities of life. For example, a woman who is frequently battered by her husband would not like to lodge a complaint against her husband and getting him arrested, yet she would like the policeman warn her husband that if he didn't change his behaviour, he would be arrested and sent to jail. A tenant would like to have police help to save from his landlord's harassment. A consumer would like that the police help him in getting the spurious article changed. Is all this 'social work'? Can such assignments be called 'new role' for the police? Is the strength of the police force large enough for giving them such new 'jobs'? All this requires not only a study of enforcement practices but also political will for introducing changes. In fact, the above-mentioned 'jobs' are 'extensions' of patrolmen's assignments. Police superiors have to give explicit directives to policemen at the lower level to render this type of 'help' to the needy people. Such 'help' can be made 'paid help', i.e., anybody using the services of the police will have to pay for such 'jobs'. Police officers themselves may describe such ideas as ludicrous but what is important is changing the attitude of the police towards the public. The policemen have to realise that their job is to serve people and not to serve politicians. They have to realise that they have not only to 'catch' offenders but also to help the victims. It is true that the police cannot be made to serve as a 'jack-of-all-trades' organisation. Without making more funds and personnel available to the police department, the new tasks cannot be assigned to them. But once it is realised that the scope of the role of the police can be and should be extended beyond the traditional responsibilities, the procedural and manpower limitations can easily be removed.

POLICE ACCOUNTABILITY AND COMMITMENT

Should the police be committed to law, or to political executive, or to people? My contention is that police should remain committed to none of these but only to the 'role' it is expected to perform. What is the difference in the four priorities and why is "commitment to role" given top priority?

The Police Act of 1861 requires the police to remain committed to the political executive. Senior and learned police officers like N.S. Saxena, (former Director General, CRPF, Delhi) expect police to remain committed to law. The National Police Commission suggested that the police should be more concerned with protecting the interests of the people, i.e., it should remain committed to society. I hold that 'role commitment' on the part of the police is more important.

Everybody knows that our political rulers use and misuse the police for their vested interests. The unscrupulous self-seeking politicians abuse the strong arm of the police for their partisan ends. The two most recent examples of this are: not arresting controversial godman Chandraswami (supposed to be very close to the former Prime Minister of India, and having global connections) in spite of several charges pending against him; not arresting the culprits of 1984 riots in Delhi in which more than 3,000 Sikhs are alleged to have been killed; and not taking any action against politicians, bureaucrats, and several other public men who are supposed to have received 65 crores of rupees in the Hawala case for about four years, and, belatedly charge-sheeting only 25 selected persons out of 111 persons named in the diaries seized from S.K. Jain in January 1996.

Politicians always like to lord over the men in uniform. MPs and MLAs are quite often seen taking undue interest in the postings of SPs, DSPs, and even inspectors and constables in their constituencies so that they could help them not only in keeping an eye on their voters but also in protecting them in their illegal activities. This has turned our police force into a tool for subverting the process of law, for prompting growth of authoritarianism and for shaking the very foundations of democracy.

Section 3 of the Indian Police Act of 1861 (which has not been reframed even after 135 years because of the vested interests of the political elite) says that the 'superintendence' of the police shall vest in and be exercised by the state governments and its administration in the Director General of Police. At the district level, the administration of police shall vest in the district superintendent under the general control and direction of the district magistrate. The degree of 'superintendence' by the state government or 'directional control' of the district magistrate intended to be exercised is not specified. In practice, the state governments have been issuing executive instructions under Section 46(2) of the Act, which are contrary to the spirit of Section 3 of the Police Act. Many rules and regulations are framed by the state governments which amount to 'interference' which the law did not contemplate and which have been prejudicial to the interest of the police department.

In England, a police officer is considered an officer of the law. In India too, the judiciary expects our police to follow the rule of law. In the Hawala case, the Supreme Court had to direct the police to consider all people equal, irrespective of the position and status of the person. Commitment of police to law would thus mean that the police has the inherent authority to flout the orders of their political houses if they considered such orders a barrier in maintaining law and order in society. In a situation of this kind, if a superintendent of police wants to arrest a highly-placed bureaucrat for violating the law and if he is asked by the minister concerned not to do so, the superintendent of police will not bother to carry out the minister's orders but arrest the officer concerned. In 1984, the police wanted to arrest 26 persons in Aligarh (Uttar Pradesh) on the basis of police intelligence reports that they were likely to arouse communal feelings and start riots. The politicians, however, 'intervened' and saw that these persons were not arrested. And when communal riots actually broke out, more than 20 of the 26 suspected persons were found involved in the riots. This is an instance of commitment of the police to political bosses. Had the police been committed to law, they would not have bothered to obey the misconceived orders of their political bosses.

Now comes the commitment of the police to people or to society. In this case, even if the policemen have to deviate from the existing laws (as they always do in a large number of cases), they would do it not only for protecting the life and property of the people but also for bringing the most corrupt politicians and bureaucrats to the notice of the people and for arresting and prosecuting them in the courts. No doubt, this is desirable, however; I would like to go a step forward and suggest 'commitment to role' which surely is broader than 'commitment to society'. Sometimes, in their desire to protect the interests of society, the police might feel handicapped in taking action against those persons who, having really worked for society all their lives (say, through their scientific researches or for establishing heavy industries and thus providing employment to thousands of persons and earning foreign exchange in millions of dollars/pounds), suddenly decide to pass certain 'secrets' to the enemy country either for huge monetary benefits or on being pressurised by threats of violence/assassination of their kith and kin and so forth. Knowing well the loss to the country, the police might avoid taking action against such persons. But if committed to 'role', the police will ignore the supremacy of the political elite, the supremacy of the rule of law, the supremacy of society's interests, and surely take the desired action against the law-violator, giving importance to their 'role'. This is what is expected of the police today. The concept of 'police accountability' has thus to change, keeping in view the new goals to be achieved. Let us hope that soon the role of police will be redefined and there would be a conscious effort to make it an instrument of service to the people.

IMPROVING THE POLICE FORCE

A number of suggestions have been made for improving our police force. The more important ones are:

- Attempts should be made for improving the police-community relations. This can be made possible in a number of ways: (a) good work done by the police must be given prominence in the media; (b) occasional meetings of policemen and citizens be organised in police stations/colleges/universities and in public places in which the citizens and police give each other 'feedback' and mutual problems may be discussed openly; (c) cases in which policemen, accused of crimes and violence, are punished must be given publicity in the newspapers; (d) 'public morality' offences should be removed from criminal law; and (e) provision should be made for handling grievances against the police.
- Human sensitivity training may be imparted. Training in sociology and psychology of human behaviour, change in social, political and economic conditions of society, moral values, habits of mind, qualities of self-discipline, flexibility in approach, etc. are necessary for all policemen. It is time, the need for higher education for police is realised and policemen are given opportunities and incentives for obtaining training in higher education. Policemen can be deputed in universities for getting certificates and diplomas in law, sociology, social work and psychology. The most appropriate thing would be that these courses are run by the police academies with control by and recognition from the universities. The curricula for police science training also needs a fresh look.
- The system of recruitment at all levels needs to be looked into. Strict screening and objective assessment alone can produce competent policemen. In training new recruits, besides giving the basic training, specialisation should be encouraged gradually. Frequent and malafide

transfers affect the morale of policemen. Transfers and promotion issues have to be handed over to a non-political commission.

- The system of accountability and imparting punishment for custodial deaths and proved brutality must be introduced.
- Rural police system should be strengthened.
- The old method of entrusting the job of co-ordinating the various components of the criminal justice system to the district magistrate still continues. With separation of the judiciary from the executive after the amendment of the CrPC in 1974, and with mounting pressure of other responsibilities on the district magistrate, he is no longer able to perform this role. It is, therefore, necessary to build a new legal and institutional arrangement.
- There is a need to examine and modify laws and procedures to reduce the widening gap between the role of the police as defined by the various laws and the expectations of the common man, who turns to police for help whenever he becomes a victim of a crime.
- The civil police needs to be sufficiently strengthened both in terms of numbers and with regard to their training and equipment.
- Seeking police personnel for protection by politicians and bureaucrats has become a symbol of status. This system needs a radical change.
- A policeman should no longer be considered on duty for 24 hours. It might have had some relevance in the past but it is meaningless today. A practical system of working hours needs to be introduced.
- Laws should be changed. Much crime is created by legislatures that insist on making certain types of social behaviour criminal.

Howsoever the police may be hated, they are essential and indispensable. The people may be harassed, threatened and verbally and physically abused but they have to tolerate it all because the police safeguard life and property, protect the innocent against deception, the weak against oppression or intimidation, and the peaceful against violence. They protect the rights of all men to liberty, equality and justice.

References

Barlow, H.D., *Introduction to Criminology*, Little Brown and Co., Boston, 1976.

Caldwell, Robert, *Criminology*, Chapter 13, Ronald Press Co., New York, 1956.

Fitzgerald, M., McLennan C. and Pawson, J., *Crime and Society*, Chapters 4, 5, and 6, Routledge and Kegan Paul, London, 1931.

Gibbons, D.C., Society, *Crime and Criminal Careers*, (3rd edn.), Chapter 3, Prentice Hall, New Jersey, 1977.

Jhonson, Elmer H., *Crime, Correction and Society*, Chapter 13, The Dorsey Press, Illinois, 1978.

Radzinowiz, Leon and Wolfgang, M.E., (edn.), *The Criminals in the Arms of the Law*, Vol. II, Basic Books Publishers, New York, 1971.

Chapter 17

Victim in Crime

SCIENCE OF VICTIMOLOGY

While judiciary is generally concerned with protecting the interests of society, liberal criminologists till recently were concerned with protecting the interests of criminals. Radical criminologists have now started talking of protecting the interests of the victims of crime. This has resulted in the growth of victimology as a science. This is a science which, on the one hand, studies the degree and type of participation of the victim in the genesis or development of the offence, and, on the other hand, evaluates what is just and proper for the victim's relief and benefit. Schafer (1977: 1) has described victimology as "the science which studies criminal-victim relationship." Drapkin (1974: 2) has defined it as "that branch of criminology which primarily studies the victims of crime and everything that is connected with such a victim."

Some scholars have described victimology as a branch of criminology but Mendelsohn (1956) views it as an independent science, as "a science parallel to it" or better "the reverse of criminology". He has also proposed new terms such as 'victimal' as opposed to 'criminal', 'victimity' as opposed to 'criminality', 'victimal receptivity' meaning "individual's unconscious attitude for being victimised" (*see*, Krishna and Singh, "Victims of Crime", *Social Change*, September 1982, Vol. 12, No. 3: 48).

Victim in crime has no separate entity. He is viewed in relationship to the offender who has harmed him. That is why, offender and victim have been described by Mendelsohn (1956) as 'penal couple'. Who is a victim.? He is generally described as "a person who has sustained physical, material or moral damage owing to an unlawful act". According to Quinney (1972). "the victim is a social construction in the subject-object relationship in a crime situation." Khan and Singh (1980: 61) have defined a victim as "a person who has sustained psychological, physical, material or social damage on account of being the object of depredation (destruction)." The victim is not necessarily an individual. It may also be a collective entity like a family, a firm, a corporation, a group, or even a whole nation.

The need for scientific study of victim has been explained by Krishna and Singh (1982: 49) on several bases: (1) The gravity of the offence can be better determined by ascertaining as to how the victim feels about it. (2) The cause of crime becomes more discernible by analysing the victim's background and the situation contributing to crime. (3) The analysis of offender-victim relationship enables us to identify individuals or groups who are likely to be the targets of crime. (4) Victimological studies provide information about crime not reported to the police. These studies along with those studies where crime is reported to the police help in developing scientific theories of crime. Such studies serve heuristic, diagnostic and prognostic functions. (5) Victimological studies facilitate the chalking out of a viable preventive policy.

Several empirical studies have been conducted on victims in India, of which four are considered more significant. One is the study of 184 victims of dacoit gangs conducted by D.P. Singh in 1978. Another is the study of victims of homicide conducted by Rajan and Krishna in Delhi and Bangalore in 1981. This study aimed at evaluating the socio-psychological background of the victims of homicide, ascertaining economic loss to the bereaved families, and assessing compensation to the victims. The third is the study of victims of vehicle accidents in Delhi conducted by Khan and Krishna in 1981. It aimed at analysing accidents as psycho-social events looking into the role of victims in accidents and enquiring into the conditions of victims so as to assess their compensation needs. The fourth study was conducted by this author on the female victims of crimes committed by males, viz., dowry deaths, rapes, kidnapping, wife-beating, and murders (*see*, *Crime Against Women*, 1987). The Bureau of Police Research and Development, New Delhi, brought out a compilation "Compensation to Victims of Crime" in 1979. This document looks into the legal provisions relating to victims' compensation in different countries. All this shows how interest in victimology has grown in our country in the recent years.

ROLE OF VICTIM IN CRIME

It is now believed that many a time the victim induces or facilitates the commission of crime. There are certain offences in which the victim plays a very important role and works towards the success of crime, e.g., abortion, prostitution. The study of victim-offender relationship is, therefore, considered necessary today for determining the question of guilt of the offender and for fixing up the nature and amount of penalty for the offender.

Ellenberger (quoted by Shultz, *Crime mid Delinquency*, April 1968) has said: "There is some degree of mutuality between the offender and the victim. To know the offender completely, we must also be acquainted with his contemporary partner-the victim. From a certain perspective, the victim may shape or mould the offender. A careful investigation of many offences reveals a psychological interaction between offender and victim that makes one indistinguishable from the other." Shultz (1968: 137) has held: "The concepts of aggressor and victim are not always absolutely opposite. The aggressor is not always guilty and the victim is not always innocent. The terms 'victim' and 'aggressor' are sometimes interchangeable. The personality of the victim as a cause of the offence is sometimes more significant than that of the offender."

How does a victim instigate the criminal? Four methods may be pointed out in this context: (1) by direct provocation, (2) by indirect provocation, (3) by omission of preventive measures, and (4) by emotional pathology. Garofalo (*Criminology*, Little Brown and Co., 1914: 373) too noted that the victim might provoke another individual or attack, and though the provocation be slight, if perceived by an egoistic attacker, it might be sufficient to result in homicide.

Wolfgang has used the term "victim-precipitated" for crimes in which the victim is a direct, positive precipitator. The role of the victim is characterised by his having been the first (in using weapon, in striking a blow, in verbal abuse) in the crime situation to use physical force directed against the subsequent offender. However, mutual quarrels and wordy altercations do not constitute sufficient provocation under the law, and these are not included in the meaning of 'victim-precipitated crime'.

A few examples of victim-precipitated crimes may be cited.

On several occasions, a man threatens to kill his wife since he suspects her of having illicit relations with his friend. One day, he assaults her with his hands and feet while she is cooking food in the kitchen. The wife suddenly picks up a knife from a table nearby and warns the husband against further beating her. In the ensuing struggle, the husband falls on the knife and gets killed.

In another case, the victim is the aggressor in a fight, having struck his opponent several times. People try to intervene but the victim persists. Finally, the offender retaliates with blows causing the victim to fall and hit his head on a stone, as a result of which he is seriously injured.

A landlord uses vile names against his tenant during an argument. The tenant tries to pacify him and even threatens to report him to the police. The landlord gives him an iron-rod and dares him to use it against him. Being repeatedly challenged, the tenant snatches the rod from his landlord and hits him.

Shultz (*op. cit.*, April 1968) explaining how a victim contributes to the offence has pointed out four methods:

1. *By provoking or initiating a hostile action on the offender*: For example, during a heated argument, one party hands the other party a gun and knowing full well the other's hostile mood, accuses him of not having "the guts" to shoot.
2. *By indirect invitation or incitation*: For example, a woman attacks her husband with a knife and snatching the same knife, the husband kills her. Or suppose a person 'A' has given a loan of Rs. 5,000 to another person Von the condition that he would return it in two months. When he fails to repay it even in six months and also tells 'A' that he has not taken any loan from him and he is free to take any action, 'A' assaults 'B', who is then hospitalised.
3. *By omission of normal preventive measures*: For example, a scooter or cycle theft victim parks his scooter or cycle without locking it. Further, in case of the scooter, the engine is left running. The thief gets an easy chance to steal it.
4. *By unconsciously inviting the offence through his/her (victim's) emotional pathology*: For example, an engineer's wife accepts gifts on the sly from her husband's contractor and tells her husband about it after a fortnight. The husband assaults her so severely that she becomes deaf and is admitted to a hospital. A case is registered with the police on the victim's brother's complaint.

Marvin Wolfgang ("Victim-Precipitated Criminal Homicide" in Wolfgang's, ed., *Sociology of Crime and Delinquency*, John Wiley and Sons, New York, 1962: 396) has said: "At present, societal attitudes are generally positive towards the victim and negative towards the offender, who is often feared as violent and dangerous threat to others. There is a great need to change this attitude."

Two types of studies may be quoted in the analysis of victim's role in crime: one on sex offences and the other on murders. In a study of 73 sex offences in 1955, Weiss found that 60 per cent victims were 'participative' in the offence; Glueck in his study of 185 sex offences in 1956 found the victims 'seductive' in 21 per cent cases; Radzinowicz in his study of 1994 sex offences in 1957 found the victims 'non-objecting' in 40 per cent cases; and Gagnon in his study of 330 female child victims of sex offences in 1965 found the victims "collaborative" only in 8 per cent cases.

On the other hand, in studies on murder, this author in his study of 136 murder cases in the late 1980s (Cf. *Crime Against Women*, 1987) found victims 'provocative' in 53 per cent cases. The victim's 'provocation' in victim precipitated murders was found in the form of infidelity in 12 per cent cases, ill treatment in 24 per cent cases, use of vile names during arguments in 18 per cent cases, striking a blow in altercation in 4 per cent cases, use of some weapon in 4 per cent cases, and victim's attempt to molest ego (offender) in 7 per cent cases. Wolfgang in his study of 588 murders found victim's provocation in 25 per cent cases, while Hentig found it in 85 per cent cases. Victims were found either collaborative, or seductive, or non-objecting, or participative.

Bender and Blau (Cf. Schultz, *Crime and Delinquency*, April 1968: 138) in their study of victims of sex offences in 1965 noted the following personality traits of the victims: (i) they are attractive, charming and seductive, (ii) they are promiscuous, (iii) they are impulsive and given to fluctuating moods, (iv) they make adult contacts easily, (v) they want pity and demand proof of affection, (vi) they have parents who encourage them to be 'sexy', and (vii) they defy their parents. Schultz, talking of the victims of sex offences, has said: "The victim is usually emotionally involved with the offender-spouse, parent, or lover. In many cases, when killers are submissive and passive, victims are domineering and active. The victim, therefore, exploits this trait of submissiveness of the offender, becomes critical, demanding, and unmerciful, or threatens to withhold love and affection. She thus instigates offender's overcontrolled hostility." Mendelsohn (Cf. *Excerpta Criminologice*, 1963) analysing the personality traits of victims in murders has said: "The victims of many assaults and homicides have what may be called an aggressive tyrannical personality and engage in acts with the offender which invite or excite assaultive response." Wolfgang (*op. cit.*: 395) analysed the previous arrest record of the victims and found that "In victim-precipitated cases, a high proportion of victims have previous arrest records than the offenders." Against 62 per cent victims having previous arrest record, only 54 per cent offenders had the previous arrest record. All these studies, thus, clearly point out the role of victim in crime.

VICTIM-OFFENDER RELATIONSHIP

The relationship between the offender and his victim is of great significance in crime. Wolfgang (1962) in his study of homicides found that family members, relatives, close friends, and acquaintances are the specific relationships between victims and offenders both in victim-precipitated and non-victim precipitated groups. In India, D.P. Singh (1978) found that in nearly one-fourth of cases, the dacoity-victim belonged to the village/mohalla (neighbourhood) of one or another gang member. In most cases, acquaintances of the gang leaders /members were responsible for the raids. In another study of murders, D.P. Singh (1980) found that a large number of murderers had murdered their family members, followed by neighbours, friends, and others. Rajan and Krishna in their study of homicides in Delhi and Bangalore in 1981 found that 22 to 39 per cent victims get murdered by relatives. Prasad in his study of female murderers in 1981 found that 40 per cent had murdered their husbands while the rest had murdered their children, husband's concubine, some family member, and so on.

This author conducted two empirical studies: one in 1967-68 on crimes committed by women (*see*, "Female Murderers in India", *Indian Journal of Social Work*, October 1970) which included 136 murders committed by women, and the other on crimes committed by males against females (i.e., one in which the victim was a woman) in 1985-86 (*see*, *Crime Against Women*, 1987) in which 33 murders were studied. Both the studies had analysed the aspect of homogeneity and heterogeneity along with various other aspects. Taking 169 murders in the two studies together, it was found that homogeneity in age between offenders and victims existed in 39.4 per cent cases and heterogeneity in 60.6 per cent cases. In terms of sex, the homogeneity was found only in 13.9 per cent cases and heterogeneity in 86.1 per cent cases. Kinship relationship was found between the offenders and the victims in 84 per cent cases. In 74.6 per cent cases, the victim was the member of the offender's family (spouse: 50.9%, child: 10.70%, secondary kin (son's wife, son's son): 10.1%, tertiary kin (husband's brother's wife, husband's brother's son, etc.): 2.9%) while in 9.5 per cent cases, the victim was a kin from outside the family. Of the remaining 16 per cent cases, the victim belonged to offender's neighbourhood in 8.3 per cent cases, to offender's village in 6.5 per cent cases, and the victim was a total stranger in 1.2 per cent cases. This underlines the need for focusing on primary relationship in murders committed by men or women.

Homogeneity and heterogeneity in sex, age and race have been studied in offender-victim relationship by scholars in the United States also. Berg and Fox in a study of 200 male murderers in Michigan in America found considerable homogeneity in victims and offenders. Harlan in a study of 500 male and female murders in Alabama in the United States in 1950 found more homogeneity than heterogeneity in offender-victim relations. Sutherland in a study of 324 female murderers in 1950 found significant heterogeneity in offender-victim relationship. Edwin Driver in his study of 144 cases of murder in Madhya Pradesh in India in 1961 found striking homogeneity.

TYPES OF VICTIMS

Different criminologists have given different types of victims on the basis of different criteria. Mendelsohn (quoted by Krishna and Singh, 1982: 48) has given six types of victims according to the degree of their contribution guilt in crime. These are: (i) completely innocent victims (e.g. small infants/children who are raped or murdered or kidnapped without their realising what is being done to them); (ii) victims with minor guilt (such as pregnant women who go to quacks for abortion and pay for it with their lives); (iii) victims as guilty as offenders; (iv) victims more guilty than the offenders (such as those who provoke others to commit crime); (v) the most guilty types of victims who commit offences against others and get harmed or killed themselves (e.g., a rapist who gets killed by his victim who acts in self-defence); and (vi) simulating (or pretending) victims (such as paranoids, hysterical and senile persons) who give evidence in the courts in order to obtain sentence against an accused person.

Walter Reckless (1961) has talked of two types of victims: reporting and non-reporting victims. The latter is one who is unwilling to report because he/she fears reprisals or social consequences of doing so; the former is one who does not bother for the consequences of reporting his victimisation but is rather interested in getting the offender punished or getting some relief for his suffering. Fattah (1967) has described five types of victims: non-participating, latent, provocative, participating, and false victims. Wolfgang (1967) has outlined five types of victimisation: (i) *primary* victimisation, involving personalised or individual victims (ii) *secondary* victimisation, where the victim is an impersonal target of the offender (e.g., a thief in a department store, a person travelling without a ticket on a roadways bus, etc.); (iii) *tertiary* victimisation, which affects the public or the administration of society; (iv) mutual victimisation, which concerns those victims who themselves are offenders in a given mutually consensual act (e.g., adultery); and (v) no victimisation, which is an act of negligible significance where there is no immediately recognisable victim.

Von Hentig (*The Criminal and His Victim*, Yale University Press, New Haven, 1948) has given four types of victims: (i) victims whose injury may be the price of a greater gain, e.g., in abortion; (ii) victims who bring about the detrimental result partly by their own concurrent effort; e.g., prostitutes; (iii) victims who provoke or instigate the offence, e.g., by challenging the opponent to kill him if he can and in an emotional state of mind, the opponent accepts the challenge and attacks; (iv) victims who desire the injury. Hentig has further classified the attitudes of victims as: (i) lethargic attitude; (ii) submissive or conniving attitude; (iii) cooperative or contributory attitude, and (iv) provocative or investigative attitude.

Talking of victim typologies, Schafer (1977) has remarked that a victim typology remains a meaningless speculation if it has no guiding application and is not linked to a theoretical model.

COMPENSATION TO VICTIMS

The idea of relief and compensation to victims is not a new one. Earlier too, our laws provided for compensation to the victims of accidents. In some cases, the law combined punishment of the offender with monetary satisfactions for the injured party as a means of forestalling enmity through counter-violence by the victim's kin. In the 1950s, an English reformer initiated a modem movement to bring the victim back into the criminal justice equation. "Victim compensation" refers to payments made from state funds to victims of crime. Advocates of victim compensation have argued that since the state is responsible for protecting its citizens from crime, the failure to do so obligates the state to indemnify those who are victimised. The state is believed to be responsible to the victims because imprisonment prevents offenders from paying damages. The general welfare policy also is cited as justification for governmental assistance to the unfortunate victims of crime.

Barnes and Teeters (*New Horizons in Criminology*, 1951) have said: "Our barbarian ancestors were wiser and more just than we are today, for they adopted the theory of restitution to the injured, whereas we have abandoned this practice to the detriment of all concerned."

Some countries, however, have accepted this demand and introduced victim compensation schemes. New Zealand introduced it is 1963, Great Britain in 1964, and Australia in 1967. In America, 28 states (including New York and California) have introduced these schemes. The compensation scheme in England is that a victim is paid compensation in accident cases if he is injured for three weeks' loss of pay. The award is sanctioned by the Compensation Board when the victim submits an application to it. In New Zealand, compensation is paid in rape, kidnapping and murder offences out of the fine levied on the accused persons. Compensation thus does not cover crimes against property. Special Compensation Tribunals have been created for this purpose. The victims are expected to lodge complaints with the police and submit themselves to medical check-up, if necessary. No compensation is paid where the victim shares the responsibility of the offence.

Victim compensation schemes have also been introduced in countries like Canada, France, Norway, Sweden, Italy, Denmark, Belgium, Japan, the Netherlands, Turkey, West Germany, Yugoslavia, Hong Kong, and Singapore. However, these countries do not pay compensation for all types of crimes. Compensation is necessarily selective. The guidelines generally followed are: (1) Compensation is payable to persons for injury resulting from crime. (2) Crime against property is not compensable. (3) Victims of inter-familial crimes are not compensable. (4) Victims who initiate or provoke the criminal assault resulting in their victimisation are precluded. (5) Offences arising from gang warfare are not compensable. (6) Trivial injuries are usually ignored, say a loss of less than two or three weeks' earnings.

In India, the principle of compensation for victims of crime has been accepted in Criminal Procedure Code (CrPC) and 1958 Probation Act. The CrPC provides for compensation out of fine levied on the accused. The award of compensation has to be a part of sentence and must be decided by the courts. Not only the victim but also his/her spouse, parent and child are entitled to compensation. But in practice, the provisions (for compensation) have remained merely on paper because it is difficult to recover amount from the offender.

S. Venugopal raised the question of compensation to victims in a seminar on "Criminal Law and Contemporary Social Changes" held at Delhi from 8-10 May 1969 by the Research Division of the Central Bureau of investigation. Another seminar on "Compensation to Victims of Road Accidents" was organised in 1980 in New Delhi and various issues like third-party claims, expeditious settlements, etc. were discussed. However, since then no serious thought has been paid to this question either by the judiciary or the criminologists.

A study in Poona city in 1960-61 by Pradhan (1965) showed that out of 510 cases of violence in one year (1960-61) prosecutions took place only in 182 cases and in 13 cases the aggrieved party was awarded compensation. In another study of victims of Fatal Motor Vehicle Accidents conducted by Khan and Krishna in Delhi in 1981, it was found that only in 22 per cent cases, some 'assistance' was made available to the victims. In third-party insurance, only 20 per cent of the bereaved families were compensated by the insurance companies.

In England, a white paper presented in the Parliament in 1959 suggested that "society has concentrated so much on the rehabilitation of the offender that it has lost sight of the equally important concern for the victim's welfare, i.e., the reformation policy is offender-oriented and not victim-oriented. It is necessary that victim's loss and offender's ability to pay should be assessed."

In America, Ralph Yarborough while introducing a private bill in the Senate in 1963 held that "while society is weeping over the criminal, it is showing no such concern for the victim of his crime. Society is brutal towards the victims of crime and not against the criminals." Katzenbach Commission appointed in America in 1966 found legislators, law-enforcement officers and the public in favour of compensation scheme.

Schafer's worldwide (29 countries) inquiry on victim compensation concerned the following questions: (i) whether the victim or his dependent has any legal right to claim restitution or damages from the offender; (ii) if so, to what offences does this right apply; (iii) whether damages are restricted to compensation for financial loss only or any other non-material injury; (IV) the nature of jurisdiction; (v) the manner of recovery. He found three systems existed in paying compensation to victims:

(a) *Damage*: awarded in civil proceedings only.

(b) *Restitution*: awarded both in civil and in criminal proceedings.

(c) *Compensation*: awarded through special procedure both in civil and criminal proceedings.

He, thus, concluded that the general situation involves the victim of crime in a helpless position with regard to his claim for compensation.

Stephen Schafer studied existing compensation schemes in 29

countries in 1958-59 and gave the following suggestions:

1. Compensation to victims of crime could be brought within the purview of criminal procedure and dealt with in the same criminal court which deals with the offence.
2. Compensation may be claimed by the victim but if he doesn't, the court should deal with it as part of its fundamental duties.
3. If the question of compensation leads to delay in the pronouncement of sentence, the court should pass a part sentence and may postpone its decision in relation to compensation.
4. Compensation should be fixed with reference to offender's economic and social position.
5. Where the offender is not in a position to compensate, the state must undertake its responsibilities.
6. The state should set up a Compensation Fund with the aid of fine and other sources of revenue.

Can these suggestions be accepted in a country like India? The five questions we have to pose are: (1) Should the concept of compensation be accepted in principle? (2) If yes, for what crime? (3) Who should pay compensation? Should it be paid by the state or by the offender? (4) How to realise the compensation amount from the offender? (5) How to pay compensation? Should it be paid in lump sum or in installments?

If we take into consideration the magnitude of crimes in India for which compensation may be considered feasible, we find that (taking average of six years from 1993 to 1998), every year about 2,94,360 cases of theft, 1,18,101 cases of burglary, 23,190 cases of robbery, 8,488 cases of dacoity, 21,248 cases of kidnapping, 38,024 cases of murder, 33,198 cases of cheating, 14,064 cases of rape, and 15,949 cases of breach of trust take place in our country (1998: 43-44). Can our state afford to pay compensation to about five lakh victims of only nine offences under the IPC every year? How much amount would be involved? Since we do not have wage scheme in prisons, how can offenders be compelled to pay compensation? This only shows that compensation scheme is not feasible in our country. A similar provision has already been made in our Criminal Procedure Code, Probation of Offenders Act, 1958, and in some other laws. The idea of extensive application of the scheme of government compensation to victims thus does not appear to be economically practicable in our country. In fact, no government can afford the cost of victim compensation which may run into billions of rupees a year; and also no government can lay claim to finding fool-proof methods for detecting fraudulent claims. There is also the fear that such programme would result in the creation of another bureaucratic paper mill, and that compensation would dampen the victims' desire to testify against criminals, increasing crime rates. Of course, there are scholars who have answers to these criticisms. They maintain that restrictions on eligibility will control expenditure. Also, there is no evidence that compensation affects the crime rate. The possibility of fraud is minimal. Even in accident cases which permit compensation according to the existing laws, the rates of compensation are very low which do not cover even the medical expenses. The court procedures are so complicated that people, even if aware of the existence of the compensation scheme, hesitate to take legal action against the offenders. It is, therefore, high time that a debate on the various aspects of victim-compensation in the country is started to protect victims' interests.

References

Ahuja, Ram, *Violence Against Women*, Rawat Publications, Jaipur, 1998.

Krishna, K.P. and Singh, D.P., "Victims of Crime", in *Social Change*, September 1982, Vol. 12, No. 3, pp. 48-58.

Bureau of Police Research and Development, New Delhi., *Compensation to Victims of Crime*, 1979.

Khan, M.Z. and Krishna, K.P., "Victims of Fatal Motor Vehicle Accidents", Institute of Criminology and Forensic Science, New Delhi, 1981.

Schafer, Stephen, *Crime and Delinquency*, April 1968.

Shultz, *Crime and Delinquency*, April 1968.

Wolfgang, Marvin, "Victim-precipitated Criminal Homicide", *Sociology of Crime and Delinquency*, John Wiley and Sons, Now York, 1962.

Author Index

Subject Index